# THE LIFE AND TIMES

OF

# SAMUEL BOWLES

BY

GEORGE S. MERRIAM

IN TWO VOLUMES

VOL. I

NEW-YORK

THE CENTURY CO.

1885

Republished, 1970
Scholarly Press, 22929 Industrial Drive East, St. Clair Shores, Michigan 48080

Standard Book Number 403-00220-6
Library of Congress Catalog Card Number: 76-108512

This edition is printed on a high-quality,
acid-free paper that meets specification
requirements for fine book paper referred
to as "300-year" paper

# PREFACE.

THIS book is an attempt to faithfully portray the life of a man. It includes, as the appropriate background of such a portrait, a sketch of the public events which wrought on him and on which he wrought.

The first interest of the general public in the career of Samuel Bowles arises from the fact that he was an eminent journalist. He was one of the representative men through whom a new power in society has been developed and exercised. His field was in one sense narrow, for the Springfield *Republican* was published in a provincial town, and limited to a comparatively small circulation; but it exercised a wide influence. The best measure of its editor's attainment was not the number of readers he reached, but the theory and ideal of journalism which he exemplified. His personal history touches the principles of the art of newspaper-making.

The justification for sketching a nation's story as part of the story of a journalist's life is that the journalist has become an important factor in national affairs. Mr. Bowles's editorial work covered the period from the annexation of Texas to the close of reconstruction under President Hayes. He was a spectator and actor in the struggle which ended in the overthrow of slavery, and also in the problems which taxed the nation in the years following the war. A great part of the significance and value of his life lay in his contribution to these debates.

VOL. I.                                     iii

Their reflex influence on him was among the strongest forces that shaped his growth. We do not rightly appreciate the history of a nation, except as we see it entering into the thought and character of the individual citizen; nor do we appreciate the citizen, especially if he be a leader among his fellows, unless we keep before our eyes the fortunes of the great community of which he is a member.

The sketch here given of the more prominent events of the country's political history makes no pretensions to profundity of research or originality of view. It follows the line of central interest,—the slavery question, the war, reconstruction, and reform,—touching collateral issues but lightly. It deals with thoughts and motives rather than with outward action; and the scenes of its drama lie more in the minds of the common people than in battle-fields or the chambers of Congress. Its materials have been drawn partly from standard works and partly from the volumes of the *Republican*. The files of a newspaper must not be trusted always to give the true proportion of the events which they narrate from day to day, and their record must be open to large correction from other sources. But, picturing the scene as it appeared to actors and contemporaries, and giving details caught by the reporter's pen before memory has had time to grow treacherous, they yield most abundant and vivid material.

The more essential part of the book is that which deals with the personal life of its subject. Few men in his generation had a more striking personality than " Sam Bowles," and few were more widely known. He was a man of strong, racy, many-sided individuality,—a man richly worth knowing even by report, if the biographer has at all succeeded in representing his true quality. It has been my desire to show him just as he was,—in his virtues and in his faults; in the successive phases of his growth; in the aspects in which he disclosed himself to the public, to his friends, to his enemies. I have tried to discern and present the underlying and governing forces of his life. Whatever has been my success or failure in this attempt, I have at least been able to show one characteristic aspect of the man, unwarped and uncolored by any misinterpreting medium, in the large selections from his private letters. One may say of them what Emerson says of Montaigne's essays: "The sincerity and marrow of the man reaches to his sentences. Cut these words and they would bleed; they are vascular and alive."

I acknowledge warmly the generosity with which his family and his most intimate friends have placed his correspondence at my disposal. In some cases with no small sacrifice of personal feelings, they have contributed the material toward showing him to the world with something of the charm which they knew in him. The reader of the book will scarcely need to be apprised that while the members of Mr. Bowles's family have given very valuable matter to the writer, he is solely responsible for the judgments which are expressed.

For the rest, the work must speak for itself. It addresses itself to the common interest of humanity. The writer says to his readers: Behold a man! Thus he looked, thus he acted, thus he grew; this was his work, these were his joys, these were his battles, his defeats, his victories; such was the front he wore to the world, and so he opened his heart to those he loved; this was the outcome of his life, and this is its significance and appeal.

# CONTENTS OF VOL. I.

# THE LIFE AND TIMES OF
# SAMUEL BOWLES.

## CHAPTER I.

### THE ANCESTRAL INHERITANCE.

SAMUEL BOWLES was born on the ninth of February, 1826, in the quiet country town of Springfield, Massachusetts, and in the beautiful valley of the Connecticut. He came on both sides of old New England stock. His father, named Samuel also, had some antiquarian taste, and made research into the genealogy of his family; faithful, patient, and exact in that as in all he did. A little pamphlet which he printed tells that the English family of Bowles, sometimes spelt Bolles, figures in the records of the genealogist Burke; but that the American family which spells its name as here printed was descended from John Bowles, an elder in the church of Roxbury, Mass., in 1640. He was one of the founders of the Roxbury Free School and a member of the Artillery Company. John the second (1653–1691) was baptized by the "Apostle Eliot," and married his granddaughter; was graduated at Harvard in 1671; became a ruling elder in the church; was elected a representative to the "General Court"—the Massachusetts legislature — and was speaker of the House. John the third (1685–1737) was also graduated at Harvard in 1703; was early and long engaged in managing the affairs of Roxbury town; and was major in the militia, and representative in the General Court for ten successive years. His son, Joshua Bowles (1722–1794) was a carver of furniture in Boston. Says the pamphleteer, the grandson of Joshua: "He never had much property. Indeed, I do not think our ancestors were ever distinguished for the acquisition of wealth. But he has been represented to me as a very benevolent, pious man. An old lady who knew him well in her youth, told me that when walking behind him in the street, she had heard him praying audibly. Like some other good men of his day, he had a queer way of intermingling religious and secular thoughts and words. My father told me that in a letter to him he once wrote: 'Dear Samuel: Strive to live in the fear of God, and write me word how the boat comes on' (a pleasure or sail boat kept to be let)." Of Joshua's sons, two served in the Revolutionary war, as sergeant and captain, but Samuel, first of the name (1762–1813), was only thirteen years old when the war broke out. In those troubled times he got but scanty schooling, at the hands of Master Tileston, a well-known Boston school-teacher. He and his wife grew up under the religious influences of the "Old South Church." He learned the pewterer's trade, found his business spoiled by the war, went to Hartford, Conn., and kept a grocery store, in which he seems to have thriven in a modest way. His son writes: "He was a man of good sense, quick wit, tender feelings, and strict honesty. Though not a member of any church, he was a faithful and liberal member of the Baptist Society, and governed by a sense of religious duty in bringing up his family."

"Good sense, tender feelings, strict honesty, sense of religious duty"—true marks these are all of his son

Samuel (1797–1851), who has part in our story as father of its hero. "Quick wit" could hardly be ascribed to him: he was slow in his mental action; cautious, canny, thrifty; a prim, sober man, respected and trusted by every one; laughed at sometimes for little stiffnesses and oddities; undemonstrative in his family, as was the wont of New Englanders, but with warm and faithful affections. He received as a boy a common-school education, went into his father's shop at the age of fifteen, and at his father's death a year later inherited nothing but an old gold watch and the family Bible. He was then apprenticed to a printer. "During my apprenticeship," he wrote in his maturity, "I was one of some ten or fifteen who formed an association for the improvement of the mind. I was one of the most zealous and steadfast of the club till it ran down. We met once a week, had discussions and listened to readings, original and selected. Here I acquired a taste for reading and mental cultivation. Before this my inclination was almost entirely for social pleasure and for evening carousals with young associates. And I was not very particular in the choice of my company. My connection with the debating club I consider an important era in my life — a sort of redeeming season, saving me from dangerous tendencies. It gave a good direction to my habits, strengthening my mind to resist temptation, and led me to prefer mental to sensual pleasure." When his apprenticeship was completed, he worked at the printing trade for six years, as journeyman and foreman, in Hartford and New Haven. These were years of struggle and dubious success; he was embarrassed by incompetent associates, got in debt, and underwent some hardships. While in Hartford he was prostrated for the greater part of a year by typhus fever of extraordinary severity; a most luckless illness for himself and his posterity, for it left him with a weak-

ness of the bowels which became chronic, and his death
resulted from an attack of dysentery; while a weak
digestive system was inherited by his children, and to
his son Samuel was a misfortune through life. But
the young printer struggled pluckily on, and in the
course of time took to himself a wife, Miss Huldah Dem-
ing, of Wethersfield, a woman of goodness, sense, and
energy, a descendant of the Puritan captain, Miles
Standish. In 1824 the young printer undertook the enterprise of a new weekly paper in Springfield. He came
up the river in a flat-boat, with his young wife and
their baby daughter, Julia, bringing a hand printing-
press and some scanty furnishing for the new home.
Friends in Springfield advanced a little money, and on
the eighth of September appeared the Springfield *Republican*. Proprietor, publisher, editor, reporter, compositor,
and pressman appear to have been united in Samuel
Bowles; and it must be owned by one who reads the first
numbers of the paper that one man might have produced
it all without any dangerous strain on his powers. But
it was the day of small things in journalism, and the
*Republican* satisfied the moderate requirements of the
newspaper readers of that day. It had at the start two
hundred and fifty subscribers, at two dollars a year; it
slowly and steadily prospered, outran or absorbed its
local rivals, and seems to have soon yielded a modest
but sufficient livelihood for its proprietor and his growing family. His first child, Albert, was born in 1823,
and lived but seven months; the next was Julia; then,
in the second year of his residence in Springfield, came
the son who was named after his father and grandfather;
and to these succeeded another daughter, Amelia, and
another son, Benjamin Franklin. All of these except
the first-born lived to maturity.

# CHAPTER II.

## THE EARLY ENVIRONMENT.

THE generation to which "Sam Bowles" belonged — for by that name every one called the magnetic and mercurial man, whom the stiff Biblical trisyllable Samuel never fitted — was the generation in which New England broke through the sheath of Puritanism, and flowered into broader and more various life. Two centuries before, certain grave and resolute Englishmen had turned their backs on the refinements and corruptions of the Old World, to found a pure spiritual commonwealth in the wilderness. They and their descendants had been trained in a conflict for existence under rigorous physical conditions. They had been compelled to win a livelihood from soil which asks a hard price for all it yields. They had battled with a climate of extreme and swift fluctuations. They had been separated by the ocean's breadth from the resources with which the Old World ministered to comfort, taste, and imagination. Three advantages attended them : — they came of picked English stock, they were free from all political inequalities among themselves, and their community was founded under a lofty religious impulse. Two hundred years had developed and confirmed them as a shrewd, serious, hard-headed people. They had grown strong in the robust qualities of manhood. Nature had said to each man, " Work or you

starve!" Society had said to each man, "Work, and
all you get shall be your own!" So they became resolute and patient to labor and careful to save. The
fields of interest open to them were the household, the
political community, and the divine realm of which the
visible symbol was the church. In these currents ran
the New Englander's life, in a stream quiet, somber,
and deep.

The ideal at which the founders of New England aimed
was a theocracy. The peculiarity of their theocracy was
that it assumed, as the authoritative interpreter of the
divine will, not any official class, but a book — and a book
on whose interpretation no one could place a limit. In
the practical government of the community they followed
the forms and usages which had grown up during many
centuries of English life, but subject to certain modifications: — there was no privileged class; the authority of
crown and parliament was remote, and when it began to
press closely was thrown off altogether; and the immediate affairs of each town and hamlet were ordered by its
inhabitants in a popular assembly. The clergy, though
not invested with secular authority, were for a long time
the most influential class in the community. With the
progress of time the political and religious life of the
community flowed more and more into separate channels. The decadence of the Puritan theology is to be
measured, not so much by open revolt against it, as by
the withdrawal of intellectual energies into other fields.
The two great and antithetical intellects which New England produced in the eighteenth century were Jonathan
Edwards and Benjamin Franklin,— the one a metaphysician and mystic, the other a man of science, of public
affairs, and of philanthropic humanity. Franklin got his
chance by going to Philadelphia and thence to England;
he would not have found room enough in Massachu-

setts. Then the Revolution brought to the front the lawyers, the soldiers, the statesmen, and left the clergy comparatively in the rear. The temper of the Revolutionary patriots was far different from that of Cromwell's Ironsides. With the next generation came the disestablishment of the Congregational churches. Then, slowly at first, began the prodigious development of the physical resources of the country; then came invention, discovery, enrichment; and men, toughened but cramped for two centuries, found a continent beckoning them to stride into possession. There was expansion of energy and opportunity in every direction.

While the collective forces of the community had thus been undergoing a gradual diversion from the ecclesiastical into the secular field, the religious life — that which was recognized as such — still remained one of the most striking features of the New England development. The "meeting-house" was the most conspicuous building in every town, and the church society ranked as first beyond comparison among social organizations.

Religion may be said in a broad sense to include three elements — theology, worship, and ethics; in other words, an intellectual explanation of the universe, a conscious relation of the human soul to the divine and infinite, and an ordering of the practical conduct of life. Puritanism made theology the corner-stone of religion. Theoretically it took the Bible as its law; but what it really offered was a scheme of the universe; — God in three persons; the race of man ruined through the sin of its first parent; a sacrificial atonement; the appropriation of that atonement through faith as the sole condition of an eternal Heaven, and its rejection the seal of an endless perdition. This view confronted the soul directly with the most tremendous realities and immeasurable issues. It was a view which in its essentials was com-

mon to all branches of the Christian church; but in its
practical application was elsewhere softened, by inter-
mediary elements of priesthood and sacrament, and venerable and beautiful forms of worship. Puritanism
steadily rejected all such aids and interpositions, and
set the trembling soul face to face with its Maker, whose
sovereign decree had destined it irreversibly to measure-
less bliss or woe. The Puritans renounced the authority
and mediation of the church on which the soul might
comfortably repose; they rejected the vision of inter-
ceding saints filling the air; angelic ministrations faded
almost out of view, while Satanic activity was vividly
imagined; and the liturgies and forms of worship which
the genius of ages had enriched were almost wholly
thrown aside. The English Puritans turned Beauty out
of the service of Religion. For their American descendants, the resulting barrenness was intensified by the
absence of all artistic creations in the New World. The
worshiper had no aid to his imagination from sculptured
aisle or swelling organ; no gracious Madonna looked
down on him; the prayers to which he silently listened
were but the improvisation of his minister; the beauty
of nature was without meaning for him. The spirit of
worship languished in so thin and innutritious an atmosphere, and the mass of the community tended to a
dry formalism in their religious observances, save when
lifted by the wave of a " revival." But the theological
spirit was very active. The founders of New England
included many clergymen among their leaders, and most
of these were Oxford or Cambridge graduates. In every
town they planted the school beside the church, and no
population in the world had so high an average of education. In the dearth of literary and social resources,
the minds of the clergy, and largely of the intellectual
class in general, continued to work eagerly and unceas-

ingly on the problems of the universe. The main line of their speculation was a series of modifications of Calvinism. The attempt to apply these abstruse speculations to the conduct of individual life produced a strange result. A highly metaphysical system was made the basis upon which every man must work out his salvation from hell, and a mystic experience of conviction of sin, self-despair, and conversion was required of the soul with the definiteness of an apothecary's prescription. It was a theory of life which gave constant exercise to speculative natures; by turns exalted and depressed the sensitive; and lost its practical hold on the mass of the community long before it was confessedly modified by the clergy.

But Puritanism, while it was narrow in its philosophy, and by its lack of beauty and of tenderness stinted the fountains of spiritual feeling, was strong in its appeal to moral purpose. It roused men with the idea of a great destiny. Its tremendous presentation of the issues of existence woke an energy like that which is inspired by man's conflict with the elemental forces of nature. The ideal of conduct which it offered was austere but lofty. It appealed to the sense of obligation rather than to sympathy or delight. It made men strong rather than sweet; it made them sober, chaste, and upright. From whatever source derived,—from Puritanism, from the older Christianity, from English stock, from Hebrew religion, from primitive humanity,—the sense of duty lay deep in the New England character. Conscience was the bed-rock of the typical New Englander, as granite is the foundation of his soil. Deficient in spiritual imagination, severely logical in intellect, he was in the practical conduct of life the loyal servant of Duty. To Calvinist, Unitarian, or Rationalist the sovereign word was *I ought*.

The interests of the state had an absorbing interest

for its citizens such as is hardly known in our modern community, whose tastes are fed from a thousand sources of literature, art, and amusement. Almost every man was a politician. It was not merely that each had a stake and a voice in the commonwealth, but in their monotonous lives the place of theater, travel, and newspaper was filled by political debate.

To the Puritan fathers, the chief end of all human doings had been the salvation of the soul from future perdition. They regarded the ordering of the state as only an incidental step in this process. But under the practical necessities of their situation, they and their descendants had worked out the experiment of political democracy, under the most favorable conditions that had ever existed for it. In and after the Revolutionary war, the sister commonwealths had entered on the vastly more difficult experiment of a great federal democracy. In this creative epoch of the new nation there were found a large group of men with rare capacity for nation-building,—men trained under the Puritan traditions of New England, in the mingled Dutch and English school of New York, in the softened Quakerism of Pennsylvania, and the aristocratic democracy of Virginia and the Carolinas. The foundations were settled ; the great question between federal and state authority reached a stable equilibrium ; then followed nearly half a century in which the young political system was exercised in only moderate difficulties, as if getting well knit for the tremendous tasks and problems awaiting it. But the struggles between Whigs and Democrats, about tariffs and national banks and internal improvements — the combats of Jacksonians and Clay men and Adams men — these, besides their intrinsic importance, shared with religion in furnishing the chief intellectual exercise of a people poor as yet in literary and artistic development; and they were a constant training in the noblest and most complex of social arts — the self-government of the community. Religion and politics were the two main subjects of thought in the community in which young Sam Bowles grew to manhood. It was these themes that gave zest and largeness to lives otherwise somewhat dry and narrow; on these topics wits were sharpened; from these came a touch of ideal greatness; from these sprang passions nobler even in their excesses than the struggle for material gain,— a consciousness of membership in a mighty body politic, and a sense of place in a divine order transcending the seen and finite.

The primitive period of New England may be taken with sufficient exactness at two hundred years,— lapping over by a quarter of a century into the nineteenth. It was not until then that its second great function began in pouring its sons forth to people the West, while from Europe there set in a tide of immigration which is changing the constituent elements of the population. Since then, too, there have come immeasurable changes in the conditions of intellectual and social life. It was just as the old was broadening into the new that the boy of our story grew up to manhood. The surroundings of his childhood retained in large measure the characteristics of the early time. He belonged to a family and a community of which the inheritance and possession were sobriety, industry, and self-control, unmodified by literature, art, and the social graces and amenities.

The Unitarian controversy had arisen in Massachusetts a few years before the elder Bowles came to Springfield, and he united with the Unitarian church, which had been established there by a secession from the old First Church that was coeval with the town. In the separation the families of higher social pretensions went generally with the new movement, and the ecclesiastical

schism divided the society of the town, not with virulence, yet to the weakening of the social forces.  Early
Unitarianism was but a ripening of a long-growing
alienation among the intellectual class from the severi-
ties of Calvinism.  It was from the beginning intellectual, decorous, reverent, rather than popular and
enthusiastic.  Its ministers kept with little alteration
the ecclesiastical tone of their Orthodox brethren, and
a solemnity verging sometimes on lugubriousness.  Of
such ministers was the Reverend William B. O. Peabody,
pastor of the Unitarian church in Springfield from
1820 to 1847.  He was a man of piety, refinement, and
intellectual cultivation, whose name is still held in
honored memory in the denomination, and by the community at large.  Dr. Horatio Stebbins's testimony shows
how one youthful mind was affected by his ministry :
" Here Peabody prophesied and prayed, and his words
fell upon my heart like rain upon the tender grass ; and
my mature experience makes no abatement from my
boyhood's impression of the singular elevation of his
mind, and the penetrating purity of his spirit."  Yet to
most of his youthful auditors, Dr. Peabody was awe-
inspiring rather than winning.  In his sermons he laid
constant emphasis on the perils, the woes, and transitori-
ness of the present life.  The sentiments of a creed outlive
for a time its intellectual form ; and the view of earthly
life as tolerable only because it may lead to something
better — a view inherited from the burdened Middle Ages
— colored much of the preaching of the early Unitarians.

Dr. Peabody used to wear in the pulpit a black gown
and black silk gloves.  His manner and tones, both in
and out of the pulpit, were to a child decidedly solemniz-
ing.  Of his church the elder Bowles was a steadfast
member ; he became a deacon and superintendent of the
Sunday-school.  His children went to church twice every

Sunday. In their home were practiced the usual religious observances, family prayers every morning, and the " blessing " before each meal.

The stream of the community's life flowed slow and tranquil as the Connecticut that glides through the level meadows. The first railroad reached Springfield when the boy was thirteen years old; and just as he was coming of age the first message was flashed over the telegraph wires. Steam and electricity are fit symbols, as well as agents, of the revolution that has gone through American society since then.

In those days Springfield was a country town, its inhabitants principally farmers, centering in a village of residences and a few shops. It was settled, in 1636, by a colony from Roxbury, Mass., shared the experiences of colonial times, and was burned by the Indians in King Philip's war. It drew its prosperity mainly from the fertile meadows bordering the Connecticut, and remained the principal town in Western Massachusetts, but with no special importance or marked growth until it became a railroad center, at the intersection of the great lines joining Boston with Albany and New York with Northern New England and Canada. The town had the characteristic features of New England life, with probably more general prosperity along the rich river basin than was found on the granite-ribbed, bowlder-strewn soil which characterizes much of the state ; while of mental activity there was less than in Eastern Massachusetts. The families which were recognized as the social aristocracy of the town derived their consequence from wealth acquired in local trade by themselves or their immediate ancestors. The United States Armory gave employment to a class of sturdy and intelligent mechanics.

The natural scenery of the region is full of various and tranquil beauty. The Connecticut, here about a

fourth of a mile in width, loiters between its verdant
banks, like a great meadow-brook; beside it, like a nest
by the brook-side, lies the town of Springfield, ascending
by gently sloping hills, and running off eastward over
dry and breezy plains.  From many a knoll and terrace
one may look upon endless variations of the broad, fair
landscape,—the placid river flowing in the midst; away
to the west, the blue hill-country of Berkshire; eastward,
the wooded and pastured slopes of the Wilbraham hills,
answering the aspects of the sky in ever-changing play
of light and shade; twenty miles to the north, the sharp
outlines of the Holyoke range, and Mount Tom lying
like a couchant lion.  Over the meadows are scattered
noble elms; elms and maples line the streets of the
town, so that, seen from the neighboring heights, it
seems to lie in a forest.  The landscape is clothed through
the summer in richest green, heralded in the spring by
marvelously delicate and various tints, and ripening into
autumnal glory.  Across the brown soil of March the
flash of a bluebird's wing and a thrilling song tell that
winter is past.  Over the waving grass-fields of June,
the bobolink, tipsy with joy, pours his bubbling laughter.
From the arbutus to the aster, a long procession of flowers mark the year's almanac,—shy northern blossoms,
hardy darlings of the frost, and hues warm as the tropics.
Up and down the river lie ancient villages, flavorous of
the olden time; the one broad street overarched with
patriarchal trees, the fine old houses dreaming over their
past.  The tall chimneys of the outlying mill villages,
growth of the last half-century, even now scarcely break
the aspect of rural peace, which steals in soothing delight over the beholder's heart.  To-day, as fifty years
ago, one looks on the homes of a thriving, free, and virtuous people;—now, as then, he looks on Nature in her
aspect of peaceful charm.

# CHAPTER III.

## BOYHOOD.

THE Bowles family formed a hard-working, frugal household; united by a deep but undemonstrative affection; pushing on with slow steps and sure grip to moderate prosperity; sincerely and decently pious; with little of recreation or social enjoyment. Their home was in a modest two-story frame house, on the north corner of Union and School streets. The oldest son was born in an earlier residence, known afterward as the "Osgood house," near the corner of Main and Howard streets. The family consisted of father, mother, four children, and several apprentices. Sam shared his bed with the youngest apprentice, Chauncey White, who afterward became his foreman, and two other apprentices had their bed in the same room. The day began with breakfast at six o'clock, the year round, and at seven the master and apprentices were at work; doing a general printing business in addition to the newspaper. The mistress of the household had a potent voice in all her husband's affairs. She was a woman of plain exterior, of quiet and prim manners, under which lay energy and spirit; even-tempered; with quicker, more incisive mind than that of her husband, and greater force of character and will; practical rather than intellectual in

15

her tastes; of decided religious character; a good wife
and good mother. "She was smart as a whip," says an
apprentice of those days; "she knew as much of the
office as her husband did." Of the two parents it was
the mother to whom the son bore more intellectual like-
ness. But it was the common remark in later years that
Sam Bowles was not like his parents,—was not like anybody but himself. In his boyhood he seems to have
given no indication of anything remarkable in mind or
character, nothing in any way salient or striking. He
was a good boy, not wayward, not infected with any
vice; obedient, in the fashion of those days when obedience was the first element of family training; making
friendships with other boys, some of which—with David
A. Wells, Charles O. Chapin, F. H. Harris, and others—
lasted through a life-time; given to admiration of one
girlish charmer after another, for the village boys and
girls met freely in the wholesome American way; with
little relish for boyish sports, but a marked fondness,
when he did take part, for being leader and captain;
with no aptitude or inclination for manual work; as a
student, faithful, rather slow in acquisition, but retentive
of what was once learned.

He went to the public high school, taught by Dr. Vail,
and afterward, at the age of thirteen or perhaps earlier,
to the private school of Mr. George Eaton, which he
attended for several years, completing there his school
education. Mr. Eaton is remembered by his old pupils
with high regard. His scholars, boys and girls, were
mostly from Unitarian families in Springfield. Young
Sam Bowles, in addition to the usual English studies,
made some progress in Latin, and read portions of Cæsar,
Virgil, and Cicero. He wished to go to college, and had
Mr. Eaton's sympathy and encouragement in that desire,
but his father did not approve of the project and it

was not carried out. In later years Mr. Bowles was wont to speak of this as a severe disappointment, and the want of a college training was a life-long regret to him.

The father's first purpose was that his oldest son should learn the printer's trade, just as he had done; but he was sometimes discouraged, and feared the boy would never succeed, because he had so little skill with his hands. If a kite was to be made, or so much as a nail driven, his younger sister was apt to be called to his help. To the end of his life, his hands—long, pale, delicate—had a look of helplessness. He did once go into the printing-room for the purpose of regularly learning its art and mystery; but a few hours of type-setting was enough for him, and he left at the end of the first half-day. At odd times he picked up, after a fashion, the mechanical part of the business, but never so far as to have any expertness in it.

The Yankee boy of those times was wont to have a regular set of "chores" to do, such as cutting and bringing in wood, making fires, and the like. But where there were apprentices in the family, custom assigned this work to the youngest of them; so Sam escaped these labors, except when his father especially allotted to him a piece of manual work, and even then he could sometimes coax one of his companions to act as substitute. Yet he was trained in various ways, as a boy in those days could hardly fail to be, "to make himself useful." He drove the cows to and from their pasture, carried the Weekly *Republican* to a round of subscribers, and had more or less outdoor and indoor work to do. One summer, when he was perhaps fifteen, his father put him in charge of the garden, and he kept it in trimmest condition, disciplining the other children if they let a paper or a wisp of straw lie in the paths. He was very neat in

VOL. I.—2

his person and clothes, not solicitous about the style and fit of his garments, but fastidious as to their condition, showing in this respect a delicacy and daintiness which was characteristic of him through life.

Mr. Eaton was in the habit of taking his scholars once a week on a ramble in the woods. The favorite resort was Blake's Woods, a noble pine forest near the town, of which a sadly reduced remnant yet lingers as one of the chief ornaments of the place. Here the teacher, enthusiastic and sympathetic, gave his pupils one of the finest and most serviceable elements of education, by wakening in them the love of Nature. Some of the boys, Sam Bowles among them, used to make up parties to bring flowers from the more distant woods and swamps. He was in those days shooting up fast into a tall, slender boy; carrying his head a little projected forward, as was also his father's habit; finding companions and favorites among the girls that visited his sisters; spending his time in school, in the family, a little in his father's office, and sometimes in evening gatherings of the young folks at each other's houses. He was never an adept at skating, ball-playing, and such boyish exercises, nor very fond of them. His comrades had hard work to coax him out to join them in coasting down the long hills near by; or if he kept them company for once in the thrilling swift descent, the long upward trudge was so little to his liking that he soon returned to the house. No doubt this distaste for hardy sports was partly due to some want of physical vigor; for though his health as a boy was fairly good, it was never robust; there was no surplus or overflow of vitality. His favorite occupation was reading. The house had a good supply of what was then considered classic English literature,—classic American literature being yet in its early beginnings,—but it was not these solid volumes that attracted the boy so much as the newspapers and magazines, with occasionally a new book, that came into his father's office. " Over these he would pore so deeply," says an old associate, " that sometimes you might speak to him half a dozen times and he would not know it." In his last sickness, Mr. Bowles said to a friend, in reviewing his busy life, "I was never much of a boy,—I had very little boyhood." The sobriety of the community and the household, with a want of full vitality and animal spirits, made his early years somewhat colorless. The first strong wakening of life came with the call to manly work.

# CHAPTER IV.

## THE BEGINNING OF THE DAILY "REPUBLICAN."

IT is almost a matter of course that a father who is fond of his own business and succeeds in it should wish his eldest boy to follow in his footsteps. So it was with Sam Bowles's father, and the boy himself was nothing loath. To be the maker of a newspaper was an attractive prospect, and the opportunity was right before him. The father had no foresight of the high power which the son was to develop, and saw no occasion for giving him a much broader and more liberal education than had fallen to his own share. When the son left school, at the age of seventeen, he began the miscellaneous duties of "office-boy," with sometimes a turn of work in the printing-room; passing on gradually to write occasional items of local news, and to practice the various duties of a country editor, except the writing of "leaders." Such few of these as the paper contained were done by an older hand, generally one outside of the office. The boy had no distinct ideal of what he was to do or be. He did faithfully and laboriously his work as it lay before him conscientious and thorough even in drudgery, as his father had been.

But in young Bowles there soon showed itself a pushing, ambitious spirit, which aimed at higher things tha had contented his father. When he was eighteen year old, a bold enterprise shaped itself in his mind. He proposed to his father to make the *Republican* a daily paper. He was at first by no means favorable to the idea. There was not a daily paper in the state outside of Boston. There was nothing in the size or character of Springfield that seemed to him to promise favorably for such a venture. He had worked through early failures and hardships to a moderate success. The Weekly *Republican* was now a well-established concern; its editor was nearing his fiftieth year; why increase his toils and risk what had been gained?

But the son was persistent and persuasive. His will was strong and his tongue skillful to plead. Railroads were coming in; already there were daily trains to Boston and Albany, and soon would be to Hartford and New York; the town must grow under their influence, and outlying towns be brought near; Hartford had its daily paper; the Weekly *Republican* was a good basis to start from. All this and much more the boy urged on his father, who at last gave consent as far as this: "If you, Sam, will take the main responsibility of working and pushing it, the daily shall be started." That was enough. The plans were made; father and son went to Hartford to inspect the methods of making a daily paper; and on the twenty-seventh of March, 1844, appeared the first number of the Daily *Republican*. It was an evening paper, a small four-page sheet, with just two columns of original matter, including prospectus, editorial, and local news. So the ship was launched and the young man's life-work begun.

Work it was from the start, and hard work. The father toiled steadily, in his slow, assiduous way: on the son it fell to break the new paths, invent methods, and carry from the start the larger part of the brain-work and pen-work requisite to meet the inexorable daily de-

mand. The alert mother used to set rocking-chairs at
the table at meal-times: "Mr. Bowles and Sam work
hard and have so little time to rest." Almost at the outset there came to the young man an ominous breakdown.
A weakness of the bowels became severe and chronic,
and it was feared that his lungs were in danger. In the
winter of 1844–5, he was obliged to seek a warmer climate,
and spent several months in the Southern states, for the
most part in Louisiana. When he left home his father
gave him a Bible, with this inscription on the fly-leaf:

"DEAR SAMUEL: Read this book often and prayerfully.
Let it be your chief counselor and friend. Let it strengthen
your heart to resist temptation. May it be your support in
affliction, and may God protect and bless you in your absence,
and restore you in health to Your Parents."

The young man was lonely and homesick, but he came
back with health restored, and having made his first
marked success as a writer. From the South he sent
home a series of fifteen letters to the paper, which gave
to the local public its first impression that "Young Sam
Bowles was a smart fellow." It was not a showy, boyish
smartness that the letters showed, but the eye of a good
observer and the pen of a good reporter. The writer
notes the climate, the productions, the business resources
of the places he visits; describes the cultivation of cotton and sugar; tells something of manners and morals;
gives an occasional bit of picturesque description;
touches observantly on local politics; and infers that
slavery is worse for the masters than for the slaves.
The letters are written in a clear and simple style, in-
elegant sometimes, but never pretentious or obscure.
They show a young man with quick eye and ear and
shrewd brain, observant of practical affairs, skillful to
gather facts and to tell a plain story.

The traveler came home,—with health so strengthened that it was seven years before he again succumbed,—and resumed the stroke oar in the *Republican*. The paper kept steadily on, gaining a little in quality and standing. It began without a subscriber, and at the end of two years claimed only three hundred. In December, 1845, it became a morning paper, and with that change came the hours of late night-work for its editors. One chief item in the younger man's work was for a good while to gather and write the items of local news. After a while he developed a talent for condensing into brief and readable form the long and heavy articles in which the great political papers of the day discharged their thunder. On these he began to practice that great art of " boiling down " which his paper afterward carried to such perfection. For original writing, beyond news, he did not know that he had capacity, and the reporting and general work of the paper gave him ample occupation.

In the last year of his life, Mr. Bowles was asked by a friend: " Do you trace your success to any special impulse at the beginning?" He answered, " Yes. Soon after I took hold of the paper there was a quarrel about the management of the Armory. The men who differed from my father made it a personal matter against him, and tried to break down his business by starting an opposition paper. That roused my ire, and I determined that we would not be beaten. I threw myself into the paper with all my might. After a year my opponents came to me, and wanted a truce, but I said, ' No ; you began the fight and now you shall have it.' And they did, till they were driven from the field. That fight got my steam up, and after that I kept on."

This hostility to the *Republican* took form in the establishment of the *Daily Evening Gazette*, changed from a weekly to a daily paper in April, 1846, when the younger

Bowles was in his twenty-first year. The trouble arose upon the transfer of the United States Armory, which was the principal manufactory in the town, from civil to military control. The new superintendent, Major Ripley, an able and energetic officer, introduced a different régime from the easy-going ways that had been in fashion. Regular and sharply enforced hours of work, marks and fines for tardiness or neglect, a military exactness and formality,— these and the like were new features to a set of independent Yankee workmen, accustomed to doing their work in their own way. There were loud complaints against the superintendent, the citizens took sides in the matter, and the dispute came to have a good deal of acrimony. It culminated in a military court of inquiry, which acquitted Major Ripley. The *Republican* had criticised him, but in a very temperate manner, and had by no means made the subject a prominent one. But feeling ran high; and just before the conclusion of the court, the *Gazette* was changed from a weekly to a daily, by way of retaliation on the *Republican*. The latter paper engaged in no wordy warfare with its rival. Its columns showed at this time not a trace of that ready and brilliant combativeness which was so marked a distinction of the later *Republican*. But one who studies the files sees unmistakably a marked and steady growth in the merit of the paper from this time on. For two years it had done little more than sustain the quality with which it began. But through 1846 it grows broader and better, and after that it does not cease to grow. It shows gradually an increase of reading matter, a better arrangement, and an abler style of discussion. During this year first appears that prompt, full, and admirable reporting of the state election returns — upon a system like that originated by the Boston *Atlas* some years before — which became one of the paper's brilliant features. The size of the sheet was repeatedly enlarged, and the subscription list steadily increased. Through these years Sam Bowles was putting into the paper his hardest work, his best life-blood. The situation appealed to his pride, his combativeness, his filial feeling, and that delight in journalism for its own sake which was becoming in him a master passion. The immediate struggle ended in victory, in July, 1848. The *Gazette* was absorbed in the *Republican*, and its editor, Mr. William Stowe, a man of character and ability, was added to the *Republican's* working force.

# CHAPTER V.

## The Old and the New Journalism.

THE first editorial, beyond a paragraph, which appeared in the Daily *Republican*, April 24, 1844, was a vigorous protest against "The Annexation of Texas," for which a treaty had just been signed by President Tyler. With that annexation may be said to have begun the new era in American politics, in which the issue was directly tried between slavery and freedom, and at last between secession and union. In the second month of the paper's life, on May 27, 1844, it told of the first telegraphic dispatch between Washington and Baltimore. Thus it was at the very point of transition between the old and the new politics, and between the old and the new journalism, that Samuel Bowles began his career.

In the great cities a new race of newspapers had begun to supplant the older dynasty. The papers of the earlier time had been in every sense heavy; big in size, high in price, dull, long-winded, intensely partisan, and mainly used as the instruments of the party chiefs. Of these journalists — represented by such names as the elder Blair, Gales and Seaton, Major Noah, Richard Haughton, and Colonel Greene — Mr. Horace White says: "These men and their generation were given over to the 'leading article' as the sole end and aim of journalism. They were a strong-limbed and hard-headed race, but they had never learned that 'variety is the spice of life,' and 'brevity the soul of wit.' The railway had not reached out its arms, the telegraph had not spread its wings for them. They were ruled by their environment, and the journalism they produced consisted of a diurnal succession of essays more or less learned, and more or less bellicose, but as regular as the succession of day and night, or of seed-time and harvest."

But within a dozen years there had sprung up in New York the first of a new class of newspapers, such as the *Sun*, begun in 1833, and the *Herald*, in 1835. They were sold for one or two cents (the older papers were not sold by single copies, being sent only to regular subscribers); they aimed at news more than discussion; their style was lively and dashing; they were swift to seize and invent new methods in every direction; they brought steam into their press-rooms and organized special service by land and by water for getting the earliest information. They struck into many veins of social interest, — trade, religion, and personal gossip, — which the older papers had ignored. They discussed politics without asking orders from the chieftains at Washington and Albany. It was in papers of this class that American journalism came of age. Hitherto the newspaper had been a minor and a servant. It had been an instrument to promote some other interest, generally that of a political party or a personal clique; controlled by the leaders of the clique or the party, and sustained by their patronage. In the new journalism the newspaper became its own master. It was an independent enterprise, as much so as a cotton mill or a cheese factory. So far as financial success was the object, — and such success was generally a main object, and always the necessary condition of any further achievement, — the resource was no longer subsidies from a political party, but the pay-

ments of its buyers and advertisers. The buyers were
to be won by giving people such a paper as they wanted.
It was, in a sense, the discovery of James Gordon Bennett,— his great contribution to the journalistic art,—
that what people most wanted in a newspaper, and
were most willing to pay for, was news. Give news, and
you gain subscribers; gain subscribers, and you will have
advertisers; that is the formula of newspaper success.

In the new journalism this solid commercial fact of a
successful business enterprise was the basis which the
journalist might, if he pleased, use as a platform from
which to say to the world his word of advice or exhortation, of preaching or scoffing. Thus there was born a
new social power. The journalist might use his position
for good or for evil, but henceforth his class must be
reckoned with as a force not less distinct than the clergy
or the law-makers.

The New York *Herald* was the first conspicuous example in America of the new journalism. Its sole object
was money-making; its creed was expressed by the editor when he wrote, " We have never been in a minority,
and we never shall be "; its political sympathies were
generally Democratic; its temper was one of rollicking
impudence; and it neither feared God nor regarded man.
Its enterprise in news-gathering won popular favor, and
drove its dull and respectable rivals either to imitation
or to death. Its mocking temper and its open worship
of material success shocked the moral sentiment of the
community, and its reckless personalities showed at full
height the virulence of a period of bitter partisanship
and low culture. By its merits as a newspaper it won
the reward it sought— wealth and notoriety.

In 1841, Horace Greeley established the New York
*Tribune*. Mr. Greeley's characteristic and best ambition
was to be a teacher of men. He was a sincere enthusiast

in social and political ideas, a master of pithy and eloquent speech to the common people, and he found in the newspaper his best instrument. The influence of the time, and the associates he found, gave prominence to the news element of the *Tribune,* but its especial service was as a social educator. He was an ardent politician, and his paper heartily supported the Whig and afterward the Republican party, though with a considerable degree of independence. But politics was not its exclusive field. Through its earlier years it gave more of education and leadership than any other American journal in literature, education, reform, and all the higher forms of social activity.

The journalistic features of the period just following the establishment of the Daily *Republican* were thus summed up by Mr. Bowles, thirty years later:

" American journalism was undergoing the greatest transformation and experiencing the deepest inspiration of its whole history. The telegraph and the Mexican war came in together; and the years '46–'51 were the years of most marked growth known to America. It was something more than progress, it was revolution. Then the old *Sun* was in its best estate ; then Mr. Bennett was in the prime of his vigorous intellect, and his enterprise and independence were at the height of their audacity. He had as first lieutenant, Mr. Frederic Hudson, the best organizer of a mere *newspaper* America has ever seen. Then Mr. Greeley and Mr. Dana were harmoniously and vigorously giving the *Tribune* that scope of treatment and that intellectual depth and breadth which have never departed wholly from it, and which are perhaps the greatest gifts that any single journal has made to the journalism of the country. Then Mr. Raymond commenced the *Times* and won for it at once a prominent place among its rivals. And then began that horde of provincial daily journals, springing up like mushrooms all over the land. Hardly a town of 10,000 inhabitants but that essayed its diurnal issue in those fertile years."

It was in this field of provincial journalism that Mr. Bowles's work was done. Of the old-fashioned country newspaper he once wrote:

" News had grown old when it was published. The paper did the work of the chronicler or annalist merely, and was the historian of the past rather than a spectator and actor in the present. It was not upon the printed column that the events of the day struck the heart of the living age, and drew from it its sparks of fire. In those times that place of contact was found in the personal intercourse of men. News ran then along the street, from mouth to mouth; the gossiping neighbor carried it; the post-rider brought it into the groups gathered at the village store. By and by came the heavy gazette, not to make its impression but to record the fact. . . . The journalism was yet to be created that should stand firmly in the possession of powers of its own; that should be concerned with the passing and not with the past; that should perfectly reflect its age, and yet should be itself no mere reflection; that should control what it seemed only to transcribe and narrate; that should teach without assuming the manners of an instructor, and should command the coming times with a voice that had still no sound but its echo of the present."

Among the country newspapers of its time, the Weekly *Republican*, before 1844, stood well. It had outlived and absorbed several rivals during its twenty years' existence, and thus had satisfied the test of the survival of the fittest. But one who now turns over its old files will find scanty material even for the chronicler or annalist. A file of the Weekly *Republican* for any of the years of its later history affords a most graphic and vivid week-to-week history of the period. These volumes will be a rich treasury to the future historian. But, between the years 1826 and 1844, the pages of the *Republican* throw little light upon the social life of the times. It has two chief staples — political discussions, and scraps of miscellaneous unassorted news. The politics are more vigorous than lucid. Personal and party names do service largely in place of rational discussion. Nothing is more characteristic of the younger Bowles's methods in his maturity than his constant reference to general principles in his writing,—the special question or incident being illumined by its relation to some broad idea. In his work we have continually, "philosophy teaching by example." But the father's paper followed largely the easier method which assumes that the editor and his readers are of the same mind, and simply reiterates under a variety of forms that they are right and their opponents wrong. Political discussion forms the central interest, and occupies half the space, of the Weekly *Republican* before 1844. For the rest it is filled generally with some selected " tale "; with an odd collection of miscellaneous news items, in which " shocking accidents," "mysterious occurrences " and " sad calamities " predominate; and with scraps of literary and religious matter. There is an occasional piece of local news, meagerly told, sometimes with mild attempt at humor. But there is nothing like a systematic presentation of the week's occurrences even in the town and neighborhood, still less in more distant fields. In reading the meager chronicle one is moved to ask, " Did nothing happen in those days? Or did no one know how to tell what happened ? "

# CHAPTER VI.

## The First Years of Work: Ashmun and Calhoun.

SUCH was the general condition of American journalism when Mr. Bowles began his work, and such was the paper which was his school and his basis to build upon. The first development which he showed was in solid rather than brilliant qualities. In the words of one who knew him long and well, " The fire, spirit, life, which in his prime he was so full of, did not appear in his early years. There was not much to develop him at first. He went away from home little, and he had not an inspiring circle of acquaintances. He was plodding, industrious, saving,—that was his reputation. But he whom in later years we knew as *Sam Bowles* was not there,—not even the suggestion of him."

In these first years, he was under the pressing necessity of unresting work. The best editorial writing at this time was done by one or two men outside of the office. Except this, almost all the business and editorial labor came upon father and son, and most heavily upon the son. He worked late at night; vacations and holidays were unknown; of recreation and general society he had almost nothing.

The first special power he showed was in the faculty of seeing a thing clearly and telling it as he saw it. He was quick to find out what was going on. His big eyes

— of so dark a brown that they often seemed black — saw everything that men were doing about him. In his news items the community began to find a little daily history of itself. Springfield was probably in reality much the same town in 1848 as in 1843; but as reflected in the *Republican* it has become a much more interesting place.

Mr. Bowles was at the outset a slow writer and a slow thinker. Even his news reports were written patiently and laboriously. His epigrammatic brilliance, his genius for terse and telling phrase, belonged altogether to his later development. So did his power of managing men, — a power compounded of magnetism and tact. His first foreman had been his room-mate as a boy, and, being a stiff-grained Yankee, was not very amenable to the management of his old companion, and gave him many a troublous hour. The editor managed to hold his own, but at home he sometimes cried with vexation over the difficulties of the composing-room.

He seems to have had no marked period of mental fermentation and deep questioning. Among his contemporaries in New England, there was much unsettling and relaying of foundations. Emerson and Carlyle were uttering their quickening words. Transcendentalism was at its height, and all manner of reforms and agitations were in the air. The Abolition movement was stirring the social and political world with thrills of wrath and of sympathy. It was a yeasty time: intellectual America was in the stage of uneasy adolescence, with its passion, self-questioning, aspiration, and revolt. A few years later, no man was more sensitive to the moral atmosphere of the community than Mr. Bowles. But in his youth he was not especially stirred by what we now look back to as the vital and prophetic forces of the time. With those forces, as social influences, he did not come in close contact. The town he lived in was provincial as no place is provincial in these days of railroad and telegraph. The movements of thought, which, as we look back on them, appear like tidal waves agitating the whole community, were in reality narrow currents, which left the greater part of society a long time unmoved. Boston and its neighborhood awoke to the new life long before the rest of the country. The social atmosphere of the Connecticut Valley was conservative and in a degree materialistic. It was little responsive to the passionate cry of the Abolitionists. That dryness of the old New England life, that want of color and warmth and spiritual insight, against which Emerson and Thoreau and the Transcendentalists revolted, so pervaded and incrusted the general community that only the more sensitive and restless spirits answered to the call for something better. At the time of life when a young man is most liable to questioning and mental unrest, Mr. Bowles was held too closely by work and responsibility to have any leisure for exploring excursions into the infinite. His whole early bent was practical rather than speculative. He found his great interest, beyond his personal work, in that broadest of practical subjects, the political life of the nation. His finest work as a reporter was his account of political conventions; and his journeys to these, with the contact into which they brought him with leading men, were a great step in that intercourse with humanity in which lay much of the education of his maturity. He had grown up in a family and a community in which the solid and practical qualities were more cultivated than the graces and amenities. He had by nature an instinct to claim the first place; and the early struggle for success, in which every foot of ground had to be fought for, was not likely to lessen that disposition. His associates found him sometimes selfish and sometimes crusty. The sweeter and

mellower traits needed years and experience for their
full ripening.

His habits were pure, and only in work was he given
to injurious indulgence. With early manhood began
the lavish, unstinted drain of nervous power through
excessive toil and shortened sleep. There appeared no
lack of nervous force until in later years this steady
drain had weakened him. Indeed, the immense activity
which in effect condensed half a dozen life-times into
his fifty-two years, showed that his original endowment
of nerve and brain power was magnificent. It seems
probable that the quiet and unstimulated character of
his boyish years was no bad preparation for the intensely
energetic career that was to follow. From the time when
the first friction of manly work and struggle struck fire
within him, the flame never ceased to burn. But through
his boyhood and adolescence nature had slowly and
quietly ripened and stored her forces within him, amid a
sedate household and a tranquil community.

The two men whose influence on the early life of Samuel Bowles and the *Republican* was most marked, were
William B. Calhoun and George Ashmun. To Mr. Calhoun more than to any other man the paper owed its
first high merit as a political teacher. The editorials in
which the little provincial sheet, even in its earlier days,
spoke sometimes with a voice as forcible and as lofty as
the best of the great journals, were for the most part
written by him. Mr. Ashmun made less immediate contribution to the *Republican*, but his was the most brilliant and impressive personality at that time in western
Massachusetts, and he fascinated and helped to mold the
young man who was his near neighbor. Mr. Bowles
once said, toward the end of his life, that the only man
he ever felt dominate him was George Ashmun. He
sketched the portraits of Calhoun and Ashmun at the

time of their deaths.   Those portraits deserve to be given
here, at least their most salient features,—not only as
among the best specimens of Mr. Bowles's style in its
maturity, but because the two men acted upon his character from different sides as strong formative influences;
and because each illustrated a conspicuous type among
the New Englanders of the last generation;—the one, a
modernized Puritan, the other a personal and political
disciple of Daniel Webster.

The obituary of Mr. Calhoun, November 9, 1865, says
of him :

"A vigorous constitution, simple habits, and great care have
long withstood sharp disease, combining consumption, catarrh,
and dyspepsia;—it was not in humanity to resist such union of
assault longer or more bravely; and he died with the dignity
and the courage and yet the submissiveness with which he had
always lived.

"Mr. Calhoun was beyond any other man of past or present
generation THE PUBLIC MAN of Springfield.  No one was ever
more truly popular among us than he; no other citizen ever
held so many high public trusts, or so long, as he; and no
man, perhaps, ever gave more satisfaction to his constituents,
or more faithfully fulfilled his duties."

There follows a summary of the events of his life.
He was born in Boston in 1796, educated at Yale, came
to Springfield a young lawyer; was sent to the legislature (House) from 1825 to 1835, and for the last two years
was Speaker; was in Congress for Hampden and Hampshire counties from 1835 to 1843; failed then in health;
went to the State Senate and was its president in 1846
and 1847; then was Secretary of State for three years;
was a State Bank Commissioner for three years from
1853; lived on his farm in the intervals of public service;
was mayor of Springfield in 1859, and again was representative in the legislature in 1861.

"This was the last of his public service. Since, his retirement has been inexorable from the growing power of his disease, now at last finally victorious. But the cordial respect and tender thought of the communities he had so long and so faithfully served waited on him in his invalid home; and never was there a party emergency, or popular want of leader, that his name was not mentioned, and his incapacity lamented.

"None of this popular confidence, none of these popular trusts, were due to what are understood in political circles as 'popular qualities.' There was no self-seeking, no placating manner, very little warming, magnetic quality, in Mr. Calhoun. We never knew him to seek an office; he yielded to the opportunities for it oftener than he would but that he was poor, and ill-health and disrelish unfitted him for the successful practice of his profession; but we never could detect the slightest element of the demagogue or the office-seeker in his character or his manners. The atmosphere of his presence forbade any such ideas. He was consistently, radically, democratic in his thought and principles; as true a republican as ever lived; but his appearance and his manner were always dignified, self-respecting, unimpassioned. When he spoke, particularly when he addressed a public audience, there was more of enthusiasm, and he was always earnest in conviction and utterance. In writing, too, his style was far more spirited, popular, and enthusiastic than would have been imagined by those not familiar with this expression of his life. He did nothing so well as this, indeed. His style was pure, the purest, yet popular and enticing. It was both vigorous and effective, simple and elevated. For many years he was an occasional editorial writer for the Republican, and for several years quite a voluminous contributor to its columns. He wrote very readily and with great perfection in detail. No copy was ever so clean as his. His electioneering paragraphs were especially admirable,—the fashion is gone out with us now; but his appeals to the old Whigs to rally at the polls, to vote early, to get out the sick, to stand by the polls till night, and generally to save their party and their country, in the pending crisis, had as much pith and ring to them as Thurlow Weed's, and more of culture and rhetoric.

" The one superior element in Mr. Calhoun's character and life was its high moral quality. It was this and the subtle magnetism of it that made him so strong with the people, that gave him such influence with them, and such power in public places. No man we ever knew was more gifted in this respect; it seemed an endowment of nature, indeed, more than a discipline of life, with him — it seemed as if he were born into it, and had always lived in it. His religious character grew out of this, and became in middle life and since a conspicuous and even dominating influence with him. He was very much absorbed in religious and theological reading; probably his library is the richest in these respects in all this region; and the old Puritan habits and thoughts appeared to grow firm into his nature with his study and experience.

" Mr. Calhoun began his public life the very season the *Republican* was started, forty years ago, and he and it have always been in political sympathy. He was an habitué of its office and writer for its columns when we began to sweep out, carry papers, and play ' roller boy.' He has been its familiar ever since ; though not so frequently a visitor as before the death of his intimate friend and contemporary, the original proprietor and editor, and his own broken health. We imagine he felt a little shy of the youthful rashness that succeeded to the helm, as we never wholly outgrew the feeling of awe and distant respect that his tall, erect form, his sober face, and his stiff, iron-gray hair, as well as the weighty and measured wisdom of his editorials, created in our boyish breast. Years and invalid experience have unlocked for us some of the mysteries of his life ; we knew him better lately without seeing him at all ;—and we knew, too, that honorable and useful as his life has been, it would have been more effective and even more successful in a worldly sense had he not ever borne torture and weakness in his body ; but that it could hardly have been nobler and more faithful, or earned a higher glory in Immortality."

Upon the death of Mr. Ashmun, in the summer of 1870, Mr. Bowles wrote of him :

" No citizen of western Massachusetts, of all her generations, ever made that impress upon his fellows, ever more stimulated

the hope and stirred the pride of his own neighbors and friends,
than George Ashmun. Other men have made larger use of
their opportunities and their gifts. The very wealth of his own
seemed to make him careless of them, and he lived and died,
himself sharing the vexation of his admirers at what might
have been."

An epitome of his life up to 1854 is given, in a note
of his own to the editor: "Born at Blandford, Mass.,
1804; graduated at Yale; studied law and began practice in Springfield in 1828; was sent four times to the
Massachusetts House of Representatives, and was its
Speaker in 1841; went twice to the State Senate; and
was in the National House from 1845 to 1851. Such,"
he writes, "is my public history during the fifty years
which are completed to-day! I have had too much of
public life for my own good, and more than is good for
any man who wisely seeks the happiness of himself or
his family, and not enough to be of any service to any
one else, or worth being put upon record."

"Early," writes Mr. Bowles, "he became both a personal and political favorite, and there never has been a
time when the people of Springfield, almost without regard to party, would not join with enthusiasm in elevating him to any public station within their power." In
his profession he was associated from 1834 until his substantial retirement in 1851 with Reuben A. Chapman,
afterward chief justice of the state. He was not a severe general student, but always mastered his cases; the
day before the trial he might be off with his dog and
gun, but the struggle found him prepared.

" He comprehended as by instinct not only the strong points
of his own case, but the weak points of his adversary's, and he
was alert and vigorous in following up every advantage. Subtle or simple, attentive or negligent, indifferent or absorbed;
vehement and overpowering in assertion and bold invective, or

calm in statement and modest in appeal, he really had no match in the profession in all this part of the state, and if he had chosen to give himself up to the law with any consistent and persistent following, his triumphs in it would have swept through the state, and gone into the higher courts of the large cities. . . .

" But perhaps his great power in trying a case, as indeed his great power in politics or in social life, was his personal influence over men. He was a student of human nature, and somewhat prided himself upon his attainments in this respect. He had all the elements of great personal attraction, and added to this a subtle and cogent way of putting a case from the standpoint of the man whom he was seeking to influence. By being master of himself and superior to the reasons which influenced his own mind, it was that he became capable of giving the reasons which should influence other minds. His career in public life is full of striking illustrations of this great power of his. Probably the most notable was the result of his interview with Stephen A. Douglas, directly after the rebels fired on Fort Sumter, and the rebellion was fully launched upon the land. Such were his appeals, such the force of the arguments he addressed to Douglas, that the great Illinoisian rose up superior to partisanship, superior to disappointment, and took his stand with the country. ' Now,' said Mr. Ashmun, although it was very late in the night, ' let us go up to the White House and talk with Mr. Lincoln. I want you to say to him what you have said to me, and then I want the result of this night's deliberations to be telegraphed to the country.' That interview at the White House between these three men — Lincoln, Douglas, and Ashmun — should be historical. Then and there Mr. Douglas took down the map and planned the campaign. Then and there he gave in, most eloquently and vehemently, his adhesion to the Administration and the country. Mr. Ashmun himself briefly epitomized the story, and it went by telegraph that night all over the country, to electrify and encourage every patriot on the morrow.

" In public life, not only by such address as this, but by ability in debate, by wisdom in council, by adroitness in dealing with the circumstances of the moment, and the prejudices and passions of friends and foes, he wielded great influence, and had in fact no peer on the floor while in Congress, and was always put forward by his friends to manage any difficult case, to discomfit any dangerous opponent. He was always true to the advanced ideas of the Whigs of Massachusetts" upon the great questions of the time. "Though his great friend, Mr. Webster, abandoned the Wilmot Proviso principle, Mr. Ashmun could not and did not. . . . His intimacy with and admiration for Mr. Webster, more than any other circumstance, perhaps, shaped his public career and interrupted his growth in public life. It always seemed to us a remarkable circumstance, as a striking testimony of the consistency and firmness of Mr. Ashmun's principles, that Mr. Webster did not confide to him in advance, as he did to many others, the character of his famous seventh of March compromise speech. The letters which Mr. Ashmun then wrote to his correspondents at home would now be regarded as valuable political revelations. ' Don't believe,' said he, day after day, ' what you hear about Mr. Webster's forthcoming speech. He will make no such concessions as are attributed to him. To use his own words, " the past at least is secure," and he will take no steps backward.' " When the speech came, Mr. Ashmun was as much surprised as any one ; it did not shake his personal loyalty to Webster, but he would not go with him in giving up the Wilmot Proviso. " But his personal feelings were so strongly in sympathy with the man that, without giving up his principles, he espoused Mr. Webster's side in the ensuing political and personal quarrels, and went out of political life in consequence. Never was there greater evidence, it seems to us, of the real personal power of Mr. Webster, than the fact that this strong man, before whom and to whom all others yielded, surrendered himself almost completely to him, shared his controversies, and accepted voluntarily his fate. Nor do we ever find the evidence that Mr. Webster truly appreciated this great tribute to his power, this great gift of self-sacrificing friendship. It seems to be the weakness of men of the Websterian position and supremacy to regard men nearly all alike, and make no true distinction between the characters of those who give them their friendship." Mr. Webster showed always a warm and high regard for Mr. Ashmun, but apparently "he did not measure the true degree of heroic friendship and generous self-sacrifice which Mr. Ashmun laid at his feet. Other men owed what they were to their friendship for Mr. Webster; Mr. Ashmun, in a sense, lost all he was and all he had a right to hope of being, by that friendship. But his devotion to his great friend truly marked the innate heroism of his nature. Perhaps it was the only occasion of his life that brought it out in full measure, but the quality was there, and no one ever came near and saw into him but detected this great instinct of heroism. . . .

"Not until long after Mr. Webster's death did Mr. Ashmun recover tone and toleration for public life. Living at Washington most of the time, he was in contact with leading men of all parties, but while he never gave up his old anti-slavery Whig principles, and early sympathized with the idea and movement of the Republican party, his views of public life were all tinged by the Websterian experience." He was induced to go to the Chicago convention that nominated Lincoln in 1860, and served ably as its presiding officer. Upon this followed a pleasant intimacy with President Lincoln, and an influential private position at Washington; but he was not acceptable to the Massachusetts congressmen, and no office was offered to him that he would accept. "We remember his bringing to us the first intimation of Mr. Lincoln's desire for re-election, long before it had been manifest to the public. Walking together under the trees of the public grounds, the President gave his confidence to our townsman. He said, in his quiet, plain way, that, now he had got used to the machine, he thought he should like to run it four years more.

"But it was in social life, perhaps, that both the power and the charm of Mr. Ashmun's character came out most fully. Sometimes he was imperious, as he was always imperial; but it was rare that he was not kindly and winning and instructive. He was not a great reader of books, though a devoted admirer and re-reader of Scott. But he knew life and nature, and his observations on the men who walked, the birds that flew, and the fishes that swam, were always original and suggestive. He had strong domestic affections, and his friendships were sincere and permanent. All his senses were keen; he was alive to the beauties of landscape, flowers, and poetry. He was choice and delicate in his food. He had a quick sense of humor, and a magnetic force in conversation. His words were loaded with conviction. He did not write much, but his letters or his newspaper contributions — for he was a frequent contributor of editorial paragraphs or communications to the *Republican* — were always in a pure, incisive English style, noticeable chiefly for their strength, and yet were not without frequent felicities of expression. He struggled in early life against the family tendency to consumption. It was this that drove him so much out-of-doors, and to his free, generous way of living. But whether it was natural or acquired, or partly both, he grew to have great enjoyment in field sports, and he drew from them a quality of happiness and invigoration which undoubtedly heightened his faculties and certainly prolonged his life.

"At his own or a friend's dinner-table he was almost incomparably felicitous. He had a thought and a word for everybody at the table, man, woman, or child, and it fitted exactly to the level of each life. Of politics; of fishing or hunting; of flowers or nature in general; of the raising of vegetables; of meats and their cooking — no housewife but could learn something from him here; of literature; of men, women, things; — while there was nothing pedantic, he yet had a thought and a knowledge upon them all. A royal night, we remember, he gave a few of his friends when Thackeray was in Springfield. He led in the feast of good things, skillfully avoiding all possible shoals, smoothing any ruffling of feathers that might come from any transatlantic prejudices or a thoughtless remark. The company floated out for hours on a tide of humor, of brilliant gossip and suggestive criticism, in which Mr. Ashmun was astonishingly seconded by his friend from Greenfield," — George T. Davis, — "the most brilliant table-talker of America; so that even Thackeray, accustomed to the finest society of England as well as of America, often laid down his knife and fork,— a thing he was not wont to do without occasion,— and listened or applauded with wonder.

" For several years, while his brain has been clear and strong as ever, and his digestive faculties healthy, there has been growing over him a palsy of the nervous system, accompanied with great suffering, and with a growing inability to move. . . . He has now passed away,— a man greater in nature and in capacity than in deeds, but yet supreme among his fellows in all action. We do not forget his failings and his misfortunes, but there arise above them all the peerless qualities of mind and heart that made him walk a king among men, and drew around him a circle of devoted and loving friends."

# CHAPTER VII.

## THE MEXICAN WAR AND THE FREE-SOIL PARTY.

THE strength of the Daily *Republican* from the first lay largely in its political discussions. While as a newspaper it was still insignificant, it often handled the political questions of the day with a breadth, intelligence, and vigor which few journals then or afterward surpassed. The most effective of these articles, during this early period, were undoubtedly from the pen of Mr. Calhoun. But the general attitude of the *Republican* upon the national questions of the time was determined by the Bowleses; others might influence, but never dictate.

The beginning of the Daily *Republican* coincided with the appearance of the Slavery question as a chief factor in American politics. In 1844, the birth-year of the paper, a treaty for the annexation of Texas was signed by President Tyler, and a joint resolution approving the treaty was introduced in Congress. This thrust upon the nation the question of an aggressive policy toward Mexico, involving the probability of war and the annexation of more slave territory. The Whig party as a whole was opposed to the acquisition, partly on anti-slavery grounds, partly as the traditional champion of a moderate foreign policy. Its presidential candidate, Henry Clay, was supposed to be hostile to the annexation, but his position was somewhat ambiguous, and he lost

the confidence of Seward and the New York Whigs. The
Democrats and their candidate Polk were for immediate
annexation, with the resulting increase of slave territory,
and at the price of war if necessary. The "Liberty
party"—organized in 1840 by those of the Abolitionists
who believed in political action for the gradual suppression of slavery, and who at that time separated
from Garrison and his immediate associates — nominated
James G. Birney for President. Their action drew enough
votes from Clay to give the presidency to Polk.

During this period the *Republican* was anti-slavery and
Whig. In its first number, March 29, 1844, an article
was quoted in regard to Mr. Clay,— already recognized
as the coming presidential candidate of the Whigs,—
representing him as a champion of protection, internal
improvements, close commercial alliances with Mexico
and the South American republics, and "a system of
American policy." The first long editorial, April 23, denounces the annexation of Texas, just brought before
Congress for its confirmation, and makes a vigorous and
stirring appeal to the North to oppose it. Through the
ensuing campaign the *Republican* heartily supported
Clay, and urged as the leading issues the defeat of annexation and the maintenance of a high tariff.

The election of Polk was a popular sanction of the
annexation of Texas, which was accordingly consummated
by President Tyler's administration as its closing act.
Texas had recently won its independence from Mexico.
It had been greatly aided therein by immigrants from
the neighboring American states; and by their influence
slavery, abolished by Mexico, had been reëstablished.
Texas, with the assent of its people, was now admitted
to the Union as a slave state. The boundary line between Texas and Mexico was in dispute, Texas insisting
on the Rio Grande as the dividing line, and Mexico

claiming the Nueces. President Polk threw into the disputed region a military force under command of General Taylor; Taylor's forces and the Mexicans came into collision; and Congress hastened to declare war. Taylor won a succession of brilliant victories and penetrated deep into the Mexican territory; and General Scott captured Vera Cruz, fought his way to the capital city, and took it. The war lasted two years, and was ended early in 1848 by a treaty in which Mexico gave up the immense region afterward organized as California, New Mexico, and Utah, and received fifteen million dollars. The acquisition of this territory was the real purpose of the conquest which the United States achieved over its weak neighbor.

The war had its chief support in the South and in the Democratic party. It roused at the North a strong protest, in the name of peace and of freedom,— a protest of which the lasting literary memorial is the "Biglow Papers." The Whig party in general, and especially its Northern wing, opposed the war throughout, and was emphatically hostile to the acquisition of any more slave territory. When in 1846 a proposal was made in Congress to give the President $2,000,000, with which to purchase an advantageous peace, David Wilmot, of Pennsylvania, moved in the House to add a proviso declaring that in all new territory that might be acquired slavery should be prohibited. The proviso passed the House, receiving almost the solid Northern vote, but it was defeated in the Senate. The "Wilmot Proviso" became the watchword of the Northern Whigs.

The *Republican* was in hearty sympathy with the anti-war and anti-slavery sentiment. Indeed, of open opposition to that sentiment there was very little to be found in the state. Webster presented in the Senate a resolution affirming the principle of the Wilmot Proviso, which had been adopted in the Massachusetts House by a unanimous vote. The political situation is well illustrated by the action of the Whig State Convention at Springfield, September 30, 1847. Scott had given the finishing stroke to the war by the capture of the city of Mexico a fortnight before, though the fact was not known until four days later. The Democratic Convention had nominated for governor General Caleb Cushing, who was fighting in Mexico; had voted down a Wilmot Proviso resolution; and in its platform had ignored the slavery question. Of the Whig Convention George Ashmun was president. Webster, the idol of the Massachusetts Whigs, made one of his lucid and powerful speeches. He declared that the Whigs of the entire country are opposed to the addition of any new territory, free or slave; that the Southern Democrats want more slave territory, and the Northern Democrats more free territory; and the two wings have combined to rob Mexico, leaving the disposition of the plunder to be settled later. He said: "I never have voted, I never shall, I never will vote for further annexation to this country with a slave representation upon it. Slave representation in a political point of view is an all-important subject. The moral view is great, I know, but it is with the former that I have only to do in my capacity as legislator." The resolutions of the convention called for "Peace with Mexico without dismemberment." They declared that there should be no addition of Mexican territory to the American Union; but should any be annexed, it must be free. Webster was named for the presidency. These resolutions having been unanimously carried, another was proposed, declaring that the Whigs of the state will support no man for the presidency who is not opposed to slavery extension. This resolution was supported by Sumner, Palfrey, and C. F. Adams, and opposed by

Robert C. Winthrop and others, and was defeated by a large majority. The *Republican* approved the convention's action and Webster's speech, but maintained that the additional resolution ought to have been adopted.

While party politics were taking this course, a little band of the most zealous Abolitionists, with Garrison at their head, were uttering fierce denunciation against the sin of slavery, but stood aloof altogether from the voter's function and from the whole political system of which Southern slavery was an integral part. Garrison, who had never acted with the "Liberty party," reached in 1844 the position of directly assailing the Constitution, by which slavery was protected as a local institution, and the Union in which a slave-holding element was a factor. Thenceforth his cry was "The United States Constitution is a covenant with death and an agreement with hell." Before this, he and some of his associates had begun to denounce the American churches, for their complicity with slavery. They thus struck at two of the most powerful sentiments among the better class of Americans, — ecclesiastical Christianity and loyalty to the nation. They smote as unsparingly as the Hebrew prophets rebuked the ceremonial system when it cloaked impiety. They denounced the churches and the Union at the same time that they were attacking one of the strongest material and political forces in the country, and defying the basest prejudices of the mob.

The *Republican*, like the great majority of Northern people, had no sympathy with the principles or methods of the Garrisonian Abolitionists. It was hostile to them in their assaults on the Union and the churches, was offended by their violence of language, was unsympathetic toward the brood of reforms with which they often made common cause, and showed little appreciation of the self-sacrificing earnestness and the grasp of one great

truth which ennobled their cause.  The early attitude of
its leading editor toward slavery may be illustrated from
his letters to the paper, when traveling in the South in
the winter of 1844–5.  In these there is little mention
of slavery ; but the closing letter contains this paragraph :

" The fact is, in regard to slavery, the owners are generally
much more the objects of pity and sympathy than the slaves ;
they suffer from its blighting curse greatly and sensibly, while
the latter are more contented, better fed and clothed, than the
free blacks either at the North or South.  This is true, if my
observation the past winter has been worth anything, and I
fully believe that a great majority of citizens of the slave
states are fully aware how great the curse is which weighs
them down, and would gladly throw it off, if it could be done
in any reasonable and proper manner, without completely im-
poverishing them, or endangering their personal safety and
success."

Evidently the young man — he was only nineteen — ob-
served and judged for himself ; but his observation did
not yet go below the surface of things.  He judged by a
materialistic standard ;— the slaves he saw were well fed
and clothed ; why pity them overmuch ?  But the system
was bad economy for the masters; trust their self-interest
to get rid of it !  This materialism, this want of moral
intuition and enthusiasm, tinged all the early course of
the *Republican* on the Slavery question, and made it constantly unjust to the Abolitionists.  Yet the *Republican's*
condemnation of slavery during these years was sincere
and earnest, and expressed that grave conviction of its
wrong and folly in which the general sentiment of
New England was agreed.  The practical difficulty and
divergence came upon the question of what political
action was advisable in the matter.  It was impossible

to make political attack on slavery where it already existed, without disregarding the Constitution and destroying the Union. To this the great majority of the Northern people — the majority too of the conscientious and intelligent — were always opposed. On the question of breaking up the whole political fabric to eradicate slavery,— or rather to relieve the North from complicity in it; since after disunion the South would still have retained slavery,— on this question the extreme Abolitionists were always a small minority. But when the question arose whether the national authority should establish slavery within the national territorial domain, and even whether new territory should be conquered that slavery might be extended,— then the most conservative of citizens, the most constitutional of Whigs, could unite to maintain the cause of Freedom.

When the presidential election of 1848 was approaching, and General Taylor came into prominence as the Whig candidate, the *Republican* urged two questions: What is his position as to the annexation of slave territory, and what as to the spoils-of-office system? But neither General Taylor nor his friends made any answer to such questions. Of his political opinions almost nothing was known; his personal reputation was that of an honest, soldierly man,— "Old Rough and Ready"; his recommendation as a candidate was the fame he had won in a war which the Whigs had from first to last denounced. But the national convention sacrificed everything to success. Webster and Clay, the brains and the heart of the party, were discarded in favor of Taylor. In deference to the party's Southern wing, the resolutions wholly ignored the living questions of territorial extension and slavery. It was a most inglorious surrender of principle to expediency. On the floor of the convention two Massachusetts delegates, Henry Wilson and Charles Allen of Worcester, declared that they would not support the party nominee. They went home, and with such men as Sumner, C. F. Adams, and Samuel Hoar, leaders of "the conscience Whigs,"— as the phrase now went,— met in convention, and sent delegates, chosen equally from the three existing parties, to the national Free-soil Convention at Buffalo. In that body were Chase and Giddings of Ohio, and a strong representation from a section of New York Democrats, who were in revolt against their party on grounds partly anti-slavery and partly personal. The Liberty party was merged in the Free-soil, whose creed was the exclusion of slavery from the territories; and Martin Van Buren and C. F. Adams were nominated for President and Vice-President.

Here was a party that stood clear and strong on the great coming question. Yet the political situation had still its grave embarrassments for the anti-slavery voter. There was no chance of Van Buren's election. The presidency lay really between Taylor and the Democratic nominee, General Cass of Michigan. The dilemma was: to assert a principle, and build up a party of the future, at the risk of letting in the worse candidate at present; or to aim at an immediate gain, by the choice of the less objectionable of two leading candidates. Fresh in mind was the election of four years before, and the disastrous result of Birney's candidacy, in the election of Polk, and the Mexican war. The Free-soil party had an unattractive element in the New York Democratic seceders —" Barnburners" in the slang of the time— who cared little for anti-slavery, and much for avenging the wrongs of Van Buren and Silas Wright. Whigs as strongly anti-slavery as Seward and Greeley thought that that party still offered the best practical ground for opposing slavery extension. It was one of those perplexing situations which must often occur in politics;— or in any other field where men seek to obtain the ideal under the limitations of the real.

It is at this juncture that we can first identify Mr. Bowles's personal work as a political writer. "For a good while," says his old foreman, Chauncey White, " he didn't do much political writing. But one evening in a presidential campaign — it was in the Taylor year — he had been out to report a speech, and he came in tearing mad, and sat down and wrote a reply to it. The article was so spicy that it pleased Ashmun, who came in to ask who wrote it. I think that was about the beginning of Mr. Bowles's political writing." This must have been the article published June 3, 1848. The occasion was a Free-soil speech in Springfield, by Joshua Giddings, fore-shadowing the nomination of Van Buren. The editorial, in comment and reply, is marked by a good-tempered vigor and pungency. It takes issue with Mr. Giddings chiefly on the question of Van Buren's fitness to represent opposition to slavery extension, and cites his record as a supporter of slavery and its aggressions.

"What then, up to the month of June just past, has Martin Van Buren done, that should win for him the praise of anti-slavery men? During his whole political life, he has been the most abject tool of the slave power. He earned by his readiness, nay, his eagerness, to serve their interests and forward their purposes, the name of 'the Northern man with Southern principles.' If he has, in the retiracy of his private life, at last discovered and forsook the errors of his whole previous existence, and come to the stool of repentance, well and good. We rejoice. No one will do so more heartily. But while the sad results of the betrayal of Northern rights, interests, and principles are so vividly before us, we cannot join in the high-sounding pæans of praise to his character that we hear from some quarters. We cannot join in efforts to elevate him to a place he once so wrongly and so injuriously to the country's

prosperity occupied.  No, not at least until his acts speak for
his repentance as well as his words.  We give in to no man in
opposing the extension of slavery.  We are for Free Soil and
Free Labor.  Our efforts are pledged to this end.  But we cannot yet see our way clear to follow Mr. Giddings' lead.  That
nasty word 'Compromise' is already introduced into the Senate.
Congress is the battle-ground of Slavery and Freedom.  We are
ready to meet the shock.  If the North stands by its rights, we
triumph; if not, we fall.  Our motto is, 'No compromise';
'*No more slave territory.*'"

Upon this ground, through the ensuing campaign, the
paper opposed Van Buren.  It supported Taylor as an
honest, patriotic, and moderate man, who could be trusted
to oppose all aggressive and dangerous measures.  The
impression generally prevailed that as a matter of personal opinion he was opposed to the extension of slavery.
But on this supreme question he made no public utterance.  This campaign brought a great access of strong
leaders to the Free-soil party in Massachusetts.  From the
Democrats came such men as Robert Rantoul and N. P.
Banks; from the Whigs, Charles Sumner, Henry Wilson,
and C. F. Adams.  The moral enthusiasts, and the men
of practical instinct for the coming future, tended to the
party which stood distinctly for freedom.  It was such a
company as the Samuel Bowles of a few years later would
have been sure to be found in.  But he had not yet got
his growth, and the influence of Ashmun doubtless did
much to hold the *Republican* among the loyal followers
of the Whig flag.  Horace Greeley, who at a late day
and with reluctance yielded his support to Taylor, was
perfectly frank in avowing his dissatisfaction with his
attitude upon slavery.  He expressed this regret in his
printed campaign addresses to the Whigs of doubtful
states; and by that very frankness, he added weight to
his appeals,— appeals in which common sense, logic and

passion were blended with an effectiveness which hardly any other American has equaled. The *Republican* made no such frank admission as to Taylor's deficiencies. It made the best of him, not with extravagant laudation, but with skillful magnifying of his strong points and silence as to the weak ones. In this it followed the fashion of loyal partisanship.

The Whigs won the day. The Southern Whig, Taylor, received 163 electoral votes, and the Northern Democrat, Cass, 127,— drawn in pretty equal proportions from the two sections. Van Buren got no electoral vote; of his popular vote of 290,000, almost a third was drawn from New York state; there and in Massachusetts he had more votes than Cass. The Free-soil party owed its strength largely to a local and temporary feud of the Democracy, which added to it nothing permanent. But it had laid a foundation for the Republican party. At present, the anti-slavery element among the Whigs was strong. Webster and his followers had given only a half-hearted support to Taylor, and were disaffected toward his administration from the first. But Seward was elected to the Senate from New York; and Seward had already declared, in a speech at Cleveland: "Slavery can be limited to its present bounds; it can be ameliorated; and it can be abolished;— and you and I must do it."

# CHAPTER VIII.

## PERSONAL AND FAMILY LIFE.

WHILE a boy in Mr. Eaton's school, Mr. Bowles had met among his fellow-pupils Miss Mary S. D. Schermerhorn, a daughter of H. V. R. Schermerhorn, of Geneva, N. Y., and grand-daughter of James S. Dwight, the leading Springfield merchant of the first quarter of the century. Miss Schermerhorn while attending the school lived in an uncle's family; she had numerous relatives in the town; and when school years were over, the two young people had opportunities for continued acquaintance, which ripened into an engagement. They were married at the bride's home, September 6, 1848. No time for a wedding journey; they were married on Wednesday, and on the following Saturday the editor was back at his post. The young wife identified herself from the first with her husband's interests and aims. Through their thirty years of married life she gave an entire devotion to his comfort and happiness, and was repaid by a loyal affection, and a constant and considerate helpfulness which the most exacting demands of his profession never abated. He had now the resource without which no worker is rightly equipped and no man is a full man. When in his later life he was asked by one of his younger lieutenants the cause of his success, he answered "I married early, and I worked with all my might."

The young couple made their home with the parents. The elder Mrs. Bowles gave a mother's kindness to the young wife, who had lost her own mother while still a child. The son was receiving from his father five hundred dollars a year for his services, and on that sum he and his wife at first lived. After a year or two, a property of $10,000 coming to him, he bought with a portion of this money a part of the block into which the paper had been moved. It had exchanged its first quarters over the Chicopee Bank, on the corner of Main and Elm streets, for rooms on the north-east corner of Market and Sandford streets. For the sum thus invested he received from his father the ownership of one-half of the paper.

After Mr. Stowe had worked with the *Republican* for a few months, he was called to another position. In his place came Samuel H. Davis, a son of Rev. Dr. Davis, of Westfield. Young Davis was a man of fine parts and good education. In him the young editor found for the first time a thoroughly competent ally in the higher department of his work. He was not only a good writer, but was able and willing to share the responsibility for the executive labor of the paper. The younger Bowles looked hopefully to him as the coming writer of the *Republican.* So he used to tell his friends, saying that for himself he did not expect to accomplish much as an editorial writer,—the general management of the paper would be his province. Mr. Davis slept in the office, and took his meals with the Bowles family, which included father and son with their wives, the unmarried son, and two or three apprentices. The working day of the younger Samuel Bowles began before noon and lasted till one or two in the morning. His wife shared in the household work, and sometimes late at night went down to the office; and when there came a little leisure, the

last " copy " having gone to the printers and the proof not
yet returned, husband and wife would read aloud to each
other from some book.   The one leisure evening of the
week was Saturday,— Mr. Bowles's ideal of "a paper every
day in the year" being unrealized till thirty years later.

   But in the early spring of 1850, Davis was taken suddenly ill.   Mr. Bowles took him home and put him in his
own room ; a sharp, brief illness followed, and the young
life so full of promise came to its end.   To Mr. Bowles
it was the loss of a brotherly comrade, and the right
hand of his enterprise.   Whoever might sicken, whoever
might die, the daily paper must go on, and go on well.
Through these hard days when Davis lay sick, and after
his death, its pages were just as full and vigorous as before.   The assistant's place was not vacant long.   Dr. J.
G. Holland, who had just come back to the town after a
year or two of teaching and school superintendence at the
South, was invited to take the place of associate editor,
and entered at once on the work.   The first year he was
paid $480; the next year, $700; and then there was sold
to him a quarter of the paper for $3500.   The elder Mr.
Bowles had come to be engaged wholly in the affairs of
the counting-room.   For four or five years the whole
editorial work of the paper was done by the younger
Bowles and Dr. Holland.

   Through these years, Mr. Bowles's family life was
eventful.   His first child, a daughter, Sarah Augusta,
was born in June, 1850.   Sometimes, coming home from
work after midnight, he would walk the floor with the
baby in his arms, to soothe it, so fatigued that he stumbled
over the furniture as he walked; but to this his wife
soon put a stop by assigning to him a separate room.
The second child, a son named after his father, was born
in October, 1851; and a second daughter, Mary, in January, 1854.

In the early autumn of 1851 came a succession of be-
reavements. His sister, Mrs. Julia Foote, lost a child,
and died ten days afterward. Ten days later the
illness of the elder Mr. Bowles ended in his death.
To the son that death brought a great sorrow, and
also heavier work. The responsibility of the counting-
room came now on him, in addition to the editorial
management. The strain was too great; his overtaxed
eyes began to suffer, and loss of sight was feared. He
went in the spring of 1852 to the home of his sister, Mrs.
Henry Alexander, in Brooklyn, to consult New York
physicians. In the middle of the night he was attacked
by terrible pain in the head; a time of acute suffering
followed, from a succession of abscesses in the head;
and to this ensued a siege of inflammatory rheumatism.
At one time there were fears for his life. His wife was
bound at home by the sickness of the two babies; but
his mother came to watch beside him. During his con-
valescence his presence brightened his sister's home. In
health he was sometimes irritable, but in sickness he was
wonderfully patient. The household remembered the
visit with delight. The moment that strength began to
return, his keen interest in public affairs revived; and
he dictated to his sister many letters about politics.
When he went back to Springfield, it was with health
still delicate, and for a year or two following he was
obliged to use his eyes sparingly. It was not the old
home to which he returned. A great project had been
consummated during his illness; his own little family
had left his mother's and moved into a house of their
own. The step had become of clear expedience, but he
had shrunk from it somewhat; he hesitated at leaving
the mother's roof and encountering the unknown cares
and responsibilities of a separate establishment while the
burdens of his work were so heavy. But he accepted

the united counsel of mother and wife, and the wife
oversaw the removal of the household goods, when by his
absence he was spared all burden of the details. Through
these earlier years, she took almost the whole of the
household care. Afterward, when children were numerous, and the enlargement of the paper's force lightened
his load, he relieved her of a part of the domestic management.

A man's establishment under his own roof-tree is
generally an era only less important than his choice of
a profession, his marriage, and his first child. It is an
especially momentous event to a man for whom mental
labor, with its sharp strain on nerves and brain, creates
necessity for a home in which his repose can be made
the first object. That advantage Mr. Bowles fully enjoyed from this time onward. The new house was on
Maple street, on the lower slope of "Ames's hill,"—a
two-story wooden structure, tasteful and comfortable,
commanding from its rear a fine view of the town, half-
hidden by trees, the river, the valley, and distant hills.
Its occupants took as rooms for constant use those in
the rear, looking toward this view. With full mutual
agreement, they furnished the house modestly, according
to their means. Now the wife had her rightful province,—a cosy nest for the increasing little brood; and
there was a quiet resting-place for the husband in the
intervals of probably the closest, hardest work that was
then done by any man in the whole region.

# CHAPTER IX.

## THE DEVELOPING NEWSPAPER.

THE accession of Dr. Holland to the *Republican* was an important event in its history. He and Mr. Bowles supplemented each other. Mr. Bowles was a born journalist, and showed early an instinct for news, an aptitude for politics, and a skill in administration. His development as a thinker and writer came later. Dr. Holland, who was seven years his senior, came to the paper equipped with more of literary culture and taste, and was always a writer rather than an editor. He was strong in his convictions, warm in his feelings, sensitive to the moral element in any question, and the master of a forcible, lucid, and popular style. His interest lay not so much in politics as in the personal conduct of life, and social usages and institutions. His editorials in the *Republican* were one of the earliest signs that the newspaper press was beginning to exercise, along with its other functions, that of direct moral instruction, which had hitherto been almost a monopoly of the church. Many of his articles were short and pithy lay sermons. They dealt directly with morals and religion, in their practical rather than theological applications. They discussed such topics as the mutual duties of husbands and wives, of laborers and employers; the principles of conduct for young men and young women, and the like. This was an innovation in journalism. It found favor among a community which takes life seriously and earnestly. It signified in truth an expansion of the newspaper's possibilities, which has as yet only begun to be worked out. Dr. Holland was admirably qualified for a pioneer in this kind of work. He was so far in sympathy with the established churches and the accepted theology that he reached and held a wide constituency, while he was little trammeled by theological or ecclesiastical technicalities. He was quite as impatient as Mr. Bowles of any assumption of authority by a party or a church, and the *Republican* early showed an independence of the clergy, and a willingness to criticise them on occasion, which often drew wrath upon its head. But its attitude toward the churches and the religion they represented, though an independent was also a friendly one. Such theological coloring as the paper had, came from Dr. Holland rather than Mr. Bowles, and was what would now be described as liberal orthodox. The tone was conservative as to the observance of Sunday, and similar questions, and even opposed the theater as an immoral institution — a position from which Dr. Holland receded at a later time, while Mr. Bowles perhaps never shared it. Toward the aggressive social and intellectual movements of which New England was prolific thirty or forty years ago,—Woman's Rights, Abolitionism, Transcendentalism,— both editors were unfriendly.

In general, Dr. Holland added to the paper a higher literary tone, and a broader recognition of human interests. He had a sympathetic perception of the pathos, the humor, the dignity, in the lives of the common folk. He wrote one article on "The little tin pails," carried by the early and late procession of laborers; the suggestion of homely fare, of wifely provision, of the long day's labor cheered by the thought of the evening welcome. He was eminently a man of sentiment and feeling. It belonged to his mind, and to his somewhat narrow education, to vividly see and present one side of a question, rather than to comprehend its entirety; and this was at once his limitation and his strength, for the average reader follows most sympathetically a writer who goes straight to a conclusion, and does not embarrass him with qualifications and balancings. Mr. Bowles, on the other hand, guided himself by his reason more than by his feelings, and had a growing instinct and capacity for looking at all sides of the question. It was he who gave its central inspiration to the *Republican*, and who held its helm, though Dr. Holland's contribution to the paper was important and unique. The two men worked together harmoniously, but never came into personal intimacy. Dr. Holland had not a little of the clerical attributes. While in his social tastes he was democratic, he avoided the companionship of men whose moral standards were different from his own. His faith, his feeling, his sentiment,— all perfectly genuine,— were freely expressed to the world; they were the material of his writing; they found expression in his conversation. He craved appreciation and recognition. He was a man of striking and handsome presence, and in his bearing there was something a little suggestive, as it were, of gown and bands,— a touch of self-consciousness. Mr. Bowles, on the other hand, was always ready to hob-nob with any man, saint or sinner, in whom he found any likable quality. His highest aspirations, his finest feelings, were not carried in sight of the world,— they were seldom openly expressed in his writings, or in his ordinary conversation. He bore himself like a man of the world. Any approach to assumption or display of religion provoked his sarcasm or scorn. No doubt Holland often thought Bowles irreverent, not to say heathenish, and Bowles thought Holland something of a prig. There were no collisions between them; each of them respected the other's rights and guarded his own; but they kept always at a little distance, and their terms of mutual address were never more familiar than "Mr. Bowles" and "Dr. Holland." Each man liked to have the first place in his world, though the one cared more for the reality of power and the other desired the outward signs of recognition. Opposite as they were in some respects, they both had the adaptiveness and the self-control to work together harmoniously and efficiently for many years, until circumstances parted them.

The *Republican* was all the time growing broader, brighter, fuller of information. It was making itself a necessity to everybody. It reaped continually from wider fields. Telegraphic news was now a constant feature. In 1850 there had come to be a regular column of "Local Items," which was probably the first thing that most readers looked at. About the same time, Mr. Bowles began a weekly column of "Religious Intelligence"—a new thing in secular journalism. By Dr. Holland, seemingly, there was given for a time in each Saturday's paper a chapter of "Sunday Thoughts,"—practical applications of Christianity. The paper showed a growing capacity for getting hold of whatever could interest its readers. Its editorial matter was less in long articles, and more in pithy and pungent paragraphs. Politics was still the chief staple of its discussions, and was treated always with lucid vigor. It had not yet come to be a pioneer of political thought. It announced itself as "Whig"— "thoroughly, devotedly, but not blindly Whig" (January 16, 1851), long after the Whig party really had no distinctive opinions on the great rising questions.

The paper's growth was won by unsparing labor, by close economy, by making the utmost of each day, yet looking always toward the future. After six years of existence, it claimed (May 8, 1850) a larger circulation than any daily paper in New England outside of Boston. " Up to the present time," it added, " the *Republican* has been no direct source of profit to its proprietors. As fast as money has been made, it has been invested in improvements, and even to a greater extent, by several thousands; but we have now reached a point where we hope to see the scale descending on the other side."

Dr. Holland, just after Mr. Bowles's death, wrote as follows :

" As I think of my old associate, and the earnest exhausting work he was doing when I was with him, he seems to me like a great golden vessel, rich in color and roughly embossed, filled with the elixir of life, which he poured out without the slightest stint for the consumption of this people. This vessel was only full at the first and it was never replenished. It was filled for an expenditure of fifty or sixty years, but he kept the stream so large that the precious contents were all decanted at thirty. The sparkle, the vivacity, the drive, the power of the *Republican*, as I knew it in the early days, the fresh and ever eager interest with which it was every morning received by the people of Springfield and the Connecticut Valley, the superiority of the paper to other papers of its class, its ever widening influence— all these cost life. We did not know when we tasted it and found it so charged with zest that we were tasting heart's blood, but that was the priceless element that commended it to our appetites. A pale man, weary and nervous, crept home at midnight, or at one, two, or three o'clock in the morning, and while all nature was fresh and the birds were singing, and thousands of eyes were bending eagerly over the results of his night's labor, he was tossing and trying to sleep. Yet this work, so terrible in its exactions and its consequences, was the joy of this man's life—it *was* this man's life; and as the best exponent of this kind of devotion to an idea and a life-work I have ever known, I give its memory most affectionate reverence.

VOL. I.—5

" His love of thoroughness was united with a firm personal belief that no one could do his work as well as he could do it himself. His strong conviction that his way was always the best way led him to fret and worry over the work of others, and to do all that he could with his own hands. I have known him in the early part of his career to sit up at night for hours that he might read a little batch of unimportant proof, which was measurably sure in the foreman's hands to come out right in the morning,—little fancying that he was selling his life at that petty price. Mr. Bowles died of overwork and over-watching, and proved that the man who, in a large administrative place, undertakes, in any considerable degree, to execute his own plans in their unimportant details, must suffer the penalty of death."

There is much truth in this criticism. Yet it was only by the closest devotion to his work, and to every part of his work, that Mr. Bowles, starting from the mea-gerest foundations, built up in a small provincial town one of the best newspapers in America. He may have done more than was needful; he may have sometimes waited for a proof when it was unnecessary; but in a broad way it was because the proof-room, the press-room, the counting-room, as well as the sanctum, all felt the ceaseless vigilance, the unresting energy, of that one man, that the paper became what it was.

The permanent inroad of overwork on his strength did not show itself for a number of years. But beyond doubt its secret effect was early wrought. The injury to his brain of which he died was doubtless begun before he was twenty-five,— during those years when he used often to take a bottle of cold tea to the office, and work till one or two in the morning; while on two nights in the week he snatched but a few hours' sleep on a lounge in the office, and was at work with the daylight. It may well be that at that time there was wrought an actual lesion of the brain, which left only a thin shell between the citadel of life and its enemy.  To this it should be added that he formed during these early years a mental habit of literally unresting activity, which he never afterward could throw off.  He was splendidly developing all his powers of work, but he lost, never to fully recover it, the power of rest.  When, in later years, circumstances gave him the opportunity of frequent abstinence from work, he had forgotten—indeed he had never learned— the art of repose, and could only exchange one activity for another.

He was spending his life-blood,— but he got a great price for it.  He knew what he was doing—at least he thought he did.  When his friend Edward B. Gillett, of Westfield, once remonstrated with him about his overwork, he answered: "I know it just as well as you do. When my friends point out that I am working toward a breakdown, they seem to think that is to influence my action.  Not at all!  I have got the lines drawn, the current flowing, and by throwing my weight here now, I can count for something.  If I make a long break or parenthesis, to get strong, I shall lose my chance.  No man is living a life that is worth living, unless he is willing if need be to die for somebody or something,— at least to *die a little !*"

He was developing as the maker of a newspaper, as a political writer, and also in the management of men. He admired Thurlow Weed's combination of power,— at the same time a journalist and a mover of the springs of public affairs through personal intercourse.  He saw that as soon as an editor became an office-seeker, he compromised the independence on which his real power depended. Both Raymond and Greeley fell into this mistake: Bennett and Weed avoided it.  Mr. Bowles used to say to Dr. Holland, " So long as you and I are on this paper, we will never accept a public office."  He came to be skillful in the manipulation of men, and to be felt as a personal as well as a journalistic power in local political circles. "I first appreciated his political ability," said Dr. Holland, "at a city election of which I cannot give the date. He carried the day, and used both the paper and his personal influence so skillfully that I saw and said he would become a political power in the state." "I think," added Dr. Holland, "that his strongest passion was the love of power."

It was during these years that he established the system of requiring advance payments from subscribers. A few of the great city papers had led the way in this innovation, but it was so contrary to the tradition of provincial journalism that many predicted utter discomfiture for the rash experiment. But it succeeded. It was a great step to a firmer business footing; and it was also a sign of the new attitude which newspapers were taking in the community. The old-time journal was very deferential to its subscribers and advertisers. It spoke of them as its "patrons." It was ready to praise the wares which they advertised, and to give all manner of friendly notices and puffs. It was patient, though sometimes plaintive, toward their delay in making payment. The possible message, "Stop my paper," hung over the editor's head, keeping him docile and respectful. All this was swiftly changing. The newspaper, strengthened by railroad and telegraph, was becoming so strong that it needed not to ask favors or depend on them. The *Republican* took the lead among provincial papers in this independent attitude, of which the advance-payment system was the commercial sign. It had never a master, either among the political chiefs or in the classes with whom its business interests lay. It depended on their support for its existence; but the editor won that support by making it for their interest to subscribe for his paper, and to advertise in it.

The great achievement of Samuel Bowles was that he built up under the limitations of a country town a paying newspaper which expressed the editor's personal opinions, bound by no party, by no school, by no clique. What began to be talked of as "independent journalism" during the Greeley campaign, in 1872, was, in the *Republican's* case, only a particularly bold manifestation of a character at which it had aimed from the beginning. Its editor was in full sympathy at first with the Whig and afterward with the Republican party; he criticised them in details, but on the general issue his convictions did not bring him into fundamental opposition until 1872. But from its early years the paper avowed its opinions and made its criticisms, with a freedom which provoked frequent and often emphatic dissent among its readers. The nature of its field made this independence hard to maintain. A great city offers an immense and various constituency, and a paper which can make itself readable to one large class, can afford to ignore even a wide and weighty disapprobation from other classes. But the *Republican* was in a small community; it could reach, at most, only a circle of country towns; the utmost number who would take a daily paper was limited; and the paper could ill afford to drive off subscribers, or incline them toward the local rivals which from time to time disputed the ground with it. Besides, a provincial neighborhood is full of strong prejudices. It has its heroes who must not be lightly spoken of, its traditional code of manners and morals which must be deferred to. There is still a deal of very stiff stuff in the descendants of the Puritans, but the community thirty years ago was far more provincial, more conservative, more set in its preferences and prejudices, than it is to-day. The environment was by no means favorable to the outspoken independence which was a growing trait

of the *Republican*. The editor conquered his environ
ment. He did it by making so good a newspaper that
the people had to buy it. By industry and skill he won
the opportunity for independence.

There grew up in Mr. Bowles's mind an ideal of "journalism,"—a combination of principles, methods, and instincts, based partly on ethics, partly on expediency.
With him, to say a thing was or was not "good journalism" was to put the final seal upon its character. It
belonged to good journalism, in his idea, to tell all the
news, and as a part of this to give every side a fair hearing. His opponents and critics could always find place
for their articles, under reasonable conditions, in his
paper. But it also belonged to his ideal of journalism
that a paper should as seldom as possible own itself in
the wrong. Accordingly, if a man wrote to him in correction of a statement, or in defense against criticism, he
generally found his letter printed, but with some editorial
comment that gave the last word tellingly against him.
It was commonly said that to seek redress from the
*Republican* did more harm than good. This trait was
partly due to deliberate unwillingness to weaken the
paper's authority by admission of error. But it was
probably more due to a personal idiosyncracy. In many
ways a most generous man, Mr. Bowles always hated to
admit that he had been in the wrong. Sometimes he did
it,—not often,—in private life; but in his paper never,
when he could help it. "We sometimes discussed this,"
said Dr. Holland, "and he once said: 'I sympathize
with the Boston editor, to whom a man came with the
complaint, "Your paper says that I hanged myself, and I
want you to take it back." "No," said the editor, " we're
not in the habit of doing that, but we will say that the
rope broke and you escaped." ' "

But it must be said that this fault lies at the door of

a good many papers besides the *Republican*. It is a
characteristic sin of journalism — one of the vices of
irresponsible power. The English press is assumed to be
more fair and decorous than the American. But Trol-
lope, that faithful photographer of English manners,
characterizes the *Times* upon this point. " Write to the
*Jupiter*," counsels Bishop Grantley to the aggrieved Mr.
Harding, who has been misrepresented by that paper.
" Yes," says the more worldly-wise Archdeacon, "yes,
and be smothered with ridicule; tossed over and over
again with scorn; shaken this way and that, as a rat in
the mouth of a practised terrier. A man may have the
best of causes, the best of talents, and the best of tem-
pers ; he may write as well as Addison or as strongly as
Junius; but even with all this, he cannot successfully
answer when attacked by the *Jupiter*. Answer such an
article ! No, Warden ; whatever you do, don't do that."

The vital principle of independent journalism, as Mr.
Bowles understood it, was illustrated by an incident
which occurred in 1856. While Mr. Bowles was out of
town, a prize-fight was attempted in Springfield, and
among those who gathered to witness it were some young
men of good social standing, among them several relatives of Mrs. Bowles. Dr. Holland treated the incident
in a very sharp article, as an instance of the coarse im-
moralities in which the rapidly growing town was beginning to imitate the worst features of the great cities.
The article stated that the matter would come up in the
police court, and those who had been concerned in it
might expect full publicity to be given to their conduct.
Before the trial, Mr. Bowles returned to town. In the
evening, sitting on the door-step, his wife said to him,
" Can't you let this thing drop ? If you publish these
young men's names, it will wound and alienate a great
many of our friends." He answered, " Mary, I have con-

sidered it all, most thoughtfully and conscientiously.
The blame must be given where it is deserved. This is
the time to put an end to prize-fighting in Springfield."
The trial was fully reported in the *Republican*, including the names of those who as attendants at the prize-
fight were called as witnesses; and the paper commented
in a few vigorous words on their presence at such a
scene. Family alienations did follow, painful and not
soon healed. But there never was another prize-fight in
Springfield. In this and similar cases, the morals of the
town were vastly the gainer by the unsparing publicity
given to the misdeeds of men who had reputations to
suffer. Just as the introduction of street-lights into
cities did more to stop nocturnal crime than constables
and courts could do, so by its reports of wrong-doing has
the modern newspaper added a new safeguard to social
morality. To exercise that great function as free from
fear or favor as the judge on the bench, was the aim of
the *Republican*. Its editor liked to make his power felt,—
he liked to use it for the public good,—but the personal alienations which it brought were none the less
painful to him.

# CHAPTER X.

## The Compromise of 1850.

MR. BOWLES'S special activity as a political writer
began at just the time when national politics were
assuming a distinctively new phase. Hitherto upon the
questions connected with slavery, there had been room
for constitutional anti-slavery men to act effectively
within the Whig party. That party had opposed, though
unsuccessfully, the war with Mexico and the spoliation
of its territory in the interest of slavery. But when the
slavery question in new aspects thrust itself upon the
nation, the Whigs fell back from their anti-slavery
ground. They yielded, or evaded, or compromised.
They planted themselves on the ground of devotion to
the Union, directly menaced by a strong faction at the
South, and denounced by a small number of extreme
Abolitionists at the North. The party was held together
by this genuine Union sentiment, by old habit and association, and by devotion to its personal leaders. Between
it and the Democratic party the differences in principle
and policy became in reality of small importance. Both
organizations strove to keep in abeyance the dangerous
question of slavery; in each, the Southern wing repressed
any active anti-slavery tendency in the Northern wing.
At the South, the disunion element made some tentative
efforts at organization, but found itself for a time in a

hopeless minority. At the North, the Free-soilers made no gains except through temporary or local coalitions with one of the two great parties. The extreme Abolitionists were very active, through press and platform, but they were few, and their denunciatory temper won for them an extreme unpopularity; their hand was against every man, and every man's hand against them. The sacred principle of *liberty to the slave* was ignored by the great parties; commercial interest sought to stifle it; the sentiment of love to the Union was arrayed against it; personal ambitions, ecclesiastical conservatisms, party associations,—all were hostile to it. It seemed scarcely to have any friends except a handful of heroic fanatics. Yet in truth, there was throughout the North a wide, deep and growing sentiment of opposition to slavery. It found voice through agitators like Garrison and his associates; through poets like Lowell and Whittier; through the mighty voice of Theodore Parker in the pulpit, and a few ministers in every denomination, who, often at heavy cost, were true to the prophetic function of rebuking national sin; through Free-soil politicians and orators, and through a few Whig and Democratic leaders who were in advance of the party lines, but had not yet broken them. The cause was strong in a multitude of men and women who did not yet see their way clear to action.

The slavery interest had urged the country into war with Mexico, and had gained Texas with the promise of four more slave states to be carved out of it in the future; and Mexico had been further despoiled of a vast area of territory, comprising what was afterward organized as California, New Mexico, and Utah. The question which now came to the front was, should this territory be slave, or free? It had been free under Mexican law, and its physical conditions were unfavorable to slave labor. As a question merely of the balance of power between the two sections, the North felt itself entitled to some counterpoise to Texas by the admission of California as a free state. The people of California adopted a state constitution which prohibited slavery; they elected state officers and Congressmen — all Democrats — and applied to Congress for admission. But the Southern extremists objected. By the Compromise of 1820, it had been established that, except the state of Missouri, all of the territory then acquired by the Louisiana purchase lying north of the line of thirty-six degrees, thirty minutes, north latitude, should be forever free; the status of that south of the line was left indeterminate. Now the Southern extremists demanded that this same line should be extended across the domain won from Mexico to the Pacific; that in all territory south of that, slavery should be established, and that California should be divided by that line; its southern portion being organized as a slave state. A more extensive demand had been made by Calhoun, who in 1847 declared that slavery was entitled to protection by Congress, throughout the whole of the national territories. The South could not yet be united in support of this claim, but the mass of the Southern politicians seized every practicable chance for a fresh advance of slavery over new territory. The Free-soilers took the logical opposite of Calhoun's position; they declared, "Freedom, not slavery, is national, and slavery, not freedom, is sectional; Congress has no more power to establish slavery than to establish monarchy." Between these two positions stood the majority of the politicians, not prepared for either extreme, seeking to settle each case as it arose by the guidance of established precedent and the special circumstances of the occasion. The present occasion seemed to Henry Clay to be one that called for mutual concessions. Both sides were bringing forward their grievances. The South was exasperated by the Abolitionists' attack, and it complained that there was no adequate provision for the return of its escaped slaves; Northern men complained that on the common ground of the national capital slavery was sanctioned, and men and women were sold at the auction block. Clay had been a promoter of the Missouri Compromise; he disliked slavery, and in the ensuing debates he declared with emphasis that he would never give his vote for the express sanction of slavery on a single foot of territory that was already free. But his greatest anxiety was, that by mutual concessions between the two sections the storm which seemed gathering and menacing the national Union might be dispelled. In the winter of 1849–50 he brought forward his famous Compromise resolutions. These provided, in substance, for the admission of California under the free state constitution; for the organization of New Mexico (including what is now Utah) as a territory, with no provision by Congressional law for either legalizing or prohibiting slavery; for a national fugitive slave law; for the continued maintenance of slavery in the District of Columbia, but the abolition there of the slave trade.

Over this scheme was fought the great Compromise debate of 1850. It was at first assailed even more strongly from the extreme South than from the North. But the great incident of the debate was Webster's famous 7th of March speech. Before its delivery there was confident anticipation that he would take ground as the champion of the constitutional rights of freedom. Mr. Ashmun — as Mr. Bowles has related — shared that confidence, and he inspired the *Republican* with it. That paper took strong ground against disunion, and still stronger against slavery. Thus it said, February 22, 1850:

" The will of the majority of these states is, that not one inch of territory now free shall ever be trod by the foot of a slave. If, therefore, the Union cannot be preserved without introduction of the leaven of corruption in a still greater proportion than now pervades it, we declare our conviction that freedom, religion, and honor demand that we allow the tie of Union to be severed by those who assume the terrible responsibility. . . . Let Northern men and all the friends of freedom, while willing to concede names and forms, yield not an inch of territory to slavery while they have it in their hands."

Two weeks later Webster spoke. He rose to the full height of his intellectual power. He held the scales even between North and South. For Southern Disunion, for Northern Abolitionism, he had equal rebuke. His plea was for the faithful maintenance of the Constitution and the Union. When he described the civil strife which any attempt at secession was sure to precipitate, he spoke with a prophet's foresight and a prophet's fervor. Toward Mr. Clay's Compromise scheme he was substantially favorable. He declared himself ready to waive the formal exclusion of slavery from the New Mexican territory, inasmuch as its soil and climate were a virtual prohibition of slavery, and a legislative enactment would therefore be a superfluous reënactment of the natural law of God, and a needless affront to the South. He affirmed the constitutional obligation of the North to return fugitive slaves. He spoke in the spirit of compromise; he spoke with a lucid, massive, and at times impassioned eloquence, which even at this distance of time lays the reader under its spell, and as he reads almost convinces him,— until he looks up from the printed page, upon the field of history and the eternal lights of justice.

A single fault vitiated his whole treatment of the question. He viewed it as a question between two territorial sections, with their respective systems of labor, both systems being entitled to equal recognition and respect, and the statesman's problem being to mete out to each its equal share, and thus keep the two sections harmonious and united in a common country. From this stand-point, his plea was unanswerable. The one fact he ignored was that the system of slavery was a profoundly wrong and mischievous system, which it was part of the statesman's business to discourage and repress. He treated the question as one between North and South, instead of between freedom and slavery;— he made the supreme object to be peace instead of right.

A storm broke upon Webster's head when that speech was read in Massachusetts. The heart of the state was shaken with indignation and grief for her favorite son. The mass of his own party supported him, but that party was at the next election driven from its long-time control of the state. His friends rallied in his defense; the magic of that imperial presence and irresistible personality won its triumph; the Whig party of Massachusetts stood by Webster,— but he had given the political death-blow to himself and to the party.

The speech fell upon the *Republican* office as a great surprise. While it was reported only in abstracts, the paper deferred its comments, pleading meanwhile for a full and fair hearing of the great chief. It published the speech in full, in an extra sheet, March 13, and made its comment: "We regard the speech as a whole as strictly Websterian — broad, patriotic, and honest. We believe that it will have a good effect, not only upon the fiery South in soothing Disunion agitation, but upon the North, in impressing upon it its constitutional obligations. We are among those, however, who wish it had been more than it is,"—who wish, in short, that more had been said in behalf of the North and of freedom. But

then and afterward the paper was steadfast in loyalty to
Webster. It was always hearty in his defense, and qualified and mild in its dissent from him. Real censure upon
him it never pronounced. Through the six months of
Congressional debate that followed, this personal loyalty
to Webster was the most salient feature of the *Republican's* politics. It did not, however, follow him in supporting the Compromise scheme, but neither did it
combat that scheme with much warmth or vigor. At no
period before or after did it deal with public questions so
ineffectively. It maintained, however, that the admission of California as a free state and without any
additional measures, was the true course. This course
was favored by President Taylor, who thus justified the
expectations of his anti-slavery supporters. But in midsummer he died. With his death the controlling influence of Mr. Seward in the Administration disappeared
wholly, upon the accession to the presidency of his great
opponent in New York politics, Millard Fillmore. Mr.
Webster became Secretary of State. His personality was
far stronger than Mr. Fillmore's, and was felt with more
decisive weight in the new Administration. The influence of the Executive was now turned in favor of the
Compromise measures, which were soon after adopted.

That one of them which provoked the strongest opposition at the North was the fugitive slave bill. Driven
to acknowledge the constitutional obligation to return
fugitive slaves, the anti-slavery Whigs based their opposition to this particular bill upon its denial of a jury trial
to the alleged fugitive. This was the ground taken by
the *Republican*, which, on this question, followed Webster unreservedly. When Webster brought in a bill of
his own on the subject, giving the alleged fugitive the
right to claim a jury trial, the *Republican* said, " We can
scarcely doubt nine-tenths of all the people in the free

states will approve of the provisions of this bill when they become known to them." Webster's bill was thrown out, and the law in its most obnoxious form was passed, receiving only three votes from Northern Whigs, and with Mr. Winthrop — the successor and representative of Mr. Webster in the Senate — opposing it. Thereafter Webster and the Whigs, and the *Republican* with them, treated it as the law of the land, entitled to loyal obedience. " That nasty word, Compromise," had been spoken with effect, and the *Republican* had made but faint opposition. The anti-slavery ground, which it had maintained until now with such heartiness and vigor, was hereafter, for a time, scarcely avowed except in a perfunctory way. The paper was governed by loyalty to an individual and a party, rather than allegiance to an idea.

Webster's position was not without elements of strength. As to the fugitive slave question, he stood on constitutional ground. His devotion to the Union was a great and worthy sentiment. But, waiving all question of ambitious or unworthy motives on his part, he was blind to the handwriting on the wall, which declared an irrepressible conflict between freedom and slavery; and he was insensitive to the moral element, the wrong of slavery, which underlay all constitutions and compromises. In supporting him through this period the *Republican* subordinated its own best instincts and tendencies.

Yet history, in its calm retrospect, recognizes that Webster and his followers were far other than the mere apostates to freedom which they seemed to the men possessed by the passion of anti-slavery. Webster was identified with a sublime idea — the idea of American nationality. He wrought a supreme service in the earlier days, when in his duels with Calhoun he overmatched the acute logic which claimed for each of the states an independent sovereignty, by maintaining with equal acumen an organic national unity, and evoking in its defense a grander and mightier sentiment. No American of the first half of this century did so much to root the love of the Union in the minds and hearts of the people as did Webster. It was that love, more than hostility to slavery, which animated the North in the war which established the Union and destroyed slavery. Webster failed to measure the evil of slavery, and the Abolitionists failed no less to measure the evil of disunion. Each of them was devoted to one great idea; and the two ideas, which conflicted for a while, were destined to blend at last into a harmonious and irresistible force. The highest distinction of the radical anti-slavery men was that they gave disinterested service, in which they had generally nothing to gain and much to lose; while in the forces which opposed them patriotism had its allies in the ambition of politicians, the timidity of churches, and the selfishness of commerce.

# CHAPTER XI.

## THE FUGITIVE SLAVE LAW.

THE Compromise of 1850, inasmuch as it did some-how put an end to the immediate open questions regarding slavery, was accepted by the country with singular unanimity. Two years later, the only party which sought to reopen any of its conclusions — the Free-soil — cast only about 156,000 votes in a total of over 3,000,000. In this acceptance, the *Republican* was in entire harmony with the general drift, and with the Whig party. Upon the adjournment of Congress, it said, October 1, 1850:

" The measures which have at last been carried form a new era in our history. Time alone can develop the beneficence and efficiency of their operations. They have been the best *that could be carried* to save the Union from dangers which threatened it, and satisfied with this we may only hope they will work out the great and happy results for which they were designed."

And it steadily advocated the observance of all the pro-visions thus adopted.

Among these provisions there was one which brought the subject of slavery home to the keenest sensibilities of the Northern people, and forced upon them the sharpest dilemma between the obligations of humanity and those of citizenship. This was the Fugitive Slave law. The constitution expressly required the rendition from the free states of fugitives who had fled from their masters. By an early act of Congress, provision had been made for the execution of this provision by magistrates in the several states. This law had not been often put in operation. Several of the Northern states had recently enacted statutes intended to obstruct its operations. There were demands from the South for more effective measures. A bill for this purpose, by Mr. Mason of Virginia, was incorporated in the Compromise scheme, and enacted. An efficient bill for this object could not be acceptable to the North. The point for which the Whigs contended—that the alleged fugitive should be tried by a jury—had its only real importance in the unconfessed presumption that Northern juries would decide not according to the facts but according to their sympathies, and so nullify the law. As adopted, the law gave the decision on the master's claim to a United States commissioner. The law went into operation. It roused throughout the North a wide excitement and exasperation. Many thousands of men and women who had braved hardship and peril in their escape from bondage were living in Northern towns and cities. They were a peaceful, inoffensive class, earning their living by humble labor, in kindly relations with their white neighbors. To every one of these the law came as a deadly menace. Men and women were carried back to bondage from Massachusetts; not by secret kidnappers, but in broad day, with the whole community looking on, with the whole country apprised by telegraph of each step in the rendition, and under the shadow and sanction of the stars and stripes.

To resist was to break the law. To organize resistance was to organize rebellion. The master was in the exercise of his legal rights. The stipulation which secured to him those rights was one of the mutual concessions through which was made possible the great American republic. If any one may break and resist a law of which he personally disapproves, there is an end of civil government, of social order, of civilization. So argued one party.

Said others: "Not all the laws in the world can justify a direct violation of the sacred obligations of humanity. Human law can no more make such an act right than it can make theft, adultery, murder, right. There is a higher law than that of Congress — it is the law of God. We will aid the fugitive to escape, and if it comes to strife we will side with him rather than his oppressor."

When the bill was under debate, a correspondent, "H.," wrote to the *Republican* (June 3, 1850) that the people of the North "will aid in the recapture of the fugitive slaves when they forget the Christian law and become callous to every human sentiment — not before. The fate of Mason's bill, or any other on this subject, is of little practical importance. . . . It is much too late to think of enforcing a law so repugnant to the public conscience. Practically and forever this question is settled. Let the slave escape beyond the slave states, and the southern border of the free states, and he will be aided in his escape by every one with whom he meets. And it will be done, not only at the spontaneous prompting of sympathy, but as a sacred duty. No more false pledges should be given to the slave-holders. It is better to tell them honestly: 'It is so writ in the bond,' but it is morally impossible; we cannot and will not do it! If your human cattle escape, we bid them God-speed in the race for liberty, and we cannot do otherwise as long as we are men."

Against this plea, the *Republican* argued at length that civil government and social order depend on obedience to the law. " The Constitution does not require us to be slave-catchers, nor to withhold our God-speed to a fugitive. Our sympathies are all with him, and they always will be with him. Our simple duty is, when ownership is proved to us through regularly appointed officers, to offer no resistance to his reclamation. If we do, our Constitution is as worthless a piece of parchment as a Mississippi bond."

Through all the exciting discussions and events which followed the passage of the law, the *Republican* maintained this ground. It earnestly opposed the " higher law" idea as subversive of all civil government. It declared (March 31, 1851) that the only legitimate resource, where the law requires from the individual the active performance of what he thinks wrong, is to decline to obey, and accept the penalty. " All sober men, and all good members of society, agree that the laws of society *must be either actively or passively obeyed;* that the behests of society, uttered through its recognized channels of authority, are to be *wrought out* by the individual or *suffered* in the penalty attached to them." Under the caption "Under which King?" (March 21, 1851), it pressed the alternative — obedience to the law, or disunion and anarchy. " We put it to every man in the community who has cheated himself, or been cheated, into the belief that it is right for him to resist the execution of any of the laws of the land, whether he is willing to assume the political position of Garrison, and thus preserve his consistency, and stand where he can alone defend himself. Will you be a friend or an enemy to the Government? Will you be a citizen or an alien? Will you be a subject, or, in all essential signification of the word, an outlaw?"

These things were not said by way of abstract speculation. A few weeks before, a colored man, Shadrach,
had been arrested in Boston as a fugitive, and a mob
had carried him from the court-room into safety and
freedom. A little later, in the same city, Thomas Simms
was arrested, and by the United States Commissioner
was remanded as a slave. The state Supreme Court was
vainly appealed to in his behalf. The city authorities
coöperated with the Federal officials to guard him from
rescue. He was marched through the streets surrounded
by three hundred armed policemen, with a body of militia
held in reserve in Faneuil Hall, was placed on shipboard,
and returned to his master. This was the *Republican's*
comment the day after (April 14, 1851):

"It is a relief to know that this painful affair has ended, and
a source of gratification that the laws of the nation, so boldly
threatened in the spirit of mobocratic resistance, have been
sustained. Yet this relief and this gratification, as they must
be to every peaceable and law-loving and law-abiding heart,
are dimmed by the sense of individual and social wrong, which
is thus brought directly home to us as the result of slavery in
our country and our constitution. It is a deep and bitter evil,
an anomaly in our Republic, giving the lie to every line of our
profession as a people and a nation, and yet a fixed fact, that
must be met and treated in a broad and catholic spirit, and not
with the cowardice of fanaticism, which would pull down the
whole fabric because it has one gross imperfection in its frame.
We find no unmixed good anywhere,—not even at the hearth-
stone of home,—and yet we do not propose therefore to destroy
our family firesides and put asunder what God has joined
together."

At this period there were two forms of occasional disturbance of the peace. Resistance to the return of fugitives was not very frequent, because these renditions
were not often attempted, so strong was the popular

antipathy to them, while the public authority was yet generally formidable enough to forbid any active resistance. The other class of disorders was much more frequent, consisting in riotous demonstrations against Abolitionist speakers. The Abolitionists — Garrison, Phillips, and their associates — stood in aggressive opposition to the strongest current of the time. When the mass of the politicians and the people were declaring that the slavery question was settled by the Compromise, the Abolitionists with fresh energy declared it to be a delusive and wicked peace. While the mass of the Northern people felt themselves to have made some sacrifice of feeling for the sake of strengthening the Union, Garrison and his followers assailed the Union itself as cemented in crime and deserving immediate overthrow. They were held in detestation by most of the conservative and respectable elements of society, and those elements did not always care to check the outbreak of popular violence from the lower class against the agitators.

In February, 1851, it was announced that George Thompson, doubly obnoxious as an Abolitionist and an Englishman who had come over to attack American institutions, would speak at a public meeting in Springfield. The meeting was appointed for Monday the 17th. It was loudly threatened that Thompson would not be allowed to appear. A committee of prominent citizens was appointed to warn him that the town was in an excited and dangerous condition. Sunday morning, an effigy of Thompson, and another labeled " John Bull," were found hanging in the principal square of the town. A handbill was widely circulated, headed " Regulators, Attention," making a violent appeal against the " paid emissary and spy of England." It was an undisguised summons to mob Thompson if he attempted to speak.

The *Republican* of Monday morning reported the facts of the situation, and said, "If Mr. Thompson attempts to fulfill his engagement, there will be a very serious disturbance. We should deeply regret such an occurrence, because it would be subversive of those principles of law and order that are at once the foundation and the safeguard of a republican government; because a gross violation of the free speech of which we boast as one of the greatest liberties guaranteed by our constitution; because disgraceful to our town and country; and because it would tend greatly to assist Mr. Thompson and his American associates in their crusade against our constitution and our government." In another column it said that Mr. Thompson, accompanied by Garrison and Phillips, was to speak in the evening, "for the purpose, we presume, of denouncing the American constitution, libeling the Christian church, and abusing the greatest and best men, living and dead, that have ever impressed their names on the country's history. We allude to this meeting more in sorrow than in any stronger or harsher sentiment, for we presume it will be made, like its long line of predecessors in this and other towns, the scene of pitiful fanaticism, blind perversion of truth, and such handling of sacred things as shall wound the moral sense like the naked blow of blasphemy." It advised citizens to stay away from the meeting, and thus consign it to insignificance and obscurity. The selectmen of the town appointed a few special constables, and notified the proprietors of the hall that the town would not be responsible for any damages; whereupon the proprietors refused the use of the hall, and there was no meeting that day. In the evening a riotous crowd thronged the streets, with bonfires, drums, fifes, bells, and crackers. "Rowdyism was in the highest degree rampant," said the *Republican* next morning; and it rebuked especially the intelligent and respectable men whose latent support emboldened the mob. It thus enforced the moral: "In the Faneuil Hall reception of Mr. Thompson, in the treatment he has received here, and in the recent fugitive slave mob in Boston" (the rescue of Shadrach), "there is a trampling upon great principles that shows 'something rotten in the state of Denmark.' We fully understand the motives which were the mainspring of each of these proceedings; we fully appreciate the strength and abstract rightfulness of the feelings that prompted the actors therein; but we mourn in bitterness the terrible lack of judgment and forecast that those professing to be and holding the places of leading men in society, display in countenancing such violation of the first principles of our government."

That day a room was obtained by Mr. Thompson and his friends, in which they held meetings in the forenoon and afternoon. The attendance was small, there was no disturbance, and the speakers were very severe upon the mob, the city authorities, and the *Republican*. Mr. Thompson charged that the inflammatory handbill was printed at the *Republican* office, and that the paper had incited the mob. Mr. Bowles addressed a note to Mr. Thompson denying and demanding proof of these statements, and Thompson replied by sharp denunciations. In the evening it was considered unsafe to hold a meeting. Again there were riotous demonstrations, and Mr. Thompson was burned in effigy in front of his room at the hotel. There was no overt violence, and no arrests were made. The *Republican* the next morning made these occurrences the text of a long editorial on the "Higher Law," an idea of which it declared the mob to be a logical and practical outcome. It recalled the fact that when, a little while before, Marshal Devens visited the town, for the purpose, as was at first believed, of arresting some fugitive slaves, there had been free talk of resisting him by violence; and this manifestation, it declared, was a precedent and parallel of the demonstrations against Thompson; both were outcroppings of the same lawless spirit. The whole stress of this article was directed not against the mob that forbade Thompson to speak and hanged and burned him in emgy, nor against the respectable classes that had encouraged and tolerated this violence, but against those who had declared that they would disobey or resist the law for the return of fugitives. Mr. Thompson's charges against the *Republican* were met by denials and rebuke, and there followed a long and bitter controversy between him and the paper. For several weeks the disturbance was a leading topic in its columns; and upon this and similar occurrences the same tone was maintained, of condemnation equally severe theoretically of those who mobbed Abolitionist speakers and those who rescued fugitives from their captors; but with the sharpest stress of rebuke against the latter.

Meantime the politics of the state had taken a singular course. The Free-soilers remained throughout the country generally in a minority, whose small number is remarkable when we consider that their principles were equally anti-slavery and constitutional, and that their leaders included such men as C. F. Adams, Sumner, Wilson, Palfrey, John P. Hale, Giddings, Chase, and others of like quality. The party was very small, but in some states it held the balance of power between the two great parties, and by a temporary alliance with one of them could win some important position. In Massachusetts, Webster's defection from the anti-slavery cause, in which the Whig party as a body followed him, offered a chance of success to the opponents of that party, if they could unite their forces. Hitherto the Democrats had been less friendly than the Whigs to Free-soil principles. In several Congressional districts, at the election of 1850, the Free-soilers and a part of the Whigs united upon a candidate. Horace Mann, who had represented the old district of John Quincy Adams as an anti-slavery Whig, lost the party renomination by his opposition to Webster after the 7th of March; he was nominated by the Free-soilers led by C. F. Adams, and was elected. There were some other similar cases. But a different plan of coalition was proposed for the legislature. Each of the three parties had its own candidates before the people for governor and state officers, but it became clear that neither would have a majority, and in that case the choice would devolve on the legislature. That body was also to elect two United States senators, one for an unexpired term of a few weeks, the other for a full term of six years. It was proposed that in the legislature the Free-soilers should join forces with the Democrats, to give the state offices to the latter and the long-term senatorship to a Free-soiler. This arrangement was opposed by some of the Free-soil leaders, including Adams, Palfrey, and Whittier, but most of their number, including Henry Wilson and F. W. Bird, favored the agreement, and an understanding was openly established with the Democrats.

Such a combination, in which the two parties are not united by a common principle for which each makes some sacrifice, but by a direct exchange of votes, one set of offices being given to men of one political creed, and another set to men of another creed, is sure to arouse severe criticism. The two parties to it will always be charged with trading their principles for office and power. The Massachusetts Whigs, no longer able to appeal to anti-slavery sentiment, assailed with effect the incongruity of the coalition against them. The *Republican* was the enthusiastic champion of the Whig party. It

attacked the Democrats as insincere, and told the Free-
soilers they were being made a cat's-paw, and would
never get their promised reward.  The enthusiasm of a
party name and history ; the claim of consistency and
sincerity, opposed to a hybrid coalition for the spoils of
office ; the allegiance to a great party chief,— these sentiments gave ardor to the politics of the *Republican*.  It
was whole-hearted in its devotion to the Whig party —
Whig *cause* cannot be said, for in truth the party stood
no longer for living ideas.  It was rich in memories, but
bankrupt in great principles, save that of devotion to the
Union, and even as to that it had at the North little distinction above its chief opponent, the Democracy.  As
had been foreseen, no one of their state tickets secured a
majority in the popular vote.  The election devolved on
the legislature.  The coalition was then made definite
and binding.  A Democrat, George Boutwell, was chosen
Governor, with Democratic associates in the state offices,
except a few minor places given by compact to the Free-
soilers.  To the fragment of a senatorial term Robert
Rantoul was elected as a Democrat.  For the long term, the
Whig candidate was Robert C. Winthrop, and the coalition supported Charles Sumner.  After a contest of some
months,— a minority of the Democrats obstinately refus-
ing to support Mr. Sumner,— the necessary votes were
gained to elect him.  The *Republican* fought the coalition
with vigor, but with no such bitterness as it expressed
toward the disunion Abolitionists.  It treated most of
the coalition leaders with personal respect, spoke well of
Governor Boutwell, and when at last Mr. Sumner was
elected to the Senate, said of him (May 2, 1851) that he
was a man of brilliant parts, a theorizer, and an honest
humanitarian, with no experience in legislation, with no
proved claims as a debater or statesman, and with his
future in his own hands.

By a strange transposition, the Democratic party in Massachusetts had become for the time more friendly to freedom than the Whig. In the Democratic convention of this year, 1851, there was a great deal of strong anti-slavery talk. But in the Whig convention held in Springfield, September 11, there was not one voice in rebuke of slavery aggression. The Compromise, the Union, and Webster, were the unanimous cry. The resolutions in one paragraph declare: "The Whigs of Massachusetts will faithfully perform every duty imposed upon them by the Constitution of the United States, and they call upon their brethren in every state in the Union to respect and observe all its constitutional provisions." The only " duty imposed by the Constitution" as to which there was the least question in the public mind, was the return of fugitive slaves. To this the resolution evidently pointed, and to enforce this duty was the chief burden of the address to the people issued by the convention. No wonder that Palfrey said, when in the following week he allied himself with the Free-soil party at its convention, that the Whig resolutions and addresses had sent him there: "No man could read those resolutions without being struck down by conviction as St. Paul was." At the Springfield convention the Webster influence dominated everything. Winthrop was nominated for governor, and Ashmun, Everett, and Seth Sprague were appointed delegates to the national convention of the following year.

The *Republican* was enthusiastic over the harmony and success of the state convention. It cheered on the Whigs through the ensuing campaign, throwing its weight mainly upon state issues, in which the coalition had by no means made a brilliant success. It also had something to say for a high tariff. The coalitionists gave prominence rather to national than state issues.

They again carried the legislature, though by a reduced and narrow majority, and with it the state offices. For governor, the popular vote was, in round numbers: Winthrop, 65,000; Boutwell, 44,000; Palfrey, 28,000,—a fair measure of the relative strength of parties.

The national conventions of 1852 were held, and the nominations made. The Democratic platform declared that the Compromise of 1850 must be accepted as the end of the controversy upon slavery. In the Whig convention, Ashmun was chairman of the committee on resolutions. The Southern delegates to the convention agreed in advance upon a resolution on which they would insist, and this resolution in substance was adopted by the committee and the convention. It declared that the compromise measures, including the Fugitive Slave law, were accepted and acquiesced in by the Whig party, " as a final settlement in principle and substance of the dangerous and exciting questions which they embrace," and that all further agitation of such questions should be discountenanced. This platform was adopted by 227 votes to 66. For the presidential nomination the rivals were Mr. Fillmore, Mr. Webster, and General Scott. The latter was supported by the anti-slavery Whigs,— for little apparent reason save that he was not as objectionable as his competitors,— but was chiefly prominent from his military prestige. Webster had little support save from Massachusetts, whose delegation stood by him, with the exception of Henry L. Dawes, who voted for Scott. The real contest was between Scott and Fillmore, and at last Scott was nominated. He cordially accepted the platform, and thereby took away all enthusiasm from the anti-slavery element of the party; while such Southerners as Stephens and Toombs of Georgia refused to support him because the anti-slavery wing had favored him. The Democrats had

in Franklin Pierce an obscure candidate, but they were
more harmonious than the Whigs. They had re-absorbed
the New York seceders to Free-soilism in 1848, and they
were more trusted than the Whigs by the South. The
Free-soilers nominated John P. Hale. Their platform
re-affirmed that freedom must be regarded as national
and slavery sectional; pronounced slavery a sin against
God and a crime against man; denounced the Fugitive
Slave law, and declared that no human law can be a
finality; and gave the watchword of "Free soil, free
speech, free labor, free men!" This became the rallying
cry of the Republican party only four years later; and
the principles thus announced closely resembled those
applied by the Republican party to somewhat altered
circumstances, save that the latter never made an issue
of the Fugitive Slave law, and was much more explicit
and careful in affirming the *local* rights of slavery than
the Free-soilers ever troubled themselves to be. But
the latter party never had much popular strength, and
now, deprived of its Democratic allies of four years
earlier, its vote fell off from that of 1848 by 100,000,
and reached only 156,000. The Democrats swept the
country, carrying all but four states (Massachusetts,
Vermont, Kentucky, and Tennessee), though with a
popular vote only a very little larger than their two
opponents combined.

The *Republican's* tone through this campaign of 1852
was unreservedly and heartily Whig. The first stage of
its political history ends here. In comparison with Mr.
Bowles's course in later years, it is noticeable how thoroughly during this period he was swayed by the allegiance and enthusiasm of a party, when that party had
no longer any distinctive principles or any inspiring
idea. The ardor of the *Republican* for the Whig party
in these years was in reality, if analyzed, an ardor partly

for individuals,—Webster, the great light of the system,
and Everett, Choate, Ashmun, Winthrop, and the rest,
revolving around him,—partly for a name, a tradition,
an association, which had imperceptibly become emptied
of any solid idea or vital principle.   This enthusiasm
for a party name and associations, in distinction from
an intelligent attachment to ideas and principles, dominated Mr. Bowles in these earlier years; in later years
it was against just such unreasoning partisanship that
he was to do effective service.   As a young man he had
not yet broken away from the materializing influences
which prevailed in the community about him.   That
ardor of intellectual and moral progress which burned
on the Massachusetts coast had scarcely kindled in the
valley of the Connecticut.   The great men of the region,
the "river-gods," were very far from moral enthusiasts.
The "respectable" sentiment of the town was stronger
against George Thompson than against the men who
mobbed him.   When on that occasion the pastor of the
Unitarian church, Rev. George Simmons, spoke manfully
for the rights of free speech, it cost him his dismissal
from the parish.   He was on a sick-bed when the church
meeting was held, and his physician warned those present that any hostile action on their part at that time
might endanger his life, but in the face of this warning
they passed a vote of dismissal.   Mr. Bowles started on
a level with his environment.   The sensitiveness to the
moral element in politics, the insight into the real meaning and drift of things, were to be developed in him later.

# CHAPTER XII.

## The Journalist at Work: His Lieutenants.

THE course of the *Republican* upon great public questions can be briefly recorded, but it is impossible to record, almost impossible to suggest, the history of the paper itself, as a daily chronicle of news and opinion. As one turns the pages of its old files, at a distance of many years, there is in them a vigor and sparkle which fascinate. Read now, it is history in its most vivid and stirring form. Read then, as the sheets yet damp from the press were caught up and eagerly scanned by thousands of eyes, it was history in the very making. These bird's-eye glimpses of the world's life for a day, these stories of myriad activities of good and evil, these quick suggestive paragraphs, stamped an influence on the mind and character of the people who read them. The newspaper was a factor in the lives of the individual and the community more potent than they knew.

The especial genius of the *Republican* and its editor lay in giving the news. Said the prospectus of December 23, 1851:

"We aim first of all to make a live newspaper,—to give everything in this region that people want, briefly, intelligently, succinctly stated—to weed out the verbiage and present the kernel. . . . After news,—which is the great distinc-

tive object of the *Republican*, and to which all other things must
bend,— we aim to discuss politics, morals, religion, physics,—
everything in fact which editors may discuss nowadays,— as
honestly, fairly, frankly, and intelligently as our abilities,
knowledge, and time will admit."

The decade in which the telegraph came into use was
the swift and wonderful adolescence of the news-gathering function of journalism.   The *Republican* had its first
telegraphic dispatches in the latter part of 1846.   An
editorial on " The Newspaper," January 4, 1851, shows
how the incoming order of things impressed the men
through whom it was wrought out.   The very style of
the article illustrates the habit of thought and expression
which the rush of news, and the swift energy it exacted,
created in the editor. when he was a man of power and
sensitiveness.

" Nothing can be more evident to the public, and nothing
certainly is more evident to publishers of newspapers, than
that there is a great deal more news nowadays than there used
to be. . . .   Publishers of country weeklies used to fish with
considerable anxiety in a shallow sea, for matter sufficient to
fill their sheets, while dailies only dreamed of an existence in
the larger cities. . . .   Now all is changed.   The increase
of facilities for the transmission of news brought in a new era.
The railroad car, the steamboat, and the magnetic telegraph
have made neighborhood among widely dissevered states, and
the Eastern Continent is but a few days' journey away.   These
active and almost miraculous agencies have brought the whole
civilized world in contact.   The editor sits in his sanctum, and
his obedient messengers are the lightning and the fire.   He
knows a fire has raged in London before the wind could waft
its smoke to him; the lightning tells him of an explosion in
New Orleans before they have counted the dead and wounded ;
the debates of Congress are in his hands, though hundreds and
thousands of miles from the Capitol, before the members who
participated in them have eaten their dinner ; a speech is

under his eyes before the hurrahs it awakened have died away;
and there he sits day after day, as if he were the center of the
world, to whom all men and things are accountable, and all
actions returnable.  These events are chronicled and explained,
and then they are given to his messengers, the rushing engines,
which carry them to thousands of greedy eyes, waiting to see,
in one brief transcript, the record of the world's great struggle
the previous day.  . . .  The appetite for news is one of those
appetites that grows by what it feeds on.  . . .  The mind
accustomed to the gossip of nations cannot content itself with
the gossip of families.  . . .  The tendency of this new state
of things has as yet hardly claimed a moment's consideration
from the moralist and the philosopher.  Nations and individuals
now stand immediately responsible to the world's opinion, and
the world, interesting itself in the grand events transpiring in
its various parts, and among its various parties, has become,
and is still becoming, liberalized in feeling; and being called
away from its exclusive home-fields has forgotten, in its universal interests, the petty interests, feuds, gossips and strifes of
families and neighborhoods.  This wonderful extension of the
field of vision, this compression of the human race into one
great family, must tend to identify its interests, sympathies, and
motives.  . . .  The press is destined, more than any other
agency, to melt and mold the jarring and contending nations
of the world into that one great brotherhood which through
long centuries has been the ideal of the Christian and the philanthropist.  Its mission has but just commenced.  A few years more
and a great thought uttered within sight of the Atlantic will
rise with the morrow's sun and shine upon millions of minds
within sight of the Pacific.  The murmur of Asia's multitudes
will be heard at our doors; and, laden with the fruit of all
human thought and action, the newspaper will be in every
abode, the daily nourishment of every mind."

This was the ideal view of the matter.  But meantime
the *Republican* was making its mark especially through
a close attention to the home field and its homely details.
At this period its especial claim was to report and repre-

sent its own section of the state. The aim it announced December 23, 1851, was "to give the gist of everything transpiring at this active period of the world's history, and to do it in such a shape and with such directness as to suit in particular the tastes and wants of the people of western Massachusetts." A special department of western Massachusetts news was organized. Dr. Holland wrote in a weekly serial the local history of this part of the state. The publication of this "History of Western Massachusetts" was begun with the year 1854, in weekly numbers, and continued for over a twelvemonth. It traced the annals of each town in the western counties from its earliest settlement, and outlined the general social history of the community. The work was done with immense industry, with strong sympathy with the local traditions and sentiment, and in that popular and readable style of which Dr. Holland was a master. It was his first large literary work, and was followed by a historical novel, "The Bay Path," of which the scenes lay in the early colonial time of Springfield and its neighborhood. These writings appealed to local patriotism, and strengthened it, and through them the paper's roots struck more tenaciously into the local soil. At the same time its range was widening and its power increasing. In the new era of politics, at the birth of the Republican party, it will be seen how it rose to a leadership of nobler quality and wider scope, and it was with ample justification that its prospectus for 1856 advanced a broader claim than before. "Its highest ambition is to be the representative of New England sentiment, and the servant of New England interests." This always remained its highest claim and its proudest boast—to be the representative newspaper of New England.

The faculty in which Mr. Bowles first showed eminence—the germ as it were from which his powers developed — was skill in gathering news. Said Mr. Bryan, who was added to the paper's force in 1852: "He and I would go into a little restaurant on Sanford street, and one and another would drop in and exchange a few words, and while we were eating our lunch he would pick up half a column of news." Said a friend in a neighboring town: "I would meet him on the street, we would chat a few minutes about the events of the day, and next morning I would find in the paper everything I had told him." In the political conventions which he attended and reported, he was in his native element. He button-holed everybody, and offended nobody; found out the designs of every clique, the doings of every secret caucus, got at the plans of the leaders, the temper of the crowd, *sensed* the whole situation,— and the next morning's *Republican* gave a better idea of the convention to those who had staid at home than many of its participants had gained. These reporting expeditions were full of education to him. His mode of growth was by absorption. Other people were to him sponges out of which he deftly squeezed whatever knowledge they could yield. As yet, the work of the paper held him pretty closely to Springfield, and allowed but few of those flying trips to the centers of intelligence which in later years he used constantly to make. But he made the most of every opportunity. In the winter of 1852–3 he was appointed messenger to carry the electoral vote of the state to Washington. It was the first time he had been there since his invalid journey southward, eight years before. George Ashmun showed him all sides of the city's life.

Another journey he made in 1854 to Chicago, and thence with a great excursion party to the Falls of St. Anthony. He wrote to the *Republican* a series of letters describing this journey. One passage, written at Niagara Falls, illustrates how in this early stage of his development the grandeur of Nature, instead of carrying him into a different realm from that of humanity, stimulated his sense of the intense human activities in which his life was merged.

"America is written all over the Falls. Its roar is that of the nation. Its majestic sweep typifies the grand progress of America. The maddening, dashing, seething, baffling, pitching, uneasy flood typifies the intensity of the American mind, and the vitality of American action. Here is the fountain of true young America — here the breast which gives it milk — here the nurture which gives it vitality. And then the rainbows hovering over and about the scene, do they not signify the promise which America gives to mankind, the hope which it implants in weary-laden hearts, the home which it furnishes to the outcast and wanderer from governmental oppression and social villainy elsewhere ? "

Gradually co-laborers and lieutenants were added to Mr. Bowles and Dr. Holland. Mr. Clark W. Bryan, previously the conductor of the *Berkshire Courier*, of Great Barrington, came as an addition to the force in November, 1854, and continued with it for twenty years, — a man of high fidelity and capacity, greedy of work, warm-hearted, and thoroughly loyal to his chief. For several years he had been employed to collect the election returns from southern Berkshire. The gathering of the returns from western Massachusetts was a special achievement of the *Republican*. Says Mr. Bryan, in the *Paper World*, April, 1880 : " The writer scoured southern Berkshire, driving personally fifty miles by horsepower and the same number on a locomotive, between the closing of the polls in the hill towns of Berkshire and the hour of eleven P. M., when the returns of every town in western Massachusetts — with only one exception, on two occasions — were in the *Republican* office." From the southern border the returns were gathered to

Great Barrington, thence fleet horses took them to Pitts-field, where they were met by a hand-car from North Adams, bringing Henry L. Dawes with the reports from the northern towns; and from Pittsfield Mr. Bryan took them by locomotive to Springfield. The river counties were covered by special locomotive from South Vernon, connecting with horse-expresses along the way. The organization of such an achievement was a congenial enterprise for Mr. Bowles, and brought him into acquaint-ance with energetic and capable men throughout the region.

When Mr. Bryan came to the paper, Mr. Bowles was still partially disabled by the weakening of the eyes which preceded and followed his severe sickness in the spring of 1852. From November to the next September, he was not much engaged in the editorial rooms, except in making up the Weekly. This task he kept in his own hands, with rare exceptions, till the end of his life. He made the Weekly always his special concern. It went to a more distant circle of readers than the Daily; it was likely to receive more leisurely reading; and the work of skimming for it the cream from the pages of the Daily was one which he seldom trusted to another hand. The general editorial work through these months was done by Dr. Holland and Mr. Bryan, with no reporter or regu-lar assistant. Dr. Holland worked through the day till eight or nine in the evening. Mr. Bryan worked in the office from eleven in the morning till four, then went to the depot for the Boston papers, returned to the office and worked on local and telegraphic news till two in the morning. After nearly a year of this, he broke down in a severe illness. On his recovery, a new arrangement was made; a job printing-office was bought, and the firm, now including Mr. Bryan, carried on a general printing and book-binding business, which became very prosperous. Of this Mr. Bryan took charge, along with the publishing department of the newspaper. He was succeeded in the editorial room by Mr. Alanson Hawley. To purchase the printing business, the partners had to unite in borrowing four thousand dollars. There was no further need to put in capital, and thereafter the profits steadily increased.

Of Mr. Bowles, Mr. Bryan wrote in the *Paper World*, some time after his death:

"Labor was his relaxation, toil his daily meat and drink, perseverance his amusement, and achievement his recompense. . . . Once placed on the high road to fame and fortune, the *Republican* made rapid strides in the way of achievement and success, but Mr. Bowles never slackened his hold on the reins of government and management, or eased his shoulders from the heavy burden of labor which he assumed at the outset. He was omnipresent. He knew everything, saw everything, dictated everything, and his dictation dictated every time."

Between Mr. Bryan and his chief the personal intercourse in these hard-working years was harmonious and kindly. There were morning horseback rides together; and walks in which plans and prospects were eagerly and sympathetically discussed. The impression made by Mr. Bowles upon his comrade was that of a winning and charming personality, yet not without occasional alternations of hardness and severity. "Yet all our early relations," says Mr. Bryan, "were most pleasant,— some of my happiest days were as we walked and talked and planned and hoped together."

In studying the files of the *Republican*, the reader notes, about the year 1856, an added breadth and pungency in the editorial writing which seemed to indicate some marked addition to the force. Such an addition there had been; for the staff was now increased to four by the inclusion of Mr. Joseph E. Hood. The few who personally knew Mr. Hood held but one opinion of his character and genius. At the time of his death that character and genius were portrayed by Mr. Bowles in a letter to the *Republican* of December 2, 1871, from Denver, Colorado, where he had been sitting by the bedside of the dying man — one of the best of the unknown servants of mankind, whose high fortune it is "to widen knowledge, and escape the praise."

"So little of personal fame and public observation, with so much of real public service, and so much of real influence, it seems to me, was never united in one life as in that of this late associate of ours. For more than a quarter of a century he had been a constant writer upon the weekly and daily press of America, — doing a greater amount of first-class work than almost any other man who has lived and labored in this generation, — yet only a very few of the men and women who daily read and were daily instructed and inspired by his writings on political, social, and religious questions, knew to whom they were indebted, or were aware even of his personal existence. . . . His ill-health was one cause of this retirement; but the main reason was a simple modesty of mind that shunned the haunts of men, and found its chief pleasures in his work, in his papers and books, and in the company of the chosen few of his home circle.

"Born at Amesbury, Mass., in 1815, Mr. Hood never saw his father, who was a sea captain and was drowned while upon a voyage, and inherited from his mother a feeble and consumptive constitution, and yet a tenacious, nervous, fibrous hold on life that carried her on to old age, and would probably have similarly preserved him under more favorable circumstances of residence and avocation. The neighbor and companion in youth, the friend in manhood, of the poet Whittier, he greatly resembled him in purity and simplicity of character, and in fineness of intellectual feeling, as he even exceeded him in breadth of culture, in capacity of expression, and in practical usefulness in life. He shared with Whittier, also, an early advocacy of the anti-slavery cause, and while in Dartmouth College made himself famous among his fellows as a leader therein. At that time, it will be remembered, the abolition agitation was unpopular; parties frowned upon it, the church was at least cold toward it, and the college authorities strove to crush out its growth among their students. To be what young Hood then was, a pioneer and leader in it, indicated high character — an independent conscience and an unflinching courage — and what did not necessarily follow, also, but what was always conspicuous in him, a sweet and unassuming modesty and personal self-abnegation in walking firmly the path of duty.

"From Dartmouth College, where he graduated in 1841, he soon went to the Andover Theological Seminary, intending to fit for the ministry; but, finding after a year's experience there, partly on account of his antagonism to the popular church organizations on the slavery question, and partly on account of an independent spirit of inquiry and thought on theological questions, that he was not likely to be in such close sympathy with the churches that Andover represented as his conscience would require of him to take a pastorate, he surrendered this purpose, and turned his attention to journalism." He began at Hanover, N. H., as editor of a small temperance and anti-slavery paper, the *Family Visitor*, which in 1844 he removed to Concord, enlarged, and re-named the *Granite Freeman*. The paper was the organ of the Liberty and afterward the Free-soil party, and was merged in the *Independent Democrat*. In 1849 Mr. Hood left journalism to engage in the telegraph business, and this employment brought him to Springfield. "It was while thus living in Springfield that his abilities as a journalist became known to the *Republican*, and after waiting a year or two to grow strong enough to employ him, it engaged his services in 1855. From that time until 1869 — full fourteen years — he held a leading position in the editorial department of that journal. He had no taste for business; he declined executive responsibilities, and had no capacity for what may be called the directing and managing of a public journal; but in the details of its columns—for writing editorials not only on the current topics of politics and life, but on abstract questions of civil and political economy, on practical and theoretical religion, on literature and science, indeed on all the conceivable questions that come within the greedy grasp of the modern newspaper, as well as in condensing and arranging news and making selections, I never saw a man who was even his equal, either in the character, variety, or amount of the work that he could and did do. Irregularity in life and labor was impossible to him; day in and day out, month after month, and almost year after year, he was as steady as a clock in attendance at the office, and in a constant and quiet and yet rapid execution of every species of editorial labor. His style was admirable,— simple, direct, pure, forcible without being passionate, pungent without being vulgar, often delicately sarcastic and deliciously humorous, never egotistical, never suggesting the writer, always representing the journal, and this as the voice of the people,— he was by nature, by culture, by experience the model modern working journalist. He saw the world without, partly through others, but chiefly through its own words, interpreted to him by his own divine instincts. The *Republican* has had many capable and faithful servants, but no one who united so much of capacity with so much of fidelity as Mr. Hood; and few of its readers knew how much of the varied charms and value of its columns during these fourteen years was due to his sagacity of thought, varied culture, lively interest in all prog- ress, and delicate deftness of expression. His life seemed very narrow; he knew as few people personally in Springfield as in Denver; yet to him it was very rich. He loved his work only less than he loved his home; he spent his time between his pet corner in the office and his family fireside; the one sustained and upheld him for the other; together they more than satis- fied all his nature. He felt the great though unseen power he was exerting through the paper; he had no ambition to stand in nearer or more personal relations to his audience; his wife and children gave him all he wanted else.

"But the infirmities of inheritance were brought out by these years of indoor labor, though long restrained by simple and regular and healthful habits of living and laboring, and in 1868 his attendance at the office began to be irregular, and he had to confront the sad necessity of a change." He passed a spring in Kansas, and in 1869 settled permanently in Colorado, where he found relief from bronchial consumption and chronic dyspepsia, and did various journalistic work, including regular editorial writing for the *Rocky Mountain News*, all of high quality. "But still he could never do elsewhere what he did on the *Republican*,—he left his heart, as he had done his life's best and great work, in it; and even these tenderer skies and drier airs could not bring him up to his old enthusiasm and delight in his labor. He loved Colorado and the few dear friends he made here, but his chief desire, almost his only hope, was to be able to go back some time to his old associates and his old work in the *Republican* office. He knew it was not to be, but it was a pleasure to him to think it might be.

"In the spring of 1871, the weaknesses of lungs and stomach obliged him to give up all work. The summer was to him that of a quiet but growing invalidism—he was better and worse, but the worse grew upon him, and within the last month he has rapidly failed. He held on till his old chief and friend,—nominal master, but real pupil in all that was sweetest and purest and noblest in personal and professional life—came to sit by his bedside and to exchange for the last time greetings and partings. Then he quietly sank away—in peace and in resignation, with sweet thoughts of the past, with sweeter faith in the future. No life was ever better lived than this; no man ever did more and better work on earth, and made less noise about it; no memory could be more grateful to friends and relatives; no example purer and nobler. He was both an honor and an ornament to the profession of American journalism—he was more and better, a glory to humanity.

"It is fit, before closing, to say something of Mr. Hood's religious character. It was both peculiar and positive; the spirit of Christ was indeed abroad in his nature and in his life; theology was a favorite study of his, and with the Scriptures he was most familiar,—few ministers are more learned in both respects; and he often said the work he could do the best was a commentary upon and exposition of the Bible; but he thought not always with the priests and teachers, and his soul was always open to every form and shade of honest and intelligent belief. Though he was attached through all his life to what is known in New England as Congregational orthodoxy, and fellowshiped with its churches, he was, in the largest and best sense, a Liberal Christian, and preached, alike in life and writings, the gospel of love and charity to all. As to his personal and practical Christianity, if there ever was a disciple of his Lord, it was Joseph E. Hood."

Mr. Hood's accession to the *Republican* may be fairly regarded as an epoch in the history of the paper and of Mr. Bowles. The presence of so able and versatile a journalist brought to the paper a strength which allowed to its chief a freer way of work, a wider range of travel and reading, than had before been possible. Mr. Hood, too, was the first instrument he found that was perfectly adapted to one of his peculiar powers—the transmission of his own ideas through another's personality. In Mr. Bryan's words: "Mr. Bowles would talk to Hood for five minutes, giving him points for an article, and then go off, and Hood would work it out perfectly." To thus use another man's brain and hand is one of the special gifts of a great journalist. Mr. Bowles had it in a high degree, and he found in Mr. Hood an almost perfect medium for such transmission. One result for him was an economizing of vital force, and a corresponding liberation of energy for other uses.

# CHAPTER XIII.

## The Awakening of the North.

IN the political field the struggle between slavery and freedom in America went on only in preparation and skirmishing until the year 1854. Up to that time, the two great parties treated it as a side issue. Then, when the truce made by the compromise of 1850 was broken by the repeal of the Missouri compromise, the contest suddenly expanded until the whole country became its theater.

When, in 1820, the state of Missouri was organized out of a part of the immense north-western territory acquired from France years before by the Louisiana purchase, there was a struggle in Congress as to whether slavery, which had a foothold in the new state, should be excluded therefrom as a condition of its admission. The question was settled by allowing Missouri to retain slavery, but upon condition that it should be forever prohibited in all the rest of the Louisiana purchase lying north of the line of thirty-six degrees thirty minutes north latitude,—the line which marks the southern boundary of Missouri. The debates of 1850 had no reference to this region, but concerned that other vast country which had just been conquered from Mexico. Now, in the winter of 1853–4, a proposal was made to organize, under territorial government,—first as one

territory of Nebraska, but soon, as the two territories of
Nebraska and Kansas,—an immense district lying west
of Missouri and wholly north of the "thirty-six thirty"
line,—a part of that very domain which it had been
decreed in 1820 should be forever free. The bill originated in the Senate, and it was a Northern man, Stephen
A. Douglas, of Illinois,—for many years a senator, and a
politician eagerly ambitious for the Presidency, to which
the road seemed to lie through Southern favor,—who,
as chairman of the committee on territories, incorporated
in the bill of organization a clause declaring that the
prohibition of slavery north of 36° 30, by the act of 1820,
had been "superseded by the principles of the legislation
of 1850," and was "inoperative and void."

This proposal—instantly and eagerly seized by the
South—stirred the North with a thrill of resentment
and resistance. From this time began a wholly new
epoch in the political action of the Northern people.
Unnoted by the politicians and the worldly-wise, the
antipathy to slavery had steadily widened and deepened
among the common people. The more it was thought
of, the more odious it became to them. The occasional
return of fugitives thrust the horrors of the system upon
their notice. The men and women of keen moral
instincts who had long recognized it as the great
national sin, served each as the center of widening
circles of conviction. Millions who had been unmoved
by the denunciations of Garrison and Phillips, had been
conquered by the pathetic story of "Uncle Tom's Cabin."
But for all this rapidly growing volume of opinion and
feeling, there had lacked a political outlet. Love of the
Union, love of peace, regard for the established social
order, had united with commercial interest and personal
ambitions to hold the North in acquiescence. Now, the
South and its allies struck a sudden blow at peace, at

ancient compact, and at liberty. Slavery grasped openly
at universal extension and supremacy in the nation.
The assault set free all that hostility to human bondage
which the North had been almost dumbly harboring,
swept into its tide a multitude who before had been
indifferent,

> "And all the long-pent stream of life
> Dashed downward in a cataract."

The aggression roused an opposition on other than
moral grounds. Northern politicians who cared nothing
about slavery were alarmed at the prospect of a prepon-
derance in Congress and the electoral college to be
gained for the South by the creation of new slave states.
The men of the Clay and Webster school, who had been
anxious to keep the peace by keeping an even balance of
power between the two sections, saw the scales rudely
jostled. Clay and Webster and Calhoun were dead.
Calhoun's spirit had mastered the South, and made
aggressiveness its key-note. The work of the great compromises was undone; and two opposite civilizations, two
opposite moralities, were to wrestle for the supremacy.

The *Republican's* tone at this time, in contrast with its
course in 1850, is a good illustration of the changed temper of the nation. From the first introduction of Mr.
Douglas's bill, it made frequent and sharp comment upon
its unprincipled and mischievous character. When the
measure had reached full development, and its adoption
by Pierce's administration foreshadowed its success in a
strongly Democratic Congress, the *Republican* (February
8) treated the subject in a masterly article of two columns and a half. It clearly and soberly rehearsed the
whole history of the Missouri compromise; and said of
the proposed repeal:

"It is a monstrous proposition. It is a huge stride backwards. It proposes to undo the work of freedom performed by our fathers. It makes the government of the great Republic of the world an engine for the strengthening and advancement of the worst sort of human slavery. It is legislation against the spirit of the age, against the spirit of republicanism, against the decent opinions of the decent part of the world.

"Besides, it is a re-opening of the slavery agitation, quieted for a long series of years, as all supposed, by the compromises of 1850. The North had acquiesced in these compromises; it sustained them and abided by them. But the South and its Northern political allies have broken the peace of the country. They make fresh and monstrous demands. These demands will arouse the whole nation; they will widen and deepen the anti-slavery feeling of the country as no other conceivable proposition could. The signs are unmistakable. No mere party or faction will array itself against this Nebraska scheme. The whole people are against it. The moral force of the North — the influence, the learning, the wealth, and the votes of the North — are against it, and will make themselves effectively heard, ere the agitation, now re-opened by the insanity of the slave-holding interest, and in behalf of the schemes of ambitious partisans, shall have ceased. *The South and its allies have sown the wind,— will they not reap the whirlwind?*

"The measure will have a potent influence upon the politics of the country. Out of it now promise to grow new and important arrangements of parties, and new and important results in our country's history. We await their issue calmly, hopefully, trustingly. But we shall not, because we cannot, be passive spectators of the strife. Our sympathies, our convictions, are all with freedom and liberty, and against slavery and oppression. And wherever it leads us, we shall battle for the right against the wrong, for freedom against slavery, for progress against retrogradation,— not with blind fanaticism, but we trust with an enlightened liberality that will give us the company of the wise and good, of the earnest and the thoughtful, of all who place country above party, throughout the free states."

VOL. I.—8

In these declarations, the *Republican* entered upon a moral leadership, such as it had never before exercised. Its chief editor's greatness lay largely in his capacity for growth, his susceptibility to enlarging and ennobling influences. The new impulse which swept through the nation found him open to its full influence. He saw with clearness and spoke with force what right-minded men were beginning to see and speak everywhere. The paper noted, February 16, that all the Whig and Independent papers of the North, with very many of the Democratic, are opposed to the Kansas-Nebraska bill. It gave for several weeks a daily column of "Public Opinion," containing the declarations of papers and men on the great question. It was largely by thus giving the *news*, of opinion and fact, that the *Republican* maintained its cause. Its own argument and appeal had their place; but the story of what men were saying and doing was the strongest weapon. Thus, there occurs from this time a frequent column of news items about slavery, under such headings as "The Patriarchal Institution," relating incidents characteristic of the system and its abuses. Among these frequently appear sympathetic notices of escapes, attempted or successful,— the "constitutional duty" to return fugitives having fallen, alas! quite out of sight. Thus we read, April 28: "The underground railroad"— the system of secret assistance to slaves escaping to Canada —"was never doing a larger business, we apprehend, than at present. We find no quotations of the stock, but it must certainly be above par. The travel is large, and there are few or no accidents. The signal success of its operations speaks well for the ability and discretion of its management."

The struggle over the Kansas-Nebraska bill continued till the end of May. In the policy which Mr. Douglas advocated, there lurked a fraudulent element. His profession was that the question of slavery was to be remanded to the (white) people of each territory to settle for themselves. This he called "popular sovereignty," and the name and the theory had a considerable attraction for a people attached to local self-government. The peculiarity of totally ignoring that fraction of the local population most interested was hit exactly by Abraham Lincoln, in his debates with Douglas four years later, when he said: "Mr. Douglas's popular sovereignty means that if one man wants to make a slave of another, a third man has no right to prevent him." But, even apart from this, the pretense of remanding the subject to the territorial population was insincere. Mr. Douglas finally made this addition to the clause declaring the Missouri compromise void: "It being the true intent and meaning of this act, not to legislate slavery into any territory or state, nor to exclude it therefrom, but to leave the people thereof perfectly free to form and regulate their domestic institutions in their own way, subject only to the constitution of the United States." This was the specious theory by which Mr. Douglas kept his hold on a part of the Northern Democracy. Yet, right upon the adoption of this amendment in the Senate, Senator Chase tested its sincerity by proposing to add this clause: "Under which the people of the territory, through their appropriate representatives, may, if they see fit, prohibit the existence of slavery therein";—and this was instantly voted down—36 to 10—by the whole strength of the Administration party, Douglas among them. In subsequent debate, Southern senators openly avowed that the bill gave slave-holders the right to take slaves into the territory and hold them there. Senator Butler, of South Carolina, declared that if in such case attempt was made to free the slaves by territorial law, the master would answer "that he held the slave as property under a higher law than the enactment of a territorial legislature,—under the great fundamental law of the country." "This," said the *Republican* (March 22), "is the Southern view of the question, and it is the view that will prevail and be sustained by the courts, if the bill becomes a law." This prophecy was more than fulfilled in the Dred Scott decision of the United States Supreme Court.

The battle went on in Congress. In the Senate, Seward, Sumner, Chase, Fessenden, and their associates, in a minority of one to three, stood their ground against Douglas, Cass, Mason, Benjamin, etc. In the House, Campbell, Banks, the Washburns, Gerrit Smith, and Thomas H. Benton, with other Whigs, Democrats, and Free-soilers, found themselves strangely associated together against a narrow majority, led by Richardson (Douglas's Illinois lieutenant), Alexander Stephens, Breckinridge, and others. Party lines went down; the Southern Democrats supported the bill; the Southern Whigs held a separate caucus, but failed to agree; the Northern Whigs were against the bill, and the Northern Democrats were divided. The decisive vote was reached in the House, May 22, and the bill was passed by 113 to 100. Its supporters consisted of 57 Southern Democrats, 12 Southern Whigs, and 44 Northern Democrats. Its opponents were 44 Northern Whigs, 43 Northern Democrats, 4 Free-soilers, 7 Southern Whigs, and 2 Southern Democrats. The final assent of the Senate to the bill was given, May 25, by 35 votes to 13. Not a vote in its favor was from Massachusetts.

The *Republican* said, May 27, " What the North should do " was to pour into the new territories a tide of immigrants whose votes would keep them free, to reëlect to Congress every member, of whatever party name, who had opposed the Kansas-Nebraska scheme, and to return no member who had supported it.  The greatest problem which confronted the friends of freedom was to unite their forces in a harmonious and effective organization.  The work was one of immense difficulty, and was not instantly achieved even under the uplifting and heroic impulses of the time.  On the morning after the passage of the bill, a meeting of about twenty members of the House was held, at the suggestion of Israel Washburn, Jr., of Maine, at the rooms of Edward Dickinson and Thomas D. Eliot, of Massachusetts; and after some discussion and a little talk of trying to identify the Whig party with the cause of freedom, it was generally agreed that the only hope of victory lay in a new party, for which the name Republican was judged appropriate.*  Michigan took the lead among the states; her Whig and Free-soil organizations coöperated to establish the new Republican party, which carried the autumn election.  In Ohio, a union was effected on an "anti-Nebraska" delegation to Congress, and the state was carried by 70,000 majority.  In New York the Whig party, controlled by Seward and Thurlow Weed, kept its organization on an anti-Nebraska basis, and elected the state officers, while in the Congressional districts all the anti-Nebraska elements united with very general success.

In Massachusetts, the Whigs had in the preceding year regained their ascendency.  The Coalitionists had proposed several constitutional amendments which were defeated on a popular vote, and the Whigs had won back the state government.  The coalition, a heartless and artificial affair, was dead beyond resurrection; the revival of the slavery issue set its two elements at hopeless discord.  The Whigs had lost by death, two years before, their great leader, Webster; the mass of them gravitated

* This is Henry Wilson's statement.  "Rise and Fall of the Slave Power," ii., 410.

to a strong anti-slavery position; but the leadership of the party was deeply infected with selfishness and timidity. Within a week after the passage of the Kansas-Ne-braska bill, the *Republican* (May 31) published a letter, urging that the Whig party was the best instrumentality for forwarding the cause of liberty; and the editorial reply discussed the situation with breadth and force:

" Will the seceding Democrats, the Whigs, and the Aboli-tionists unite into one party to effect success on this point against the Administration ? United they will succeed; di-vided as now, and the Administration maintains itself over them. The opponents of the Administration have got to hang together or they will hang separately. What is the objection to their hanging together ? What have the Northern Whigs to hope by spurning association with other opponents of the Administration ? The national Whig party is surely a defunct organization. It has been tottering for some years, resorting to various devices to sustain itself, but has finally gone by the board. Those of the slave states who represented it in Con-gress have, with two or three honorable exceptions, deserted its colors, turned traitors to their Northern associates, and gone over body and soul to the administration of General Pierce and the embrace of Stephen Arnold Douglas. The Northern Whigs cannot and will not, of course, have anything to do with such men. The Southern Whigs having gone to the Administration, where will the Northern Whigs go ? We trust they will not stand still and suck their thumbs, because of old prejudices and old quarrels with those who, formerly in opposi-tion, are now animated by the same sentiments, and burn with the same desire to defeat and overthrow the Administration. For ourselves,—whatever others may do,—we shall advocate the sentiments we have enunciated, party or no party. In the great internal struggle between slavery extension and slavery non-extension, we plant ourselves with the non-extensionists, and we shall join that organization, whatever its name, what-ever its leaders, that promises most successfully, most safely, and most surely for the common weal, to carry out and estab-

lish the non-extension principle. Past enmities, past prejudices — let them go. The times demand it. The North and
Freedom demand it. Every right which Slavery enjoys by the
constitution let it have, and be protected in to the fullest; but
beyond that let Freedom rule. Here we stand. Here the
great bulk of the people at the North are ready to gather,
if those who direct public opinion and lead the masses will only
let them do it."

The teaching of events came fast and hard. On the
very day that the Nebraska bill finally passed the Senate,
Anthony Burns was arrested in Boston as a fugitive
from slavery in Virginia. The warrant was issued by
C. G. Loring, United States Commissioner, and also a
Massachusetts Judge of Probate, and by him the case
was tried, a week intervening before the final decision.
The city and the commonwealth were stirred with pity
and indignation. Mass meetings were held; the fiery
eloquence of Theodore Parker and Wendell Phillips summoned the people to armed resistance; with them united
such men as Samuel G. Howe, Albert G. Browne, Jr., and
T. W. Higginson, to plan a forcible rescue of the captive.
The attempt was made prematurely and failed. In the
closely guarded court-house, the prisoner was defended
by R. H. Dana, Jr., and Charles M. Ellis. When Simms
was sent back, three years before, the mass of the people,
the *Republican* among them, had grudgingly consented
that Shylock should have his pound of flesh. But the
times and the people's temper had changed. Said the
*Republican* (May 29):

"The embittered feelings of the North receive fresh irrita-
tion, in the new instances of the execution of the odious fugitive slave law. The peril of the Union in 1850 was nowise so
great as that in which it lies at this moment. The bold aggressiveness of slavery is striking fatal blows at the perpetuity
of our Republic, and accustoming the people of the North to

serious calculations of the value of a connection which produces
scenes so revolting to humanity and so odious to every decent
feeling of liberty, while its government disregards and destroys
other and higher interests that it may stimulate and extend
that which is the parent of such scenes, and about whose existence clusters every form of evil, social degradation, and anti-
republican doctrine."

The final scene was thus characterized (June 3):

" The fugitive has been remanded. Law and order and
slavery and bayonets and slave-catchers triumph. The decision of Commissioner Loring was on Friday morning rendered,
amid such scenes as God forbid shall ever be witnessed in
Boston again."

The captive was marched down State street, surrounded by a hollow square of one hundred special
deputies of the United States Marshal, armed with cut-
lasses and pistols, escorted by marines with a cannon, a
thousand militia, and the whole police force of the city.
He was placed on board a revenue cutter assigned by the
President, and carried back to Virginia. The *Republican*
said:

" The world now understands, if it never understood before,
that the interest cherished most warmly by the American government is property in human flesh. . . . Is there no call
for the burial of all past differences among good citizens, for
the one great object of changing the spirit of the legislation of
this country ? Slavery rules to-day — blacks and whites alike.
Shall it always do this ? Aye ! so long as we fraternize politically with men who have made us their slave-catchers, and use
our halls of justice for slave pens."

The people of Massachusetts looked upon the return
of Burns with bitter, brooding indignation. Constitution or no constitution, never again would the state lend

her officers, her militia, or her soil, for man-hunting. The leaders in the attempted rescue were held for trial, but the indictment was quashed. The next year the legislature passed by an overwhelming vote a statute which, without expressly nullifying the Fugitive Slave law, aimed to prevent its enforcement, and, had a case arisen under it, might have brought the state into direct collision with the general government. But no one cared to try further experiments in slave-catching on New England soil.

Political union of all the opponents of slavery,—this was the moral the *Republican* constantly drew from the events of the time; this was the end it sought with earnestness, with sagacity, and in a broad and concilia- tory temper. It forbore from recriminations toward its former opponents, and was in nowise exacting as to means or as to details. When an anonymous call for a Republican state convention was issued, the *Republican* expressed regret that it had forestalled a more promising movement led by well-known names, but said (July 10): "Things being as they are, however, we advise men of all parties to coöperate heartily and zealously in the gathering on the 20th, at Worcester." It urged its old friends, the Whigs, to throw themselves cordially into the movement. But the event showed that the Whig leaders were not ready for it. Of the convention of July 20, the paper said: "Though respectable in both numbers and character, it was in neither respect a just indication of the sentiments of Massachusetts. It was wanting altogether in leading representative men." Al- most all of its members were from the Free-soil party. "We do not think the impracticable folly and short- sightedness of the Whig organization justified the Free- soil leaders, who, in consequence thereof, found them- selves in control of the convention, in further impeding

that concentration of action among the friends of freedom in Massachusetts, which they professed so earnestly
and so sincerely and solely to desire." It especially
blamed the hasty call for a delegate convention to nominate state officers. The true course, it argued in subsequent articles, was to seek a union upon Congressional
candidates only, as was being done in New York,—the
time being clearly unripe for a full consolidation, extending to state officers, such as was possible in Michigan.
As the Whig convention drew near, a month later, it
urged upon that body—clearly tending to a narrow and
selfish policy—to rise to the height of the situation. It
pointed out (August 14) that the course of the Southern
Whigs had broken up the party as a national organization, and that the supreme necessity was union against
slavery extension. "We must realize the altered condition of things, and meet the crisis with generosity, with
boldness, and with wisdom." It urged that if the successful ticket of last year was renominated, it would, as
a matter of fact, be taken by the Free-soilers as a gaunt-
let of opposition; and that new candidates, such as
Julius Rockwell and John G. Palfrey, would draw
together the elements whose union was needed. But
the convention satisfied itself by passing strong resolutions as to the aggressions of slavery,—including a
demand for the amendment or repeal of the Fugitive
Slave law,—and made no advance toward union with its
old opponents. It renominated Governor Emory Washburn and the other incumbents of the state offices.
Upon this untoward result the *Republican* made scanty
comment, but yielded a late and cool support to the
party nominations. It reiterated that the old Whig party
alone could not hope to overthrow the Administration,
and that its only place was as a body-guard and nucleus
for the army of the opposition. The Republican con-

vention (September 8) had among its members, Sumner,
Amasa Walker, and John A. Andrew. It nominated
Henry Wilson for governor; and its constituency proved
to be hardly other than a small minority of the old
Free-soilers. Upon state issues the Whigs had a better
record than their opponents, and were the advocates of
desirable reforms.

But meantime a side current had swept suddenly and
silently upon the advancing tide of anti-slavery politics.
A wholly different issue seized for the moment the public
attention. The preceding years had witnessed an immense increase of foreign immigration. The immigrants
of this period were chiefly Irish Catholics. At various
points they came into somewhat irritating collision with
the feelings, tastes, and convictions of the native population. They tended to settle in masses in the great
cities, where their numbers and ignorance made them an
injurious element in the body politic. Their subjection
to the Catholic Church gave offense to the intense Prot-
estantism which America had inherited from England.
That church was shrewd to push her own interest, and
on some subjects, especially the public schools, that
interest was clearly hostile to the ideas cherished by
most of the American people. The political support of
the foreign element was assiduously cultivated by dema-
gogues, notably by those of the Democratic party.
Against these tendencies, a reaction and protest took
form in the organization of a secret society, called the
"Know-nothings," which originated in 1853, and spread
with extraordinary rapidity. Its secret ceremonies fed
that love of mummery and mystery which so often
lingers in man, a sort of survival from childhood; and
it found a great opportunity in the disintegration of the
old parties. In the South, where anti-slavery politics
were not tolerated, and Whiggism was dead, Know-

nothingism became a rallying-place for the opponents of the Democrats. At the North, the party was joined by multitudes of anti-slavery men, eager for political revolution, and impatient at the delay of the old leaders. It fell largely under the control of obscure and inferior men, but there were some prominent politicians who seized it as an instrument for their own ends. When, as "the American party," it took the field in 1854, it surprised the country by its strength, winning many local and municipal elections; and in the next two or three years it carried a number of state elections both North and South. Its success was very brief; its permanent effects upon legislation extremely slight; but it played a prominent part in the transition era. In Massachusetts, the elements it included were, first, men who honestly believed in its avowed principles; secondly, men who were impatient to break down the old parties; thirdly, a great many who joined the "lodges" for curiosity or amusement; and last, but not least, a few leaders like Wilson and Burlingame, who made it a tool to serve their personal ends.

The *Republican* first took note of Know-nothingism as a serious movement March 31, 1854, when it said of it:

"We are as much opposed as any one can be to a sectarian or foreign influence in the affairs of the government, but the means adopted by the Know-nothings to put it down are just as objectionable, in every way. Secret political organizations, in a Republican government, are in the last degree reprehensible, though we doubt whether they ever become dangerous in America, for the principles and good sense of the people must be against them. Besides, the policy is bad. It is good policy to Americanize everything resident in America; and organized opposition to any portion of our population must beget opposition, and tend to keep alive prejudices and influences which it is for the interest of all to do away with."

From this position the *Republican* never swerved, steadily opposing Know-nothingism as un-American, and hostile to the spirit of religious equality.  The political strength of the party first began to appear in Massachusetts after the barren results of the Whig and Republican conventions.  The party nominated for governor Henry J. Gardner, whose political record was that of a conservative Whig.  The *Republican* said that the nomination was managed by Henry Wilson and Anson Burlingame, as part of an arrangement by which Wilson was to be sent to the Senate, and Burlingame to the House.  The approach of the election found all the prophets at fault. But the result came as an amazing surprise.  The Know-nothings swept the state like a hurricane.  Gardner received 79,000 votes; the Whig candidate, Governor Washburn, came next with 26,000; Beach, Democrat, had 14,000, and Wilson 7000.  Every one of the twelve Congressmen chosen was a Know-nothing, and the state legislature was almost solidly of the same party.

The *Republican* treated the result with the good-natured philosophy which it always showed under defeat; and the people generally seemed to pause from their accustomed seriousness, to indulge in a great laugh at their own escapade.  The paper thus interpreted the event (November 15):

" The result of Monday's voting means that the people were out of humor with the old political organizations, and desired to extinguish them, break down the differences, unite and re-divide as the new and more important practical questions of the time shall indicate to be necessary or appropriate.  This was the voice of common sense and the feeling of the great mass of the people.  They sought satisfaction in a fusion upon the slavery question; but the quietists and the velvet-footed philanthropists on one side, and the selfish schemes of party leaders and committee men on both, brought effort here to nought." The people, it continued, disappointed and vexed, seized on Know-nothingism as an instrument for breaking to pieces the old parties. This involved the misfortune of displacing many good and tried public servants and putting novices in their stead. Thus in the Springfield district the Whig candidate for re-election to Congress, Edward Dickinson, whose course on the Nebraska question had been above reproach, was replaced by an untried man, Dr. C. C. Chaffee. "But the aggregate popular mind is apt to go straight to its object like an army in battle, without much regard for the incidental injustice it does, or the new dangers it creates."

But the broad result was favorable to freedom. The Massachusetts Congressmen and legislature were strongly anti-slavery. In the country at large, the anti-Nebraska movement had triumphed. Under various party names it had won a plurality of the national House. It lacked consolidation; its elements became partially separated again before their final fusion; but a great beginning had been made.

The battle being over, the *Republican* gave its interior history, so far as the Whigs and itself were concerned, with great frankness,— a frankness which it never after this time postponed till after election. It referred to the first outburst against the Kansas-Nebraska scheme.

"We reproached ourselves that we had stood thus gazing stupidly on the deepening shadows of that overspreading despotism. We felt that the danger was one that trifled all former knowings — and that union of all friends of freedom was the imperative necessity. The Whigs ought to have initiated a catholic union of all the opponents of slavery. But certain sagacious men had discovered a more excellent way. Under the plurality rule we might crush out all opposition. How desirable to be done! We might keep everything. The party would be saved. The offices would all be ours. And this was to be our reward, this our satisfaction, our answer when the multitudes of the unborn shall stand up to curse us! . . . These councils prevailed, and by them the state convention was governed. . . . For ourselves, it was not possible to act with any other association. We resolved to remain where we were. Yet our moral strength was gone. There was left nothing worth contending for. Thousands of young men, ready to have thrown themselves into the Republican movement with an energy that could have defied opposition, had left us for a new connection. We felt that the ship was sinking. And yet when that odd-looking Know-nothing craft came up under a press of sail and offered us a free passage and good berths, we refused to leave. We stood at our post, and fired the signal guns over the settling wreck."

But, it concludes, the power of names is broken; there exist the material, the motives, the opportunity, for a new order of things; the Know-nothing creed is far too narrow to last long, and a better future is near.

# CHAPTER XIV.

## The Struggle in Kansas and in Massachusetts.

THE struggle for slavery extension was begun in Congress, and gained its victory in the passage of the Kansas-Nebraska bill. This transferred the contest to the territory of Kansas, while at the same time an appeal was taken to the great tribunal of the American people. Through the succeeding years the strife lay in these three fields,—Kansas, Congress, and the popular elections.

While the Kansas-Nebraska bill was still under debate, a movement had been initiated in Massachusetts for promoting an emigration that should determine the political and social character of Kansas. Under the lead of Mr. Eli Thayer of Worcester, the New England Emigrant Aid Society was incorporated by the legislature in February, 1854; and in the following July, its first colony, of twenty-four members, founded the town of Lawrence. In two weeks came another company of seventy, whose outfit included a steam saw-mill. Similar societies were founded in other free states, and a moderate but steady stream of emigration was poured into the new territory. The South was wholly unable to compete with the North in this direction. It had no such material of hardy and enterprising yeomanry to send out as settlers. But right upon the Kansas border, and across the direct route to the free states, lay Missouri, whose western section abounded in a lawless and ruffianly element, devoted to the slave-holding interest, and encouraged and led by men of high political standing. It was with this material that the attempt to make Kansas a slave state was urged on. The first settlers of Lawrence, while still living in tents, were visited by a band of two hundred and fifty armed Missourians, and ordered to leave the territory. They held their ground, and the invaders retired without attempting force. There followed a long series of incursions, murders, and outrages. A systematic attempt was made to usurp the government of the territory. At the first election of a delegate to Congress, in November, 1854, bands of Missourians poured over the border, distributed themselves at the voting-places, cast their votes for the pro-slavery candidate, J. W. Whitefield, and then returned to their homes. In this way three thousand votes were cast, though it was afterward proved that there were only half that number of voters resident in Kansas. Senator Atchison of Missouri, formerly presiding officer of the United States Senate, took a leading part in these operations. In March, 1855, at the election of a territorial legislature, the invasion was repeated on a larger scale and under such systematic arrangement that every legislative district was carried, except one which lay far remote from the border. The legislature chosen by such means proceeded to enact a code of laws with the especial object of establishing slavery. Decoying slaves from their masters was made punishable by death, or hard labor for not less than ten years; the circulation of books or writings inciting slaves to revolt was punishable by death; the assertion by speech or writing that slavery was not lawful in the territory, or the introduction or circulation of any book or paper containing such denial, was made felony, and punishable by hard labor for not less than two years. The free state settlers — almost the entire population — refused to acknowledge this legislature or its laws. In the autumn of 1855, they elected a convention, adopted a state constitution, and petitioned for admission to the Union as a state. The acts of the pro-slavery legislature were systematically vetoed by the territorial governor, A. H. Reeder, who had been appointed by President Pierce as a Democrat. The bills were passed over his vetoes, and a legislative memorial for his removal was addressed to the President, who finally recalled him and appointed as his successor Wilson Shannon, who gave his support to the usurping legislature. During this period of misrule and anarchy, the Administration and its party in Congress gave their fullest countenance to the faction which by fraud and violence was trying to fasten slavery on Kansas. Franklin Pierce was a man of fair ability but no strength of character. In his cabinet were William L. Marcy of New York, Secretary of State, who held aloof from the Kansas controversy; Jefferson Davis, Secretary of War, who by no means held aloof; and Caleb Cushing, Attorney-General, who gave his adroit and conscienceless brain to the service of the slave power. In the Senate, the Administration had still an overwhelming majority. In the House, which assembled in December, 1855, parties were so evenly balanced — the Americans being an uncertain and divided element — that only after many weeks of balloting was N. P. Banks elected Speaker, — the first great national victory for the party of freedom. But the House, almost evenly divided, and overborne by the Senate, could give no substantial relief to Kansas. In that territory slavery remained in a nominal ascendency, but with no real foothold; the legislature, backed by the national authority, was not acknowledged by the people; murder and outrage were frequent and unpunished;

peace and order as well as liberty were at stake. Congress was divided; the Executive upheld the wrong; the only resource lay in appeal to the highest court,— the vote of the whole people. To make clear the issue, to bring the friends of freedom into harmony, to inaugurate the Republican party and lead it to victory — this was the great work which fell largely to the newspaper press.

There was in Massachusetts during this period a singular mixture of political elements. The mass of the people entertained a deep dislike of slavery. But Boston long remained friendly to the South and its " peculiar institution." This was due partly to commercial interests, partly to the course of Webster and his followers, and the timid conservatism of elegant scholars like Everett, and Winthrop, and Hillard. The Whig party of the state was the inheritor of honorable traditions, and retained to the last a kind of genuineness and dignity, but its managers proved fatally narrow and short-sighted in face of the new emergencies. They who should have been the leaders would not lead. The Democratic party contained some men of ability, but it had little numerical and less moral weight, and, whatever useful ideas it might have represented in the past, was now animated chiefly by a fixed hostility to anti-slavery of any sort. The distinctively anti-slavery men were divided into two sections, of widely different characteristics. The non-voting Abolitionists sacrificed all immediate results in politics to an abstract idea; while the Free-soil managers pushed their cause with less scruple as to methods than honorable politicians are wont to have. The body of the party were men of pure intentions, but its active conductors in Massachusetts relied too little upon appeal to the moral sense of the people, and too much upon artifice,— and to this was probably due its failure to gain

strength among the common people of the state.  This
was largely owing to the influence of Henry Wilson.
Wilson thought anything fair which served his purpose.
He was at home in trades and coalitions.  He was skillful
in public affairs, generous and kind-hearted, of popular
manners, and a firm friend.  Having gone into the Know-
nothing party, and thereby got the senatorship, he was
ready to betray the order to which he had sworn fidelity,
if he could advance the anti-slavery cause by doing so.
Sumner was in many points the opposite of Wilson,—
high-minded, little versed in practical affairs, by taste a
scholar, self-conscious, making few friends.  He originally owed his seat in the Senate to a bargain made by
other men, but during his long service there he represented an unswerving, often unpractical, devotion to
high aims.  If Sumner's principles and Wilson's tact
could have been united in one man, he would have
been a statesman.  Of all the Republican leaders the
greatest — regarding moral and intellectual qualities
together — was John A. Andrew.  Banks was too much
devoted to his own ends, and the ability he seemed to
show during the years before the war was not evinced in
later time.

Out of the mixture of principles and policies, old organizations and new, honest and timid leaders, shrewd and
demagogic leaders, earnest and groping people,— it was
slow and puzzling work to build up a party which should
do the work that the time demanded.  The Know-nothing victory — filling the legislature and offices with
untried and generally incompetent men — was like a
land-slide which had buried the old and crooked paths
and forced the cutting of new ones.  The road had to
be cleared foot by foot.

The rendition of Burns had its political consequences
in the legislature of 1855.  By that body a memorial was

addressed to the governor, asking him to remove Commissioner Loring from his state office of judge of probate, on the ground of his action in returning the fugitive.  This movement the *Republican* supported.  Its argument was that a man who voluntarily acted as the instrument of a cruel Federal law ought to feel the just resentment of the state by being shut out from its places of public honor and trust.  In its reply to a correspondent who argued against the removal, it said (February 17, 1855):

"We have great respect for law.  We mean to abide by it. But it is not the perfection of human reason, nor the beginning or end of all things, though it be one of the great instrumentalities of good order and civilized society.  We believe that there is something besides and something higher.  We are not ashamed to say that we believe in a higher law.  We would not resist law, unless we were prepared for rebellion and revolution.  But we would refuse to obey or execute some laws, and the Fugitive Slave law is one of them.  Coleridge was not much of a lawyer, but he was something of a man; and he says: ' With our grandfathers " the man who squares his conscience by the law " was a common synonym for a *wretch without any conscience at all.*'

" There is a conservative justification of the proposed removal of Judge Loring.  The state should be and we believe will be content with establishing the principle that she will neither obey nor resist the Fugitive Slave law.  To the clear establishment of this principle, the removal of Judge Loring seems necessary, as making evident the feeling of the commonwealth, as an example to such other officers and citizens as are lawyers and nothing else, and as proclaiming to the world, in unmistakable terms, the position of Massachusetts.  Failing in this, there will be new strength added to the efforts already making for a law of resistance and active nullification.  And Massachusetts most likely would find herself in open rebellion against the general government.  For that we are not ready.  That proposition we deprecate.  But there is a strong popular demand for the expression of the convictions of Massachusetts. The state seeks to declare itself. It is better that Judge Loring should fall a victim to his own want of sympathy with the great heart of the commonwealth than that the state should be more strongly tempted to go beyond the true doctrine of state rights and place itself in open opposition to the general government."

It further urged the matter thus (March 10):

"About the independence of the judiciary: Do we hold it desirable as an end or only as a means? Do we wish our judges placed above accountability — legal accountability, for acts that indicate shameful obliquity of moral sense? Have we made them independent, not only of sudden and fitful popular impulses but of those strong, radical, and abiding sentiments which, marking the race of men, mark also the will of the Supreme Law-giver? Is it meant, in short, that they should be the independent administrators of justice or of wrong — of the law of God or the law of the devil?"

After a long consideration, the petition for removal passed the legislature, but Governor Gardner declined to accede to it. Judge Loring's offense however was not forgotten or forgiven; when Banks became governor in 1858, he assented to the renewed petition of the legislature, and removed the judge of probate, who was then placed by President Buchanan on the bench of the Court of Claims.

The *Republican's* anticipation of more radical legislation was fulfilled. A "personal liberty bill" was passed, aimed directly against the Fugitive Slave law. It forbade any state official to take part in the rendition of a fugitive, disqualified any attorney who should advocate a master's claim, provided for the appointment of state commissioners to defend the interests of any alleged fugitive; and, in addition to other particulars, provided that any one arrested as a fugitive might be brought by writ of habeas corpus before any state judge or justice of the peace, and by him be given a jury trial for his liberty. This bill, one of a class which at this time became law in several states, was passed by the legislature, but vetoed by the governor. He pointed out that to thus by summary process remove a prisoner from the legal jurisdiction of the United States was in direct contravention of the legitimate authority of the general government. But the legislature passed the bill over the veto by overwhelming majorities.

The *Republican*, from the first, characterized the bill as practical nullification, at once wrong in principle and useless in effect. In reply to an Alabama correspondent who represented that this class of laws had strengthened the Secession element at the South, the *Republican* declared (July 14), that the South had no right to complain,— it had received only a fair reprisal for its own course in regard to Kansas. "But," it continued as to the personal liberty laws, " we can see neither the wisdom nor policy of such action. The cause of liberty needs not to be aggressive or unjust. It rests on no such foundation as slavery,— it needs no such instrumentalities to advance its power. It *cannot afford* to resort to them. Not from regard to the South, but from regard for its own unity and power should they be avoided. They divide the North and thus secure its defeat." The law in question is of no practical use; " it is only an expression of feeling, and practically impotent at that. It is worse,— it is mischievous, by dividing the sentiment and action of the state, and of all the free states. Massachusetts cannot be united upon it — the North cannot be united. It is among the impracticable schemes upon which the free states have spent their energy and dissipated their sentiments. Twenty saw-mills, a like number

of school-houses, and one thousand Sharp's rifles, sent to
Kansas with men at the back of them, would be a more
valuable contribution to freedom than all the personal
liberty laws that the ingenuity of Abolition lawyers
could devise, or legislators enact in a generation of time.
The first is action,— the latter impotent words. How
much more valuable too than such an act would be an
organization of one hundred thousand voters in Massachusetts, pledged to union, harmony, and action in behalf of *no more slavery outside of the slave states ?*"

Up to this year, the *Republican* had been politically
hostile to Henry Wilson. It had charged the failure to
consolidate a party of freedom in 1854 largely to his personal ambition, which was gratified by his election the
following winter to the United States Senate. But, once
in the Senate, his course on the slavery question was
such as to win approval from those who were disposed to
look forward rather than back. The paper declared
(March 10):

" Never was the voice of Massachusetts so well and so boldly
uttered in the United States Senate on this question as General
Wilson uttered it during the great debate on the bill to
strengthen the Fugitive Slave law." It gave him the right hand
of fellowship in saying, April 7 : " He does not carry with him
the moral feeling of Massachusetts as Mr. Sumner does, though
we believe he is a truer representative of its practical opinions,
and will prove a more effective operator in their behalf. . . .
Animated by no personal enmity in our opposition to his election ; seeking only the best good of Massachusetts and her
most effective and truthful representation at Washington ;
fearing not to denounce General Wilson as the mere politician
and party trickster,— we have no more hesitation in approving
and praising General Wilson as the senator of the commonwealth, faithfully and boldly announcing and defending her
views to the representatives of the nation. The press has a
higher ambition than to perpetuate old feuds, and a wider

faithfulness to truth than that which denounces indiscriminately the good and bad deeds of a political opponent."

The unknown quantity in the political problem was the Know-nothing or American party, which had sprung up almost in a night, like Jonah's gourd. A National Council of the party was held at Philadelphia, in June, 1855, which was the scene of an exciting struggle. The members were bound by their oath of secrecy, but from some source, which could not be discovered, the proceedings were reported each day with much fullness and accuracy in the New York *Tribune;* another excellent report was given in the Springfield *Republican,* and dispatches of a similar tenor appeared in the Boston *Atlas.* The sympathy among the Northern Know-nothings with the movement against slavery extension had injured the party in the South, and, in consequence, it had just been defeated in Virginia by the Democrats, under the lead of Henry A. Wise. The Southern members of the Council, with strong support from the North, and especially from New York, tried to commit that body to resolutions denying to Congress the power to exclude slavery from the territories, and approving all the existing legislation in favor of slavery. An opposite resolution was offered, demanding the restoration of the Missouri compromise, the protection of actual settlers, and the admission of Kansas and Nebraska as free states. A hot battle was fought in the convention. Wilson led the party of the North. After a session of eight days, the Southern platform was adopted, by a vote of eighty to fifty-nine. The next morning a meeting was held by Northern delegates, who adopted an address to the people, avowing the sentiments of the minority resolution. The result was a temporary division of the party.

The result at Philadelphia gave great encouragement to the anti-slavery sentiment, which had there proved strong enough to break the ranks of the new party, and make itself felt as the issue which dwarfed all others. The *Tribune's* correspondent wrote (June 16):

" Thank God! There is a North. The South is aghast. It does not know what to make of it. The North never acted so before. They beg, they implore, they plead; but the North is inexorable. It is not a child to be toyed back by sweet words. It asked simply the restoration of what the South had stolen: it was insultingly denied, and, as if that were not enough, it was told the robbing was right in spirit and substance, and forbidden longer to complain of it. . . . No man went into the council with more elements of distrust and opposition combined against him than Henry Wilson; no one goes out of it with such an enviable fame, or such an aggregation to his honor. He is worthy of Massachusetts, and worthy to lead the new movement of the people of that state, which the result here so fitly inaugurates."

Mr. Bowles stood in intimate relation to the events in Philadelphia. He was himself the correspondent of the *Tribune*, the *Republican*, and the *Atlas*, and the author of the daily revelations which focused public opinion upon the proceedings meant to be shrouded in oath-bound secrecy. The moral scruple against getting information from men in violation of oaths of secrecy was probably outbalanced in his mind, not only by the temptation to a brilliant exploit in news-getting, but by the advancement of the cause he had at heart, and the belief that the attempted secrecy was against all public interest. But to most minds it will seem a notable instance of a warping of conscience by the ruling passion.

He was on terms of intimate association with Mr. Wilson, and through him and other Massachusetts members exercised a direct influence upon the council. It was Mr. Bowles, as Mr. Wilson relates, who wrote the resolution on which the Northern members planted them-

selves. When the end was reached, a conference was
held between Mr. Wilson, Mr. Bowles, and Ezra Lincoln
of Boston, a prominent Whig leader, and it was agreed
that the time was ripe for a united Republican movement
in Massachusetts, and that Robert C. Winthrop was the
man to lead it. Mr. Winthrop proved unwilling to
renounce the old gods of Whiggism. But Mr. Bowles
bent his whole energy to effecting a general union in the
new party, not only through his paper but by private
influence and action.

The paper declared, June 26, " The Republican fusion
movement failed last year in Massachusetts, because the
Whig organization, proud of its supposed strength, insisted that everybody should come to it. It invited concessions, but made none. The result was the utter
overthrow of that organization. Fusion and Whiggery
were buried in a common grave." This year, it continues,
the Know-nothings must avoid a like mistake. Three
days later it recorded that the state Know-nothing council had decided to continue its organization, which it
pronounced a great blunder. It was the same mistake,
it averred (July 3), which the Whigs had made the year
before; and now the best resource was a call, broad and
catholic, signed by men of recognized influence and
representing all the past organizations, for a state convention, to inaugurate a party of freedom. The new
party must originate spontaneously from the people. It
stated (July 7) that all the old Whig press, all the Free-
soil, and all the independent journals but two or three,
in the whole commonwealth, were in favor of a new
party. Such a union had been accomplished in Ohio,
and had nominated for governor Mr. Chase, whose creed
on slavery was in one word " Denationalization." A
private consultation was announced as impending (July
21), of two or three hundred representative men, to fully

discuss the ways and means to Republican fusion. But this conference was delayed to await the action of the state Know-nothing council, which met in Springfield, August 7th. That body virtually abolished the secrecy of the order, including all the oaths of membership. Its main proposition in regard to the foreign element was that a residence of twenty-one years should precede naturalization. It took strong and satisfactory ground against slavery extension; but on the practical question of a union on this issue with those who were indifferent to "Americanism," its attitude was ambiguous, though apparently favorable. It gave this matter in charge to a committee. This action did not satisfy those who had begun to move for a new party, and a call was issued for the proposed conference for August 16th. Mr. Bowles's name headed the call, but the *Republican* stated (August 13) that this was done by mistake, in his absence (he was engaged in reporting the Amherst and Williams Commencements); and that he would have preferred a previous consultation with the American committee. However, it says: "The way is open for the right result. Let us all, disregarding private views as to the best means, rally to the accomplishment of the great and glorious end." The conference was held at the United States Hotel in Boston. Mr. Bowles, in consequence of the position of his name at the head of the signatures, called the meeting to order. A committee was appointed to summon a state convention; among its members were Mr. Bowles, Samuel Hoar, R. H. Dana, Jr., C. F. Adams, George Boutwell, Stephen C. Philips, George Bliss, and H. L. Dawes. This committee at once consulted with committees representing the Know-nothings, the "Know-somethings"—a short-lived rival society—and the Republican organization of 1854. These all favored the new movement, except the Know-nothings, who were evidently reluctant, and a call was issued for a mass convention at Worcester, September 20, with a recommendation for a delegate convention at the same time and place;— the latter proving to be the more important gathering of the two.

The spirit which gave dignity to these details of maneuver was expressed by the *Republican* (August 24) under the heading of " Confidence Necessary to Union":

" The imminent danger in which the country is placed by the recent movements in behalf of slavery has elevated men's minds, and brought them up above the low level of petty party and personal prejudices. Scarcely any of us who feel at all upon the outrages of Congress and the mob in Kansas, have failed to experience this purifying, elevating emotion; and while we recognize its presence in ourselves, we should recollect that other men have passed through a like experience. If we are led to feel like forgiving and forgetting all for the sake of united effort against the common danger, we must think that others are moved to like conciliations, and are elevated to a like sincerity and honesty of motive. . . . We must open a new set of books with all who say they are ready to move together against the strides of slavery into free territory, watching one another closely, if the past has led to distrust, but never convicting upon the past, or by the help of its prejudices. Let us stand or fall one with another, not by the past, but by the future."

The Massachusetts Democratic Convention (September 5) praised the Administration, denounced Know-nothingism and Sectionalism (meaning Northern opposition to slavery), and indorsed " the great doctrine of popular sovereignty for territory and state, whether violated by the unjust action of Abolitionists of the free states, or by border aggression from the slave states." It nominated for governor E. D. Beach, of Springfield, already the candidate of the opponents of liquor prohibition.

Over the coming Republican Convention hung a cloud which was indicated (September 16) by the editorial declaration that no man ought to be nominated who will not sink or swim with the new party. This was aimed at Governor Gardner, whose position was fully discussed in the paper the next day. Gardner, the *Republican* declares, is not honestly identified with the Republican party. If it does not renominate him, he will be a candidate in opposition. His friends make plain their purpose to either rule or ruin the Republican movement. A nomination thus forced upon the convention will discredit its work from the start, and have no binding force.

"There is but one way to carry forward this movement; that is honestly, fairly, openly. . . . If Republicanism cannot start right, fair and honest, it had better wait. It can afford to wait rather than start otherwise."

On the morning of the convention, the paper said:

"But one man stands in the way of the successful inauguration of Republicanism in this state, at this moment. That man is Henry J. Gardner. With him withdrawn all would be peace, confidence, faith, success."

The convention was a spirited and vigorous assemblage. N. P. Banks was its president. The resolutions rose to the height of the occasion. They declare, "That slavery as a state institution is not within our power or responsibility; but slavery in its relations to the nation, is the concern of every man in the nation; in its relation to the free states is the concern of every man in the free states"; that the aggressions of slavery, and especially the repeal of the Missouri compromise, "have made slavery in its national relations and its relations to the free states, the paramount practical question in the politics of the country"; that "the repeal of the Missouri compromise renders every inch of the national domain a battle-ground between freedom and slavery. It makes the admission of every new state a conflict between freedom and slavery. The issue thus forced upon us we accept; we commit ourselves to God and our country; and may it be by no fault of ours if another slave state is added to the Union, or any of the territories left open to the possibility of slavery."

There was much debate upon the nomination for governor. The alliance of the Americans evidently depended on whether Gardner was nominated. To many it seemed sound and legitimate policy to thus conciliate them. But it was obvious that Gardner and his immediate friends were with the new party only on condition that it served his personal advancement. A call for an American convention had already been issued, and the signatures included nineteen of the members of the Republican convention. By a close vote, the convention gave the preference over Gardner to Julius Rockwell, an old Whig, whose ability and sincere attachment to the cause were alike unquestioned. He illustrated his sincerity by declining in advance a supplementary nomination from the Whig convention, which met twelve days later. That body represented the dignified and respectable conservatism which was still blind to the new issues, and shrunk from the "abolitionism" and "sectionalism" of the Republican party. Its candidate was Samuel H. Walley. Of the resolutions, the *Republican* said (October 3) that heretofore Whig conventions had always had something to say against slavery; but now, with slavery rampant and aggressive, "not a word escapes the lips of those pretending, *par excellence*, to be the Whigs of Massachusetts, on this subject—not a syllable is uttered against the administration that permits, sustains, and encourages these aggressions."

The Americans renominated Gardner.  Up to the day of the election, the *Republican* declared with confidence that either Rockwell or Beach would be elected.  Mr. Bowles's expectations of what was to be were often colored by his conviction of what ought to be.  Rockwell and Beach represented the two sides of the only great question before the people; Gardner represented no definite policy or idea; he had not even a strong and attractive personality; he had behind him only a personal following, an organization, and the prestige of the last year's victory.  But when the votes were counted, he had (in round numbers) 50,000, to 37,000 for Rockwell, 35,000 for Beach, and 14,000 for Walley.  The *Republican's* comment was: "A man has triumphed over a principle.  And at his feet lies wounded the cause of freedom."

Elsewhere, too, the confusion of the true issue caused by the American party, together with some reaction from the first great enthusiasm that had carried the North for freedom the year before, gave a set-back to the Republican movement.  The Americans were successful in New York and California, the Democrats in Pennsylvania, New Jersey, Indiana, and Illinois.  The *Republican* drew the inference (November 17) that the American party was to play a part in the coming presidential contest. Its own support of the Republican party was neither at this time nor afterward a blind and unreserved allegiance. When for the city election nominations were made by the Republicans, Democrats, and Americans, its word was (December 3), "We exhort every voter to go to the polls, and, acting independently, vote for those whom he considers the best men, and only those."

So closed the year 1855, with some reaction and confusion, and little visible progress toward the triumph of liberty.  But good work had been done by the *Republi-*

*can.* No more useful work was ever done by it than in
these years when old things were passing away, and the
forces were being harmonized and organized for the
decisive struggle. In this year Mr. Bowles took a much
more active part in the personal conduct of politics than
was his habit. For the difficult and essential work of
drawing men once antagonistic into friendly coöperation,
for shaping the lines of a new party at once broadly and
distinctly, for keeping the main issue and the details in
right proportion,—for all this he had high qualifications.
While in his paper he often by his outspokenness gave
offense, he had in personal intercourse a tact and magnetism which few could resist. Never a public speaker,
he was in private gatherings skillful to plead, to harmonize, to adjust. From the beginning of the Kansas
struggle he exhibited a power to take broad and statesmanlike views, an appreciation of the moral elements
involved, and a large wisdom and efficiency in reaching
practical results. In his later period his reputation was
largely that of a critic and iconoclast. But in these great
and decisive years he showed an eminent power in the
line of harmonizing, constructive political work.

# CHAPTER XV.

## THE FREMONT CAMPAIGN.

THE year 1856 opened with an annual message from President Pierce to Congress in which he elaborately justified the repeal of the Missouri compromise, and ignored the outrages in Kansas. The message of the Governor of Massachusetts was equally silent regarding those outrages, pleaded for the repeal of the personal liberty law, and discussed at length the favorite topics of Americanism. The national House of Representatives sent a committee to investigate the situation in Kansas, and their report of facts had a power beyond all argument to teach the Northern people what they had to deal with. A still more startling lesson was given them. Charles Sumner made a speech in the Senate, in which the rhetorical finish and observance of parliamentary forms made only more effective the biting severity against the slave power and its leading representatives. His sharpest edge was turned against Senator Butler of South Carolina. A day or two later a nephew of Mr. Butler, and member of the House, Preston S. Brooks of South Carolina, came upon Mr. Sumner as he sat at his desk in the empty Senate chamber, knocked him down with a heavy cane before he could rise or resist, and beat him so severely that he was incapacitated for senatorial service for four years afterward. Indeed, he never after-

ward was the same man,— to splendid physical vigor
there succeeded a life-long struggle with ill health. Mr.
Brooks was punished only by a paltry fine in the local
court. In the House, a motion of expulsion failed to receive the necessary two-thirds vote. Receiving a formal
censure, he resigned, but was instantly and triumphantly
reëlected and resumed his seat. He was a Southern gentleman, and his standing among Southern gentlemen was
not impaired by his act. From many places in the South
he received votes of thanks, and canes marked " Hit him
again." In Congress, only the mildest disapprobation
was uttered by his political allies from either section. It
was left to Republican congressmen to rightly charac-
terize the assault. Wilson, in the Senate, called it " bru-
tal, murderous, and cowardly." Brooks sent him a
challenge, and in reply he refused to withdraw his words,
and repudiated the duelist's code. In the House, Burlingame denounced the assault, in the name not only of
humanity and civilization, but of " that fair play which
bullies and prize-fighters respect." Brooks challenged
him; he accepted, and named a meeting-place in Canada,
but Brooks declined to follow him there. The duelist's
way of redress was not the Massachusetts way. Burlingame lost nothing at home by his action. But when
after five years more of patience the state struck her
blow, it was not against an individual, but against
slavery, and by the arms, not of one man, but of sixty
thousand.

At the South, Brooks was treated as a hero. At a
gathering to do him honor in the following October,
Senators Butler and Toombs participated, both of them
taking occasion to utter threats of disunion in case the
Republicans elected their President. Senator Mason of
Virginia wrote of Brooks: " I know of none whose public
career I hold more worthy the full and cordial approba-

tion of his constituents than his," and added that if a
Republican President was elected, but one course remained for the South, "immediate, absolute, and eternal
separation."

The *Republican* (May 29) treated the assault as an
illustration of the reigning influence in the country. It
sought to turn the passionate resentment of the hour
into the practical channel whereby alone redress was possible. It said:

" There is no denying the humiliating fact that this country
is under the reign of ruffianism. Ruffianism has become national. It is the policy of the Administration, the policy of the
Democratic party, and decidedly and confessedly the policy of
the ruling interest in the country. The Administration backs
up ruffianism in Kansas, and, under its sanction, ruffianism practices its cowardly acts in Congress. Free men are denied a settlement on the public domain, are denied the privilege of making
their own laws, and have even to struggle for life against a ruffianly mob and a ruffianly Federal government. Free speech is
denied in Congress, and may only be indulged in at the cost of a
broken head. The highest representative of the noblest of the
' Old Thirteen' wins laurels for himself and the commonwealth
only to have them soaked in his own blood. What do you think
of this, O men of the North? The remedy for ruffianism resides in
a united North. Old party names must be forgotten, old party
ties surrendered, organizations based upon secondary issues
abandoned, momentary self-interest sacrificed to the country
and its welfare, and all must come together and fight and labor
side by side until the great question which overshadows all
others has found issue in the triumph of justice."

The great need of the time, the great service of the
press, was to bring into clear light the question on which
the people must divide and decide. Two influences were
at work to obscure and confuse the main question. One
was the American party; the other was the duplicity of

the Democratic leaders upon the subject of "popular sovereignty." Another National Council of the Americans was held in Philadelphia in February, and again Mr. Bowles reported its proceedings for the *Republican* and the *Tribune,* but this time the convention made no attempt at secrecy. The Southern element was victorious; a substantially pro-slavery platform was adopted, and Millard Fillmore was nominated for the presidency. Again there was a secession of Northern members. The organization in Massachusetts hung doubtful. A majority of the state council—differing from those of all the other New England states—accepted the nomination of Fillmore. A secession—such as had become a regular incident of almost every Know-nothing gathering—took place, and delegates were sent to a Northern American convention in June.

The Democratic Convention met first, in Cincinnati. Mr. Bowles reported it for his paper. Pierce and Douglas were discarded as candidates in favor of James Buchanan,—an old Pennsylvania politician, who had been Pierce's minister to England, and had engaged in discreditable maneuvers toward gaining Cuba for America and slavery, but otherwise had not been involved in recent controversies, and was of good personal repute. The *Republican* (June 10) gave the reason why Pierce and Douglas, faithful and efficient servants of the South, had been rejected and Buchanan preferred.

"There is a game to be played with the people. The respectable name of James Buchanan—the name of one who, with becoming prudence, has contrived to keep himself dissociated from the acts which have made that of Franklin Pierce execrable—has been put forward as a gilded bait to troll upon the political waters, to make the simple fish forget that it is tied to a string of resolutions every strand of which is either a cheat or a falsehood."

The convention declared in its resolutions for "non-interference by Congress with slavery in state or territory, or in the District of Columbia." What interpretation this was sure to receive in practice, Mr. Bowles pointed out (June 9):

"The right of the people of territories to decide upon the existence of slavery in the administration of the territorial government, which was the original intent and meaning of squatter sovereignty as expounded by Mr. Cass, is nowhere stated. The power over slavery in the territories is denied Congress and given to no other authority. The rights of the citizens over it are not supposed by this platform to begin until they proceed to form a state government, and in the exercise of such a right then no party has denied them, or proposed to deny them, full power. The Republican doctrine is simply that Congress has the right and should exercise it, of excluding slavery from the territories while they are territories. The Democratic platform solely, in terms, denies this. But in its purpose and meaning it goes farther, and justifies and protects slavery in the territories if slave-owners choose to carry it there. So it will be translated at the South, — so it was accepted by the unanimous vote of the South in the convention to-day. The substance of the resolutions in this respect is that slavery is the equal of freedom everywhere under the constitution and in the administration of the general government."

But the resolutions had been so worded that it might be maintained at the North that the Democratic theory was that of a real, bona fide self-government by the people of the territories. Thus stated it seemed to put the territorial residents entirely on a level with the residents of a state, in the control of their local affairs. This was undoubtedly the plea by which the Democratic ticket won most of its votes at the North. The candidate for Vice-President was John C. Breckinridge, of Kentucky.

The first National Republican Convention met at Philadelphia. It nominated for President John Charles Fre-

mont, of California; for Vice-President, William L.
Dayton, of New Jersey. Colonel Fremont was a man of
small political experience, but with high reputation as
an intrepid explorer and soldier; regarded as a prompt,
resolute, and honorable man of action, and a chivalrous
gentleman. His youth, his freedom from the soils of
political intrigue, a certain personal fascination, and
the dignity with which he bore himself under a torrent
of bitter calumnies, made him a sort of ideal hero, most
congenial to the high enthusiasm with which the young
party of freedom fought its first great fight. He was
wholly untried in statesmanship, was in reality little
known to the country, and his subsequent development
showed him little fit for any high trust. But his personality caught the popular fancy. Yet the fight was
for a principle, not for a person, save as he seemed to
embody the principle. Said the *Republican* (September 6):

"Pure as is the life of Colonel Fremont, spotless as is his
reputation, noble as are his traits of character, high as are his
accomplishments, and devotedly as the people love him, his
name in any public assembly of Republicans awakens no
responses like those which greet the annunciation of the sentiments which he represents."

The Republican platform declared it to be "the right
and the imperative duty of Congress to prohibit in the
territories those twin relics of barbarism, polygamy and
slavery." It demanded the immediate admission of Kansas as a free state, and denied the authority of Congress
or a territorial legislature to give legal existence to
slavery in any territory. Of the temper of the assembly
Mr. Bowles wrote (June 24):

"Certainly we never saw a political convention in which
there was so much soul as in that at Philadelphia. It was politics with a heart and a conscience in it. . . . Cincinnati

gathered the remains of a once powerful national party, and contributed to its further sectionalization and destruction. Philadelphia called together the heart, the independence, and the brains of all parties, to establish a broader and juster nationality. Such a fusion of contradictory elements was never witnessed in this country before since the times of the Revolution. Nor could it happen now save under a great emergency, and from a controlling necessity. Such a combination of the material and mental forces of the Republic as was represented in the Philadelphia convention, and united in its enthusiastic and harmonious results, has more power than any political combination ever formed before in this country, and cannot in the nature of things be long kept in the background. There is no law more certain than that which will throw such a union of the moral strength, intellectual activity and youthful energy of the nation, into supremacy, and that right speedily. It may be delayed for a season, but its course is onward and its victory is certain."

The Northern American Convention, meeting before that of the Republicans, nominated Mr. Banks, who declined the position; he had been very active in securing the Republican nomination for Fremont, and to him the anti-slavery American support was transferred.

Side by side with the presidential campaign went on the struggle in Kansas. The Free-state settlers, disowning the pro-slavery legislature, organized under a Free-state constitution, and chose a governor of their own whose authority was only nominal. The purpose of the Administration was to have its territorial governor a Northern Democrat, but presence on the scene of action had a tendency to convert each governor to the Free-state side. So it had been with Governor Reder; his successor, Wilson Shannon, was unstable in habits and character, and wavered between the parties. The scandal of his administration, and of the anarchic state of affairs, was too heavy to be carried by the Administration in the

face of the coming elections, and with the great state of
Pennsylvania hanging doubtful. As Shannon's successor
the President appointed, perhaps at Mr. Buchanan's suggestion, John W. Geary, a Pennsylvanian of good character
and ability. Following his private instructions, he did not
force matters to extremity with the Free-state men, and
some degree of temporary pacification ensued. The
pro-slavery legislature was sustained by the Federal
territorial court, under the presidency of Chief-Justice
Lecompte, and the Free-state leaders had been judicially
harassed, while the lawless ruffianism of their enemies
went unpunished. In September, the *Republican* had for
some time a standing paragraph in italics: "Keep it before the people that to this day no man in Kansas has
ever been punished by law for offenses committed against
members of the Free-state party,— not one!" The facts
in Kansas were too strong for many men whose theories
had made them adverse to the Republican movement.
Thus, a prominent Conservative Whig, Reuben A. Chapman, of Springfield, afterward chief-justice of the state,
wrote in September to the Boston *Advertiser* to disclaim
a participation assigned him in a meeting of the Fillmore
party — a party which was appealing not without some
success to the old Whigs. Mr. Chapman expressed un-
mitigated dislike for the "Free-soil agitators of the
North." But he saw in the American party a sectarian
and proscriptive organization; while as to the Kansas
legislature "every intelligent man and every lawyer
know that such a government has no legality." A study
of its statute-book had mightily wrought upon the Massachusetts lawyer. "I have been amazed that any body
of men could be collected from any quarter, without robbing the gallows and the penitentiaries, who could enact
laws so atrocious." The Democratic policy, he concludes,
is dictated by a purpose to make Kansas a slave state at

whatever cost of violence or fraud; that conservative and national party for which he longs can come only when the Democracy has been buried; and Fremont he esteems not an unsafe man for President.

The presidential struggle was doubtful until the October election; then the scales were seen to incline to the Democracy. Pennsylvania was carried for the Buchanan ticket over a coalition between the Fremont and Fillmore men, but by a majority so narrow that the result in November was by no means sure. The Republicans had been hopeful to the last of winning the state, but there, and in Indiana, the Democrats lavished money in bribery, while the Republican party was young, virtuous, and poor. Fillmore lost ground: his friends fell off to one or the other of the two candidates who represented an idea. In the Springfield congressional district (then the tenth) the Democrats, the old Whigs, and the Fillmore Americans, all united on a congressional and county ticket against the Republicans. So it goes all over the country, said the *Republican* (October 10): "The débris of all the old parties, the office-holders, the old hunkers, the weak, wicked, and old-womanish, are huddling together to make a last effort to avert the impending storm, and save themselves and the slave power from overthrow." That power was beginning to loudly threaten to break the Union if it could not rule it. In Virginia the election turned on the question whether if Fremont was elected secession should follow: Henry A. Wise leading the Democratic and disunion party, and John M. Botts the Unionists,— himself for Fillmore but not unfriendly to Fremont. The *Republican* pointed out (August 4) that while all Southern Disunionists were for Buchanan, the few Abolition Disunionists at the North — Phillips, Pilsbury, and their associates — were all against Fremont, because he represented a constitutional opposition to slavery, which was unfavorable to their war on the constitution. The Southern threats of disunion the *Republican* treated as insincere, and meant only to frighten the North into submission; in which view it illustrated its characteristic insensibility to panic, which led it sometimes to underrate real dangers. But in truth the South had so often cried disunion that most people at the North had little belief in its sincerity.

In state politics the American party remained a stumbling-block. In July their convention in a tumultuous session renominated Governor Gardner, who was as yet non-committal between Fremont and Fillmore, though the Fillmore men seceded from the convention after his nomination. The remnants of Whiggery met and nominated Luther V. Bell for governor, and approved Fillmore for President. The Republican convention was not called by the representatives of the last year's party, but, like that, was summoned from independent sources. It was proposed that Governor Gardner be made its candidate, and this course was urged in the convention by Banks and Wilson, the latter saying that the Republicans could afford to be liberal in dealing with an expiring and substantially defunct organization. The *Republican's* grounds of opposition to Gardner were thus summed up (September 15):

" He is a positive man and has made a positive administration. No administration in this state for ten years has been so full of important schemes and important results as this [his two annual terms]. None has so swollen the expenses of the state. His vetoes of important measures, involving high questions of principle and state policy; the creation of numerous unnecessary offices for the multiplication of executive patronage and personal retainers; his active interference in the peculiar province of the legislature; his fatal opposition to the proposition for an appropriation for the relief of our fellow-citizens in

Kansas at a time when such an appropriation would have been an immense benefit to the cause of free Kansas; the overriding of an express constitutional provision to make a new batch of executive appointments,—these, with other corresponding features of his government, unite to make it the most extravagant and corrupt which this commonwealth has ever experienced, and have established issues of state policy which can only be kept out of the canvass by keeping him out." The Republicans, it concludes, may perhaps make no state nominations,— not the highest course to pursue, but not essentially wrong, as would be the nomination of Gardner.

The convention (September 16) deliberated whether to accept Gardner, to nominate Charles Sumner for governor, or to refrain from nominating; and the latter course was adopted by a large majority. This signified that Gardner's election as an American was to be allowed, rather than to risk the alienation of American votes from Fremont. A union with that party upon an electoral ticket was agreed on, and provision made for an agreement on congressional and local nominations.

In the tenth district Dr. Chaffee received a renomination from the Republicans and Fremont Americans; all the other parties uniting on W. A. Fowler. The eleventh district, including Berkshire and a westward strip from the river counties, became the scene of a contest into which Mr. Bowles threw himself as heartily as into any of the many battles of his life. The Republican candidate was Henry L. Dawes. Rev. Mark Trafton, chosen two years before as a Know-nothing, and a rival of Mr. Dawes in the "Fremont Union" Convention, took the field as an independent candidate, while the Democrats had a popular nominee in Dr. Weston. Mr. Bowles had become acquainted with Mr. Dawes when the latter wrote for him a series of letters from the legislature, about the year 1852, and the foundation had been laid for a life-long friendship. ˙ He was deeply interested in Mr. Dawes's success. His letters, given in the next chapter, will illustrate the keenness of his interest, and the thoroughness of the electioneering work in which he was the chief organizer and inspirer. Dr. Holland, his efficient co-worker in the general contest, although habitually not active in political management, took an energetic part in the canvass for Mr. Dawes; and on the Saturday before the election visited every one of the Hampden county towns in the eleventh district, to give the last word of encouragement and exhortation to Dawes's friends.

Never had a party approached an election in a nobler mood than did the Republican party in 1856 — never afterward did it rise to a grander spirit, save when with a fervent and solemn resolution, wrought out in four years of war, it reëlected Abraham Lincoln in 1864. The *Republican's* editorials on the eve of the decisive day were filled with the high spirit of the time. They rose above passion,— they read events with that broad and clear view to which men of disciplined mind and high purpose are lifted by an emergency. Thus the paper spoke (Nov. 1) of the Republican party :

" It is a vital party. At its heart burns a great truth, of which each member feels the thrill, and to which each nerve and filament responds. It is the party of the country, and it holds within itself that principle by which this Union can alone be perpetuated — the true democratic principle. If the principle upon which this party is established do not prevail, then the days of this confederacy are numbered ; for slavery is not right, slave rule is not right, the whole policy growing out of wrong is wrong, and a government which recognizes wrong as the controlling force within it fosters the seeds of its own absolute and inevitable dissolution. The great political sea is covered with the floating fragments of defunct organizations.

Disappointed leaders are clinging with a death-grapple to the wrecks, and many of their crews, bound to them by ties of interest, or borne to their side by an impulse of not ignoble chivalry, cling with them, determined to save something or go down together. Some cling to the wreck of the old Whig ship. A crowd still tumble among the frail timbers of Know-nothingism. A still greater crowd sail with the piratical craft of modern Democracy, unaware of her crazy condition, and unthinking that in the next rough sea she must go down even if mutiny on board should not break out before the storm comes on. It is amidst this turmoil of dissolution, and the beating of governmental policy against the foundation stones of the Republic, that the Republican timbers have been laid, and the stanch bark launched upon the sea.

"Who form the strength of this party ? Precisely those who would most naturally be expected to,— the great middling-interest class. The highest class, aristocratically associated and affiliated, timid, afraid of change, and holding in their hands the sensitive cords of commerce ; and the lowest class, igno-rant, deceived with a name, fed by the rich man's money and led by the rich man's finger — these are the forces arrayed against Republicanism as a whole. The horde of office-holders and office-seekers, and the slave interest, these are what the party serves. Those who work with their own hands, who live and act independently, who hold the stakes of home and fam-ily, of farm and workshop, of education and freedom — these as a mass are enrolled in the Republican ranks. They form the very heart of the nation, as opposed to the two extremes of aristocracy and ignorance, and their will and word cannot be disregarded."

On the morning of the election (November 4), the situ-ation was thus reviewed :

"The real abstract question at issue between the two parties is, whether Congress shall control the destinies of the territo-ries, and dedicate them as of old to freedom, or whether they shall be left for bitter and bloody struggles between the settlers, like those which in Kansas now shock the moral sense of civilization everywhere. Practically the question is whether the influence of the national government shall be used to extend slavery, and aggregate its political power, or to limit its bounds and weaken its hold over the politics, the business, and the religion of the nation. Were the issue thus plainly known of all men, there would be no dispute of the result. . . . The American party stepped in at an inopportune moment, overwhelmed the true issue before the country, and turned aside the minds of many men by the glittering success which it momentarily won. And if the Republican party fails to-day to inaugurate that revolution in the national government,— which must come ere this generation passes away, or the government itself perishes,— the responsibility cannot be escaped by the American organization. To its door must the defeat of John C. Fremont and the election of James Buchanan be laid. By implanting in many minds a weak substitution for the strongest issue, and by keeping temporarily in the Democratic ranks many who but for their opposition to Americanism would have rallied around the Republican standard, it has given fresh strength to the Democracy, and enabled them to contest this election with a fair prospect of success. . . . The result of the struggle is in great doubt, and the eagles of victory are as likely, perhaps, to perch on the one side as on the other, to-morrow morning. Of the two contestants, the Republicans can alone afford to be beaten. With the Democracy, defeat is destruction. The party is only held together by its alliance with the national treasury, and the slave-holder. Separated from one, it becomes useless to the other, and its power is gone. But a reverse cannot break the Republican column. It has an enduring vitality in its principles, and a glorious destiny, as sure as the Republic has an existence. Whether it enters upon the affirmative exercise of its mission now, or four years hence, is to all seeming the only question of to-day. Time will only vindicate its truthfulness, its necessity, and its strength. It can afford to wait, if the country and the world can afford to have it. But the country cannot afford to wait for its healing, peaceful mission, and though we look not upon the day's struggle

with confidence of victory, we await its result with a buoyant
hope that the day and the hour of redemption have come."

The next morning's tidings were of defeat. The states
on which the result hung—Pennsylvania and Indiana—
had voted for Buchanan. New England was solid for
freedom; New York gave its vote to Fremont; so did
Illinois and most of the states of the great West. Massachusetts had given Fremont a majority of two to one
over both his opponents. But the next national administration was to be Democratic.

The *Republican* in the same issue that told the first
sharp news of the defeat thus addressed itself to the
future:

" The sturdy hickory sapling, bent to the ground by the
incumbent snows, snaps back to its thrifty altitude when the
jar of a passing host removes the load. So the great party
of freedom, pressed down and chilled beneath the accumu-
lations of defeat, with firm roots and well-knit fibers, springs
backward, as the great results of the election sweep by. It has
taken its position for 1860,— stronger to-day than ever before."

Governor Gardner's reëlection was a matter of course:
he fell about 13,000 behind Fremont's vote. The tenth
district sent back Dr. Chaffee by 6000 majority; and in
the eleventh, Mr. Dawes was nearly 3000 votes ahead of
each of his rivals.

The *Republican* (November 8) laid stress on the power
and responsibility of the Republican party, in its capacity
of a minority in the government; and thus enforced one
lesson of the defeat.

" We are beaten by the ignorance of the people. The excellent common-school systems of the New England states and
New York have given those states to Fremont. In every section of those states where a great mass of ignorance existed,

the votes showed that Buchanan was in advance. Pennsylvania, with no common-school system worthy of the name, New Jersey, notoriously behind the times in all matters pertaining to popular education, Indiana, with its large settlements from the South of individuals to whom common schools are entire strangers,— these have gone for Buchanan. The public mind is thoroughly to be educated, the public heart to be Christianized, before they yield to the claims of justice and right, and before they will comprehend and rationally and conscientiously decide upon the issues before them."

# CHAPTER XVI.

## LETTERS: 1851–1856.

THIS chapter might have its title in the form of a stage direction: "Enter *Sam Bowles*." For in this he first speaks freely and at length in his own person. In selecting these letters, the aim has been to show him in his every-day guise, just as he appeared to his friends. Some of the letters are slight and even trivial in their contents,— they are given as the best practicable representation of the lighter moods, which have perhaps as much of human interest as the hours of graver cares and conflicts.

*To Charles Allen, of Greenfield.*

SPRINGFIELD, June 10, 1851.

Were you ever in love, fortune favoring, smiles a plenty, and everything considered sure, when to the one great question of life you got an unexpected and bewildering *no?* Or, as this is hardly a supposable case with so fresh and buoyant a young gentleman, did you ever get a shower-bath when you least of all expected it and were least of all prepared for it ?

If so, if either, but especially the first, you may perhaps "phansy my pheelinks." I am dished,—can't go a fishing,— must stay at home,— disappoint myself, disappoint my friends, and a' that. Well, it's always so. I'm the poor victim of the accidents and incidents of a daily newspaper. This morning our pressman broke down, the foreman must take his place,

162

and I must stay to make up deficiencies and drill all hands. Besides, I am wounded in my own household.  My wife's Irish girl, who takes care of the baby, took it into her head, as Irish girls will, to take herself off last night, and in pursuance of the love-honor-and-obey contract, I ought to help my wife out of the scrape.  Moreover,— but I won't rehearse the long-drawn tale of sorrows,— "the sorrows of Werther" were no touch to them.  Suffice it, that misfortunes never come singly, and I'm their victim.  I don't care for myself, for I fancy that ten years of this galley-slave's life has used me to disappointment and self-denial of this kind, but you, whom I have troubled, bothered, and promised so much,— bah, I couldn't look you in the face. I feel mean, and like vowing as I have a hundred times already in my editorial life that I never will attempt to go away again, or make an engagement to go away, for I am sure to have something turn up and disappoint myself and my friends.

Now forget me and all my promises,— go off and catch your fish, and don't ever invite me to come to Greenfield again, or if you do, don't believe me when I tell you I'll come.  It's no use.

Thy provoked and ashamed friend,

SAM'L BOWLES, Jr.


May 19, 1852.

Have you any recollection of one Bowles?  If so, give me some evidence of it.  Burnish up your memory, and when found make a note of him for the benefit of future generations.

Are you dead or in love?  Here I've been sick these five weeks, here and in Brooklyn, and I have not had the first word of condolence, nor the first trout of sympathy, from you.  Why, man, where's your humanity?  You would not treat a nigger so bad, especially if he was a voter in Franklin county.  Come and see me, write me, blow me up, traduce me, insult me, review me à la Eugene Batchelder, anything in short — but don't forget me.

Rode out to-day for the first time since my relapse into the Slough of Despond.  Getting better slow, but I trust sure.  Am as weak as the mother of six new kittens, and am

Yours truly.

November 20, 1854.

You seem to have a somewhat similar idea of the use of
newspapers to that one of the old fathers had of language. He
said it was an invention to conceal thought. You think newspapers machines to suppress information. You tell me lots
of good news, and then put on the stopper with "don't you
print!" So I hold in, and have the satisfaction of seeing the
news trotted out in Boston, Greenfield, and all along shore,
and of hearing it talked about in great detail by my friends,
who wonder at the stupidity of the *Republican* in not printing.
Thanks to Chapman and *my imagination*,* I have done, I hope,
partial justice to your Know-nothing row, but not until it was
old news—confound you.

February 22, 1855.

I would not on any account abridge the freedom with which
you may be pleased to write me privately, and I will not hereafter use any of your private correspondence for the benefit
of the world at large, except by your expressly obtained permission.

Judge Loring's removal I look upon as a decided piece of
conservative legislation. If it be not done, the advocates of
an elective judiciary for short terms will double instanter in
Massachusetts, and our judiciary will be placed where every
passing popular breeze can reach them, which I would deprecate as much as you. Nor can I admit the distinction you
make between morals and law. It seems to me that they possess intimate connection and dependency; that every law, in a
country like ours, can really be no law, certainly no wise or
useful law, unless grounded in the moral convictions of the
people. The laws of the country are the mere exponents of the
virtue and morality of its people. That is a phase of the question which I would like to discuss.

* The phrase "thanks to *my imagination*" may perhaps refer to an occasional practice of Mr. Bowles when he did not feel at liberty to relate as
fact what had been communicated to him, yet wanted to give the public an
inkling of it, and would write "We surmise," "we imagine," or "we predict" that so-and-so is the case.

I am just from a two days' visit to Norwich, Ct., with Mrs. B.; and when I next come to Greenfield — if that ever is — I shall bring her with me.

To his wife, while reporting the Know-nothing Council in June, 1855, Mr. Bowles writes :

PHILADELPHIA, Wednesday.

Your letter of yesterday came this afternoon, and rejoiced me by its various good news. I continue well, but feel lazy and stupid, and have loafed about quietly all day, accomplishing nothing as yet but a letter to the *Tribune*. I am going to stir about more to-morrow, and see the various interesting sights of this beautiful city. You would be very much pleased to be here with me, and I should be very pleased to have you. What a pity we can't both be pleased! Philadelphia would gratify you more than either Boston or New York. The streets are so much neater, are so regular, and bear such a finished look in their stores and dwellings, and the stores are the most magnificent in the country. The great number of large and elegant stores is surprising. Broadway does not compare in this respect with Chestnut street. . . . The ladies get themselves up here on a magnificent scale, and the number of beautiful women magnificently dressed who may be seen up and down the great street — Chestnut — is beyond what any other city can furnish. They are all arrayed in their summer costumes, and some of these would quite " stun" our country folks if displayed on Main or Maple St. How long I shall stay here is uncertain. If the *Tribune* people desire it, I may stay through the farce, for such it is getting to be. I shall consult my own ease and comfort about it very largely.

Give my love to A——, and congratulate her for me on her new step forward. It is a happy day in any one's life that records such a step,— that finds the heart fitted to lay hold on eternal life. Heigh-ho ! I do not know as I shall ever get to such a pitch of goodness and right feeling; and yet I should be unhappy if I did not believe I should " some time or other."

Kiss the "childer"; remember me to Mother, Amelia, and Hannah, and reserve for yourself a generous share of all the loving and husbandly affection which the subscriber respectfully places at your disposal. Write me often, and, remember, take good care of yourself. You can't be too prudent.

PHILADELPHIA, Friday night.

MY DEAREST MRS. BOWLES: Trusting that the fact that the letter due from you to-day did not come does not augur any abatement of affection, or any return of ill health (dire calamities both!), I proceed to make my daily bulletin: pulse regular, appetite fair, though little dulled now by a pint of strawberries and cream and several mutton chops; temper happy "as could be expected under the circumstances," viz., absence from the benignant light of your presence, only partly counterbalanced by two glasses of "fine old port," accomplished with the aforesaid mutton chops and strawberries; personal appearance as bewitching as usual,— fill out the balance to suit yourself.

Yesterday was quite warm — to-day is cool and delightful. I am enjoying myself passably, and politics in a quiet way, but am impatient to be off, partly because people are beginning to suspect me as the correspondent of the *Tribune*, which is not so pleasant as an *incog.*, and partly because I have had enough of it for play, though as work it is amusing enough. . . . I hope affairs continue comfortable at home, and that your strength and health mend together. You can hardly tell what a relief it would be to me to have you well and strong again. I try to believe that what is, is right, unless we can see it to be the result of some negligence or imprudence of our own. . . But we will try not to repine, for though everything is not as we would have it, still our sources of happiness are above the average of humanity in richness and deepness.

Give my love to all, including the rosy-cheeked and good-natured Hannah; kiss the babies,— tell A—— I hope the new responsibilities will not make her any more solemn or severe,— and accept yourself what a wife ought to have from her affectionate, and he hopes faithful, husband.

PHILADELPHIA, Monday evening.

Your long and piously disposed letter came yesterday morning, and had to answer the purpose of going to meeting, as I believe it did, and more too.  For though I staid at home, and wrote a long letter to the *Tribune*, I nevertheless believe that your kind preaching more than made up for the wickedness of that performance, which is more than I could say of the discourses I ordinarily get of a Sunday.  The subject to which you allude with so much appropriate earnestness is one I often think of, though, as you are aware, rarely if ever speak.  I have not much faith in myself, but I would encourage you to go forward in your determination.  I never could get up much interest in the forms of devotion, though I know they are essential—more, however, to some minds than to others, more perhaps to yours than to mine.  The essentials of manliness and goodness, of justice and mercy, I put first.  In them I always feel an interest, and strive, though at a distance, to follow.  I will readily join in such simple acts of religious devotion as are consistent with my feelings and position, if you desire it, in the hope, also, that it may prove more a source of satisfaction and improvement than I have found before.

I am detained here still, but expect now to get off some time to-morrow.  The thickest of the fight is now on, and if it comes to an end to-morrow morning I shall quit immediately. I am impatient to return home, but I feel that I am greatly useful to myself and the paper by remaining here, and I mean to make the *Tribune* pay all the bills.  We have had a good deal of excitement here, and much fun.  I have made some very pleasant and very valuable acquaintances, and done some good to the right side of the political questions of the day, and so ought to feel satisfied that I came on.

*To Henry L. Dawes.*

August 6, 1855.

.  .  .  I put into my paper all I know and all I feel as to politics.  I have an abiding faith in fusion, and don't allow myself to be disheartened by open opposition, lukewarm friendship, or timid advocacy.  I am very certain it has got to come, and the means by which it shall be achieved are of little moment to me, so that they succeed. There will be a quarrel in the K. N. convention to-morrow, perhaps a split. I am indifferent to it. It cannot put off the end long. If it denies fusion, it will kill itself, as the Whigs did last year. I confess it is up-hill work bringing people together, and the state is reaping in the harvest of ill feeling, bitter prejudices, and unconquerable aversions, the evils of Coalitionism, Know-nothingism, and hunker Whiggery. Thank God, I do not feel responsible for either. I shall keep the *Republican* untrammeled and inde-pendent, doing everything it can for fusion, favoring any proposition that looks to it, and denouncing everybody against it. We get plenty of abuse for our course, and myself am per-sonally and weekly denounced and vilified in the Anti-fusion American papers, but I can stand it, and am only troubled by the reflection that it may inspire me with the ridiculous idea that I am an important individual, and breed that meanest of all delusions, a political ambition.

Everybody is holding back and waiting for something to turn up. If fusion does come, as I am sure it will, and I have any influence in its future operations, I hope to remember with effect some of the cowards of the day.

I am glad the agony has given place to the joys of maternity. I am glad it is a boy. Boys are institutions. They have a future, a positive future. Girls are swallowed up,—they are an appendage,—a necessary appendage, it may be,—probably they are,—but still they are appendages. I hope the boy will live, will grow up, will be worthy of his father and mother, will inspire in them hope and confidence and trust, and moreover that he won't always live in North Adams, so long as there are such fine places as Springfield outside of it.

And so hoping, believing, and trusting, and wishing that you may so hope, believe, and trust, I am yours truly——

*To Charles Allen.*

September 11, 1855.

Have you deserted your old friends? Or are you not recov-ered from your sea voyage to Nantucket? I never had my

promised letters, nor have I learned even indirectly the experience of that journey, yet I have a severe suspicion that it
was a bad failure. We have sad accounts of the sickness of
your brother's wife. How is she?

I see old Aiken is on the side of the righteous, while you
and George T. remain out in the cold for the present. Well,
the gallery has its advantages, but I am not permitted to enjoy
them if I would, and I would not if I could. I have an abiding faith that out of the present chaos of political debauchery
we shall get some decent politics by and bye. May be not this
year, but sooner or later. And I can afford to wait, since I
already have all the reward I seek,— the consciousness of being
right, making a mark, and securing an enviable position for
the *Republican*.

But if you are in the land of the living, shout, if but to say
" damn."

*To H. L. Dawes.*

October 10, 1855.

Croak, croak, croak! Why the devil can't Berkshire do
something besides? Let those who are right go to work.
The K. N's are playing the brag and lying game most awfully.
That story you mention is all a lie. There never was any
arrangement about bolting at Worcester on the part of the Republicans, that I know or heard of, and I certainly should know
it if there had been.

We shall elect Rockwell. If not, I shall invite the foreign
missionary society to look into Massachusetts. How many
speeches may I promise you for in this region during the three
weeks preceding election?

If there had been such a bolt as the K. N. story says the
Republicans threatened at Worcester, it was all right and justifiable. Gardner's speech proves this. And though there was
no concert, no arrangement, no nothing except individual
opinion that such must result if Gardner was forced upon the
convention,— a bolt was justifiable and proper and necessary,
if it could be useful. That is the only question — and I am
prepared to accept any issue the enemy choose to make on this
question. Gardner sustains us all. I will not deny there would

have been a bolt. I only deny that any preparations were made for one.

Wilson says we are sure to carry the state. I do not see how any other result is possible. The partisans of Gardner do not know of what they speak. They are stronger now than they will be at any future day. The K. N's are all broken up. In a few places like Amherst, Palmer, and North Adams,—where courageous villains and timid saints dwell,—they are strong, but elsewhere I cannot find they have any power worth fearing. They are weak in character, bankrupt in respectability, rotten in morals, and can only succeed by frightening other people. With such a cause as ours, we shall only be beaten by our own inaction, want of confidence, and timidity. The heart of Massachusetts is with us. The head will be, if we only dare to claim it, and teach it. Hampshire county will do nobly,—we perhaps badly, through rum. The *Republican* says no more than it believes. We haven't any private opinion. The canvass is changing daily, and the changes are all on our side and in our favor. Do, for God's sake, stop this croaking and do something up in Berkshire. Eastern Massachusetts is winning all the laurels. We shall beat if we will. We can conquer if we will deserve to. Five such Whigs as John Z. Goodrich and five such Free-soil Know-nothings as Wilson would give 'us the battle.

I am weak and sinful and cross enough, anyway, but such epistles as yours to-night, after all day chasing cattle-shows and buttonholing every second man on politics, make me swear. I have resolved to keep cool this campaign. I shall in my paper, thoroughly so. But that renders more necessary a little private explosion now and then. So excuse this. I don't know all that's in it. I won't read it over. Thank you for your liquor law exposé. It is what I wanted, only stronger. I am not clear yet **where or when** to use it.

*To Charles Allen, after the birth and death of a child.*

November 20, 1855.

It is over, and sadly over. . . . I should be sorry to feel that you are never to be blessed with wife and children; with-

out, there is little really worth the living for; but I pray you
and yours may be spared the agony of our last twenty-four
hours. Mrs. Bowles is perhaps less comfortable than is common, but with good fortune she will mend rapidly. She feels
her loss terribly. Though a disappointment, it is a small matter to me, only as it affects her.

*To H. L. Dawes.*

April 19, 1856.

I still live, I thank you, and had been thinking of you lately
and wondering why, since I heard you had been in Boston, you
did not lay over a train and see your Springfield friends, either
going or returning. Perhaps you took warning by the *Bee.*
Indeed, I think it is rather dangerous to cultivate my friendship, and I shan't blame my old friends if they are a trifle shy.
However, thank God, there is a future. I do not think there
was a purpose beyond crushing me out in the Gardner and
Brewster articles in the *Bee,*—nothing whatever. The American paper here was just expiring, when the two came up this
week, and wound up the machine again. But spite to the *Republican* cannot keep it up long. Newspapers demand healthier food. B——fluttered badly—was it not a good hit? That
is the only paragraph I am really proud of in the whole controversy. There are no laurels to be won in such fights. One
only gets dirtied. I aimed only to show my indifference, and
point out the sources and motives of the assault. This last I
know I did, spite of denials. Did you see the *Bee's* last article?
I feel well enough that I am "under a cloud"; that even those
disposed to be my friends feel that there was more or less of
truth in the *Bee's* assaults; that my rashness makes me a dangerous intimate and an unsafe leader. But I bide my time. I
know I am not prudent—I don't want to be—but I know
what I am about. I know, too, my motives, and I am not
afraid to make comparison with those of open enemies and dis-
trustful friends. I don't wish anybody to be responsible for
me or my paper. The more thoroughly independent I can
make it, the better I shall be satisfied, and the more really

influential and prosperous will it be. But I do not feel it necessary to vindicate myself to you. So let that pass.

Massachusetts will go Republican this fall anyhow, though it may be after a hard and nasty fight. I shall not trouble myself about home politics, nor make any particular fresh efforts at conciliation. My ambition fattened last year in caucusing and management. But everything looks bright outside. If this Fremont movement holds, we shall sweep the country beyond peradventure. We shall take from twenty to thirty per cent. of the Northern Democrats, and come in flying. That's the way things look now. The secret of the campaign is at Cincinnati [the Democratic national convention]. The Republican candidate will really be nominated there. My letters from Washington, both from our own and Western members of Congress, are very encouraging. Sam Galloway of Ohio, just returned from home, says the Fremont movement is going like prairie fire there, taking in Americans and Republicans and one-third of the Democrats. Stopping at Harrisburg, as he came along, he found the fever high in the Pennsylvania legislature, possessing Americans as well as Republicans, and ten or twelve of the Democratic members, who looked upon him as the Moses to lead them out of captivity. Galloway is himself against Fremont, and for Judge McLean,— so this report is impartial. Fremont is thoroughly with us, and if we can win with him we must put him on the course, for victory is indispensable to freedom. Greeley is for him. The other *Tribune* people rather cool, but keeping their eyes open. Seward wants to be the candidate, and Dr. Bailey of the *National Era* is for him, content to wait till 1860 for a victory. But that won't do.

What friends had Mrs. Mary Hinman Graves, in North Adams? Twenty years ago, when I was ten, she came, a bride, to my mother's to board, and I remember her with a great deal of interest and affection. I wish I had known she was dying in your village. But I had not even heard of her for many, many years.

My family are well,— business never better,— I keep cool and grow saucy; and would like to see you.

June 25, 1856.

The tunnel trip I'll make. The other and longer I want to, but am doubtful. If the obstacles to Fremont's election can be removed within a few days, or put in train for removal, I shall feel it alike a pleasure and a duty to devote myself to saving the Union for the season. If not, I shall play as much as I can.

I think the chances are rather against my accepting the *Tribune* offer, yet it presents so many inducements that I shall not decide against it at present. It would take me to Washington as my home, the place being the head of a Washington editorial and correspondential bureau for the *Tribune*, and of course one of much responsibility and influence.

*To Charles Allen.*

August 26, 1856.

. . . There is a great pressure on our folks to nominate Gardner, or set up nobody against him. Clifford, Banks, and the Boston *Atlas* are in it. I think it cannot succeed. If it does, Lawrence will be elected governor by Fremont votes. The only difficulty is, there is not a candidate on whom we can command a union of the Fremont vote against Gardner,—none but Sumner, and I suppose it would be hard to get him. If we could get him to stand, everything would be plain sailing. Gardner would be lapped up in a moment. I think, too, we could easily put Davis on with Sumner. But everything is at loose ends. The fellows are putting the screws to me to go for Gardner; they got Dana of the *Tribune* to believe that opposition to Gardner will endanger Sumner's reëlection, and he has written to me that we must treat with the devil rather than lose that. I mention this to show how they are managing. But I will see them in a very hot place before I will support Gardner.

September 17, 1856.

Can't you come down over Sunday? Or if not, then next week? I have much to say to you, and your letter provokes

more. Come, and let us cuss and discuss these political antics,
which, however, have a deeper meaning than you attach to
them. With you, I shall support Dr. Bell as the best man in
nomination, unless some other man is in the field with whom
there may be a chance to defeat Gardner; and not only support him by my vote, but urge him in the *Republican*. And I
can do this cheerfully and honestly. I am glad, too, that I am
not a Republican to be sold out. I wish there were more of
your and my kind of Republicans as to that. And yet your
denunciations of our Free-soil friends are not altogether equal
and exact justice. Some of the most determined opponents of
Gardner's nomination, or even no nomination, were old coalition Free-soilers,—Alvord (who was perfectly raving on the
subject), Erastus Hopkins, Rodney French, and a dozen others
I might name; while Banks and Wilson were supported for
Gardner by some of the most old-fogy and conservative Whigs,
Homer Bartlett, Linus Childs, Ezra Lincoln, George Bliss,
George Dwight, etc., who all worked for Gardner, and used as
a principal argument that it was only the ultra "long-heel"
Abolitionists who opposed Gardner, and that because he was
conservative (of the truth!), etc. The truth is, these coalitions,
bargains, etc., are incidental to the destruction of the old
parties and the reorganization of the new. You see them
everywhere. The Whigs are "selling out" to the Fillmore
Americans, the meanest of the breed, and *vice versa;* and now
the Buchanan and Fillmore parties, each of themselves fresh
compounds of factions of old organizations, are meditating a
grand national and natural bargain and sale for the purpose
of defeating Fremont; and I hope it will succeed, that is, in
the union proposed, for it is legitimate and proper and might
as well come now as next year. You and I never lived in such
a time as this before, for parties have been regular and established all through the previous day; but the history of the
former changing period — 1824–32 — has similar pages of coalitions, bargaining, etc. Every man must be his own judge how
far he will engage in such things. When done with decent
men and to secure great and important results — in triumphs of
principle — they are not unworthy of any man. Though I saw

at Worcester men going in for Gardner, because, as I thought, it would help them to certain offices, great and small, I met many others who believed it a matter of patriotic duty, as necessary and important to the great object of defeating Buchanan and electing Fremont; who took Gardner as a mere incident, a dose of medicine, because in order to get the good results they must take it, determined and expecting to get rid of him next year. There is much force in the view of these men, and did I believe that it was necessary, as they affected to, for the great results, I should at least acquiesce quietly in the adoption of Gardner, though I never could vote for him. I would pursue towards him the policy you pursue towards politics in general. But I do not believe in the necessity or policy of swallowing Gardner, at least to any further extent than of making no nomination as a party against him. That on the whole will have a good effect in certain states on the presidential election. It shows the overriding importance of the national election, and the depth of feeling as to that in Massachusetts, that such men as met at Worcester yesterday were willing to throw away their certainty of flaxing out Gardner, for the sake of the moral effect abroad of a grand union and peace here in Massachusetts, against the Administration party.

October 29, 1856.

. . . Say to Dawes I find great encouragement to work in Berkshire. The result in No. 11 depends on the work done on Saturday and Monday. I wish you and he would arrange for an old Whig and an old *Democrat* to visit every town in Franklin county in the district, on those two days in addition to all other work done and being done. I want them to pray with the leaders, and make 'em promise to do everything possible for Dawes on Tuesday. This is the work that tells, and he who does the most of it on those two days wins the victory.

Southern Berkshire looks better. Senator Wilson has sowed good seed. Banks's letter amounts to little or nothing — does not take ground for Trafton as against Dawes. I have arranged a meeting of the faithful at Pittsfield, Friday, with the assurance that the county shall be mapped out afresh, and every town visited Saturday and Monday. Dawes is gaining, and so is Weston. The fight is between them, it seems to me, and Weston's friends are quite confident of victory. Dawes is the only man that can beat him,— that is the word to pass along the line.

*To H. L. Dawes.*

November 10, 1856.

What with forty-two hours continuous work Tuesday and Wednesday and Thursday, without sleep, and getting over it, last week, I had not time to write you. But you know what I would say,—and how I felt, and how I whooped, and how good all over I felt; so good that not even Fremont's defeat could take the joy out of me. Was not the vote great, and the result magnificent, and that Berkshire should do the best part of it too! I had faith, strong faith, after I saw how your friends responded to the final call for work, but I was not prepared for *such* a victory. Your friends everywhere worked well and with a hearty good will. It is something to have such friends. All deserve appreciation, and no one above another, and I know all will have it from you.

It seems now as if you *must* have been elected any way; but there's no doubt that both Weston and Trafton thought they were ahead a week before the election, and with reason. You gained rapidly in the last six days, and immensely in the last three. Our fellows went over the district after Weston and Trafton had got through. I verily believe that every town in the district was visited on Saturday and Monday. It was certainly so this side the mountains.

You shall pay the bill now that you are elected — that is, all the *expenses*, for it is right. Had you failed it would have been different, for I felt we could well afford to invest $50 or $100 in your behalf at a venture. The principal item is for the 5500 extras, which being printed in the night in order to get them out, cost more than they ordinarily would. I have paid some bills at Northampton, and have some to pay at Greenfield. The whole will be within $75,* but pay all the rest first and let this remain till you have cash on hand and "owe no man anything." Please do this. I'll take a mortgage on your first mileage.

*To Charles Allen.*

SPRINGFIELD, December 21, 1856.

. . . I had just settled down for the winter, determined not to be seduced out of Springfield for the present, when I got, on Saturday, the note I enclose [the suggestion to establish a newspaper in Philadelphia]. I hardly know what to think about it, much less what to say. It's flattering, of course, and appeals somewhat to a proper ambition, and yet I have a dread of deep water. I feel a good deal as did the bashful boy, whose father was urging him to go and marry a certain girl of the neighborhood. " I was married — your mother was married — and you must expect to be." " But," blubbered the youth, " you married mother, but you want me to go and marry a strange gal ! " I can edit a paper in Massachusetts, but the strange gal in Philadelphia I have some horror of. However, I shall hear what they have to say. If I could dictate the terms as to capital, etc., and have supreme control, and make an independent paper with Republican leanings, and not a Republican paper with independent leanings (like the *Tribune* and *Republican)* I should like to see what I am made of somewhat more than I am likely to here. Please return me Dana's note, and of course say nothing of the suggestion in its present shape, unless it be to G. T. D., whose opinion I should respect.

December 25, 1856.

The compliments of the season ! . . . My Philadelphia man came yesterday, but I told him I could and would do nothing with him ; that I could only talk seriously of the matter when I saw a combination of capital, of which I was to be the

* Characteristic of the region and time,—the chief manager in a hot congressional contest spends less than a hundred dollars ; and the sharp decisive work of the final rally is done on Saturday and Monday, without infringing on the intervening Sunday.

representative and salaried agent, taking such interest of course myself as to inspire confidence in my fidelity. He says Dana, Snow, and M'Elrath, of the *Tribune*, are ready to invest in the enterprise if I will take hold. I said, very well: when you and the other Philadelphia gentlemen and Dana & Co. want to talk with me on my basis, summon me to New York for consultation, and I will come down. And so he left after half an hour's talk, evidently full in the faith that the combination would be made, and that I should be summoned to its head. But we will see. There is undoubtedly a chance to make a property costing from $30,000 to $50,000, worth $100,000 within one to two years, with good and resolute management; but I shall be stiff with 'em,— depend upon it.

# CHAPTER XVII.

## THE BOSTON "TRAVELLER."

AT the close of the presidential campaign of 1856, the
*Republican* had fairly achieved the position which
the New York *Tribune* soon after accorded to it, of "the
best and ablest country journal ever published on this
continent." It had won its place by the hardest work,
by its editor's natural genius for journalism, and by the
opportunity of a great political epoch. It had for several
years been steadily earning money for its proprietors; it
was constantly increasing the quantity and quality of its
matter; it had won a high reputation, had made
many enemies, and was acknowledged by both friends
and enemies as a power in public affairs. But it seemed
to have reached a limit which forbade much further
growth. It had gained almost as large a circulation
as was possible in the country neighborhood to which it
was necessarily restricted. After several more years of
prosperity, in 1860, the entire circulation of the Daily
was 5700. Of this number 1850 copies were taken in
Springfield, of which the population was about 15,000;
giving one paper to every eight inhabitants,—a very
high rate, and one from which scarcely any advance
could be expected, though in fact within two or three
years the circulation of the Daily was more than doubled
owing to the rapid growth of the town through the

enlargement of the Armory, and the increased demand for news in time of war. The Weekly had, in 1860, a circulation of 11,280, of which 7271 were in Massachusetts. The special field of the paper was in western Massachusetts, though both editions had a limited circulation elsewhere; and there was no state or territory, except Mississippi and Utah, in which the Weekly had not regular subscribers. But the substantial paying circulation was necessarily confined to the immediate neighborhood, and could never rise beyond a small fraction of the constituency possible for the journals of a great city. The advertising patronage, of course, was under a like limitation. All this implied that the *Republican* must be published upon a very economical basis : that it must deny itself many of those resources by which a wealthy newspaper can increase its attractions ; that its chief conductor must spend his own vitality freely to make up for the limitations of his exchequer, and that he must content himself with a far scantier measure of influence than the journalist who numbers his readers by the hundred thousand.

This was the barrier which Samuel Bowles had now reached in his career. It was impossible but that such a spirit as his should seek to pass it, and to find a wider field. He was only thirty years old,—an age when the best of a man's work should be still before him. He had in himself every qualification for filling a large place. He might well feel a strong self-confidence when he looked toward a wider field. From the great established newspapers, under the recognized master-journalists, advances were repeatedly made to him. Propositions more than once came from the office of the *Tribune*, a paper with which the *Republican* was largely in sympathy, and with whose staff its editor was on friendly terms. In 1856, as one of his letters has shown, a project was discussed for his taking the head of the *Tribune* bureau at Washington. But probably no situation as lieutenant, under however great a Cæsar, would have suited him.

Early in 1857, a scheme was planned in Boston, and broached to Mr. Bowles, of a great newspaper enterprise there under his direction. The Boston *Traveller* was to be taken as a basis, and its name retained; the *Atlas* and the *Telegraph and Chronicle* were to be bought up and consolidated with it; there was to be a large staff, with distinguished correspondents; the paper was to be Republican, independent, progressive, and Mr. Bowles was to be editor-in-chief.

The plan seemed full of brilliant promise. It proposed such a paper as Boston had never seen before, and offered to its editor a leadership of the whole New England press, and a place in the little group of newspaper kings of America. Ambition made quick response to the call; imagination fired at it; prudence took a hasty survey, and said, "Try it!" A favorable decision was quickly reached, and the details settled without delay. The editor was to receive about one-tenth of the stock of the new company as a bonus, and a salary of three thousand dollars. He took in addition ten thousand dollars' worth of stock, paying for it with money he had laid up from the *Republican's* earnings. The subject was first suggested to him in February, and in April the new *Traveller* was launched. Its ambitious programme was thus stated:

"The grand idea of the new paper is that of universality—a full presentation and a liberal discussion of all questions of public concernment, from an entirely independent position, and a faithful and impartial exhibition of all movements of interest at home and abroad."

It was a hasty step on Mr. Bowles's part. Yet he was not altogether deserted by the caution which he had inherited, and by which he had thus far kept secure every step once gained. He avoided the risk taken by many a brilliant journalist who stakes all he has won in a long course of subordinate labor, upon a doubtful venture. Mr. Bowles staked only his surplus earnings. He kept unimpaired his interest in the *Republican* establishment. He did not break up his Springfield home, but left his family there, though it involved for him the discomfort and loneliness of a bachelor residence. The *Republican*, too, was well enough equipped in its editorial and business departments, with Dr. Holland, Mr. Hood, Mr. Bryan, and the sub-editors, to maintain itself fairly, while it was troubled by no considerable rival in its local field. So, its old chief said his farewell in a brief editorial, transmitting his authority to Dr. Holland, and regretfully leaving the paper into which he had " freely and honestly poured the second and best fifteen years of his life." The phrase is noticeable,— at thirty-one a man's best fifteen years should not be behind him.

The new *Traveller* made a good though not a brilliant beginning. It was a sheet of eight pages, a form then unfamiliar to Boston journalism. It was fairly good in its various departments, but strongest in the editorial page, which showed on political subjects the vigor and independence which were characteristic of the chief editor; while it gave also a variety of topics and breadth of treatment, which, if they did not fulfill the ambitious promise of universality, were a marked advance beyond the ordinary newspaper field. But the paper lacked the good work in every detail, the individuality, the spice, the unique charm of the *Republican*. It was not to be expected that the Boston paper should be a mere enlargement of the Springfield journal, and for it to develop a homogeneous and powerful character of its own there were needed time and growth. The public found the *Traveller* a strong, readable, and well-informed paper; but while it was still "in the gristle," before it had gained a symmetrical, impressive individuality, or got a firm hold on its constituency,—in a little more than four months,—came the withdrawal of Mr. Bowles and the relinquishment by the paper of its new character.

The general verdict by the wise ones was that "Sam Bowles and Boston did not suit each other"; that the stronghold of tradition, propriety, and mutual admiration, was no place for an audacious and irreverent fellow who was perfectly ready in the way of debate to crack the crown of his dearest friend, or to stab under the fifth rib the greatest man of his party; and who was quite capable of speaking disrespectfully of the State-house dome. But it would probably be juster to say that his personality offered the very elements then most needed by Boston journalism. In no other respect was the city so deficient in leadership as in its newspapers. It stood, as it still stands, preëminent above all other American cities as the home and mother of scholars, thinkers, and reformers. It was then as now the disseminating center of the best influences inherited from Puritanism, and the most hospitable port to the adventurous craft of modern thought. Nowhere else will one see so large a proportion of intelligent and earnest faces as in the crowds that throng its narrow streets. Even with all its modern degeneracies, and the deterioration due to its later importations from Europe, the town still shows itself the true descendant of the Puritan fathers. If "holiness to the Lord" is not written on the bells of the horses, yet the horse-car passenger is warned by placard to follow the prescribed way of paying his fare, with an appeal to his conscience, "*Not to do it is wrong*"; and the sign above the bootblack's stand on the Common impressively addresses the patriot : " It is a discredit to you, and a *disgrace to the commonwealth of Massachusetts,* to let your boots be dirty."

Thirty years ago, the newspaper press of Boston, while representing in its different journals a wide variety of ideas, was in its methods of journalism very unprogressive. It was far behind the press of New York in enterprise of news-gathering, in intellectual force, and in influence upon the country at large. The superiority on which it chiefly prided itself was that of decorum. Such a free lance as Sam Bowles was sure to considerably startle his new constituency. But in his principles of journalism and his own powers, there were, as it would now seem, the very elements to supplement and enlarge the traditions of the Boston press, and to make a newspaper which should be to Boston what Horace Greeley's *Tribune* was to New York.

But the *Traveller* enterprise was ill-planned, and predestinate to failure. The three newspapers which it amalgamated were financially weak and morally incongruous with each other. The old *Traveller* had not had any decided character as a newspaper, except perhaps that it was semi-religious; and it had not obtained any commercial patronage or advertising,—this was all absorbed by the *Advertiser* and the *Post.* The *Atlas* had formerly been the leading Whig paper of New England. It had gone heartily into the movement for a new party of freedom, and had thereby alienated a part of its old supporters ; it had lost subscribers, advertisers, and prestige. The *Chronicle* had been started as an anti-prohibition paper, and its stock had never been worth anything. The new *Traveller* added to these original elements a moderate financial capital, a brilliant editor-in-chief, and inharmonious owners. It started with a flourish of trumpets, proclaiming that Boston had never had a good newspaper, and was now to see a *ne plus ultra*. It had powerful rivals in the *Journal* and the *Transcript*. A paper begun on the scale of the *Traveller* needs either an ampler capital than that paper possessed, or an extremely able management inspired by perfectly united councils. The councils of the *Traveller's* conductors were not and could not be united, because there was among them a radical difference as to the fundamental principles of newspaper management. From the day he began his work in Boston, Mr. Bowles found that his associates, who represented the principal capital and business management of the concern, were out of sympathy with him both as to the principles and details of their joint enterprise. He was in nominal control of the editorial department, but while some good and satisfactory workers were secured, other employees owed their position to the favor of the other partners in the business, and gave neither the amount nor kind of work that was needed. Deficiencies of this sort were in part made good by the editor, who threw himself into the breach and did what other men ought to have done; in part they could not be made good at all. Other trouble arose. With a limited capital and heavy expenses, the necessity was felt for wise and delicate financial steering. Gardner and his friends were looking about for newspaper help to strengthen his tottering estate. Under such circumstances, a clear and full agreement among the paper's owners was needed, as to what class of considerations was to be paramount in its conduct; whether financial or moral success was the prime object; whether and how the necessary means of financial support could be obtained without any compromise of principle. As soon as these questions began to come up, Mr. Bowles found himself at odds with his principal associates in the ownership, to a degree that ere long resolved these questions into the single one of how to dissolve their ill-mated partnership. There was a time of painful and wearying discussion and negotiation, and then the end was reached,— Mr. Bowles withdrew from the editorship and management; the money he had invested was left in the concern with the other capital until such time as it could be safely withdrawn; and a new organization was made for the conduct of the paper. Bankruptcy was avoided, and the *Traveller* continued its existence, but sailing under other colors and on a different course from that so hopefully entered upon a few months before.

Mr. Bowles's brief card announcing to the public his withdrawal said:

" The explanation of this change lies in the different principles of newspaper economy held by the respective parties. Mr. Bowles, finding from this cause and his own health that the expectations under which he was induced to take the editorship of the *Traveller* were not likely to be realized, has insisted on withdrawing, in justice to himself and in order that his associates might without embarrassment conduct the paper after a policy in which they have great confidence, but which he cannot approve."

His associates rejoined next day, laying chief stress on the non-success of the eight-page form and professing entire content with their own "principles of newspaper economy." The paper returned in a few days to the large four-page sheet and to the old style in general. Under Mr. Bowles the *Traveller* had supported the Republican party and opposed Governor Gardner. It said (July 10) that the governor was trying to secure some newspaper organ in Boston: " Time works wonders, and it would surprise no one who is acquainted with the under-currents of the political sea to behold his Excellency's name at the head of columns now devoted to anything

else than the setting forth of his claim to excellence."
The paper of September 10 — the same in which the
retiring editor took leave — spoke of Gardner's impending renomination by the Americans as directly hostile to
the Republican and Anti-slavery cause, of which Banks
was already and worthily the candidate. The next day
the paper spoke of Gardner in a different tone, and before
the end of the month it was the active advocate of his
reëlection.

To Mr. Bowles the issue could not but bring deep
chagrin. He had made a great venture and had lost.
The financial loss was inconvenient, but not distressing.
But his ambition had met with a check, and his pride
was deeply touched. He bore himself steadily, without
wailings or reproaches. He took by way of rest a brief
trip to the West with Charles Allen and his sister; and
then came back to his home, to the quiet little town and
the beautiful Connecticut valley, and before very long to
his first and last love, the *Republican*. The paper had
undergone no marked change in his absence. It had
lacked something of breadth and brilliance. Dr. Holland had impressed it more than before with his own
special vein, of direct and vigorous preaching on the
personal conduct of life; he had fairly maintained, with
his associates, the character of the paper, but his gift
and taste (and this was also true of Mr. Hood) lay rather
toward writing than toward general editing. He volun-
teered to relinquish to Mr. Bowles the editorial control,
at the same time selling his interest in the paper, and
withdrawing from all editorial work except writing.
The offer was accepted, perhaps with a little regret
and reluctance by both men, the one at resigning the
place of power, the other at assuming without inter-
mission the full burden of responsibility, yet each drawn
by true instinct toward his right place. Dr. Holland

devoted himself hereafter partly to contributions to the
paper, partly to lecturing and book-writing.  Mr. Bowles
threw himself into his old work with a new energy.
Whatever he felt of regret or of wounded pride at the
failure in Boston, was alleged neither by spoken complaint nor by brooding, but by harder work.  He had
sought a more favorable environment, and, failing in
that, he essayed the higher task of making a narrow
environment serve his purpose.

# CHAPTER XVIII.

## THE RIPENING JOURNALIST.

A MAN'S life may be measured by two great tests,—
his work and his character; what he does and what
he is. Mr. Bowles's return to Springfield in the autumn
of 1857 may be taken as a point whence in some marked
respects his life became broader, deeper, and more diver-
sified, and gives fit opportunity for a review of his personal development. There was an immense educating
force in the public events of the time for one whose business it was to report, to discuss, and to help to shape the
course of things. The civil contentions about slavery
afforded not only a moral but an intellectual education.
Whoever reads the history of the Republican movement
against the extension of slavery will see how different
it was from a simple moral crusade against wrong. It
was allied with other sentiments and motives — a perception of the economic folly of slavery, a sense of
injury to Northern white men by the aggressions of
slavery in the territories, a growing resentment at the
domineering temper of the Southern leaders, a determination that the country should no longer be governed
by an arrogant sectional faction, with Northern politicians for its allies, and patronage and corruption for its
instruments. It was political self-respect, and care for
white men's rights and interests, more than regard for

the slaves or moral condemnation of slavery, which brought the Republican party into power. Yet Abolitionism had no monopoly of the conscience of the North. The obligation to support the existing form of government, as the bulwark of social order, was felt honestly and keenly by a great class of minds, many of which were at the same time fully alive to the wrong of slavery. To find the practical reconcilement of the two sentiments was as hard a problem as the brain and heart of a people ever struggled with. If the motives of Republicanism were less single than those of the Abolitionists, its methods were more practical. Abolitionism was a passionate sentiment; Republicanism was statesmanship. The task of the Abolitionist was often heroic, often perilous, but it was extremely simple, being simply to reiterate "Slavery is a crime." How to free the slaves the Abolitionists hardly attempted to show. The only course they indicated for Northern voters was to abstain from voting, and to dissolve the Union. Their chief apostle, Garrison, was as much opposed to war as he was to slavery; and when at last the slave's fetters were cut by the sword, the way was as hostile to his lifelong teaching as the result was congenial. The Abolitionists as a class were as brave, intense, and narrow as the early Puritans, but without the Puritan aptitude for state-building. But the Republican leaders were men of affairs. They took it as their business to sail the ship of state. The Constitution and the established forms of government were the instruments by which they were to work: these were the organic framework of civil society. The framework might not be altogether of the best, and might need gradual improvement; but to discard or ignore it outright was to plunge into anarchy and chaos. Seward, Chase, Wilson, Lincoln, and their associates had that large wisdom in adapting means to ends which is statesmanship; with that especial wisdom in ascertaining public opinion, educating it, leading it if possible, and in the last resort obeying it, in which consists the statesmanship of a democracy.

A similar wisdom, at once philosophical and practical, must belong to the journalistic leader of opinion. Greeley and Raymond had it,— the one with more of moral sentiment and passion, the other with greater breadth and adroitness. Mr. Bowles too grew eminent in this statesmanlike quality of mind. In a democracy the people are greater than the government, and the journalist who influences and educates the people, and in their name points out the ends which government ought to seek, often fills a place of larger power than representative or senator.

The limitation of the moral power of politician or journalist is that in order to lead he must in a degree conform. In a democracy no kind of leadership is free from that necessity, save that of the pure idealist — the poet or the prophet. On all others conformity lays its heavy hand. But under the firmest rein of all does it hold the man who makes it his business to take active part in government. Agreement with the majority is the inexorable price of his personal success. As often as election day comes round, he must have the approval of a majority of his constituency or be turned out of his work. The journalist's necessity, on the other hand, is to make a paper that men will buy. One way to that end is to express sentiments agreeable to his readers,— to soothe them with assent and approval. Another way is to make a newspaper so attractive by its general merits that men will buy it even though they dissent from its doctrines. That was the path which Mr. Bowles chose for the *Republican*. Not till near the end of his life was the paper confronted with the severe test of directly

opposing, in a presidential campaign, the party to which
the mass of its readers belonged. But at a much earlier
stage it committed itself to the then novel position of
criticising with entire freedom the special measures and
the individual leaders of the party to which it gave a
general support. The old theory of party allegiance —
a theory still substantially practiced in this year of grace
1885 by a large majority of American journals — is that
the individual, or the newspaper, shall support the party,
as the patriot stands by his country, or the believer by
his church. Interior discussion and guarded criticism
are allowable, but are always to be subordinated to the
prime object of victory over the foreign foe, the heretic,
or the opposing faction. The approved temper toward
the party is to

> " Be to its faults a little blind,
> Be to its virtues very kind."

Three obstacles must be set aside or overcome by the
truly independent journalist. He forfeits his freedom if
he becomes a place-seeker — whether for the presidency
or a post-office. Next, he must not be afraid on due occasion to give offense to his subscribers ; — he must either
counteract such offense by the irresistible attractiveness
of his paper, or he must put up with a diminished sub-
scription-list. Lastly, and this is by far the hardest, he
must, in his own mind, rise above the domination of the
public opinion environing him. The worst despotism of
party is exercised within a man's own mind. It consists
in his proneness to believe that all truth and goodness
are found in his own creed or sect.

The *Republican*, after it became a daily, was never
extreme in its partisanship. But for its first decade it
virtually owned allegiance to the Whig party. When, for
example, the Whig party leaders in 1854 adhered to its

organization, against the *Republican's* remonstrance, the paper, still considering the party preferable to the Know-nothings, or the then abortive Republican party, took during the campaign the course now taken by moderate party organs when similarly dissatisfied. It professed no enthusiasm, but forbore to hurt the cause by " speaking out in meeting" till election was over. But that was its last act of perfunctory allegiance to the Whig party, or any other. The editor's ripening comprehension of the journalistic idea fell in opportunely with his paper's established financial success, and with a time of political disintegration which weakened all party bonds. The *Republican's* declaration of independence was made on the third of February, 1855. At that time the paper took a forward step by making its regular Saturday paper one of double size, with eight pages instead of four. It began at the same time with a new press and new type, and marked the occasion by a review of its own history from the start, and a notice of the general advance of journalism, dating from the invention of the telegraph. It continued:

" With the dawn of a new national growth upon the press of America, at the period of which we speak, came also a more perfect intellectual freedom from the shackles of party. The independent press of the country is fast supplanting the merely partisan press. Parties are taking their form and substance from the press and pulpit, rather than the press and pulpit echoing merely the voice of the party. A merely party organ is now a thing despised and contemned, and can never take rank as a first-class public journal. The London *Times*, the great journal of the world, is the creator, not the creature, of parties. There is not in New York, where journalism in this country has reached its highest material and intellectual perfection, a single party organ in existence. All are emancipated. None conceal facts lest they injure their party. None fear to speak the truth lest they utter treason against merely partisan power. The true purpose of the press is understood and practiced upon. They are the mirrors of the world of fact and of thought. Upon that fact do they comment with freedom, and to that thought do they add its freshest and most earnest cumulations.

"Such in its sphere, does the *Republican* aim to be. Whatever it has been in the past, no more shall its distinction be that of a partisan organ, blindly following the will of party and stupidly obeying its behests. It has its principles and purposes. But these are above mere party success. To these it will devote itself. Whenever and wherever the success of men or of parties can advance those principles and purposes, the *Republican* will boldly advocate such success; whenever men and parties are stumbling-blocks to the triumph of those principles, they will be as boldly opposed and denounced."

To one who bears in mind the character of the New York press, and the American press in general, during most of the thirty years since this was written, this description of its impartial character reads like a sarcasm. The era of journalistic independence was as brief as that of the disintegration of parties. When the new lines had been drawn, the newspapers fell into place on one side or the other,— not upon the whole with the old subservience, yet with a degree of partisan fidelity which grew with the growth of party discipline, as the Republican party matured and the Democratic party recovered from its successive disruptions; so that in 1872 " independent journalism" was greeted by the general public as a new phenomenon. There were of course exceptions among the press, to trace which would belong to a general history of journalism. But through the intervening period, whether heartily favoring, or criticising, or opposing the general course of the Republican party,— Mr. Bowles's paper never hesitated to pronounce a frank, independent judgment on the measures and men of that party and of all parties. Its political news was honest. Its readers could always find the views of its opponents fairly quoted and ungarbled. Its regular correspondents at Washington and elsewhere were always under instructions to give the facts as they were, whether they suited the editorial views or not. In the correspondents' galleries in the capitol, one may sometimes hear such remarks as this: " The situation looks to me so and so—but the old man at home will not let me say so in my dispatches." The *Republican's* correspondents had no occasion to say that. They were chosen with due regard to their general agreement with the paper's views, but the instructions given them were to tell the truth. They were allowed, too, to tell it largely from the stand-point of their personal convictions. It was often the case that the paper's Washington dispatches were considerably more radical in their tone than the editorial columns; while the biting criticisms of " Warrington," the Boston correspondent, fell often on the measures and men that the *Republican* editorially approved.

One great source from which the chief editor drew his knowledge and power was his personal intercourse with public men. Among these he cultivated so wide an acquaintance that in his later years scarcely another journalist or politician in the country had so large a personal knowledge of the leading men of the time. He was thus able to judge of public questions, not as abstractions, but with a keen appreciation of the personal factors involved in them. Through all these years it was his habit to visit and report the national conventions of all parties, as well as the important conventions in his own state. In times of special crisis, he made flying visits to the state or national capitol, felt the beats of its pulse, and came home to judge more clearly and correctly the drift of things than those who either remained in the

central heats or had no contact with them. Whenever
he left his home it was always to go into the midst of
people, and the most interesting people he could find.
He had a rare faculty for penetrating direct to the real
man. He caught with quick and subtle instinct the
characteristic quality, the true self; and he exercised a
magnetism and charm which drew people to open themselves, to talk of what they cared most for, and show
what was in them. Men and women were to him a perpetual education and inspiration; they were his uni-
versity and library, his teachers and pupils, his work
and recreation. He lived always in the atmosphere of
humanity.

His estimates of character were swift and, as a rule,
sagacious, but by no means unerring; his likes and dis-
likes were quick, and he sometimes took strong fancies
or unreasonable prejudices.

His change of attitude toward Henry Wilson has been
described. They remained on excellent terms with each
other; in each there was a strong element of good-fellowship; and Wilson had a communicative disposition which
fitted Bowles's thirst for news as a spring of water
fits with a pump. With Charles Sumner Mr. Bowles
had much slighter personal acquaintance, but Sumner's
sincerity and ability won for him a hearty and warm
recognition and a steady support. Of Mr. Banks, after
his distinguished success as speaker of the House, Mr.
Bowles had great expectations, which were strengthened
by his able administration as governor. He discerned
no more than others the promise of Lincoln's greatness,— in truth, evidence of it was scarcely visible to
human eyes until tested by the event. Nor did he fully
recognize the quality of John A. Andrew until the war
showed the man; he thought his nomination in 1860
unwise, and was at first inclined to disparage his judg-

ment and ability. But, when the exercise of power showed their true quality, the *Republican* gave a stanch support to Governor Andrew and to President Lincoln, and cordially recognized the power and integrity which each showed in his own sphere and way. A friend who was with Mr. Bowles when the news came of Andrew's death relates that he was almost overcome by it,—though he had known him only in his public capacity, he felt his death like the loss of a friend. He was for many years on very cordial terms with Schuyler Colfax; was his companion in several tours in the far West, and inscribed "Across the Continent" to him.

If some of his political estimates and predictions illustrate Mr. Bowles's fallibility,—and infallibility was the last thing to be claimed for him,—they illustrate, too, how completely some great men of a day or a year are dethroned by Time, and how imperfectly the most sagacious observer fathoms the drift of public affairs. Seldom has political foresight been more baffled than by the outcome of the struggle over American slavery. Its issue in a gigantic war, which left the Union impregnable and the slaves free, was wholly beyond the presage alike of the fathers of the republic; of Webster, Clay, and Calhoun; of Seward and Greeley and Douglas and Lincoln; of Garrison and John Brown. When the war came, the whole nation, like one man, was held sternly to that tremendous discipline in which the only possibility is to meet the hour's duty, and leave all beyond with the unseen power that rules human destiny. It is the presence of this mysterious power as the supreme actor in the drama, which gives the deepest impressiveness to that critical period of the nation's life. The suspense and agony of the conflict lifted men into a sense of sublimer relations than they had felt in quiet days; and now we look back with wonder to see how a result was

wrought out transcending all human plan and calcula-
tion; men's wisdom or folly, heroism or cowardice,
counting always as potent factors, yet as instruments to
an end which no human eye foresaw.

Among the influences which molded Mr. Bowles's
mind, there is to be considered the effect of his work as
a daily editor, with its ceaseless activity and stimulus.
One quality which this pressure developed in him was
an extreme rapidity of mental action. He had been a
slow boy, but he became one of the swiftest of men.
An editorial writer in the New York *Times* — evidently
one of his old pupils — said after his death : " His thinking was like the working of a perfected machine. The
apt conclusion came quickly, without groping or exterior
suggestion. He was not in the habit of waiting till he
had read his exchanges before writing his leading articles. He wrote, as he thought, with astonishing facility.
If with his own pen, it flew over the page with a dreadful disregard of legibility that tortured and impoverished the unhappy compositor; if by an amanuensis, he
kept him at the stretch of his powers. But the literary
excellence of his style was remarkable. The apt word,
the terse, incisive phrase, and the sentence full of present meaning and later suggestion, were in his ready
control."

There grew the aptitude and desire for something
always new. The constant freshness of the *Republican*
was one of its most marked qualities and strongest
charms. The editor said to a friend: "It is no trouble
to me that the paper contradicts itself. My business is
to tell what seems to me the truth and the news to-day,
and the same to-morrow. That is one of the paper's
fascinations. It's a daily journal. I am not to live to
be as old as Methusaleh, and brood in silence over a
thing till, just before I die, I think I have it right!"

He seemed almost to become weary of having the sun rise every morning in the East. He was constant always to his principles, but he was so ready for a change of method that it put him in a degree outside of the sympathies of the mass of men who like to move in channels and ruts. His judgment of political situations was somewhat warped by his own impulse toward novelty. He was constantly looking for such a break-up and new crystallization as comes but once or twice in a generation. He took part in one such grand re-formation, and assisted in the unsuccessful attempt at another; but he predicted them a great many times when they did not come.

He was growing constantly in the power of condensed and telling expression. The editorial of a column, or a column and a half, grew less frequent and prominent. The paragraph was superseding it in the place of honor, and the column of brief "Note and Comment" was getting always stronger and brighter, till it became the most characteristic feature of the paper. The editor had a genius for pregnant and terse diction. He knew how to condense an editorial into a paragraph, a paragraph into a two-line item, an item into a word. As he came to his full growth, hardly another hand in the profession equaled his in shaping phrases which "make a hole in the target." His epigrammatic sentences went the round of the press. They snapped like a whip and sometimes cut like a knife.

It is often difficult or impossible to distinguish with confidence the editorial writing of Mr. Bowles from that of his associates. They caught something of his style. He had "the masculine faculty of impregnating other minds." Some writing in the paper seems indicated as Mr. Hood's by a certain scholarly ease and grace; a finished style as of one who when he is writing his article is doing his day's sole work, instead of having a

hundred other things to attend to; and a philosophical
quality which firmly grasps and clearly presents the
central principle underlying the immediate question.
This philosophical habit grew with Mr. Bowles as years
advanced, and the obligation to Mr. Hood which he so
warmly expressed may have lain partly in this direction.

Dr. Holland's distinctive contribution to the *Republican* was twofold. He was more a man of books than his
colleague, and gave to the paper in its early years the
discussion of literary topics which did much to broaden
it beyond the field of politics and news. But he added
too a more novel and striking feature. It was said of
him at the memorial service following his death:

"Dr. Holland was essentially a preacher. He was ordained
by natural endowment, and by steady, enthusiastic purpose, to
the ministry of moral guidance and inspiration. That vocation has hitherto been largely exercised by personal speech from
pulpit or platform, and largely through the instrumentality of
the church. But his life fell at a time when a new engine of
influence is supplementing and in a degree supplanting the old.
While those who speak from the pulpit are glad to number
their hearers by hundreds, the daily editor counts his by tens
of thousands. While the church is anxiously debating how it
can reach and hold the people, every man looks on his door-
step for his morning paper before he goes to his breakfast.
The newspaper beyond any other teacher now comes home to
men's business and bosoms. The limitation upon that influence is that it too often lacks that clearness and emphasis of
moral purpose which has largely characterized the ministry of
the pulpit. It was the especial distinction of Dr. Holland that
he used the newspaper's power to serve the preacher's purpose.
He enlarged and ennobled the function of journalism, by putting it to a new and higher use. He showed that a newspaper
might do something more than tell the news; something besides discussing affairs at Washington; something more even
than to act as guide and judge in literature and art and public
affairs. He used the daily or the monthly journal to purify
and sweeten the fountains of personal and family life. He

spoke continually the word that should inspire young men to
be pure, and women to be strong; the word that shed poetry
over the home life; the word that threw on every interest the
light of conscience and the warmth of moral feeling."

The innovation in which Dr. Holland was perhaps beyond any other man the pioneer consisted not in using
periodical publication for the moralist's purpose,—such
use is as old as the time of Addison,—but in successfully
grafting that function upon the modern daily, and making religion compete successfully there for men's attention with the press and throng of other interests. He
opened a noble field which has as yet been but scantily
worked. Much of his editorial writing had this quality,
but his conspicuous success began when he wrote
"Timothy Titcomb's Letters to Young People." He
had previously contributed to the paper some series of
letters on light social topics, and Mr. Bowles one day
suggested that he should do something more of the same
kind. "I thought at first," said Dr. Holland, "that I
had written myself out, but without premeditation I
made a dash at another line of subjects, and wrote that
forenoon the first of the 'Timothy Titcomb Letters.'" It
shows how little expectation he had of attracting marked
attention, that he borrowed a pen-name which had been
used by Thackeray in one of his minor writings. His
unexpected success was an illustration of Cromwell's
saying: "A man never rises so high as when he knows
not whither he is going." The letters were in three series,
the first addressed to young men, the next to young
women, and the third to young married people. They
were plain, familiar talks on the conduct of life, aimed
neither too high nor too low for the average reader,
familiar in illustration, pervaded with practical and
undogmatic Christianity. They met with instant and
wide favor. When gathered into a book, they had a

sale which at once gave Dr. Holland rank with the most popular authors of the country. Many a man and woman to-day remember them with gratitude. They were followed by other serials in a like vein, which proved equally popular, and won for the *Republican* a new hold on public regard.

These contributions, of which the authorship was soon known, gained for Dr. Holland a personal reputation in connection with the paper which for a time rivaled that of Mr. Bowles. Yet he did not find in daily journalism his most congenial field. After 1857, he gradually diverted his labors into lecturing and book-writing, and his contributions to the *Republican* ceased entirely about the year 1864. The culmination of his career was as one of the founders and the editor-in-chief of *Scribner's Monthly* (now *The Century Magazine*). In his later years, sitting on a piazza overlooking the Hudson with a friend, he said, pointing to the river, that his present life was to his earlier like the Hudson to the Connecticut.

With the exception of the brief *Traveller* episode, Mr. Bowles was from first to last identified heart and soul with the *Republican*. It was his hand that shaped its course, and assimilated the elements of its strength. It is the course of national events on which the historian of a newspaper naturally dwells most, and which was always the leading topic of the *Republican*. But the paper was continually seeking other and widening fields. Religion, social reform, literature, nature, amusements, personalities—it took them all as its province. In a little country town it presented the amplest range of human interests; it was as broad and various as humanity. It drew from many a worker who gave to it the best of his heart and brain. But it took its central inspiration and distinctive character from one many-sided and intensely vital man.

# CHAPTER XIX.

## Personal Relations.

" SAM BOWLES," as he was known to the *Republican's* readers, and the "Sam Bowles" whom his friends and acquaintances knew, were the same, yet different. In truth, if almost any one of us could be seen as his image exists in the minds of different people,—if he could be seen successively as his wife sees him, as his children, his servants, his business associates, his enemies, his intimates, see him,—the result would be a portrait gallery of many different people, with sometimes not even a family resemblance.

All his readers recognized Mr. Bowles's power, but all by no means admired him. He gave frequent and wide offense. Thoughout the Connecticut valley, the sentiment toward the paper was a strange mixture of admiration, pride, and hostility. Every one wanted to read it, and those who declared they did not, and stopped their papers, were drawn back to read it again, even while they abused it. To those who had grown accustomed to its well-flavored repast, it was a necessity. Any vigorous and outspoken paper, like any vigorous and outspoken man, will make enemies. The quality in the *Republican* which roused most hostility was its free criticisms upon institutions, parties, and every person and event of public concern. This freedom of judgment, subject to no limitations save those of truth, the editor claimed as his right, asserted as his duty, and exercised with a width of range and deftness of stroke which increased as the years went on. There is nothing which almost any man so quickly resents as unfavorable criticisms upon himself, his friends, or the institutions he believes in. When the criticism is public, it has a tenfold sharper sting. There was not a day in which the *Republican* did not touch something or somebody with the thong of its whip. Its vocation was to make report and comment on the whole course of events, and frequent blame was its necessity. If it had been as just as Omniscience, it would still have given frequent offense. Being entirely human and fallible, it gave offense continually.

By the mass of the paper's readers this critical, sharp-speaking quality was probably regarded as the chief characteristic of Mr. Bowles. But to his personal acquaintances he showed a side as different from this as May from January. Many of them saw and felt both sides by turns, but to some he was always May.

From the earliest, his family affections were deep-seated and constant. His father's was one of those New England households in whose undemonstrative and outwardly meager life the domestic attachments strike tenacious root, like pine-trees in rocky soil. In later years his own family was the first object of his care and the center of his dearest affections. His chief aim in life was not to make for himself a career, a name, or a fortune, but to provide for the happiness of his wife and his children. His wife's aim in turn was to make their home above all else a resting-place for the husband. The habit and law of the house was that " Father's " rest was to be shielded and made comfortable. "I remember," says one of the children,— there were now two daughters and a son,— " how we used to be kept quiet through the early forenoon,

because Father was asleep, and how we were taught to
look out for the first early delicacies of spring, to tempt
his appetite.  I recollect his late breakfast,— Mother
roasting oysters for him at the grate, and we children
standing around expecting some of the juice, like
open-mouthed birds." It was not in his nature to be a
mere passive recipient from any one, least of all from
those he loved most.  He charged himself with a close
oversight of the welfare of wife and children.  In his
absences, however full of occupation he might be, his
letters to his wife were as constant and devoted as any
youthful lover's.  At home, his care for the various interests of the household was as vigilant as for the management of the newspaper.  To spend and be spent, in
every direction, was the law of his life.

In some of the chapters of this biography, extracts
from his domestic correspondence are given with a good
deal of freedom.  It is impossible to do justice to the
portraiture without giving these glimpses of the richness and sweetness of his household affections.  Were it
permissible to draw the portrait without any reserves,
the fuller light would only bring out more distinctly the
fineness of the traits.  Browning says:

> "God be thanked, the meanest of his creatures
> Boasts two soul-sides — one to face the world with —
> One to show a woman when he loves her."

And the side which Mr. Bowles showed to the world
made no disclosure so fine as the sweeter side he showed
at home.  Only in that intimacy were fully revealed
the tenderness, the patience, the self-control which were
in him.

His sojourn in Boston during the *Traveller* experiment was a painful exile to him.  He once said to a
friend who was about to be married : " You are going

to live in Boston. Now you know I once lived there awhile,— if it was living,— and I was about the most wretched creature in that little city. Social life did not touch me anywhere, nor I it. I want you, for my sake, to have an eye out for such poor, forlorn creatures as I was,— away from wife, babies, everything that makes life sweet. Take them in; let them sit by your fire, talk about their home, take up your children — if you have any — and kiss them for their own. I have walked through the streets in Boston, and seen families seated at their table, in the bright light, and it seemed as if I couldn't bear it. I wanted to ring the bell and say, 'For heaven's sake take me in and comfort me.' Why didn't I take letters of introduction? I didn't believe in them. I didn't wish to be thrust upon people to dine and wine,— there was my work before them every day; my name was in the paper. I would not speak of this if it were not to show you where you can tread in the path of the saints and do good."

At home he went between his house and his office with hasty or with tired step; tall, his head bent forward a little; with shaggy, projecting brows; luminous dark eyes, that noted everything, and seemed always to look straight to the heart of whatever they fixed on; and with passing words of direct, alert address. In the town — which grew from three thousand to thirty-five thousand inhabitants while he lived in it — he knew and was known by everybody. Outside of the town he had a circle of acquaintances which widened until it reached from England to the Pacific. His main recreation was traveling, and wherever he traveled he found his chief interest in humanity. He would talk with every man upon his own subject, and get all that he could give. He was a master of that supreme secret of education, the art of listening. He listened so recep-

tively and engagingly, and the contact of his mind was
so stimulating, that people as they talked with him were
put at their very best. The characters thus opened to
his eye won from him a quick and warm admiration for
whatever was fine or lovable. Thus from an observer
he grew to be a lover.

In his newspaper he regarded himself as a public censor,
bound to render to every man his strict desert. In private life he welcomed to his acquaintance every man who
had any attractive or interesting trait. He was as charitable and catholic in his personal relations as he was in
his public relations austere. The range of his taste was
wide : people of high culture, plain country folks, statesmen, backwoodsmen, artists, actors, business men, literary women, boys and girls, babies,— none came amiss
to him, so they were genuine and human. He had his
resentments and his quarrels, but a good lasting hatred
he could keep up against nobody except a liar or a hum-
bug. If, in any matter of public moment, he saw in a
man a single fault, the *Republican* named and blamed it
though the man might possess all the other virtues. In
private life, if a man had one agreeable merit, and only
one, Mr. Bowles would give him fellowship on the
strength of that. In his newspaper he was a judgé on
the bench ; out of it, and toward the same people, he was
the most appreciative and tolerant of companions.

From the plain and unpolished bearing acquired
through his early experiences, he grew to have at his
command a singularly winning manner. There was
nothing about him of diffusive and cheap geniality, no
stereotyped or meaningless smiles. He not infrequently
carried himself with a slight reserve and dignity.
" Billy," he said to one of his special friends, " why don't
people clap me on the shoulder, with a ' How are you,
old fellow,' as they do you ?" " Because," was the plain-

spoken answer, "you go along with a look that says
'Keep away from me—d—n you!'" But this touch of
unconscious hauteur belonged to his dyspeptic turns more
than to his habitual bearing, and at the worst was quick
to disappear. He could always assume at will an easy
and charming manner. An occasional political associate
says: "When, in arranging some point together, we
would see that some man was going to be rather trouble-
some to manage, he would say, 'Send him up to me';
and after a talk with him the man would go away
pleased with himself and delighted to feel he was doing
Mr. Bowles a favor." In his visits to Washington, especially in the later years after the war, he was on good
terms with every one he met. He would encounter some
congressman whom he had been pounding in his paper,
and in half an hour would have that man his friend and
telling him his secrets. He delighted to thus conciliate
people whose friendship was of no earthly use to him
except for its own sake. This charming address came to
be his spontaneous habit whenever he was free from
the absorption of work and the depression of suffering
nerves. He conquered hearts like a charming woman,
and with a feminine sense of power and pleasure in his
conquests. Nor did he lightly abandon them.

To the world he was a great journalist, but to many a
man and woman he was known as the truest and most
generous of friends. Those whom he loved felt that his
friendship was inspired by an appreciation of their inmost self; that he saw what was best in them and ideal-
ized it. Such recognition is in itself one of the dearest
tributes and one of the strongest inspirations to excellence. His friends felt that they were worth much to
him; that he counted on them, depended on them, drew
from their friendships the fullness of his life.

He had a great command of the language of affection; his letters sometimes display a mastery of what Dr. John Brown calls "that language of love which only women, and Shakespeare, and Luther, knew how to use." On lighter occasions he could pay a compliment so charmingly that its grace pleased more than the tribute to self-love. There was "just a soft tang at the tip of his tongue," when he chose. But with his real friends he oftener used a pungent and piquant way of speech, never cloying them with sweetness. Where he felt at home he liked to exercise an entire freedom, and an off-hand brusqueness that had a laugh behind it. Said the mistress of a house in Springfield where he was a familiar visitor: " He used to come in for a few moments, on his way back and forth between his home and his office, and would perhaps sit with both legs hanging over the arm of a chair, his hat low down over his eyes, and talk *sarse* as he called it." Says another lady : " I remember how my acquaintance with an intimate friend began by his introducing us to each other on the street,—'This is Lizzie R——, and this is C—— W——, one of the Roxbury saints. You are going to be friends,—I ordain it,—I predict it. Now don't go looking each other over, but pitch in, and talk. Yes, of course,'—reading our glances with his quick eyes—' Lizzie R—— is orthodox, and you are a kind of come-outer, but you will like each other for all that,—better for that.' "

In his friendship he was very free from egotism. He sought to converse on his friends' subjects rather than his own. Closely wedded as he was to the *Republican*, he left it behind him when he talked with his intimates, unless they turned the conversation that way. With some of them he scarcely ever discussed it; there were some who even disliked the paper. This was the sentiment of one man who knew the editor through twenty-five years, whose home was his frequent resort, and who said years after his death: "The two great losses of my life have been my father and Sam Bowles." Yet this same man, a New Englander, stanch and stiff in all his convictions and prejudices, said at the same time, "I never liked his paper. I was an old Whig, and after the *Republican* left the Whigs it was always ready to denounce them. Its course on many subjects was distasteful to me. I pitched into him so sharply about the paper sometimes that at last my wife cautioned me to stop or I should endanger our friendship. But Sam Bowles was to me like a brother. I discussed with him the most intimate and personal affairs of my life." Said another life-long friend, an active man of affairs, "I loved him as I never loved any other man,— as I never supposed I could love."

Henry L. Dawes, in a private letter written some time after his death, speaks thus of their early intercourse :

"When I first knew him, he and I were both young, and in our respective spheres ardent and ambitious. We were never tired of talking together over our respective callings, sometimes visionary in our notions, but always sincere. Notwithstanding his usual buoyancy of spirit and courage, I have known occasions when he was ready to give up, when he would be just as far over on the dark side, and everything and everybody seemed to go wrong. He would come out of these moods, however, as the sun comes out of a cloud, and light up every idea with the brilliancy of his conceptions. In those days he used to come up and see me very often [at North Adams], and on those occasions he seemed to me to be as entertaining and fascinating as at any other period in his life. His passion for news, and for currents of thought, which has ever been the distinguishing characteristic of the *Republican*, was among the earliest developments of his character. He would go everywhere, he would write everywhere, and he would ask everybody everything, in order to be the first to get sight or sound or sign of something new. Then he would sit down and talk over matters of personal interest in one's private affairs, just as if he had nothing else to think of. I never knew a man who knew him who wouldn't rather have him at his table than any other man in the world."

Intercourse with him had always the charm of keen vitality. There was never an empty word or a dull moment. He gave the kind of stimulus which, instead of fatiguing, refreshes and cheers. By his unceasing mental activity he wore himself out; for the last twenty years of his life his nerves and stomach were in chronic rebellion; heavy clouds, of dyspepsia, sciatica, sleeplessness, exhaustion, came often and staid long. It was impossible that the shadow of these clouds should not sometimes tinge his intercourse with those about him, and the edge of his suffering sometimes wound others. But whatever was felt of this fell almost entirely on those who were associated with him in work or business. Outside of the paper and its concerns, he maintained habitually a wonderful kindness and good cheer. Overworked as he was, other overworked people found rest and refreshment in him. No man under like pressure ever "burned his own smoke" more bravely and successfully. His easy talk, with its shrewd comments and quick wit, his sensitiveness to nature and humanity, his unexacting cordiality, his strength and delicacy, were to a tired brain as restorative as sunshine. A woman who sometimes visited in his family, a teacher and writer, said : "I used sometimes to go there when I was so jaded I felt as if I could never write anything again ; and after a day or two I would come away rested, all ready to write an essay or two,— not so much from anything he said as from the vital impulse he gave."

He exercised toward his friends a considerate generosity. He did not wait for help to be asked, but planned
and offered it unsought, in counsel and in deed. He had
some friends who kept a school in Springfield, and
one day coming to them, he said: "I have learned that
Mr. —— is to give up his school" (a rival of theirs)
"at the end of the year. That will give you a new opportunity, and you must meet it half-way,"— and then
went on to suggest changes and enlargements, planned
as wisely as kindly. A woman, worn to exhaustion and
illness by the hardest and best of work as a teacher, was
taken by him and his wife into their home, nursed and
cheered, until after several weeks she went home reno-
vated. His life was full of such acts. He learned that
an old friend was embarrassed in his business, and going
to him said, "I know you are in difficulties,— now, I can
afford to do for you so much," naming a sum, "and I
want you to take my help." Such help he gave repeatedly
even to men who were not his near friends. To young
men especially he was generous in lending his indorse-
ment on their notes. He was ingenious and fertile in
benevolence to his friends, and aided them with an un-
obtrusiveness and grace which sweetened the gift.

All old ties and old associations were dear to him. He
loved the familiar localities, and whatever recalled the
early ways. "When I go by your house," he said to a
woman, "I always stop to lean over your fence and take
a good look at your *sarse-garden*,—you've got the only
old-time sarse-garden in Springfield!" The town itself,
its varied loveliness of view, the river, the guardian
hills, all had a hold on his affection that tightened as
years went by.

Of the men who had relations with him both as a
friend and in the conduct of his newspaper, almost all
agree in saying, "There were two men in him; one

gracious, charming, delightful,—the other hard and
severe." The existence of two opposite natures in one
man need not appear strange to any self-observant person, who may have found in himself twenty different
selves, resolving themselves on the whole into two ; and
may have found it to be the chief and proper business of
his life to bring one of these two selves into due ascendency over the other. In Mr. Bowles's case, the contrast
between his different sides had the vividness which belonged to his whole nature, so that it impressed men as
something unique. His faults lay almost wholly on the
side of self-will and pride. He was by nature masterful—fond of having his own way and the first place.
His life as a journalist in some respects confirmed that
disposition. The *Republican's* attitude of entire independence sometimes ran into excess and caprice. It was
never servile, but it was sometimes arrogant. In the internal administration of the paper, Mr. Bowles was, and
always would be, master and chief ; and the man has
seldom lived in whom absolute mastery did not breed
something of despotism. Among his business associates
and subordinates he was like a captain on his quarter-
deck. As soon as he entered his office, his whole frame
seemed to grow tense ; his orders were directly and
briefly spoken ; his mere presence kept the whole staff
up to concert pitch. His genial ease of manner was laid
aside as a man throws off his dressing-gown to take hold
of work. He did not indulge in scolding—a word or
look was enough. The men who worked under him
felt admiration, loyalty, and a touch of fear. While
work was going on they were to him like parts of the
great engine he was driving, and he urged them as
remorselessly as he did himself. He always meant to
be just, but he had a strong feeling that the *Republican* was his creation and possession, and within its

sphere he recognized no man's claims as on an equality
with his own.

When his personal friends received public criticism
from the *Republican*, it was not in human nature that
they should not frequently resent it. But, besides the
plea of public duty, Mr. Bowles was apt to assert in his
defense a distinction which nobody recognized but himself,— that he was not to be held responsible in his private
capacity for the paper's utterances. No journalist ever
identified himself more closely with his paper; yet, when
a friend complained of comments in its columns, he would
answer, " The *Republican* is one thing and Sam Bowles is
another, and you mustn't identify them." This, as the
aggrieved person perfectly knew, was a distinction without a difference. Once engaged in combat, too, he always
became aggressive and struck hard. " The *Republican*
will not be put on the defensive!" he used to say — " We
shall carry the war into Africa." So, a public retort
from a man who felt himself aggrieved often drew out a
severer attack, and it was when thus provoked that the
*Republican* said its most unjust things. When the
quarrel was over, Mr. Bowles was quick to forget and
ignore it — it became to him as though it had not been.
He was too proud to make open amends, but his resentment quickly died away, his old friendliness returned, and
he looked for equal readiness on the other side to forgive
and forget. It was frequently an unreasonable expectation. Most memories are as tenacious of an injury as a
kindness. An injury from a friend seldom heals perfectly without some open word of reparation or regret.
So, in a long succession of controversies,— controversies
which in their public aspect were often the *Republican's*
best contributions to the common good,— many a private
hurt was given, of which the memory rankled in him
who received it; and from some close friendships a bloom

was brushed which never quite came back. This was a deep pain to him. And if he gave some wounds whose scars did not heal, it must be said that the wounds he received — and no man got more hard thrusts — were wont to heal quickly and kindly. If he was loath to express regret or reparation, neither did he exact it from others. To any overtures of reconciliation he made prompt and winning response. " The pleasant-est man to *make up with* that I ever knew," said a life-long acquaintance. Such collisions as he had with his friends and acquaintances were almost always connected in some sort with the *Republican*. In the conduct of the paper, he meant to have his own way. Its success was the object of his life; its character he prized dearly as his own; its independence was his glory. Hardly even for friendship's sake would he permit it to swerve a hair's-breadth from its wonted course. To make an explicit correction, or to withhold a piece of news which he thought the public entitled to, was a great and rare favor. A friend relates one such experience with him. " A man here got into a disreputable scrape, and many people knew it, but the papers hadn't got hold of it. His wife was a good woman, and I wanted to spare her the dis-grace of having it all spread before the world. So I went to Mr. Bowles, and, seeing he knew nothing of the story, I gave it all to him. ' Thank you,' said he, ' you have given me a valuable bit of news; we'll use it at once.' Said I, ' I don't want you to print it.' We argued a while, but it did no good. At last I got up from my seat and said, ' Mr. Bowles, suppose your daughter had married, and her husband turned out a scoundrel, and it was proposed to spread it all out before the whole coun-try — how would you feel ? " He gave me one of his infernal looks, black as a thunder-cloud, and said nothing for half a minute; then he said, ' Well, if the other papers will say nothing, we will say nothing.' So it was kept quiet. After that I'd have gone through a block of burning buildings for him ! "

He was a man who could unite an entire and life-long loyalty to one woman, the partner of his life, the mother of his children, and the mistress of his home, with intimate and mutually helpful friendships with other women. People often said of him that he was irreverent, but no one who knew him ever charged him with irreverence toward womanhood. He honored good women, he learned of them, and he used to say that the best wisdom and inspiration of his life had come through them. His attitude toward them in personal intercourse was manly and delicate. In the homage he paid, there was nothing of perilous sentiment, no philandering or flirtation. He met them with chivalrous appreciation of what was womanly, and on a footing of entire equality. His closest intimacies were with women of a characteristic New England type. There is in that section a class of such who inherit a fine intellect, an unsparing conscience, and a sensitive nervous organization; whose minds have a natural bent toward the problems of the soul and the universe; whose energies, lacking the outlet which business and public affairs give to their brothers, are constantly turned back upon the interior life, and who are at once stimulated and limited by a social environment which is serious, virtuous, and deficient in gayety and amusement. There is naturally developed in them high mental power, and almost morbid conscientiousness, while, especially in the many cases where they remain unmarried, the fervor and charm of womanhood are refined and sublimated from personal objects and devoted to abstractions and ideals. They are platonic in their attachments, and speculative in their religion;

intense rather than tender, and not so much soothing as stimulating. By the influence of such women Mr. Bowles's later life was colored—his views were broadened, his thoughts refined, his friendships exercised in offices of helpfulness and sympathy. By their acquaintance he was educated to a conviction of the entire equality of the feminine with the masculine mind, and its claim to an equal place in shaping the public and private life of the community, as well as its need of larger outlet and freer scope than society had hitherto assigned to it.

Among the strongest shaping influences of his life were those of the men and women with whom he came into intimacy. The formation of these friendships was among the chief epochs of his history. He owed to them something like that which the Mississippi owes to the Missouri, the Ohio, and all the streams that swell its waters from their early obscurity to an imperial flood. He was indebted less than most intellectual men to books. Newspapers were his chief literary food; and newspapers, with all they teach, teach but little of the heights and depths of humanity, and hint but scantily at its sublimity and tenderness. These higher lessons he learned by what was wrought out in him as he manfully did his work and bore his burden, and in no small degree from the human souls which opened their wealth to his insight and sympathy.

He gave his friends of his very best in thought and labor, but above all other gifts was contact with his own vital, fructifying personality. All analysis will seem cold and all praise meager to those who knew and loved him best. Their common sentiment toward him was expressed by one who wrote, "Not to see you sometimes, not to hear from you, is a kind of eclipse." There were not a few whose feeling was akin to that expressed by a Massachusetts judge, now dead, who wrote to him after a critical illness:

"As you know better than any one else, I do believe I should have gone over the dam from sheer depression, but for my wife and the cheerful words of half a dozen friends, of whom I put your name first on the list. God bless you for that, Sam Bowles! Now, I don't think you have committed many sins in the *Republican*" (this was in 1873, after the paper had brought on itself wrath and tribulation by its support of Greeley). "There is the same old tone to your paper, always on the side of honor and honesty, and I stand by you even in your mistakes, if they are mistakes. But you may perpetrate what you please from now till doomsday, in the columns of your paper,—you shall never make me feel you are any other than the kind sympathetic friend, who took his friend by the hand and with singular appreciation of his condition ministered to him as no one else could."

# CHAPTER XX.

## The Dred Scott Decision.— The Lecompton Constitution.

IT was under Buchanan's administration that the tide turned decisively against slavery. His election was its last victory. He was elected by an alliance of three powers,— the slaveholding interest, the Northern Democratic party, and those Northern conservatives who dreaded a sectional and aggressive tendency in the Republicans. His inauguration was closely followed by a decision of the Democratic Supreme Court which was a shock to all real conservatives. His Administration gave countenance to such usurpation in Kansas that a revolt was provoked among Northern Democrats. Then John Brown's attack on Harper's Ferry filled the South with fears of Northern invasion and negro insurrection. This was the logic of events which united the North, and by its vote chose a Republican president, and led the South to leave the Union in which it had lost the mastery.

President Buchanan's inaugural, on the fourth of March, affirmed the right of the people of a territory to determine their institutions; but as to whether that right was to be exercised prior to their action in organizing a state government,— the only real point of controversy,— he referred deferentially to the arbitrament of the Supreme Court. On the sixth of March the

Court pronounced its decision on a suit which it had
long held under consideration. It was brought on an
appeal to determine the status of Dred Scott, a slave in
Missouri, who, twenty years before, had been taken by
his master into the free state of Illinois for a term of
residence, and also to Fort Snelling on the Mississippi,
within the territory where by the Missouri compromise
slavery was prohibited ; and who now as plaintiff in this
suit claimed that he was made legally a free man when
his master took him upon free soil. The Court's decision,
stripped of all technicalities, was to this effect : it dismissed the case for want of jurisdiction, on the ground
that no person who was of slave descent or African
blood could ever be a citizen of the United States, or
have a right to sue in the courts. Nevertheless, the
Court proceeded to discuss the grounds on which the
plaintiff claimed his freedom, and declared that the prohibition of slavery north of 36° 30' was unconstitutional
and void, Congress having no power to exclude slavery
from the national territories. As to the effect of the
residence of a slave, by his master's will, in the free state
of Illinois, followed by a return to the slave state of
Missouri, the Court held that the question belonged to
the Missouri courts, and that their renderings were
adverse to the claim of freedom.* There was a considerable division among the judges as to various points in
the decision, and Justices Curtis and McLean — the two
Northern Whigs upon the bench — dissented emphatically both from its reasoning and its conclusions. The
chief spokesman of the majority of the Court was Chief-
justice Taney. His dictum, that no person of African
descent could become an American citizen, was based
on the inferior and degraded condition in which these

---

* Dred Scott afterward became the property of a daughter of his master,
and was by her manumitted.

people were held when the Declaration of Independence and the Constitution were adopted, they being regarded at that time, said the chief-justice, " as so far inferior that they had no rights which the white man was bound to respect"; so that there could have been no intent to include them in the "all men" of the Declaration, and similar phraseology.  The unconstitutionality of the Missouri compromise was maintained by an argument which was thus tersely summed up by Lincoln : The Constitution of the United States forbids Congress to deprive a man of his property without due process of law ; the right of property in slaves is distinctly implied in the Constitution ; therefore, if Congress shall undertake to say that a man's slave is no longer a slave when he crosses a certain line into a territory, that is equivalent to depriving him of his property without trial or verdict.

The whole dispute as to slavery under the Constitution is involved in this statement of the master's claim, admitted thus by the Supreme Court.  Once granted that a man's slave was absolutely his property,— as much so as his horse,— and his right to take him into the national territory, just as he might take his horse, was indisputable.  That a slave was in this absolute sense his property, was, to the slave-holder's mind, a fact beyond denial or doubt.  The answer was, that a slave was property only by the creation of *local law*, and that when a slaveholder took his human chattel into a territory, he did not carry with him that state law by which alone, in exception to the general usage of mankind, property in man was recognized.  As to the other main point of the decision, that negroes were incapable of American citizenship because that incapacity existed at the era of the Constitution, Justice Curtis pointed out that at that period free negroes had the right of suffrage in five of the thirteen states.

But, whether on just grounds or not, the highest Court in the nation had decided that no negro could be an American citizen, and that slavery could not be legally excluded by Congress from any territory. How that decision was received by moderate men at the North, may be illustrated by the *Republican's* editorial of March 11:

"We cannot overrate the significance of the recent opinion of the majority of the Supreme Court, as given in the case of Dred Scott. The history of judicial decisions in this country contains nothing so important as this. . . . The case on which the new opinions were given did not necessarily call for them. It could have been disposed of without discussing or disturbing the great principles of slavery which the Court has undertaken to settle. . . . The majority of the Court therefore rushed needlessly to their conclusions, and are justly open to the suspicion of being induced to pronounce them by partisan or sectional influences. The decision was of the utmost importance to the slavery interest and to the Democratic party, as based upon it. They were in desperate circumstances. The present territories of the country are almost certain to become free states. Nothing but violence can prevent them from coming to this decision." The new rule, the paper proceeds, is designed for practical effect more especially in those further acquisitions of territory in Mexico and Cuba which the slavery interest is bent on gaining. But, " the expectations of the perpetrators of the new scheme for protecting and advancing slavery, that it will be acquiesced in by the country because it is the voice of the Supreme Court, will not be realized. It will widen and deepen rather than allay agitations. It will be heeded in practice only by those who approve of it in theory. The people are the court of last resort in this country. They will discuss and review the action of the Supreme Court, and if it presents itself in a practical question will vote against it."

The Dred Scott decision showed how far the forms of law could be wrested, not only against justice and hu-

manity, but against the traditions and spirit of judicial
procedure. The authority of the Court was invoked by
a trick which removed the mooted questions from the
arena of legislative and popular debate, where the people
were giving judgment against slavery. The weakness of
the decision, from a purely legal standpoint, was thus
characterized by the *Republican* (March 18):

"There was but one question before the Court, and that was
a question concerning its own jurisdiction in the case. In fact,
the Court gave no judgment and simply dismissed the case for
want of jurisdiction. . . . There is probably no rule in law
more firmly established and widely recognized, than that the
opinion of any court, touching any question outside of that before it, is of no binding force whatever. The question before
the Court was whether it had any jurisdiction in the case. It
decided that it had not. Everything beyond this uttered by
the Court is just as binding as if it was uttered by a Southern
debating club, and no more. It undoubtedly shows how the
Court will decide in cases involving the questions which it
argues, and this gives its extra-judicial opinions their only power
and significance."

These quotations illustrate the general temper of the
free states. The New York legislature promptly enacted
that neither color nor African descent shall disqualify
from citizenship; that every slave brought by his master
into the state becomes free; and that any attempt to retain such persons as slaves shall be punished by from
two to ten years' imprisonment. It passed a resolution
declaring that the Supreme Court has lost the confidence
and respect of the people. A year later, Seward said in
the Senate: "The people of the United States never can
and never will accept principles so unconstitutional,
so abhorrent. Never, never! Let the Court recede.
Whether it recede or not, we shall reorganize the Court,
and thus reform its political sentiment and practices and

bring them in harmony with the Constitution, and with the laws of Nature." Lincoln said at Quincy in 1858 that while the Republican party did not propose to declare that Dred Scott was a free man, they did not believe the Court's decision was a political rule binding the voters, Congress, or the President; and they intended so opposing it as to have it reversed if possible, and a new judicial rule established on the subject.

President Buchanan surrounded himself with a cabinet as much identified with Southern interests as his predecessor's. Its members were Lewis Cass, Isaac Toucey, and Jeremiah S. Black, from the North, and Howell Cobb, Jacob Thompson, Aaron V. Brown, and John B. Floyd, from the South. He was a very weak man, despotic, but without the skill to rule; arbitrary when he should have been tolerant, and yielding when he should have been firm. He sought to enforce a rigid party discipline, and to that end made freest use of all the weapons of patronage; but he had not the breadth or tact to harmonize his party, nor the strength to keep his own pledges. He held a strongly Southern view of the Constitution, and lent himself to an unscrupulous scheme to make Kansas a slave state. He had no sympathy with the disunionists, but he was utterly powerless to check their intrigues. He was the luckless mariner who opened the bags of Æolus, and the storms which issued drove the ship far over seas.

Governor Geary had done his best to promote justice in Kansas, but found himself abandoned by President Pierce, and resigned just as the new Administration came in. For his successor, Mr. Buchanan selected Robert J. Walker, of Mississippi, a man of character and ability. Walker was very unwilling to take the place, for it had been the political ruin of every man who had held it. But the President gave him the strongest assurances that he should be supported in giving the Kansas people a perfectly fair opportunity to organize their own institutions. Thus fortified, Walker went to Kansas. The usurping legislature had provided for the election of a convention to form a state constitution. The delegates were to be appointed upon the basis of a census, which the legislature intrusted to certain county officials. In many of the counties the free-state party disowned altogether the existing territorial organization, and kept the form of a state government, under a constitution framed by themselves at Topeka, so that there were no officials recognized as competent to take the census. For the approaching convention, no voters were registered and no representation allotted in fifteen out of the thirty-four counties; thus half the territory was disfranchised, and a predominance was given to the districts which lay conveniently for an invasion from Missouri. This confirmed the disposition of the free-state party to keep wholly aloof from all proceedings instituted by the territorial legislature. The new governor did his utmost to induce them to take part in the coming election, but as he was powerless to change the apportionment, his appeals were unheeded. The convention was elected by a very small vote, and postponed its action for a time. In the interval came the election of a new territorial legislature. Walker's appeals and assurances to the free-state men began to take effect. Senator Wilson had visited Kansas and counseled with the leaders, and given them the shrewd advice of a practical politician,— to take part in the legislative election, trusting to their overwhelming numbers even under the unfair apportionment; and to get hold of the working machinery of government, rather than stand too long on theory and punctilio. Most of them finally followed this course, and in October, at a peaceful and undisputed election, in which both

VOL. I.—15

parties participated, the free-state men, by a majority of two to one, carried both houses of the legislature. But the fruits of their victory were snatched at. From the Oxford precinct — a place with eleven houses — a return was sent in with the names of 1624 persons; copied, as it turned out, in alphabetical order from a Cincinnati directory. An equally fraudulent document was sent in from McGee County. The two would have transferred the balance of power in the legislature. Both these returns were rejected by Governor Walker. The authority was used against him of the territorial Chief-justice Cato,— a creature of the Administration, like his predecessor Lecompte,— but the governor disowned his jurisdiction in the premises. From this time the Administration threw its whole weight against the governor.

The convention met at Lecompton and drew up a constitution, in which was one section affirming that the ownership of slaves was a right of property, higher than any constitution, and inviolable; and forbidding legislation hostile to such ownership. Among the other provisions, one forbade the residence of free negroes in the state, and another prohibited any amendment of the constitution before 1864. The convention ordered that a vote of the people should be taken, not on the acceptance or rejection of the constitution, but as between " constitution with slavery" and " constitution without slavery." Except this single section, the whole organic law of the new state was assumed as fixed and beyond amendment for six years, by the convention itself — a body whose authority most of the people disowned, and in whose election only a small minority had taken part. The free-state men refused to sanction this proceeding by taking any part in the vote on the slavery clause. They staid away from the polls, so that, practically without opposition, the slavery clause was fixed in the Lecompton constitution.

The Administration now bent all its energies to obtain the admission of the state by Congress, under that constitution. Already discontent was finding loud voice within the party. Strong appeals were made to the President, by men like Forney,— to whom probably, beyond any one else, he owed the decisive vote of Pennsylvania,— not to make Lecompton the test of party fidelity. But Buchanan was obstinate, misled by the flatteries of office-holders and office-seekers, and wholly committed to the effort to make Kansas a slave state. In December he forced Walker into resignation, but the governor, in an indignant letter, exposed the President's treachery to him, narrated his own policy of reconcilement and justice, and declared that " insurrection and civil war, extending, he feared, throughout the country, were alone prevented by the course pursued by him ; and the whole people, abandoning revolutionary violence, were induced by him to go for the first time into a general and peaceful election."

It was amid the rising of these angry clouds, toward the end of 1857, that Mr. Bowles took again the laboring oar in the *Republican*. Congress was just assembling, with a Democratic majority in both Houses. The situation was perilous. While the struggle was going on in Congress, February 8, 1858, the *Republican*, never an alarmist, said : " It seems to us that the issue of civil war is involved in the questions which now agitate the country." The course of wrong, it continues, has gone on step by step, till forcible resistance seems near at hand. " All these operations are like the demonstrations of a problem in Euclid. A moral certainty is made of as stern and unrelenting stuff as a mathematical ; and so truly as this Lecompton constitution is attempted to be forced on the people of Kansas, and the people of Kansas, driven to the wall, retain their manhood, will there be a civil war, for which alone the Administration will be responsible."

Either from such an issue, or from the political subjugation of Kansas, the only resource lay in a division of the Democratic party. When Congress met, it was known that Douglas was hostile to the Lecompton scheme, and might even break with the Administration upon the question. " Mr. Douglas," said the *Republican*, December 1, 1857, " better than any other man, now stands in a position to dispose of the Kansas question at once and forever ; while in doing so, he would go far toward installing himself in the confidence and respect of the country, without regard to party. He has heretofore turned toward the public his demagogue side ; he has now but to show some of the qualities of the statesman, to be useful alike to the country and himself."

When a few days later the President in his message declared unreservedly in favor of the Lecompton scheme, the *Republican* said that he had lost the golden chance for leading the party to throw off the yoke of the Southern extremists, and the opportunity of the future lay again with the Republicans.

" But to occupy this position they must open wide their doors, accept new leaders, and cease leveling the Philadelphia platform, revolver-like, at everybody who seeks admission into their ranks. They must make it easy for old opponents to join them. Mr. Buchanan's assumption of the quarrels and rascalities of Fernando Wood has already given them New York City. Forney can transfer to them Pennsylvania, Douglas holds out Illinois and Indiana. Blair has Missouri already ; Bell can give them Tennessee, and mayhap Breckinridge will offer Kentucky, and Wise, Virginia, while Kenneth Raynor is eager to transfer North Carolina, and New Orleans's attachment to the Union will surely give them Louisiana. The Administration, in omitting its golden opportunity, has thrust another before its opponents. Will they rival its stupidity or profit by its blunder?"

Such a programme was very characteristic of Mr. Bowles,—critical of associates, hospitable to opponents, impatient of party lines, and eager for new combinations. But the central figure in the kaleidoscopic picture— Douglas as a Republican leader—was at this time attracting many of the wise men of the party. Douglas took issue with the Administration on the Lecompton question, and carried with him enough followers to render the battle in Congress a doubtful one up to the very end. Meantime, very friendly relations were established, though no open alliance, between him and the Republican leaders at Washington. In truth, Douglas was a coarse-grained, self-seeking man, to whom politics was merely a game of personal advancement. He had for many years been subservient to the Southern interest; he had proposed the repeal of the Missouri compromise, and had sustained the usurping Kansas legislature, and the whole course of slavery propagandism in the territory, until the refusal to submit the constitution to a vote of the people. For him to assent to this last outrage would have been a self-confessed abandonment of every vestige of that "popular sovereignty" which had been his whole stock in trade before the Northern people. He saw that the tide was turning at the North, and his place in the Senate depended upon a reëlection in the following year. In the winter of 1857–8 he opposed the Administration upon its leading measure, and induced such party chiefs as Wilson, Colfax, and Burlingame, and such editors as Greeley and Bowles, to warmly favor his return to the Senate unopposed by the Republicans.

The struggle in Congress was long and sharp. Finally the Senate voted to admit Kansas under the Lecompton constitution. Senator Crittenden, of Kentucky, elected as an American, and one of the best representatives of the moderate Southern sentiment, had proposed a bill, submitting the constitution to a direct vote of the people, its acceptance to be followed by immediate admission, or its rejection by the choice of a new constitutional convention. This bill, defeated in the Senate, was in substance passed by the House, the Republicans and their friends supporting it. A committee of conference was appointed; for a while each House insisted on its own measure; finally the committee reported a singular compromise. Mr. English, of Indiana, who had hitherto been a leader among the Douglas Democrats in the House, was the author of this measure, which was known as the "English bill"; and it was accepted by the Administration party, as the best they could get; while enough Anti-Lecompton men supported it to secure its passage through both Houses,— Douglas and a part of his allies uniting with the Republicans in opposing it. Its purport was the submission of the entire constitution to a vote of the people; if they accepted it Kansas was to immediately become a state, and to receive an immense land grant from the general government; while if they rejected it, the territory was not to become a state till it had the full population requisite for a representative in the House,— 93,340,— and no land grant was offered. It is, said the *Republican* (April 22),

" An attempt to drive the people of the territory into assuming for themselves what the Administration has failed to force upon them; and the hopes of its success with them are based on the supposition that a majority of the voters care more for getting into the Union, and fingering the rich grants of land offered as a bribe, than they do for their own consistency, honor, and inherent right to fashion their own institutions."

The English bill was in appearance a lame and illogical conclusion to a great controversy.  But, substantially, it was a half-retreat from the four years' struggle to make Kansas a slave state.  The election under the bill a few months later was the end of the contest.  The Lecompton constitution was defeated by a heavy majority.  The destiny of the state was too obvious to be longer resisted, and Kansas ceased to be a battle-ground.  A new constitution was framed at Wyandotte, ratified by the people, and the final admission of the state—delayed by a sullen Democratic opposition—was effected when the departure of the seceding Southern members left the Republicans with a majority in the Senate, as well as in the House, in the winter of 1860–'61.  The effort to make it a slave state had resulted in making it not only free, but the most tenaciously Republican state in the Union.

# CHAPTER XXI.

## DOUGLAS AND LINCOLN.

"IT was notorious among well-informed politicians," said the *Republican* of March 15, 1860, " that for weeks and months "—early in 1858 — " Mr. Douglas was in full consultation with leading Republicans at Washington, openly seeking their influence to get the Illinois Republicans to make no opposition to his re-election, and making plenty of promises for coöperation to depose not only the Administration but the ' power behind it.' It was, ' *we* could do this, and *we* would do that.' All the leading Eastern Republicans responded to his ideas; nearly every Republican senator, and most of the representatives, were desirous that the Republicans should withhold their fight, and let Mr. Douglas come back to the Senate with the Republican mark upon him. He sought this himself in every way consistent with the outside independent position which he had taken, and which was necessary to his purpose of dividing and breaking down the Democratic party. But the Illinois Republicans could not if they would, and perhaps would not if they could." Now that the lives of Douglas and Lincoln are finished, it is easy for us to pronounce wisely on this question. But it was not so clear when the sole way to Republican victory seemed to lie through Democratic division, and Douglas was the leader of a revolt which in its effect had turned the scales in favor of free Kansas. The argument of policy was stated by the *Republican*, June 19, 1858, in reply to a correspondent who pointed out with much force that Douglas was the same man who had given leadership, support, or connivance to every aggression of the slave power up to the preceding winter. Its reply was: " The Republicans of 1856, in order to turn out the present slavery administration of 1860, must have help from somewhere — from men who voted for Buchanan or for Fillmore, or from both, and who, if they did not applaud the Nebraska bill and the assault on Sumner, at least acquiesced in them both and were silent." Former opponents, it continued, stand ready to become allies,— such Americans as Crittenden, Bell, Marshall, Fillmore, and the Brookses,— such Democrats as Douglas, Broderick, Stuart, Haskins, and Montgomery. " Shall we step in and ask them what they think of the repeal of the Missouri compromise, the brutality of Brooks, and the capacity of Fremont, before we join hands in a beneficent and patriotic duty of to-day ? "

The *Republican* had, too, a reason of its own for countenancing Douglas. Its editor hated the rule of party almost as heartily as he hated negro slavery. The paper protested against party tyranny vigorously in behalf of Seward when, in the preceding winter, some attempt was made to discipline him for voting against his associates in favor of an Administration bill for the increase of the army. Now, its hearty sympathies went to the brilliant rebel who had defied the tyranny of the President and the Southern leaders, and was like to pay the penalty in political ruin, unless the Republicans welcomed him to their ranks. Only when Douglas had dexterously united the Democratic party in his support at home, against the spiteful but feeble opposition of the President, did the

*Republican* yield a reluctant approval to his opponents. It recognized then that, " through his own timidity and the folly of the Illinois Republicans," he had become again the most formidable of Democratic chiefs, and his defeat desirable.

The weak spot in the plea for accepting Douglas as a Republican leader lay in his moral untrustworthiness. Two years later, the *Republican* judged him with entire correctness when it said, April 14, 1860 :

" There is one essential deficiency in his political character. He does not recognize the moral element in politics in the slightest degree ; makes no account of it ; never appeals to conscience, and in effect despises and scouts its authority. Yet as a politician he is successful, and no man carries the masses with him so easily. In his own state and at the West everywhere his success on the stump is perfect. Yet his arts are those of the demagogue and the sophist, and the fame and influence built on such foundations must necessarily be perishable. Yet, with a courage amounting to audacity, a will that marches scornfully over every obstacle, and a magnetic power to inspire and control men, his ambition may reach its goal, in spite of the great moral deficiencies which make him an unsafe leader, and which will give him a much lower place in history than he will hold during the period of his vigor and influence. It is precisely this lack of the moral quality that stands in the way of his aspirations more than anything else. Men do not trust him. Nobody can be sure what he will do to-morrow. If placed in the presidential chair, those who elect him will tremble for the result. They can never be sure of him for any given period of time, and this notwithstanding the tenacity, amounting to doggedness, with which he sticks to his own purposes."

The Illinois Republicans in 1858 already knew their old foe far too well to accept him for their leader. They were willing, as Senator Trumbull said, to " take him on probation"; but they by no means proposed to make him at once the head of their church. So he rallied to him his old party, and was proclaimed its senatorial candidate. Against him the Republicans pitted Abraham Lincoln. They knew Lincoln as "Honest Abe," a shrewd politician, a thoroughly trustworthy man, and a moderate but resolute opponent of slavery. To the country at large he appeared as a backwoods lawyer, who had served one term in Congress a dozen years before, with little distinction. No one yet recognized in him the typical and foremost man of American democracy.

Mr. Lamon, the fullest historian of Lincoln's ante-presidential life, gives a graphic portraiture of the circumstances under which he grew to manhood. His father was an immigrant from Kentucky to Indiana, an ignorant, thriftless, coarse man. Left with two motherless children, he returned to his early home, and brought back to his cabin a second wife, in every way his superior, who found that she had married poverty and degradation. She improved the one possibility which her lot offered, by becoming a true and tender mother to the ragged and neglected boy and girl. Her love and care exercised a gracious influence over their lives. The boy grew up, working now on a farm, now on a flat-boat, now as clerk in a country store; read voraciously the few books he could get hold of; studied law-books, lying stretched at full length before the store with his heels raised against a tree; went as a volunteer in the Black Hawk war; was sent to the legislature; served one term in Congress as a Whig in 1847-8, and then gave way to another aspirant of his party; practiced law, and, in his own words, "was losing interest in politics when the repeal of the Missouri compromise roused him again." As a young man, in the rough backwoods country, he was known as the most powerful wrestler and fighter of the region, when driven into a fray; but a peace-lover

prompt and skillful to allay incipient brawls by his tact
and good nature. He was full of good-fellowship, yet a
solitary man. His humor was a refuge from underlying
sadness. There was in him a deep constitutional melancholy. In his youth the death of the woman to whom
he was betrothed depressed him so that for a few weeks
he was insane. His ambition met with no great success. His domestic life was clouded. His nature on one
side impelled him to activity in large public affairs. He
was a shrewd, long-headed politician, with sagacity to
read men, and tact and patience to manage them. On
the other side that nature was deeply meditative. He
brooded in solitude over the problem of human life. In
his youth he had accepted the hard materialistic infi-
delity of the West. Its loud-voiced negations did not long
satisfy him; he was weighed upon by the heavy mysteries of human existence, and found no wings to rise
above them. Said his partner, Herndon : "His melancholy dripped from him as he walked." But if a friend
met and heartily saluted him, he would answer with a
cordial " Howdy, howdy," and detain him to hear a com-
ical story, the fun dancing in his eyes and playing over
every feature.

The popular title of " Honest Abe " hit a central trait
in the man. His character and his mind were veracious
to the core. This is the quality which gives to his written
speeches their power and charm. One feels that the
speaker is always going as near as he can to the heart of
the matter. There are no mellifluous nothings. Every
word stands for something. His mind laid hold with
firm grasp on every fact it could reach. It combined
and interpreted its facts in the daylight of plain common sense. It confined itself to the solid earth ; its
movements were slow, but without pause or retreat. The
man was true, with a painful fidelity to the facts of each

present situation, weighing, testing, hesitating, while prophets and theorists rushed with fiery energy to their conclusions. But his path of action once chosen, he moved on as inflexibly as gravitation. Personal ambition he had in abundance; but he held it subject to a profound sense of justice and a sensitive humanity.

Lincoln's attitude toward slavery was that of the humane and conscientious men throughout the North who were not Abolitionists. He hated it; he opposed its extension; but, as existing in the Southern states, it had to him the sanction of an established political order, which could not be defied without inviting anarchy. In 1855 he wrote to his friend, J. F. Speed, of Kentucky :

"I acknowledge your rights and my obligations under the Constitution in regard to your slaves. I confess I hate to see the poor creatures hunted down, and caught, and carried back to their stripes and unrequited toils ; but I bite my lips and keep quiet. In 1841, you and I had together a tedious low-water trip in a steamboat from Louisville to St. Louis. You may remember, as well as I do, that from Louisville to the mouth of the Ohio there were on board ten or a dozen slaves shackled together with irons. That sight was a continued torment to me ; and I see something like it every time I touch the Ohio or any other slave border. It is not fair for you to assume that I have no interest in a thing which has, and continually exercises, the power of making me miserable. You ought rather to appreciate how much the great body of the Northern people do crucify their feelings, in order to maintain their loyalty to the Constitution and the Union. I do oppose the *extension* of slavery, because my judgment and feelings so prompt me ; and I am under no obligations to the contrary."

A mind which is deeply tenacious of concrete facts and chary of theories and abstractions, when it sometimes rises, perhaps suddenly, to a broad and commanding view, speaks with a deliberate weight of inmost conviction. It

is this feeling of solid reality which gives their majesty
to Lincoln's Gettysburg address and second inaugural.
Those utterances stand for us among the noblest chapters of that national history which Carlyle says makes
for every people its own Bible. It was with some such
illumination that Lincoln spoke in the address with
which he began his campaign against Douglas in 1858.

"A house divided against itself cannot stand. I believe this
government cannot endure permanently half slave and half
free. I do not expect the Union to be dissolved,—I do not
expect the house to fall; but I do expect it will cease to be
divided. It will become all one thing or all the other. Either
the opponents of slavery will arrest the further spread of it,
and place it where the public mind shall rest in the belief that
it is in the course of ultimate extinction, or its advocates will
push it forward till it shall become alike lawful in all the
states—old as well as new, North as well as South."

This declaration was followed by a lucid exposition
of that march of aggression by which successively the
barrier of the Missouri compromise had been thrown
down; then the permission to a territorial population to
exclude slavery had been refused by Congress; next a
Supreme Court decision given that slavery had an in-
alienable title to exist in all the territories; and a door
carefully left open in this same decision for a future
ruling that the master might take his slaves into the free
states. In the whole speech there was no passion and no
exaggeration. He summoned the North to resistance only
through the ballot-box. He went no further than opposition to any extension of slavery. The extinction of
slavery where it already existed, he anticipated as a
probability on broad philosophic grounds, but did not
for a moment regard it as the legitimate object of political action on the part of the North.

Lincoln, as Lamon narrates, read this speech in advance to a council of his friends, and they all, with the single exception of Herndon,—an old Abolitionist,—protested against it, as far in advance of the time, of doubtful truth, and full of danger to his prospects. Lincoln made sober answer that he was convinced its opinions were true, and needed to be spoken; if he was to go down because of saying it, then he chose to go down. " This nation cannot live on injustice !" The speech did injure his standing with the people of Illinois, and tended to his defeat in the immediate contest. It was arranged that the two rivals for the senatorship should address the people at the same place and time, in a series of joint debates. These debates were watched with great interest not only in Illinois but throughout the North. The subject discussed was mainly the question of congressional exclusion of slavery from the territories, as against "popular sovereignty." Each did his best to drive his opponent to disadvantageous positions. Each offered a series of questions to which the other was bound to reply. It was a tug of skilled wrestlers. Douglas's appeal was to the coarsely selfish man, jealous for his own rights and not sensitive to the rights of others. Democracy of the vulgar and self-assertive kind has never found a better mouth-piece. He was loud in proclaiming his own indifference to slavery; he " didn't care whether slavery was voted up or voted down." His plea was, in substance, " You have a right to go into a territory, and there you and your neighbors have the right to settle your own affairs as you please, and neither Congress nor anybody else has a right to interfere." He made great capital out of the prejudice, strong in Illinois, against the negro race; he represented Lincoln as a negro-lover, an Abolitionist, a foe to the South. Against these attacks, and in reply to Douglas's questions, Lincoln took ground—

which was quite consistent with all his utterances and sentiments up to that time — against any equality of the two races. He said, "I am not, nor ever have been, in favor of making voters or jurors of negroes, nor of qualifying them to hold office, nor to intermarry with white people; and I will say in addition to this that there is a physical difference between the white and the black races which I believe will forever forbid the two races living together on terms of social and political equality. And inasmuch as they cannot so live, while they do live together there must be the position of superior and inferior, and I, as much as any other man, am in favor of having the superior position assigned to the white man. I say upon this occasion, I do not perceive that, because the white man is to have the superior position, the negro should be denied everything."

The *Republican* said of the debates, two years later: "The judgment of all men of mind upon the Illinois canvass is in favor of Lincoln as against Douglas. Caleb Cushing said but recently that these debates showed Lincoln the superior of Douglas 'in every vital element of power'; and Mr. Cushing added what we believe is equally true, that 'the world does not yet know how much of a man Lincoln really is.'" "He handled Douglas," said the *Republican*, "as he would an eel — by main strength. Sometimes perhaps he hugged him so strongly that he slipped through his fingers." But the eel did not get away on the occasion when it most behooved him to do so. The weakest spot in Douglas's position was the contradiction between the Dred Scott decision — to which he had expressed his adherence — which carried slavery by its own right into every territory, and the idea of "popular sovereignty" by which each territorial population was its own master on the subject. About this inconsistency Douglas habitually threw a cloud of sophistication; his genius lay in covering up the real facts as much as Lincoln's in disclosing them. But among the questions which Lincoln in the course of debate was entitled to propound, he slipped into the middle of a series, of which the other inquiries were harmless conundrums, this query: " Can the people of a United States territory, in any lawful way, against the will of any citizen of the United States, exclude slavery from its limits?" It was a most legitimate question; it simply probed home the position of Douglas on the main topic at issue. But it impaled him on a fatal dilemma: if he said Yes, he lost his Southern support; if No, his Northern. Douglas so answered as to win in the field where he was then fighting. "It matters not," he said, " what way the Supreme Court may hereafter decide as to the abstract question whether slavery may or may not go into a territory under the Constitution,"—the weight of the already pronounced decision, as most people construed it, Douglas always belittled. "It matters not," he said; "the people have the lawful means to introduce or exclude it, as they please, for the reason that slavery cannot exist a day or an hour anywhere, unless it is supported by local police regulations. Those police regulations can only be established by the local legislature; and if the people are opposed to slavery, they will elect representatives to that body who will, by unfriendly legislation, effectually prevent the introduction of it into their midst." The reply might be satisfactory to the audience who heard it, but, as Lincoln had foreseen and predicted to his friends, it put Douglas in a position where the South would never accept him. That phrase, "unfriendly legislation," was fatal to him as a presidential candidate in the party controlled by the South.

At the opening of the canvass, Lincoln was aware of the dubious regard with which the Republican leaders elsewhere looked at his opposition to Douglas. In his opening speech he said :

"They remind us that he is a very great man, and that the largest of us are very small ones. Let this be granted. But 'a living dog is better than a dead lion.' Judge Douglas, if not a dead lion for this work, is at least a caged and toothless one. How can he oppose the advances of slavery ? He don't care anything about it. His avowed mission is impressing the 'public heart' to care nothing about it."

Meantime congressional and state elections were approaching throughout the country. The Dred Scott decision, the Lecompton scheme, the divisions in the Democracy, the weakness of Buchanan, had greatly strengthened the hands of the Republicans. In most of the doubtful states they were on more friendly terms with the anti-Lecompton Democrats than in Illinois, though not enough so to satisfy the *Republican*, which was eager for a more comprehensive policy. It went so far as to actively favor, for a time, the adoption of a bona fide "Popular Sovereignty" doctrine in place of the party's original dogma of congressional exclusion. It urged that Kansas had shown how certainly the Northern immigration would predominate in the new territories ; that practical results were more important than a theoretical consistency, and that it was equally safe and politic to meet half-way the anti-Lecompton Democrats. But as to these, most of the Republicans evidently opined that it was not necessary for the mountain to go half-way to meet Mahomet. The popular wind was blowing too fair and too strong for them to care to go upon the other tack. Moreover, the theory that Congress should leave the territorial populations to settle the slavery questions for themselves never found favor among either the most strenuous foes or friends of slavery. Both of these were

eager to grasp and wield the full power of the central
government on the question they had most at heart. In
the Republican ranks, voices were becoming louder and
clearer as to the magnitude and intensity of the whole
struggle. Seward in New York made a declaration which
was equivalent to Lincoln's "House divided against
itself." Said he:

"The United States must, and will, sooner or later, become
either entirely a slave-holding nation or entirely a free-labor
nation. Either the cotton and rice fields of South Carolina
and the sugar plantations of Louisiana will ultimately be tilled
by free labor, and Charleston and New Orleans become marts
for legitimate merchandise alone, or else the rye-fields and
wheat-fields of Massachusetts and New York must again be
surrendered by their farmers to slave culture and to the pro-
duction of slaves, and Boston and New York become once more
markets for trade in the bodies and souls of men."

He declared that one of these alternatives must be the
issue of the "irrepressible conflict" between slavery and
freedom. The *Republican* (November 13, 1858) said that
these utterances had been widely misinterpreted, as if
they conveyed a menace of direct political action against
slavery in the slave states; although in this very speech
Mr. Seward disclaimed any purpose or expectation of
giving universal freedom "otherwise than through the
action of the several states coöperating with the federal
government, and all acting in conformity with their respective constitutions." Nevertheless, the *Republican*
held his bold prediction to be incautious, improbable of
fulfillment, and likely to injure Mr. Seward and the party.

Massachusetts had in 1857 chosen a Republican state
government. Banks, fresh from his brilliant career as
Speaker of the House, had been nominated with enthusiasm by the Republicans and one wing of the Americans, and elected over Gardner, whom the rest of the

Americans supported. His administration was able and successful, and an easy victory fell to him and the party in 1858. He could scarcely be claimed by the Conservative, certainly not by the Radical, wing of the party. The *Republican* was his cordial supporter. In this year the intensifying anti-slavery sentiment of the party — though it still in its resolutions stood steadily on constitutional ground — found voice through the president of the state convention, John A. Andrew. "I believe," said he, "in the Republican party, because I believe that slavery, the servitude of humanity, has no business to exist anywhere; because it has no business to exist and no right to be supported where the sun shines or the grass grows or water runs."

The *Republican* foretold ill to the party in the doubtful states for want of a broader policy. On the 12th of October — election day in Pennsylvania, Ohio, and Indiana — it said: "The undertow of politics is running against the Republicans." But the next day's news was of victory along the whole line. The voice of the great central states was decisive. "Mr. Buchanan," said the *Republican*, October 16, "has been in office a little less than two years, and his Administration and himself are practically overthrown. The popular voice is declared against him and his policy, and he falls no more to rise. The South, which has flattered and fooled him, will forsake him in the end, for his power is gone. *Sic semper tyrannis!* . . . It is now plainly seen that it is in the power of those who are opposed to slavery, and in favor of free labor, to elect the next President of the United States."

The November elections confirmed the October verdict. The Republicans had obtained a majority in the House of Representatives. The Senate was still Democratic. But Kansas was free beyond reversal, and the Republican party was on the high road to possession of the government. In Illinois, the Republicans had a small majority of the entire vote, but by the apportionment of districts it fell out that a Democratic legislature was chosen, and Douglas was reëlected. He returned to Washington, to be deposed from the chairmanship of the Committee on Territories by the Southern and Administration influence, but still the foremost man of his party in the estimation of the people. Lincoln returned to private life and to comparative obscurity.

# CHAPTER XXII.

## JOHN BROWN.

IN reality, as we now see, after the elections of 1858 the slave power began to feel itself on the defensive. Yet it still grasped at fresh conquests. A demand was urged by some of the leaders that Congress should enact a code for the regulation and protection of slavery throughout the territories; it being clear that whatever abstract right it possessed there under the Dred Scott decision would avail little without active Federal protection. The Administration conducted some ineffectual negotiations with Mexico for the purchase of more territory. There was a little talk about buying Cuba. An American adventurer, William Walker, made repeated attempts at conquests in Nicaragua, without effective hindrance from the Administration, and with considerable sympathy from the South. There was a greatly increased activity in the importation of African slaves to Cuba, and numerous vessels were sent out from New York for the traffic. Our government had been notably remiss in fulfilling its treaty stipulations with England for coöperation in the suppression of the slave trade; but when some of the English cruisers in the West Indies went a step beyond discretion, in examining suspected vessels under the American flag, our government bristled with wrath, war vessels were sent, and congressmen of both parties threatened loudly. England conceded the rights of the flag; and the exemption from search, for which we had forty years before fought a war, that we might protect our sailors from impressment, without gaining a word of explicit concession, was now formally recognized in order to guard our sensitive honor against the inspection of ships which from their appearance might be slavers. But the Administration was roused to bestir itself against the trade, and a number of captures were made by our cruisers. The crew of one slaver, the *Echo*, captured with her freight of misery on board, were, against the clearest evidence, acquitted by a Charleston jury. One or two cargoes of Africans were landed at the South, and there was some agitation by Southern newspapers and politicians in favor of legalizing the traffic.

But none of these projects, for a congressional slave code, for the acquisition of slave territory, or for the re-opening of the African slave trade, had any prospect of success. The power of successful aggression had passed away from the slave-holding interest. The leaders of that interest saw in the steady march of the Republican party to power the approaching end of their own long control of the government. Meantime fresh events were teaching to both sections the irreconcilable hostility of their sentiments.

On the 16th of October, 1859, a company of nineteen men, led by John Brown, entered the little town of Harper's Ferry in Virginia, seized the United States Armory, killed, wounded, or captured several of those who resisted them, and maintained their position for thirty hours, when they were overcome by a company of United States marines. Eight of them, including two sons of Brown, were killed in the fighting; five escaped; and six, with Brown among them, were captured. The first news of the event — in a time of absolute civil peace and comparative political quiet — amazed the whole country. Then, as its significance, as an attempt to free slaves by force and on the widest scale, was perceived, the South was filled with alarm and anger. The chronic latent dread of every Southern household was that of a negro insurrection. Brown was at once believed to be the product and representative, if not the direct agent, of the Republican party. Behind his single form the imagination of the South saw looming the whole power of the North. It read in the Harper's Ferry affair the menace of invasion, united with the horrors of servile insurrection. The Southern people did not credit the loyalty of the Republicans to the Constitution. That strong anti-slavery sentiment should co-exist with scrupulous respect for the legal rights of slavery was beyond their belief, and perhaps beyond their comprehension. Their own friends at the North, of the Democratic and "Union" parties, habitually encouraged this distrust by their charges against the Republicans. These political allies of the South now made haste to fix the responsibility for John Brown on the Republican party. What they said insincerely for political effect, the South believed with passion and with fear.

The majority of Northern people could ill comprehend the alarm of the South. They did not appreciate how slavery was interlinked with every usage and sentiment of Southern life; how much of kindliness and mutual attachment softened its rigors and quieted the master's conscience; nor, on the other hand, how the dangers attendant on it, both real and imaginary, environed every plantation and every fireside. The alarm which Brown's raid inspired was to most Northerners inscrutable and almost despicable. The Republicans, too, were so far from any responsibility for Brown, or any disposition to favor projects like his, that they scarcely felt solicitude even to defend themselves against the imputation. Their attention, and that of the whole country, was soon closely fastened on John Brown himself.

Brown was a man of conscience, courage, and simplicity. Living amid a complex civilization, he was governed by ideas few and simple as those of an ancient Hebrew. He was a devout Presbyterian, and his library was the Bible. He had gone with his sons to Kansas, where he became a leader in the border warfare. Most of the free-state settlers had the aversion to violence which characterized the people of the Northern states, they stood on the defensive, and fought only when obliged to. Brown was of a different make; peaceful and inoffensive when not assailed, yet in a worthy cause of quarrel he was as ready to take up arms as the ordinary citizen is to take his case to the courts. He was prompt not only to repel the invaders but to retaliate on them. He accepted the situation as one of open warfare. Among other reprisals he crossed the Missouri line, and set free a few slaves; and this seems to have suggested to him the demonstration at Harper's Ferry. He fell into disfavor with his party; his way of settling the issue was by arms, theirs was by first exhausting all civil remedies. Leaving Kansas, bereft of a son in the conflict, he meditated an attack on the whole institution of slavery. The moral question was entirely simple to a mind like his: Slavery was wrong,—then make war on it. His plan was to seize the arms at Harper's Ferry and establish in the mountains of western Virginia a fortified camp of refuge, to which the slaves should be invited to flee. His ultimate expectation seems to have been to so unsettle and disturb slave property that the institution would not be worth maintaining and would collapse. It was a scheme that miscalculated almost every element

in the situation,—the temper of the slaves, the strength
of the government, the disposition of the Southern and
Northern peoples. The attempt broke down at the very
outset: if it had gained a brief success, it would have
been put down by the whole power of the nation. The
Northern people, two years later, showed themselves ready
to fight in defense of the Union, but scarcely a handful
of them would have opposed the Federal government in
putting down a slave insurrection, had Brown's attempt
gained headway. That attempt in its failure contributed
to great results; but there is no reason to suppose Brown
foresaw those results. There was no large forethought
in his plan;—it was inspired by a generous heart, a
brave will, and an erratic mind. He had in his confidence
only a few Massachusetts men, who were impatient of
debate and delay and longed to see a blow struck—Dr.
Samuel G. Howe, George L. Stearns, T. W. Higginson,
and F. B. Sanborn. They were not Republicans, nor in
any sense representative either of the Republican party,
the Abolitionists, or the Northern people. Several years
later, Mr. Sanborn was a writer for the *Republican;* at
this time he had no connection with it.

It was Brown's failure which immortalized him. As a
helpless prisoner the grand traits in his character shone
clearly. In counsel short-sighted, in action baffled, he
suffered with heroism and faith. During his imprisonment the simple courage which marked every deed and
word impressed the imagination and won the heart of
all mankind, except that section to which his act was
a menace. He was a fanatic, as all men recognized;
but to the South the inspiration of his fanaticism
appeared to be hostility to their rights of property and
their social order, while the North recognized that, in
however crude a way, he was aiming at obedience to the
Golden Rule. The North, disowning his act, yet hon-

ored him as a hero and mourned his death as that of a martyr. The South saw the sympathy, and disbelieved the disavowal. The hearts of the two sections were so far apart that the unclasping of hands was sure to follow.

The impression which John Brown made at this time upon the Northern people at large is fairly illustrated by the comments of the *Republican* — wholly dissociated as that paper was from the extreme anti-slavery men. On the same day when it reported the conversation of the wounded old hero with the political leaders who gathered about him — in which his nature towered above self-seeking and worldly men like "the conscience of a saint among his earthly members" — it said of him, after referring to personal knowledge of him through his residence at one time in Springfield:

"He is so constituted that when he gets possessed of an idea he carries it out with unflinching fidelity to all its logical consequences, as they seem to him, hesitating at no absurdity and deterred by no unpleasant consequences to himself personally. He is a Presbyterian in his faith, and feels that it is for this very purpose that God has reared him up. This is evident in the answers given to his catechism, as he lay chained and bloody, with fierce eyes against him and hearts thirsting for his blood. His perfect coolness and self-possession, his evident truthfulness and transparent sincerity, and the utter absence of fear in his manner, commanded the respect of all about him. The universal feeling is that John Brown is a hero, — a misguided and insane man, but nevertheless inspired with a genuine heroism. He has a large infusion of the stern old Puritan element in him."

The paper protested, October 24, against the haste and unfairness of his trial.

"The whole manner in which the trial is conducted shows that the Virginians have not recovered from their original fright. They scent a rescue in the air, surround their poor wounded and worn prisoners with bayonets, and promise to bring them to the gallows within thirty days. Let them go ahead in their crazy cowardice, and see if their 'ain roof-trees' are any firmer for it."

Of his speech on receiving his sentence, it said, November 4:

"In calm dignity, in the conscious rectitude of good intentions, in an honest and hearty faith in Christianity, it has in it heroic elements that elevate it toward the sublime. . . . If he had been a weak man or a wicked man, a felon in the common acceptation of that word, when the sentence was pronounced upon him there would have been a general and tumultuous demonstration of satisfaction in the Charlestown court-room. Instead of that, the impressive silence was broken only by the clapping of a single pair of hands, and the people were shocked and mortified that even one man should have been found in Virginia who appreciated so poorly the character of the prisoner and the nature of his condemnation. This scene shows the wonderful impression made by Brown upon those about him. It is this great sincerity and heroic self-sacrifice to what he believed to be right that gave him such influence over the men who enlisted in his scheme, and that has so impressed the Virginians with respect, from Governor Wise down, and that will make it a difficult thing to hang him."

And again, November 12:

"We can conceive of no event that could so deepen the moral hostility of the people of the free states to slavery as this execution. This is not because the acts of Brown are generally approved, for they are not. It is because the nature and spirit of the man are seen to be great and noble, and everybody feels that he acted from feelings that do honor to human nature, and that are to be condemned only because they were not directed by wisdom and soundness of mind. John Brown is neither a traitor nor a murderer in intention. His death will be a result of his own folly, to be sure, but that will not prevent his being considered a martyr to his hatred of oppression, and all who sympathize with him in that sentiment will find their hatred grow stronger and deeper as they contemplate his death. Nobody can respect an institution to the safety of which the death of the too ardent lover of liberty is essential. If Virginia were wise she would see this and be magnanimous; but she is neither wise nor magnanimous in anything that concerns her property in human brains and bones, and so we suppose the appointed hanging will occur."

Defiant responses came from the Southern press. Said the Richmond *Whig*, November 16:

"Virginia and the South are ready to face all the consequences of the execution of old Brown and his associates. Though it convert the whole Northern people without exception into furious, armed, abolition invaders, yet old Brown will be hung! That is the stern and irreversible decree, not only of the authorities of Virginia, but of the people of Virginia without a dissenting voice. And therefore Virginia and the people of Virginia will treat with the contempt they deserve all the craven appeals of Northern men in behalf of old Brown's pardon. The miserable old traitor and murderer belongs to the gallows, and the gallows will have its own, in spite of all the threatenings and maledictions of the North and the world combined."

Upon the morning of his execution, December 2, the *Republican* said: "The calmest man in all Virginia to-day will be he who knows that he will be in another world before the sun has reached its meridian." And so it was. The old hero walked serenely out of his prison; said, when asked if he suffered from fear, that he had always had a constitutional insensibility to physical dread, and had suffered far more from bashfulness than he ever did from fear; and, with demeanor as simple and unconscious as a man going to his night's rest, ascended the gallows and met his death. His fellow-prisoners were executed a few days later.

On the day on which John Brown was hanged, the church bells were tolled in Springfield, as in many another Northern town. Said the *Republican*, next morning:

"John Brown still lives. The great state of Virginia has hung his venerable body upon the ignominious gallows, and released John Brown himself to join the 'noble army of martyrs.' There need be no tears for him. Few men die so happily, so satisfied with time, place, and circumstance, as did he. . . A Christian man hung by Christians for acting upon his convictions of duty,—a brave man hung for a chivalrous and self-sacrificing deed of humanity—a philanthropist hung for seeking the liberty of oppressed men. No outcry about violated law can cover up the essential enormity of a deed like this."

When the Northern voice thus applauded John Brown, the South believed that the Northern heart fully approved the act. It discredited all disclaimers of such approval as insincere or half-hearted. If we can imagine a permanent alienation and hostility between the poorer and the richer classes of New England; the sympathy of the Western people given to the New England operatives, and their employers denounced as criminals; and a peaceful town like Springfield invaded by a band of armed men from the West, its citizens shot down, and its operatives called on to rise in arms;—if we can imagine the leader of the invaders treated by the Western people as a hero, and his execution as a judicial murder, though with disclaimers of any intention to follow his example,—we may then appreciate how the South was affected by the act of John Brown and by the spirit in which the North regarded it.

And in truth, John Brown's death went far to reveal to the North itself how irreconcilable was its hostility to slavery. Its loftiest and serenest thinker, Emerson, said :

"Our blind statesmen go up and down, with committees of vigilance and safety, hunting for the origin of this new heresy. They will need a very vigilant committee indeed to find its birth-place, and a very strong force to root it out. For the arch-Abolitionist, older than Brown, and older than the Shenandoah Mountains, is Love, whose other name is Justice, which was before Alfred, before Lycurgus, before slavery, and will be after it."

JOHN BROWN. 255

# CHAPTER XXIII.

## THE ELECTION OF LINCOLN.

THE session of the new Congress which followed close on the John Brown raid was full of wordy storms. The Southern members interpreted Republicanism in the light of that event. Their leading men declared that sooner than submit to the rule of the Republican party, their section would leave the Union. No great questions of practical legislation were under debate. In the House the chief text of discussion was the election of a Speaker, and a resolution condemning the approvers and indorsers of a noted book, Helper's "Impending Crisis," a vigorous exposition of the folly of the slave system, which had been used as an anti-slavery campaign document in the border states. The resolution was especially aimed at John Sherman, the Republican candidate for the speakership, who had given to the book a qualified approval. In the Senate, the main discussion was upon resolutions introduced by Jefferson Davis, and embodying the Southern ultimatum;—the rebuke of all anti-slavery agitators, the enforcement of the fugitive slave law and repeal of the personal liberty laws, and the recognition of property in slaves as an indefeasible right of territorial settlers, entitled to congr ssional protection. The Senate finally adopted these resolutions, nearly by a party vote. Only six Republicans opposed

256

the resolution as to fugitive slaves. Douglas stood upon his Popular Sovereignty ground, but unsupported except by Senator Pugh of Ohio. He professed entire deference to the Supreme Court, but could find nothing conclusive in the Dred Scott decision, and declared that whenever a territorial legislature should prohibit slavery, and the prohibition be brought before the Court, the decision then pronounced as to its constitutionality should be final. He also introduced a bill to prevent invasions of one state from another; and on the whole steered the bark of his personal fortunes with wonderful skill amid the storms born of genuine convictions and passionate sentiments. In the House, meantime, the Republicans had left the talking mostly to their opponents, and had shown the discipline and tactics of a powerful young party, educated in opposition and confident in the near prospect of full victory. They at last exchanged Sherman for a candidate regarded as more conservative, William Pennington of New Jersey, and at once gained the necessary votes to elect him Speaker. The salient feature of the session in both houses was the emphatic declaration of Southern leaders that their constituents would never submit to the government of the country by the Republican party. They gave the loudest warning of impending secession and disunion, should Seward, or any man of like principles, be elected president. Most of the Republicans regarded this talk as mere bluster. Almost the only men at the North who treated it seriously were those who were in close political affiliation with the South. The New York *Herald* was fanning the flame of excitement. A Washington correspondent of the *Republican* — Mr. Bowles apparently — wrote, December 9 :

"It is amusing to see the greed with which the *Herald* is snatched up and devoured on its earliest arrival here in the evening; and, what is worse, to see the simplicity of these

Southern fellows who seem to pin their whole faith upon it. Where Northern men look at it only for amusement, as they would look at *Punch* or *Frank Leslie*, Southern men swallow it gravely with a sigh and a knowing shake of the head."

The *Republican* declares, December 13, that the "Union meetings" held in the great Northern cities are worse than useless, because they are managed by an insignificant clique of men, whose aim — with a few patriotic exceptions such as Everett — is to save trade and make Democratic votes; and they mislead the South by representing that their little coteries have a monopoly of love of the Union in their section. At the North, said the paper, December 14, there are but two disunion papers, the *Liberator* in Boston and the *Standard* in New York, — and they advise a dissolution by the harmless means of staying away from the ballot-box. No politician, no Democratic or Republican paper, no caucus or convention, in the North raises a voice for disunion, while at the South disunion is rampant everywhere, and unrebuked.

The South was in deadly earnest, and gave ample proof of it. The proscription of anti-slavery men went on with such vigor as never before. From Berea, in Kentucky, a whole company of anti-slavery men were forcibly driven away. Cases of expulsion and violence all over the South were constantly reported during the winter. The exclusion of anti-slavery documents from the mails was enforced with new zeal, and with the assent of the Post Office Department at Washington. In many of the states, postmasters refused to deliver to subscribers papers like the *Tribune* and the *Republican*. John Brown had sent home to the "business and bosoms" of millions, as a keen personal apprehension, ideas which had before been hardly more than the politicians' stock in trade.

The South wrongly believed that the North meant aggression, and stood ready to grasp at secession as a remedy. The North wrongly believed that the Southern excitement was a transient fever fit, fostered as a political maneuver. The few Cassandras of the time were discredited; their sentiments were so alien to the Northern heart, that their predictions fell idly on Northern ears. In Faneuil Hall, in December, Caleb Cushing declared of the Republican party:

"A band of drunken mutineers have seized hold of the opinion of this commonwealth — the avowed and proclaimed enemies of the Constitution of the United States. . . . And so the good ship of state drifts,—drifts, with the storm still howling around her,—drifts into the gulf of perdition, with the black flag of the pirate hoisted at the mizzen,—aye, and the piratical death's head at the fore,—black, black, black, from deck to keelson,—I say the good ship of state drags on to perdition."

At such talk, as at the threats of disunion by the Orrs and Wises and Davises and Toombses of the South, most Northern people only laughed. The presidential campaign, the decisive game in the long controversy, went on at the North like the campaigns before it; — with the maneuvers and intrigues of aspirants and their friends; the wonted play of ambition and office-seeking; while the people continued their farming and trading, discussed good-naturedly the parties and their candidates, and cast their votes with their wonted confidence in the finality of a popular decision.

The Democratic Convention met at Charleston in the last days of April. Douglas, ostracized by the Administration, and almost alone in the Senate, was very strong with the people. He had for them the attraction which a virile, audacious man — a dominant personality, a natural leader — always exercises upon the crowd, whatever may be the ideas which he represents. He had behind him that great element of the Northern democracy, which, like the Republicans, was provoked to resistance of the South's dictatorship, but, unlike the Republicans, cared very little about slavery. At the same time he had trimmed his sails so shrewdly to conciliate the South, that it was by no means without hope of using him eventually as a subservient ally. But it insisted that the convention must first of all pronounce the pro-slavery shibboleth. There was a hot fight upon two sets of resolutions. The friends of Douglas favored a reaffirmation of the Cincinnati platform of 1856, with the addition only of a clause declaring that doubtful points as to constitutional interpretation were to be decided by the Supreme Court. But the thorough-going Southerners insisted on an explicit declaration that slavery could in no way be excluded from the territories. For the Douglas men to accept this would have been humiliation for them and sure defeat for the party. Neither he nor any other candidate could carry the doubtful Northern states on such a platform. On the other hand, the deference to the Supreme Court which his friends offered to pledge left the old convenient ambiguity on which to win votes, with an open door for all the South wanted, through a Democratic Administration and Court. If the question were merely one of dexterous strategy for winning the presidential election, the advantage lay all on the side of the Douglas resolutions. But the South was in dead earnest for something more than the presidency, — for an absolute, unequivocal guaranty that slave property should be as fully recognized and protected as any other property. The Douglas resolutions were carried, and thereupon the members from the Gulf states left the house, and organized a separate convention.

Even then Douglas was not at once nominated; the Administration had still many friends left in the convention, including its president, Caleb Cushing; and it was decided that the old rule making a two-thirds vote necessary for nomination should be construed as including in the canvass of membership the places of the seceders,—and Douglas could not obtain a two-thirds vote in this case. Finally the convention adjourned for several weeks, to meet in Baltimore.

When it re-assembled there at the end of June, there was another struggle. Douglas delegations, which had been elected from some states to fill the places of the seceders, were admitted against a protest of a minority of the convention. Thereupon this minority, including Cushing, General Butler, and a majority of the Massachusetts delegates, added themselves to the original seceders. Those who remained then nominated Douglas. The second place on the ticket was given to Herschel V. Johnson, of Georgia.

The rival convention also adjourned, to meet in Baltimore, at the same time with the other—the two bodies being nearly equal in numbers. It re-affirmed the Cincinnati platform, but dispelled its ambiguity by added resolutions, declaring that so long as the territorial government exists—being in its nature temporary and provisional—all citizens of the United States have an equal right to settle, without the impairing of any of their rights of person or property, either by congressional or territorial legislation; and that Congress is bound to protect those rights—including the slave-owner's—until, upon organization as a state, the people decide the question of slavery for themselves. The convention nominated John C. Breckinridge, of Kentucky, for the presidency, and Joseph Lane, of Oregon, for the vice-presidency.

The *Republican*, June 25, said:

" We rejoice that there has been at last a determined and successful North in a Democratic National Convention; and we honor Stephen A. Douglas, that he has had the firmness and the will to lead it. We rejoice, not chiefly because this fact dissevers and destroys the Democratic party, and renders a Republican triumph easy and welcome to the country; but because, party aside, it is an important element in the political revolution now rapidly coming to a head, and in the pacification of the sectional strife which has raged so bitterly for the past twelve years. . . . The fight and the victory of the Northern Democracy are an anti-slavery fight and an anti-slavery victory. . . . The way is now easy to the completion of the revolution by the entrance of the Republican party into the possession of the government, with the acquiescence of the great mass of the people of the nation, and with the disposition on all sides to give it a fair practical trial."

Between the Charleston and Baltimore conventions, the Republicans had met at Chicago. George Ashmun, of Springfield, was made president of the convention. It adopted a long series of resolutions, which condemned disunion and inter-state invasion; were silent as to the fugitive slave and personal liberty laws; and on the territorial question took direct issue with the Southern position, by denying the right either of Congress or a territorial legislature to legalize slavery in a territory. The great interest of the gathering centered in the struggle for the nomination, a struggle principally between the friends and foes of Mr. Seward. He was unquestionably the foremost man of his party. All that could prevent the nomination was the doubt whether he could be elected. Thurlow Weed led the party of Seward, Evarts was its foremost spokesman on the floor, and Greeley was active among his opponents. Mr. Bowles, who reported the convention for

his paper, was an admirer of Seward and of Weed.
But he thought that the consideration of expediency
should under the circumstances be decisive, and that to
nominate Seward was to seriously imperil the victory of
the party. The *Republican's* favorite candidate had been
Governor Banks, but he found no support in the convention. Seward's leading rivals had been supposed to
be Senator Chase, and Edward Bates of Missouri — the
latter supported by the *Tribune*. Lincoln became prominent only at the last. He had an enthusiastic support
from the West. Simon Cameron was a nominal candidate, and controlled the Pennsylvania delegation. Lamon
circumstantially narrates that Lincoln's friends, without
his knowledge, made a bargain with Cameron's representatives for the votes of the delegation, to be repaid
by a place for Cameron in Lincoln's cabinet; and that a
similar compact was made in behalf of Caleb B. Smith,
of Indiana, — both agreements being reluctantly kept by
Lincoln when he was told of them. The argument that
he could carry the doubtful states was effectively used
with other delegations. The great crowd of spectators
were loud for him. On the first ballot, Seward was far
ahead; on the second, Pennsylvania changed from Cameron to Lincoln, and he came up abreast of Seward; on
the third, four votes from Ohio turned the scale, and,
with universal acquiescence, Lincoln was nominated.
Experience in administration he had none, and in legislation very little. For the problems which a Republican
president would encounter, his capacity was almost unknown. He was recognized as an able debater, a man
thoroughly honest, by origin and associations identified
with the common people, and very popular in his own
state. His nomination over Seward was supposed to be
the preference of unobjectionable mediocrity to greatness
which had made dangerous enemies. For the vice-presi-

dency, Hannibal Hamlin, of Maine, was nominated. That the two candidates on the ticket were both from the North—in 1860 as in 1856—was contrary to the general usage of parties, and was an illustration of the "sectionalism" urged against the Republicans. If they had nominated a vice-president from the South, he would have been fortunate if he met with nothing worse than exile from his home.

There was a fourth ticket in the field. John Bell, of Tennessee, and Edward Everett were nominated by a "Constitutional Union" convention which met at Baltimore early in May. It was a sort of remnant of the old Whig party. Its resolutions were simply a declaration for "The Constitution of the Country, the Union of the States, and the Enforcement of the Laws." It represented an attempt to make the preservation of the Union and the Constitution the supreme issue, and to wholly ignore the slavery question. The result showed that this was the predominant sentiment in the great tier of border slave states. But the party was laughed at by the strenuous combatants on either side. "Its ticket," said the *Republican*, "is universally respectable. It is worthy to be printed on gilt-edged satin paper, laid away in a box of musk, and kept there. . . . It is the party of no idea and no purpose. . . . It might as well have taken the multiplication table and the decalogue for its platform as the Constitution and the Union." Yet this party recognized what the *Republican* and its party wholly failed to appreciate—that the Union was in imminent danger.

The campaign at the North was a quiet, decorous, and almost languid one. The election of Lincoln was foreseen from the first. There were no "burning questions" of immediate practical administration, such as Kansas had furnished in 1856. The broad question at issue was whether a party disposed to restrict and discourage slavery wherever the Constitution gave it scope to do so, was to administer the government. Specific questions other than that of the territories were little discussed on either side. The South gave the most substantial issue to the canvass, by the threat of secession if the Republicans were successful. Douglas, being questioned during a speech at Norfolk, Va., declared that the election of Lincoln would not justify secession, and he would support a Republican administration in putting down nullification by force. He asked that Breckinridge would state his position on this question, but Breckinridge took no notice of the inquiry. The North remained incredulous of the South's purpose of disunion, but the menace of it was recognized as giving significance to the election. The *Republican* thus spoke, August 25, of " The Issues of this Campaign":

" The South, through the mouth of many of its leading politicians and journals, defies the North to elect Abraham Lincoln to the presidency. It threatens secession in case he shall be elected. It arrogantly declares that he shall never take his seat. It passes resolutions of the most outrageous and insolent character, insulting every man who dares to vote for what they call a ' Black Republican.' To make a long matter very short and plain, they claim the privilege of conducting the government in all the future, as they have in all the past, for their own benefit and in their own way, with the alternative of dissolving the Union of the states. Now, if the non-slave-holding people have any spirit at all, they will settle this question at once and forever. Look at the history of the last two administrations, in which the slave interest has had undisputed sway. This sway, the most disgraceful and shameless of anything in the history of the government, must not be thrown off or else the Union will be dissolved. Let's try it! Are we forever to be governed by a slave-holding minority? Will the passage of four years more of misrule make it any easier for the majority to assume its functions?

"There are many reasons why we desire to see this experiment tried this fall. If the majority cannot rule the country without the secession of the minority, it is time the country knew it. If the country can only exist under the rule of an oligarchy, let the fact be demonstrated at once, and let us change our institutions. We desire to see the experiment tried, because we wish to have the Southern people, who have been blinded and cheated by the politicians, learn that a 'Black Republican' respects the requirements of the Constitution and will protect their interests. Harmony between the two sections of this country can never be secured until the South has learned that the North is not its enemy but its best friend. We desire to see it tried, that the whole horde of corrupt officials at Washington may be swept by the board, and something of decency and purity introduced there. We desire to see it, that the government may be restored to its original integrity. And any Northern man who has not pluck enough to stand up and help do this thing is a paltroon. It will be tried, and our minority friends may make up their mind to it."

Just before the State Republican Convention, Governor Banks declined a renomination. The *Republican* enthusiastically declared for Mr. Dawes as his successor. Against John A. Andrew's nomination it objected that his "more than Republican position" on the slavery question made him an inappropriate representative of the party, and would repel some moderate men. In the convention, the western Massachusetts delegates were not fully united upon Mr. Dawes, and he received but 326 votes to 723 for Mr. Andrew. The *Republican's* comment was, August 30:

"We do not believe this a wise or politic nomination; yet we have no doubt he will prove a wise and politic governor. He has a warm heart but a cool head; he may be hot and extreme in individual expression, going beyond, as he often does, the lines of the Republican organization and platform, but he feels keenly the responsibilities of power and follows kindly the conservatising influences of position. . . The Republicans can lose 10,000 votes on Mr. Andrew and not endanger his election. His John Brown sympathies and speeches, his Garrisonian affiliations, his negro-training predilections and all that sort of extreme anti-slaveryism with which his record abounds, will be trumpeted far and wide in the state to injure him, and out of it to harm Lincoln; and though it will doubtless have its effect in frightening timid and conservative recruits, it will strengthen others to labor, and can hardly anywhere change or endanger results."

But Andrew was the man for the time. From the days of the Liberty party he had been identified with constitutional opposition to slavery. He was lion-hearted and woman-hearted. He represented the purest conscience, the clearest intelligence, the most earnest purpose, of New England — and at last the New England idea was to be tried out against the South Carolina idea.

While the South was imputing to the North the most hostile designs against slavery, no other action against it was intended or expected among the Republicans than the gradual appearance of emancipation as a local political issue in the border states, and their slow conversion to freedom, and the encouragement of a Republican party at the South by the influence of the Administration. "What changes may occur within the next half-century," said the *Republican*, October 20, 1860, "to hasten the work of negro emancipation on this continent, no one can foresee, but present appearances indicate its gradual retreat southward, and an irrepressible conflict in the slave states, protracted long after the question has been completely removed from national politics."

It was the division of their opponents that gave the election to the Republicans. Of the popular vote,

Lincoln received about 1,860,000, Douglas 1,370,000, Breckinridge 840,000, and Bell 590,000. In the electoral college, Lincoln had 180 votes, Breckinridge 72, Bell 39, and Douglas 12. Lincoln had the electoral vote of every Northern state save New Jersey, which was divided between him and Douglas; Douglas had in addition only the vote of Missouri; Bell carried Kentucky, Tennessee, and Virginia; and the other Southern states were for Breckinridge. Massachusetts gave Andrew 104,000 votes, Beach (Douglas) 35,000, Lawrence (Bell) 24,000, and Butler (Breckinridge) 6000.

" To completely remove the question of slavery from national politics," leaving each state to slowly work out the problem for itself — that was the expectation with which the *Republican*, a sagacious, representative New England newspaper, welcomed the approaching presidency of Abraham Lincoln. The North for the most part looked for a subsidence of all slavery agitations, and the direction of the government's energies to promote the material prosperity of white people in general, instead of as heretofore the exclusive interest of the slaveholding states. The Abolitionists were little elated — freedom for those in bondage scarcely looked nearer for a Republican victory. The South was looking forward to a career as an independent nation. The four million slaves looked for no change in their lot, and were either unconscious of the struggle or indifferent respecting its issues.

# CHAPTER XXIV.

## SECESSION.

THE result of the election was no sooner known than the South Carolinians began to take action for the secession of their state with a vigor which allowed no doubt of the seriousness of their purpose. An energetic movement in the same direction began at once in all the Gulf and cotton states. The North was almost as much surprised as if it had received no warning. Mr. Seward had said toward the close of the canvass: "I do not think these threats before election are evidences of revolution and disunion after election, for the simple reason that I have always found that a man who does intend to strike a fatal blow does not give notice so long beforehand." Such reasoning was good as against the idea of a secret plot of a few conspirators, to which the North was long inclined to impute the origin of secession. But in truth the movement toward it was as open, and its causes as patent, as in the case of any other revolution. The South saw in the election of Lincoln the triumph of a party whose central principle and motive was hostility to the South's most characteristic institution. The avowed doctrine of the Republican party was the exclusion of slavery from the territories. The sentiment which underlay and inspired that doctrine was dislike to slavery in itself and everywhere; — so much

the South knew, and it had no faith that the sentiment
would be restrained in its expression by that loyalty to
the Constitution which the Republicans professed. Its
unbelief was not so totally unfounded as the Republicans
themselves supposed. The sentiment which lies deepest
at the heart of a man or a party has a constant tendency
to draw into line with itself the workings of the mind,
to convert the head, and finally to direct the act. Beyond
question, a Republican administration would give effective aid to any party of emancipation that should grow
up within a slave state. Such a party was already
formidable in Missouri, and was likely soon to spread
through the border states. An influence vast though
indirect would be exerted to loosen the hold of the slave
power on the Southern people. So far the Southern
leaders were right in their apprehensions,— slavery was
menaced in its own home by the election of Lincoln.

But the menace was a remote and indirect one, and at
this point the Southern people misjudged. They imputed
to the Republicans sentiments and purposes of active
aggression such as even the Abolitionists had never entertained. Thus in Georgia's declaration of secession, one
of the ablest documents of its class, and attributed to
Toombs, it is said of the party which had just elected
Lincoln:

"The prohibition of slavery in the territories, hostility to it
everywhere, the equality of the white and the black races, disregard of all constitutional guaranties in its favor, were boldly
proclaimed by its leaders and applauded by its followers."

This was the ordinary tone of the Southern politicians
and newspapers. Charges of disloyalty to the Constitution and indifference to the Union were constantly and
freely made at the North by the Democratic and "Unionist" opponents of the Republicans. Douglas said in the

Senate in January, 1860, that the Harper's Ferry outrage was the natural, logical, and inevitable result of the doctrines and teachings of the Republican party, as expressed in the party platform, by the party presses, and in the speeches of the party leaders. Up to the election and afterward, the Boston *Courier* — the representative of a party which included such men as Everett and Winthrop — habitually charged the Republican party with John Brownism and disunionism. And thus the South, misled by this rage of party spirit, grossly exaggerated and misconstrued the purpose of the Republican party.

Such was the immediate provocation, real and imaginary, to secession. It is to be remembered that slave labor was the chief element in Southern industry; the foundation of its agriculture and of its commerce; the environment of its family life, with personal relations often of the kindliest; the corner-stone of its social system. That system was thoroughly aristocratic, with the slaves as its base, an intermediate stratum of poor and debased whites, and at the summit a proud, luxurious, and brilliant aristocracy, made up in the country of planters, and in the cities of their mercantile and professional allies and associates. For this aristocratic class politics was the highest field of energy and ambition, and engaged the best ability of the community, such as at the North found outlet largely in great industrial enterprises or in literature. Thus the South was far more dominated by politicians than the North, and the personal ambition to rule, which in the one section had to fit itself to the sentiments of the common people, could in the other section dictate to the people. Throughout the community public sentiment had for many years been intensifying in support of slavery. The position of toleration or apology had been exchanged for one of enthusiastic advocacy. To this change two main factors

had contributed — the growth of the cotton-raising interest and the denunciations of the Abolitionists. The
practice of the latter, for thirty years continued, of denouncing slave-holders as the worst of criminals, had
somehow failed to convert them from their sins. What
the Abolitionists said passionately, the civilized world
was beginning calmly to say and to feel. The South,
thus criticised, was stung to self-justification until it exalted slavery, on grounds economic, social, and religious,
as among the greatest of earthly blessings, and for the
benighted Africans the providential opening of eternal
salvation.

The ruling power at the South was intensely intolerant.
All dislike of slavery, however mildly expressed, was
frowned upon, all open dissent was crushed out. Purse
and passion were on the same side; the South's great
industry was agriculture, and of its agriculture the staple
was cotton raised by slave labor. In a word, the South
gloried in slavery, and the North abhorred it. In a
democracy such convictions tend to express themselves
in political action,—and so the two opposite sentiments
drifted irresistibly toward collision. The North, having
on its side the forces of nature, and finding political
ascendency coming within its reach,— being moreover by
habit patient and law-abiding, and also having no immediate contact in its interior life with the subject of dispute,— was well content to trust the issue to time, and
to established and peaceful procedure. The South, having for ten years found its victories barren ones, and
having now lost the control of the Federal government;
feeling itself endangered more or less, in the chief muscle,
the most sensitive nerve, of its social organism; and
being always of a masterful temper and hot blood,
was prompt to cut the knot of a union that had grown
irksome and hateful.

Ready to its hand for the purpose of separation stood a political theory long cherished at the South and repudiated at the North,— state sovereignty. The North in general held that while the powers of sovereignty were divided between the individual states and the Federal Union, yet that the latter was an organic union of the whole people, and indissoluble. The South in general held that the Union was an alliance of independent states which might separate at will. To the Southern mind, therefore, secession was not revolution; the issue which it presented to the state was not of loyalty but of expediency; and when the state had decided, the obedience of the citizen was due, not to the Union, but to his state, whether in the Union or out of it. It was this conviction, that paramount allegiance was due to the state, which was decisive after their states had left the Union, in the minds of men like Robert E. Lee,— men as conscientious and high-minded as any who fought against them. But in the original Secessionists the motive was the maintenance of slavery and of the political power of the aristocracy.

The South Carolinians, then, being pretty much of one mind in the matter, proceeded immediately on the election of Lincoln to dissolve the connection of their state with the Union. The Federal judges, marshals, and other officials throughout the state resigned their offices. The United States senators, Hammond and Chestnut, resigned. A convention was called by the legislature, chosen by the people, and before the end of December it had declared the state independent of the Federal Union. The other Gulf states moved more slowly. There was some debate and division among their leaders; some waiting to see what Congress would do —waiting that ended when, early in the new year, their congressional representatives telegraphed home in favor of prompt

secession; and, before the end of February, Georgia,
Florida, Mississippi, Alabama, and Louisiana had followed South Carolina's example, and organized with her
a Southern Confederacy, with a constitution closely re-
sembling that of the United States, and with Jefferson
Davis as its president.

The secession movement found the North unprepared,
amazed, and distracted with conflicting views and purposes. There were no precedents for such an emergency,
no clear principles for dealing with it. The Administration was utterly helpless. The Republican party had
never contemplated such a state of things, nor agreed on
even the most general attitude toward it. There was a
chaos of opposing counsels. Men did not know their
own minds, and changed from day to day. The Secessionists had a clear purpose, and followed it steadily and
successfully. They made all the Gulf states their own;
they gained a strong and growing hold on the border
states; forts and navy yards fell into their hands; not a
shot was fired against them, not a blow was struck;
their Confederacy was organized; within four months
they could boast of creating a new nation. The Federal
government had done nothing to protect itself; the
North did not even know what it wanted to do, was not
resolved to fight, was not willing the seceding states
should go, was unsure of its own people and its own heart.
Yet, hesitatingly, gropingly, its mind was working to a
clear purpose, its heart was nerving itself for a mighty
effort.

When, within a week after the election, South Carolina
made evident her purpose to secede, there was on the
part of some Republicans a willingness to let them go if
they wished to. The *Tribune* said:

"If the cotton states shall decide that they can do better out
of the Union than in it, we insist on letting them go in peace.

. . . Whenever a considerable section of our Union shall deliberately resolve to go out, we shall resist all coercive measures designed to keep it in. We hope never to live in a republic whereof one section is pinned to the residue by bayonets."

Thus, one strong sentiment of the hour was that of the impossibility of maintaining by force a Union which should have any value; the impossibility of self-government without the consent of the governed. The *Republican's* first position was (November 10) that all the Southern states except South Carolina would decide against secession; that it was obviously against their interest to secede; that South Carolina might go if she would, but must not touch the Federal forts in her borders, or refuse to pay the Federal duties on her imports, under penalty of armed coercion. It held (November 15) that if South Carolina would seek a dissolution by peaceable negotiations and mutual agreement, it would be and ought to be granted. "A Union that must be maintained by force is not desirable." No such withdrawal, it continues, is contemplated or provided for by the Constitution, but it would be legitimate and expedient to grant it if South Carolina lays her grievance before the country and seeks a peaceable dissolution of partnership. But South Carolina, it was soon apparent, would do nothing of the kind; she did not ask a favor, but claimed a right, and drew her sword to enforce it if resisted. She at once began to arm. Throughout the neighboring states the martial fever spread, among a population accustomed to the use of arms and fond of military glory.

Of the former political allies of the South, many were loud in calling for conciliations and compromise. Among the Republicans in general the disposition was strong against any material concession. The prevalent temper of Massachusetts was against any concession whatever. When the *Republican* advocated the repeal of the personal liberty law, it had against it almost the whole strength of the party. The paper urged that the law, while perhaps not in its letter unconstitutional, was intended to thwart the execution of a United States statute; that it had never been of the least practical use, and that by repealing laws of this class, the North would remove the one real grievance of the South, and would show not cowardice but a manly willingness to do right. Governor Banks, in his parting message, argued in the same direction. But the inaugural of his successor, Governor Andrew, took opposite ground, and Andrew and not Banks was the representative man of the party.

Thurlow Weed, in the Albany *Evening Journal*, was urging as a basis of agreement, the restoration of the Missouri compromise line, and instead of the rendition of fugitive slaves the payment of their money value. The *Republican* (December 11) objected to any proffer on the part of the North of a restoration of the boundary line which had been overthrown by the South's own act; but it was willing that if the South would propose such restoration, and be content with it, it should be accepted. The yearly number of escaping fugitives, it remarked, was not above 2000, at an outside value of $2,000,000, and the payment of such sum, as a commutation for a distasteful obligation, was legitimate, and was preferable to the consummation of secession.

But it was soon apparent that no such concessions as these would satisfy the South. Congress met; the President's message argued that secession was not permissible, but that there was no authority to prevent it or to coerce a state; and in both Houses the leaders of the two sections met each other with final question and reply. The North saw at last that the South, the Gulf states at least, were serious in their purpose to leave the Union; would the North pay the price they demanded as their right and as the condition of their remaining? That price was — as Toombs summed it up in the Senate — that slave-holders should be allowed to take their property into the territories; that slave property should be recognized by the government in all its departments as equally sacred with any other kind of property, save in states which excluded it; that offenders against the laws of slave states should be surrendered to justice in those states; that fugitive slaves should be returned; that Congress should prohibit and punish insurrection and invasion. In a word: Will the Federal government take slave property under its immediate and special protection; shall slavery be made national and general, and freedom be the sectional exception? "Never!" said the North, through its congressmen. "Then," said the men of the Gulf states, "we will leave you!" That was the sum and substance of a month's debate, and early in January the senators and representatives of six states bade a stern farewell to their associates in Congress, left their places vacant, and went home to organize and arm a new nation.

"How shall we deal with the seceders?" was a question sorely puzzling. "Say to them, 'erring sisters, go in peace!'" was the counsel of some, like the *Tribune.* "Yes, go — but touch the national forts in your harbors, or refuse to pay the customs duties, at your peril!" So said Senator Wade, a representative spokesman of his party in the Senate. "Be patient; give them time to cool; offer a national convention to talk matters over," said men like Weed and Seward and Adams. But within two months from Lincoln's election, the tide of feeling had swept the nation to the verge of war. Charleston harbor was the focus where the rays of passion centered. A little company of troops under Major Anderson held forts Moultrie and Sumter. The Carolinians threw up around them a circle of menacing fortifications. Would the government reënforce them, as they lay almost at the mercy of their besiegers? "Oh for an hour of Jackson!" cried the *Republican*, December 17, when Buchanan declined to risk bloodshed by sending reënforcements. Cass left the cabinet in disgust at the refusal. Major Anderson, December 26, deftly withdrew his handful of men from Moultrie on the mainland, and planted himself in water-locked Sumter; and the watching North cheered his successful maneuver. The President changed his mind and sent the steamer *Star of the West* with troops and supplies; the forts at the harbor mouth (January 9) opened fire on her, and she turned in silence and went back. Those guns woke in the North a pulse of wrath; compromise had failed at Washington; the Gulf states were seceding,— now the South had struck at the flag. "Thus," said the *Republican*, January 12, "the final act of the disunion drama has opened upon us by the perversity of South Carolina." Three days before it had said, "There is but one voice from men of all parties in the free states, and it calls imperatively for the defense of the Union and the enforcement of the laws."

But the tide which seemed about to sweep away all barriers of peace once more ebbed for a little. The nation's heart might be hot, but while Buchanan was President its hand was as forceless as an empty glove. The Southern members of the cabinet had resigned, after doing their utmost to aid the seceders; their places were filled by Northern men of character and force,— Dix and Stanton and Holt,— but the President shrank from all vigorous action. It was scarcely to be regretted; for the Northern mind was not yet clear nor its purpose fixed. Seward, regarded as the foremost man in the coming administration, spoke in the Senate, January 12, and his voice was weighty for a calm, patient effort toward peaceful reunion. He yielded nothing of Republican principles, but he offered a programme of conciliation. He proposed that all unconstitutional legislation against the return of fugitives be repealed; that non-interference with slavery in the states be guaranteed, if the South desired, by a new article in the Constitution; that, secession being abandoned, and after a year or two's interval, there be held a constitutional convention; that any proper legislation against inter-state invasion be granted; and that as a material bond of the whole country, two Pacific railways be constructed. The temper of the speech fell on the North like oil on troubled waters. Congress, calmed by the withdrawal of the fiery secession element, labored assiduously with great special committees to devise some scheme of restoration. The most conspicuous project was that of Senator Crittenden of Kentucky, of which the salient feature was the restoration of the Missouri compromise line, as applicable to all territory present or hereafter acquired; each new state to determine its own institutions. To this, as contemplating future acquisitions of slave territory to the southward, the North would not consent. Another plan was that of Charles Francis Adams, then in the House, which proposed the immediate admission of New Mexico as a state, her people deciding the slavery question for themselves (there were, said Mr. Adams, but twenty-two slaves held there),—and thus virtually restored the old line for all present territory. While Congress debated such plans, a convention was held at the call of Virginia, to which the states, except the six seceders, sent delegates, to discuss the situation and devise remedies. In all these discussions it was recognized that the immediate object was to retain the yet unseceded Southern states. Those which had already formed a confederacy were scornfully indifferent to all such mild palliatives. But if the other Southern states could be held, there was hope that after a time the "wayward sisters" would get tired of their isolation. The border states were the prize for which both parties were now working. On Virginia were now centered the strongest hopes and fears. In Virginia,— and largely also in Maryland, North Carolina, Kentucky, Tennessee, and Missouri,— there were two powerful conflicting forces, attachment to slavery and love of the Union. Strong sympathy drew Virginia toward her sisters of the Gulf; strong ties, of revolutionary traditions, of a proud place in the whole history of the nation, bound her to the Union and its flag. She wanted the North to concede the Southern demands; failing that, she wavered as to her choice. A state convention was called; immediate secession was rejected; the representatives of the confederacy were strenuously persuasive; the compromisers did their best. But all compromise came to nothing. The fugitive slave law, the personal liberty laws—nobody really cared much about them; the Missouri compromise talk was only galvanizing a corpse. The South wanted just one thing—that property in human beings should be put on an equality with property in cattle or horses. Lincoln went to the bottom of the matter when, in a speech at the Cooper Institute a year before, after a sober and searching review of the whole field, he said:

"What will satisfy them? Simply this: we must not only let them alone, but we must somehow convince them that we do let them alone. . . . What will convince them? This, and this only: cease to call slavery wrong, and join them in calling it right. And this must be done thoroughly—done in acts as well as in words."

So, now, all the talk brought matters no nearer a settlement. Out of it all a single measure was finally adopted. Congress, at the close of the session, approved an amendment to the Constitution, prohibiting any future amendment to authorize Congress to interfere with slavery where it was sanctioned by state law. That—as the Thirteenth Amendment—was the last proffer of the North to the South. It was a quite different Thirteenth Amendment which met the South on its return after four years.

Any who had believed, as many did believe, Mr. Bowles apparently among them, that the new President was to be but the instrument of Mr. Seward, were undeceived by the first words he spoke after assuming his office. "No one," said the *Republican*, March 5, "can doubt that Mr. Lincoln is the sole author of his own inaugural." One thing was clear, that the country had at last a *man* for its chief ruler,—a man most genuine and veracious, whose effort and longing were toward peace, but who held a steadfast purpose toward national unity. The inaugural was a sober, calmly reasoned, and weighty appeal to the seceding states; the avowal, firm, but without a spark of passion, that secession cannot be recognized, and that the President will if necessary use his authority to hold the national forts and property and to collect the imposts, though he will not use force for any other purpose; and the assurance that if the Southerners will submit their grievances to peaceful arbitrament, they shall be met with the fullest regard for every moral and constitutional right. The language of the address, while lawyer-like in its carefulness of statement, was yet homely and familiar as the talk of a plain man by his own fireside. At the end it rose to a strain of pathetic sublimity:

"I am loath to close. We are not enemies, but friends. We must not be enemies. Though passion may have strained, it must not break our bonds of affection. The mystic chords of memory, stretching from every battle-field and patriot grave to every living heart and hearth-stone all over this broad land, will yet swell the chorus of the Union, when again touched, as surely they will be, by the better angels of our nature."

The cabinet appointments were such as on the whole gave encouraging assurance as to the President's catholicity and courage. It was not then known that he had offered places to such Southerners as Guthrie, of Kentucky, and Gilmore, of North Carolina. Among his official councilors, he chose his foremost rivals, Seward, Chase, and Bates; the other places were filled by Montgomery Blair, Gideon Welles, Caleb B. Smith, and Simon Cameron. The new Administration was instantly engaged with an army of place-hunters. Lincoln remarked that the office-seekers would not leave him time to attend to the country; he was, he said, like a man obliged to negotiate with lodgers at one end of his house when it was on fire at the other end.

While this had been the course of events, the mind of the Northern people had been struggling with contradictory impulses, and had by no means come to a clear conclusion. The pages of the *Republican* reflect many of these phases. Through the perplexities of the immediate situation, the great substantial fact — the supreme fact, as history now makes account of it — is recognized, December 22, in an article which thus begins:

" Slavery seems to be gathering itself up for a decisive struggle. The moral forces of the world have long assailed it, and everywhere religion, morality, and politics are against it. . . . Its stronghold is in the Southern states of this Union. . . . Only in this country is an attempt made to throw around the system the sanction of religion, and to uphold it as a good and proper thing in itself, and worthy to be cherished, protected, and extended over other lands. Here it seems to be rushing upon a decisive battle-field."

With the closing year, December 25, comes the first avowal, clear and firm, of "The Stern Purpose"—to put down rebellion by arms. But the question was speedily obscured again. The fighting temper ebbed at the North. With Mr. Seward's conciliatory speech, and with the subsequent effort toward a peaceful settlement, the *Republican* was in warmest sympathy. Mr. Bowles's optimistic temper, his strong reliance on the prevailing power of reason and self-interest, made him skeptical of a warlike issue, and strenuous to avert it. The *Republican* did not compromise its anti-slavery principles; it would by no means concede the Crittenden plan, or anything beyond the Adams proposition. But it criticised the readiness of Governor Andrew and the legislature to prepare for war, as overzealous and injurious. The state was forward and prompt to meet the worst that might come. The legislature, in January, by a unanimous vote, called on the President to enforce the laws and maintain the Union, and offered him whatever support of men and money he might need from Massachusetts. The *Republican* deprecated such measures, as showing a disposition to meet the South half-way on the war-path.

Men far less sanguine than Mr. Bowles were slow to believe that the issue could come to actual war. Even Lincoln said on his journey to Washington: "This crisis is all artificial. It has no foundation in fact. It was not 'argued up,' as the saying is, and cannot be argued down. Let it alone and it will go down itself!"

In the mind of the North, two sentiments were strong, —that the government must not give up its own to the seceders, must not surrender its forts or renounce the collection of customs duties; but that it was impracticable. to compel by arms the submission and return of the seceded states. The practical contradiction resulting from these two propositions was not for a good while appreciated by the North. In reality it was out of the question for a people claiming independence — like South Carolina or the Southern Confederacy — to allow a foreign power to collect duties on its imports, — by war-ships outside of its harbors for example, as was sometimes gravely proposed. Any such attempt meant certain war, and in case of war defeat to the seceders must mean their subjection to the national authority. But this, so plain in the light of events, was not so plainly seen beforehand; and men went on saying that the government must not give up Fort Sumter, but must not invade the seceded states.

There was another very grave uncertainty. It seemed more than doubtful whether the Northern people had any strong and passionate sentiment of love for the Union, such as would inspire them to fight for its maintenance. There had grown up in truth a great alienation between the two sections of the country. Many anti-slavery men besides the Abolitionists thought the national partnership with slave-owners, if broken by the act of the latter, was by no means worth restoring. The sentiment of common country, the pride in a great national destiny, had been dimmed by the hot struggle of recent years. Said the *Republican*, November 22, "The fact is not to be disguised that the feeling at the North in respect to the Union has considerably changed within a score of years." Certainly, it says, the North does not care enough for the Union — however orators may glorify the name — to made any further compromises to save it. The South has destroyed all liberty within its borders, and denies to Northern men upon its soil the rights which the country would exact in the case of a foreign power.

As late as March 23, the paper declared, in a gloomier mood than usual, but with a misgiving from which few then were wholly free, that loyalty, as an enthusiastic sentiment, does not exist among Americans.

In the first month of Lincoln's administration—while as yet no blow had been struck; while commissioners of the Confederacy were at Washington trying to negotiate for a peaceful separation; while the Virginia convention still debated whether the state should secede—one great fact was becoming clear to the North. It was expressed in a sentence of the President's inaugural: "The central idea of secession is the essence of anarchy." It was not— so the North slowly perceived—a question merely whether several states were to part company with the rest. It was a question whether the bond of all national government was to be dissolved; whether a principle was to be admitted which in its ultimate application would reduce the country to a chaos of discordant states. The fact of a common nationality, on whose preservation depended ultimately the peace of society, the happiness of every household, the hopes of future generations, was asserting itself in the hearts of the common people.

The character of the seceders' act had been obscured by that feature in our system which places very many of the functions of civil government in the state, and only a few in the Federal Union. In a centralized nation, a revolt against governmental authority brings the insurgents into immediate collision with the civil authority, at every point where law touches the citizen. The revolt of the Gulf states from the Union had not disturbed the relations of their citizens to that frame-work of local law which covers most of the questions and interests of civil life. Business contracts, police, the state courts, the ordinary functions of government, went on as before. The scanty machinery of Federal administration, in its local forms, had dissolved by the consent of the people; Federal judges and marshals had resigned; the post-offices had been easily transferred to the new authorities. From their share in the government at Washington the senators and representatives had withdrawn. But at one point the relation was not effectually severed; the supreme right of government, the right of taxation,— exercised then by the Federal government only through the customs duties,— remained fully asserted by the North in theory, and practically expressed by the two or three forts over which the stars and stripes still waved. This brought the whole matter to an immediate practical test. To withdraw from the forts would be a virtual renunciation by the government of the one remaining function which testified to a vital, organic, indissoluble relation between itself as an authority sovereign within its sphere, and the seceders as rightfully its subjects within that sphere.

This was the logic of the situation. The concrete fact was, a beleaguered fort, garrisoned by a company of United States soldiers, with rapidly diminishing supplies, menaced on all sides by the batteries of a people exultant in their new independence, and eager to be free from the last symbol of the authority they had cast off. On that fort and its flag the eyes of both sections were fastened; and as men watched, the tide of feeling rose higher and higher. Unrelieved, it must speedily fall. Would the Administration reënforce it or withdraw from it? To hold it, said the military counselors, would require twenty thousand men. It is worthless to us, said Seward and others of the cabinet, and by holding it we risk a collision which destroys the last hope of a peaceful victory. Once the report went over the country from Washington that the garrison was to be withdrawn. Such retreat was bitter for patriots, even for

those who sought peace. " The moral effect of the abandonment of Fort Sumter," said the *Republican*, March
12, " will unquestionably be a degree of disappointment
and chagrin among loyal citizens of the North." Yet, it
adds, if it will deprive secession of its last opportunity,
it is a good move. Lincoln, as it now appears, was hoping to gain a substantial advantage by a small sacrifice,—
to keep Virginia in the Union, by giving up Sumter. He
told a representative of the Virginia convention (so says
Henry Wilson) that if that body would immediately
adjourn, he would order Sumter to be evacuated. The
reply was that both Sumter and Pickens must be evacuated at once, and assurance given that no attempt would
be made to collect revenue in Southern ports. This was
more than Lincoln could grant. At last, a relieving
squadron was secretly ordered to sail from New York
for Sumter. The government, keeping its promise to
the Confederate commissioners, that if Sumter were not
first attacked, no relief should be sent it without notice
being given, sent private word to the Charleston authorities that supplies were to be introduced into the fort,—
peaceably if possible, otherwise by force. Throughout
the country, meanwhile, the hopes of peace which had
followed Lincoln's inaugural and Seward's pacific
counsels had been obscured by swiftly gathering clouds.
We read, April 6, that a warlike aspect has suddenly
come over the whole face of affairs; that the Secessionists are getting ready to strike, and the Administration is on its guard. The tension of suspense was
nearing the point where something must break. It
paralyzed business,—so said the *Republican*, April 11.
With food abundant, with money plenty, there yet was
universal stagnation. Men felt thunder in the air, and
waited for the storm. " The time is come when the
North is entirely ready to see the issue decided as regards

Fort Sumter. If the Confederate conspirators refuse to
let food be conveyed to a starving garrison of American
soldiers, the friends of the Union everywhere are ready
to know the reason why, and it will be a joy to the
country to have that question settled." Between Charleston and Montgomery, the Confederate capital, secret tele-
grams were flying. Doubtless, the Secessionists counted
on the effect of a conflict of arms in sweeping the waver-
ing border states into union with the South. The effect
in uniting the North they did not foresee,— they believed the North to be divided, half-hearted, and without
spirit to fight. The decisive order was given by President Davis; the fort received a summons to surrender,
and Major Anderson refused; then from the surrounding
forts a circle of fire opened upon it. For two days, April
12 and 13, the people North and South listened breathlessly to the pealing of the guns. Then the overmatched
garrison yielded; Major Anderson agreed to evacuate
the fort, and its flag went down. One great passion of
grief, resentment, and purpose united the North as one
man. Hesitations, doubts, theories, vanished. Party
lines were forgotten. There was but one thought, one
feeling — to make the flag supreme again over the whole
land. The President called for seventy-five thousand
volunteers, and the loyal states rushed to arms. Virginia,
North Carolina, Tennessee, Arkansas, and Texas joined
the Southern Confederacy. Pennsylvania troops were
thrown instantly into Washington to defend it, and close
after them came the Massachusetts Sixth Regiment. The
country was wrapped in a whirlwind of war.

# CHAPTER XXV.

## LETTERS : 1857–1860.

TO turn from the story of a nation's crisis to details of personal life gives at first an impression of abrupt descent. It is like coming from the distant view of a city in which its far-away grandeur charms the eye and fires the imagination, into immediate contact with its scenes of prosaic reality. But the deeper look sees under these homely aspects the great drama of humanity. The pictured tapestry of a people's fortunes has for its warp and woof the thread of every-day lives — their toils, pleasures, discomforts, losses, successes. Of the letters in this and other chapters, not a few are given for their incidental revelations of traits in the writer. Often the thought may not be weighty, the judgment, perhaps, not correct, but if the reader is helped to see the man as he really was, something is gained.

*To Charles Allen.*

January 11, 1857.

With what meat are you consoling yourself in L——'s absence, and the want of my delightful chirography for the last ten days? I have been to New York and Boston, have gone to a ball, and have sat up till four o'clock printing Governor Gardner's message, besides experiencing several other unusual sensations, since I last wrote you. I had a delightful breakfast with Dana at Delmonico's in New York, during which we settled the Philadelphia matter. He took it in hand, and told them that I would go on and see them if they would agree to raise a $50,000 cash capital, to which I should contribute $5000 — then make the nominal capital $100,000, and give me twenty of the new shares, or one-fourth of the whole concern, which he calculated would be worth the $100,000 at the end of the year, or when the $50,000 was used up ;— and besides give me supreme control and $4000 salary. This was rather more magnificent than I should have demanded myself, but he said they ought to do it, if I went, and I told him to go ahead. The reply I have not heard — probably it will end the matter, at least for the present. I am content. On such terms I could hardly decline running the small risk proposed. Rather than accept less, or much less, I would remain here, or go to Boston, or go on the *Tribune* itself. I shall get $4000, perhaps $5000, out of the *Republican* this year, and had best stay unless I can make a ten strike.

L—— I saw a few moments in Boston. She seemed in capital spirits, and promised to come around this way home. Is it not about time for you to come down and see us again ? I feel sort o' leisurely, have got a new anecdote or two, and the blissful fountains of ale are overflowing, while with a lemon and some hot water we might save the Union after the more approved fashion of the season. What say you ? L—— being away, you must be lonely, and disposed to do something desperate. If my wife were away, I'd come up and see you — I would.

January 18, 1857.

. . . The Philadelphia people have replied, coming nearly to my standard, but I have declined to abate a jot. I think the only real point is my demand for supreme and absolute control; there are one or two people who have an interest in the movement, who, though willing and desirous to have me lead, are yet bent on attaching themselves to the enterprise and going to glory with it. This is all right if they are worthy, but if they prove drags I must have the right to slough them off.

I think here is the sticking-point. I am more and more indifferent to going unless on my own terms.

*Monday.*— My eyes, what a storm! One of my ears was nipped by the frost last night going home at eleven, and it burns to-day like a bad conscience. But that last hot whisky, at the noon of night, with Mrs. Bowles, was like meat to a strong man. It only needed you to make the thing complete. By the way, Mrs. B. and I have been indulging in the weakness of being crayonized this last week by Kimberly. The result is rather a success. Come and see 'em.

### To H. L. Dawes.

February 16, 1857.

. . . Our friends in the legislature are getting somewhat exercised, but are not half so frightened as I wish they were. Gardner wants to make the legislature long and unpopular, and cast upon it and us the extravagance of himself and crew, and give the hunkers aid and comfort in their combination for "reform." But it won't work, unless our fellows are natural fools, which they are not quite, though I sometimes think near it. If we had a decent press in Boston, it would straighten the trouble out directly; but we must only kick and cuff the legislature into appreciating their responsibilities, and trust in Providence and the people to bring the matter out right during the summer.

In national politics, matters seem to be drifting still, and the exact form of the future no one knows. The Democratic party cannot go unitedly through Buchanan's Administration. The men that elected him will never choose another president, because their organization is worn out, effete, and cannot stand the rocks before it.

I wish you would come down here and go to Boston with me. I think there will be a gathering of the "saints" early in March, perhaps after Congress has adjourned, and then you must appear on parade. We should get those amendments out of the way before we strike out for the summer campaign. We want two planks;— non-extension of slavery, and state reform.

*To Charles Allen.*

April 9, 1857.

. . . I am here for a day, and return to-night, to launch
the *Traveller* next Monday. My editorial staff is about made
up, and is rich and abundant, though not in all respects to my
taste. But that will work out in practice. It will number
in all some fifteen, and be such as no Boston journal ever yet
dreamed of.

Charley Hale [editor of the *Advertiser*] has nothing to fear
from us, but more from the revival of the *Courier*. He ought
never to have allowed it, but should have bought it up when
he could, a few weeks ago. Now it disputes places with him
boldly. I have not had time to talk with him, but shall seek
occasion. We seek to be the popular, progressive journal; his
place is the conservative, respectable, high-toned; and there is
no better or richer field than that before him, if he will only
properly cultivate it, and get the *Courier* out of the way. We
shall combine with him, because he is no rival of ours. Indeed,
if he feels properly his saddle, ours is the best move for him
that could be made.

*To his Wife.*

BOSTON, Sunday afternoon, April 26, 1857.

Your first letter was received yesterday morning, and I
meant to have replied by last night's mail, but was too busy.
Just now I have got your yesterday's letter, and rejoice to see
evidences in it of improvement in health and mental resignation. The only thing we can well say now about our new
enterprise and separation is that it is undertaken, that it is not
as hard as it might be, that it may work for good, that it must
result in good if we only insist on turning all there is in it to
good account. With a weekly meeting, and the promise of
permanent reunion in a few short months, I think — with
plenty for mind and heart to do — we can endure till the good
time coming. Separation even has its uses. We enjoy one
another the more when we meet, we learn to discipline ourselves, to depend upon ourselves, to develop the inward powers;
we concentrate happiness, and learn the better to appreciate it.

So let us neither repine nor quarrel with fate, but out of seeming evil educe good. That is the true philosophy of life, and without philosophy there is vastly little of life but a passion and a struggle.

I have got down into my new room, and am slowly getting out of chaos. But it must be a long while before affairs get settled and everything works easy. I feel, however, that I have passed the two hardest weeks, and I no longer feel any serious question as to my ability, in health or otherwise, to master my position, in all good time. I have had a little cold for several days, and that and the *tire* in me gives me some headache to-day, but both are trifles, and only inspire caution. I expect an easier week this, and feel now pretty certain that I shall be able to go up to Springfield next Saturday.

. . . I did not get up this morning in season to go to church, though I had intended to. So I have spent the morning in reading and walking on the Common, which begins to be very pleasant already. Colonel Lincoln has sent for me to dine with him at five, and at seven I must come back to the office and work. My new night editor commences this week, and as soon as he gets broken in I shall be relieved of late work. Things move along very well on the whole; of course there are annoyances and rough places, but they will be overcome all in due time; and though I often think I was a fool for leaving old Springfield, still the undertaking has been begun, and I cannot and shall not turn back until it is thoroughly tried out. Thank fortune, I can *afford to fail*, but I don't mean to.

*To Charles Allen.*

BOSTON, May 14, 1857.

I make slow progress in commanding order, but the world moves. I am not at all satisfied with the paper, yet I can see it is an improvement upon what went before. I am trammeled by old engagements, and seek in vain for such men as I want to gather around me. But I have courage and hope, generally. Our daily circulation is 21,000, about neck and neck with the *Journal*, and no more; weekly, 16,000; semi-weekly, 4000 to

5000 ; all fair and promising, but not supreme enough to indulge in a general bray. I am, of course, busy, yet can get
off for the theater, or a long dinner with a friend ; and I should
like above anything to see your face in these parts. I do wish
your mother or L—— would go down and spend a week with
my wife.

He writes to Charles Allen, June 2, to meet him in
Boston or Springfield, in regard to possible difficulties :

"As I think it a duty to be prepared for emergencies and
accidents, I desire to talk with one who is both a lawyer and
a friend."

June 9, he writes :

"The matter of which I spoke to you is not so pressing as to
justify a journey. Indeed there is nothing specially new ;
nothing which I need not have expected, but yet as the course
is long on which I have entered, and the result is doubtful, I
have thought I should, like a good general, 'protect my rear,'
and how to do it is that which I desire to talk with you about.
I shall not increase my interest here until everything is in my
own way, or the result is absolutely certain. I can afford to
lose what I have put in, but I do not want to endanger what I
have in Springfield."

The next two months brought the internal difficulties
of the *Traveller* to a crisis. The letters are full of the
perplexing and worrying details of negotiations for a
dissolution of the partnership. The matter drags to an
end in September. He writes to his wife :

"There is nothing in my business troubles to give you any
serious annoyance. They are mortifying and disagreeable to
me, and I shall run the risk of losing a few thousand dollars —
beyond which, nothing. . . . The loss of the money is the
smallest of the sources of regret to me,— even if I do lose it,—
for I have no fears that I cannot easily replace it in good time.
. . . If I do not lose too much money, I do not intend to

go to work anywhere for a year, but to play for that time, if I can afford to, and it is not too hard work."

A little later he writes to Charles Allen:

" As to going West, I must wait a few days at least. I dare not start on a long journey in my present health. I am terribly used up."

A letter of October 29 marks the return to the old work.

" Holland is ready with an offer to vacate and go into a literary and lecturing life. He really wants to resign his place, he chafes under the drudgery and responsibility. I hold the matter under advisement, yet I think it is destined to result in my taking hold at once. I would rather be ' fancy-free ' for a few months or a year longer; but how can a man in these times ? "

*To H. L. Dawes.*

February, 1858.

You *are* an apt scholar. The stunning accounts of your speech come to us by every wave of the electric current. [It was Mr. Dawes's first speech in Congress, in favor of a concession of time to an unwilling witness before a House committee.] And to-day Hanscomb sends a letter " all about it," setting it out with the accompanying " sound of hew-gag." I wish you had made your first speech for something else than in behalf of a man who wants to escape telling the truth ; but I congratulate you that the agony is over, and that the hall has kindly echoed the sound of your voice. Go on and conquer. You cannot win a victory that I shall not glory in, no more than suffer a defeat, or experience a sorrow, that I shall not take unto myself.

*To Charles Allen.*

[1858.]

I take it you have a fresh disgust with politics. So have I. Banks has, on the whole, made a failure in his appointments for the new court; that is, a considerable portion of his judges have yet to vindicate the wisdom of their selection. He has made down here, too, some bad justice selections, if I may believe what the people say. However, the great world lays no stress on the disappointment of individuals. So long as their offices are decently filled, they are well enough satisfied. . . . I have the gratifying satisfaction of knowing that all the men I went for are defeated. Now, I hope nobody will ever ask my aid again; it is the meanest business I do, asking for offices for people, and if I didn't love my friends I never would do it. Now that they see I damage them, I guess they had better leave me to enjoy the independence of asking no favor of anybody, and grumbling at everybody.

The trout came, cold and fresh. I shared 'em with Deacon Stearns—poor man—and we were both filled with gratitude. We are in an awful plight at the house, just now in the thick of it, and I have to eat at the cellars around town and wait upon Irishmen, carpenters, masons, painters, *et id omne genus.*

April 8, 1859.

I had the present of a bottle of wine this week, from a woman, with an affectionate note. We had some good food Fast-day, and we drank the wine. We thought of you, lamented your absence, and concluded to send you the label on the bottle — much good may it do you. Otherwise, Fast-day was rather stupid. —— came around before I was up, and was willing to talk about being judge, which I have no doubt he will be if —— is not reappointed. It will be so invidious and difficult making distinctions that I have thought and still think that the whole common pleas bench will go by the board. I should chiefly regret Aiken of this lot. I have imbibed a good deal of respect for that man. Ben. Butler says he is an exaggeration of the stage Yankee; but he is fresh and hearty, and keen and human, and says civil things about me — and of course I like him. It seems to be a weakness of human nature to like those people who like us and praise us. But about the judges. . . . I am prepared for some good and some bad appointments —I don't think Banks's forte lies in filling offices well. But it seems to me —— expresses himself as to him with uncommon

and needless severity; especially as we Unitarians don't believe
in a hell.   I have no reason to believe he has shown any bad
faith towards Chapman,—nothing worse than lack of appreciation; and that ought not to be held in this erring world a
deadly offense.  I think it is generally conceded here, and even
by Chapman's friends, that Hoar is the best appointment.  My
knowledge is limited, yet I am inclined to agree.  Hoar has
genius, insight, an edge to his mind, that I never discovered
in Chapman. . . . I meant to say about the judges that
I am determined not to write to Banks for or against any
one.  He has never seemed to place any value on my views
as to appointments, heretofore, and he won't have them
hereafter, without seeking them.  Probably he will be able
to do without them.

April, 1859.

. . . My cold is only better, not cured.  I have a heavy
back yet, but am mending, unless this night " on "—I don't
expect to be through till four or five—gives me a set back.
It was well perhaps I could not go up to Greenfield, for we had
a Saturday night call which ended in a Sunday visit from a
young man in Williams College, who writes poetry and stories
for the *Republican,* and is going to be a minister; and seems to
have come on purpose almost to get some Christian, fatherly
advice, which I gave him.

I have taken violently and resolutely to horseback riding;
went yesterday, and again this (Tuesday) morning, and mean
to follow it up till it kills or cures.  On the whole, I am
liking it.

It is a long way ahead to Saturday.  I wish you would think
you could come down here — there is really no reason why you
shouldn't.  But if you insist on holding me to my promise, I
shall go up, I think, unless something now unforeseen happens
to forbid.  Of course Mrs. Bowles is always ready to say go;
you know she would give up any gratification, or endure any
suffering, to give me a pleasure, or get me out of the way of a
half-day of work.  But that doesn't make it always right that
I should take her at her word — by no means.

*To H. L. Dawes.*

April 20, 1859.

I consider it more the duty of the members of Congress from Massachusetts to secure the defeat of the two years' amendment [to the state constitution, requiring that citizens of foreign birth should after their naturalization wait two years longer before being allowed to vote] than any other set of men. The standing of the state in national politics is in their hands; and they have to meet their brethren from other states at Washington, and answer for the conduct of their constituents. I can have no doubt that you agree with me in this, as in the conviction that that amendment should be rejected. And I presume you are doing all you can, both publicly and privately, to convince the people of Berkshire that they should vote against it at the election on the ninth of May. Why, then, do I write? Simply because I am asked to do so—to stir up your pure mind to labor, to faith, and to work.

And I am yours truly, at three o'clock in the morning.

*To Charles Allen.*

July, 1859.

Our ride to Northampton was rather savage from the heat, especially the last half of it, but the horse had the worst of it. He was in trim at six, however, for a night ride to Springfield. On the whole, we had a delightful excursion of it, and Mrs. Bowles enjoyed it greatly. Our friends were all exceedingly civil to us, and then the country was fine, and most of it new to both of us. Of course I had to undergo a blistering at Northampton for touching with profane hands the local gods, combined in this case with the immaculate gentlemen of the bar; and even Mr. Delano himself, whom I met at the Mansion House, gave me the satisfaction of showing he was wounded, though putting me to the awkwardness of defending myself by word of mouth. I am not good at talking—but in the long run even the lawyers don't get the advantage of us. When I have done anything mean, I generally find it out as soon as anybody—but I don't discover it in this case of the Hampshire bar and the new court.

I am aching to pitch into Choate, and shall do it yet, un-gracious as Boston will think it. I don't believe he was a bright and shining light to the profession in at least one very important particular. And I hate the "*Nil de mortuis*," &c. What do men die for, except that posterity may impartially judge, and get the full benefit of their example?

November, 1859.

I go to New York Friday or Saturday for a few days, partly for a little recreation, partly on business and to see some friends, and partly to see that I am not put in a false and dis-agreeable position as to the printership of the House. I hear nothing particular about the affair lately, and shall be quite content to learn that Weed & Co. have abandoned their idea. In the first place, for them to try me and fail would be unpleas-ant; and I am not so sure that the appointment would be a good thing for me. I am content, however, in all these things to let affairs take their course. I should like some money. I should like to enlarge my position and power in the next cam-paign. But I can be content with what I have of both.

I am very busy indeed. I never get through, nowadays. Something of every day's work goes over, and I have submitted to this as a sort of law of my life. My correspondence is sadly neglected, and I cannot pretend to follow my friendly exchanges with regularity or fidelity. Yet it seems to me that I accom-plish much less than I used to ; but the range of work widens, and the care of the paper grows greater and greater. And yet I like it first-rate. I only wish it paid better, so that I could have better assistance, and have more steady reliance on my men.

Your early rising is a great achievement, but good if you will go to bed in proportionate season. You can't burn the candle at both ends, and make anything by it in the long run ; and it is the long pull that you are to rely on, and whereby you are to gain glory.—A tender turkey and fixin's to you all at the "Hotel de Allen."

[November or December, 1859.]

. . . I have much to do this fall, and must ask my friends to come and see me rather than exact my presence. The printing business I shall leave to the men who suggested it, Weed, Greeley, and Dana; I shall neither expect nor seek it; and I question even if, on such conditions as will accompany it, it is worth my having. It will lead me out of my independent position, and with my disposition and the demands of those who will elect me, if I should be elected, I suspect the bulk of the profits will be contributed to the party funds for the presidential election. I did intend to go to Washington at the opening of Congress. The suggestion of me for printer will keep me at home — I will have no hand in the dirty work of election. [This came to nothing.]

Our differences in politics, etc., do not oppress me. I trust our friendship can stand them all; and indeed I am inclined to believe that it is somewhat through our differences that we like each other. It would be stupid to always agree. Yet I would not that we should drift too far from one another — we must preserve sufficient points of sympathy for contact, and I have sometimes thought that, in my disposition to respect your independence, and leave you to work out your own views of men whom I respect and am disposed to follow, I was not doing quite the fair thing either by them, you, or myself; especially as other men who know them less, or no better, and who have no better right to influence you, are yet apparently doing so against them. For instance, I think my opinion of Banks is quite as likely to be correct as your Mr. ——'s. I know him as well as ever he did, and that in his riper years and character; I think my capacity for judgment is quite as great as ——'s, and I should be sorry if I had so narrow and prejudiced a soul as he; and yet you rather take his estimate of Banks than mine, — and simply I suppose because I have taken no pains to instill mine into you, while he has his. Isn't it so?

Horace Mann had qualities which by themselves deserve a statue, by way of commemoration and example. Whether as a whole he deserves a statue in the State-house yard next to Webster, I am not so clear. I think his labors for the schools would entitle him to it, if anything. He was not a statesman, but a reformer and a teacher. He was not lovable, like Choate, but he had sterner and more enduring stuff, and has left his mark for a longer period. The bad thing about the Mann statue business is that it has a chief impulse in the fact that he quarreled with Webster, and Webster is on the other side. But as the money is not subscribed, nor the artist engaged to make the statue, we may trust that feeling to wear out. The movement will not go on long, or to success, upon such capital as that. Let us have patience, and look all around a question.

Brown was *insane* on this point of his mission. He was courageous, conscientious, a real old Puritan, but a pure monomaniac, like George Lunt ; and I am inclined to think you as a lawyer could wish for no better case than to defend either of them for a murder committed in the line of their mania. The Harper's Ferry affair will appear to kill Seward — but he was dead before. He has no chance, and his apparent strength has for some time lain greatly in the fact that other men were not ready to be brought forward, and that everybody wants to please him and his friends, and have their reversionary support when he breaks down. Banks stands the best chance to-day. There are many obstacles to his nomination, which, if powerfully combined, may prevent it; but I think that he will succeed both at the convention and before the people. None of our politicians more thoroughly appreciate "the epoch" than he, and no man in the country will make a more powerful and brilliant administration. There will be plenty to quarrel with in it ; but it will have great features and decided character.

December, 1859.

I am waiting for Congress news, at 2 A. M., and in a dull moment write to say there is nothing new about the printing or the other thing. I am somewhat puzzled by the *Tribune* offer, and what is best for me under the various aspects of present and future. But I shall make no positive conclusion at present.

I do not think you judge Parker's book on Choate quite impartially. It seems to me that it is a book we should all be glad has been written, while we may more or less quarrel with the man who wrote it. We may say as the man said when he

declined to go bail, he had no conscientious scruples against it
— he would as lief somebody else would do it. I wrote our
notice of the book, and I believe it gives a better idea of Choate
than any other man in the country than Parker could (or
would) have given. Our children will appreciate it, as they
will John Brown, more fairly than we.

The ducks — my own raising — were as fine as any I ever saw
or ate, and I felt somewhat disappointed that you did not
come,— especially as you had no better reason. It is never
"ridiculous" to seek good food. Come Saturday, if you can
and will.

In our editorial to-day, you will recognize some of your ideas
and expressions as to Brown's final taking off. I didn't mean
my man should adopt the language, but only use the idea, with
the others that I fished up for him — but he said he could not
spoil yours, and brought it to me, as a quotation from a private letter. This would not do,— and as there wasn't time to
wholly remodel the article, I made a nice piece of patchwork
of it,— only shrewd people will be amused by the abrupt
changes in style from feeble to forcible and back to feeble again.
However, I think it is a good article all around, and if you
aren't ashamed of it I shall be relieved.

February 9, 1860.

Mrs. B. and I came back from Albany to-day, after a pleasant visit. I saw various people, and learned a few new things.
The most interesting thing however was a dinner with Thurlow
Weed, and a long private talk with him. He is a great man —
one of the most remarkable men of our time — one whom I had
rather have had such an interview with than with any president
of our day and generation. He is cool, calculating, a man of
expedients, who boasts that for thirty years he has not in
political affairs let his heart outweigh his judgment,— and yet
a man with as big a heart, as quick to feel and as prompt to
act, as the best of the men you and I have seen. He is quite
encouraged as to Seward; if Douglas is not nominated, and a
Southern man is, at Charleston, he says Seward's election would
be a sure thing — he *knows* it. But enough of Lord Thurlow—
you shall have more of our talk when I see you if you want it.

*To his Wife.*

CHICAGO, May 18, 1860.

I have just received your letter of Monday night, for which I
had been anxiously waiting for two days. The excitement is
tremendous, and the nomination of Abe Lincoln has just been
made. Mr. Seward's friends are disappointed and sad, but
everybody else feels that it is a right result, and that the Republicans will succeed with him. We hope Mr. Banks will be
added for Vice-President to-night, but are content any way.
With Mr. Lincoln we shall have an administration that will
recognize him, and give him a chance for 1864, which is perhaps early enough.

I am now disposed to go over to Burlington (Iowa) to-morrow, and spend Sunday with Mr. Fitz-Henry Warren. Colonel
Lincoln and Mr. Hooper, of Boston, are going, and earnestly
desire me to accompany them. I shall be home in any event
next week, from Wednesday, but probably not till Friday or
Saturday. My cold is much better to-day, but I am wearied
out, and must rest a day or two somewhere before starting for
home. I shall probably be in Chicago on Tuesday or Wednesday next, and may be reached there by telegraph if occasion
requires. If rain is not abundant, have the trees in the yard
around the house, and in the lot, newly set out, freely watered.
The strawberries should be watered every day if the weather is
dry, and every two or three days any way. Water is their need.
The grape-vines, too, must be freely watered.

*To Charles Allen.*

June, 1860.

As usual, I came home sick; indeed, but for the threatened
boil which disciplines me as Job of old was not comforted, I
should probably have remained in Washington over Sunday.
As it is I am unhorsed, literally and figuratively.

The news of Mr. Ripley's death followed quickly your fore-
shadowing; but I did not know of it until I read Vose's paragraph this morning,— for I did not go to the office, and it was
not known I was home. There were some things wanting to
the perfect man in F. R., but it is rare you find so much ster-

ling stuff in one life as he has put into his. We may well be happy to compromise with our aspirations on such results as he has shown — results, I mean, of life and character rather than of worldly endowment. We shall hope to be softer — shall we be able to be as just? To your mother this must come with sad and serious suggestion; and you all have our sympathy and thought. Singular, is it not, — or would be, if not so often illustrated, — that his wife, hovering so long on the brink of the grave, survives him, who bade fair for years more?

I shall keep at home pretty closely now for six weeks, partly because Hood goes off for a month, and partly because it is best for me. With horse, and regular habits, and the consolations of wife and babies, I can mend better here than away. We want to see you, and you will come as early as you can, advising me in advance, that we may have a clear field.

Once only, so far as is known, did Mr. Bowles "drop into verse." Middle-aged people will remember a certain kind of album once in vogue, with leaves of different colors, devoted to autographs and friendly or sentimental effusions. One of the women employed as compositors on the *Republican* brought her album to him for a contribution, and he gave her this:

> Our Lucy's album! Come and write,
>   Young men and maidens all;
> Put dainty thoughts in phrases trite,
>   And make the pot-hooks small.
>
> Lovers may write their hopes and fears
>   On leaves of blushing hue;
> Wise women, getting into years,
>   Will scribble on the blue;
> White for the girls; — why! bless the dears!
>   They've left the green for you.
>
> Pass round the book, and let it claim
>   Free gifts from generous souls.
> An album only asks a name,
>   Here, take it,
>                     SAMUEL BOWLES.

"REPUBLICAN" OFFICE, September, 1860.

# CHAPTER XXVI.

## ILL HEALTH.

NOT long after Mr. Bowles's return to the *Republican* in the autumn of 1857, he began to suffer from violent headaches,—Nature's sharp signal that the engine had been overdriven. But he held close to his work, and for three years more his power of labor was not perceptibly impaired. From that time on to the end of his life, he was in constant battle with physical infirmity. By avoiding such close application to his work as had been his previous habit, and by a succession of journeys longer or shorter, he kept himself equal to the main guidance of the *Republican*, and to a life very full and rich in its activities. Yet through it all he was a crippled man. The full delight and power of health he never tasted, after the tide of vitality began to ebb when he was only thirty-four. It was after that age that he did his best thinking and writing, fought his greatest fights, carried his newspaper to its highest attainment, and ripened in his most characteristic personal traits. But much of the work was done at sore cost, by strain of will instead of free spontaneity, with penalty of suffering days and restless nights. The actual achievement was tantalized by the sense of higher possibilities, seen but unachieved.

There was really but one resource and hope for full recovery,— rest, complete and long-continued. But he felt the necessity, first, of winning a competence for himself and his growing family. He felt, too, as editor and as citizen, the absorbing demands made by the swift succeeding acts in the great national drama. When, returning from the *Traveller*, he took again the working oar in the *Republican*, he wrote to a friend, October 19, 1857: " I would rather be 'fancy-free' for a few months or a year longer, but how can a man in these times?" In "these times" the Buchanan Administration was trying to force upon Kansas the fraudulent Lecompton constitution. The Supreme Court had just denied the possibility of American citizenship to any man with a black skin, and given slavery a legal foothold throughout the territories. Liberty, opposed by the government, found its champion in the press. To take part in the debate,— to express, and by expressing intensify, that public opinion which was to dethrone slavery,— was a task for which a man might well be willing to spend his life-blood.

The circumstances of his early life had wrought into Samuel Bowles like a second nature the habit of unresting activity. He had almost lost the power of mental quiescence. In his own house, sheltered and watched over, he might for some brief hours sink into the languid torpor which the overtaxed system craved. But no home in the same town with his newspaper could be to him a refuge from the cares and thoughts connected with it. The best resource was in going away for a time. But he could hardly find any place where his social nature would not soon engage him in stirring conversations with old friends or new. How can a man get mental rest who hates solitude and who stimulates every mind he meets? This man had no taste for solitude, no genius for lonely contemplation; no aptitude for that inward leisure in which the mind lies fallow, and in almost unconscious repose accumulates the energy for new harvests. Even Nature could not long hold him in silent communion. If there be a spot on earth where all soothing influences unite to woo man into self-forgetful passivity, it is Mount Desert. But even there, between mountains and sea,— with the lulling dash of the waves to soothe the weary head,— the air strong with ocean's salt and fragrant with the breath of pines,— amid the enchantment of sparkling bay and island cliffs and sun-steeped hills,— the restless child of action could not be still. Said a friend who was with him there in 1863: "If we lay down on the shore to watch the waves, he would jump up in five minutes and be off to something else. He used to say to me, 'I wish I had your power of enjoyment.' The fault of his composition was, as Carlyle says of Sterling, that he had no inertia."

Chronic ill health was henceforward the burden of Mr. Bowles's life. Of his bearing of that burden, the most significant circumstance is this, that neither the paper's readers nor his personal friends were ever wont to think of him as an invalid. To those who every morning scanned his work, it seemed to issue from a fountain of exhaustless vitality. It was almost impossible to believe that the alert, courageous, various newspaper had as its central inspiration a jaded and suffering brain. It was almost as hard for the great circle of friends, to whom his presence brought reviving cheer, to think of him as a man harassed by sleeplessness and all the subtle torture which wrecked nerves inflict. It was not in human nature that some of it should not have vent. His daily associates in the office found him sometimes moody and severe; to his home he often returned, pale, silent, and exhausted, but self-controlled and gentle.

Ill health was not without its inner compensations to him. It enforced something of leisure, and with leisure, even though it be that of invalidism, comes a deeper and more delicate sense of things passed by without notice in the midst of strenuous activity. It taught him lessons of patience, sympathy, and charity. Scarcely any human experience is harder to bear than the torture of mind and body, the suffering and the weakness which are caused by nervous exhaustion. Yet out of these depths the soul may bring an enlarged being,—a wider reach of sympathy, a finer tenderness, a strength of endurance. In the later half of Mr. Bowles's life, there was an alternation of heavier shadows and softer lights. Whoever compares the letters which immediately follow this chapter with those that precede it, will recognize in the writer a different man. If there is a loss of outward power, there is a gain of something higher.

His nervous malady came upon him gradually. It had begun to make itself acutely felt in the early part of October, 1860, when he wrote to Charles Allen :

" I am going through a ' crisis.' I don't know whether it is religious, mental, or physical, but I shall be better or worse when I get through. Whatever it is, it is awful night-mareish ; not even twenty-three miles of saddle on Saturday drove it off. If it doesn't move soon I shall send for Mrs. Cook to come back and write my obituary, and for you to write my will."

Against the assaults of disease, his chief resources were a careful regimen, horseback exercise, and occasional absences from Springfield. His physician was Dr. David P. Smith, a man with a genius and passion for his profession, a commanding will, and a volcanic temperament, whose power showed itself best in cases requiring surgical or heroic treatment. He never took rest himself, and it was not his habit to prescribe it for others. He

used to tell Mr. Bowles in his stammering emphatic
way, "K-k-kill a horse and it will do you good!" Mr.
Bowles learned of necessity to be more regular in
his hours, more careful in his diet, and to take more
open-air recreation. But the regimen which is ample
for preserving health is often quite insufficient to
regain it.

It was a time when no man whose business touched
public affairs could afford to be sick. Through the
winter of 1860–61 the air was stormy and electric. One
after another of the Southern states was seceding; the
President was imbecile and his successor inexperienced
and almost unknown; councils were divided, and the North
did not know its own mind and heart or the temper of
its opponent. Mr. Bowles inclined to a hopeful view of
the situation, and looked to see the clouds blow over
without a storm, as they had so often done before.
Then came the day when news went over the country
that Fort Sumter was under fire,—then, while from
hour to hour men held their breath and waited, word
came that the stars and stripes had been lowered in
surrender. In one instant the nation shook off its
paralysis. One great impulse swept all doubt and uncertainty to the winds. To restore the flag,—to save
the Union,—was the passionate desire of all. The
guns before which Sumter's flag went down had dealt
the blow "that turns the coward's heart to steel, the
sluggard's blood to flame." The inspiration of that
day—its grief and resentment, its sudden revelation,
like a resurrection from the dead, of a mighty love for
the endangered country; the fusion of white-hot passion
into inexorable purpose — was the baptism for a life-
and-death struggle of four years. Into those years
was crowded for the actors the equivalent of an ordinary
life-time.

The chief place in the drama belonged now not to legislator, orator or journalist, but to the soldier. But every man at home who could worthily act or speak or write felt the call to give the best that was in him to the common cause. How the *Republican* bore its part will be told hereafter. Its chief editor shared to the full the intense feeling of the time. But amid the tremendous rush of public events he was a disabled man. He had gathered and trained the assistants who could carry on the paper's work without any very marked flagging in its quality. But for himself, his ebbing strength had almost

"Amid the Muses left him deaf and dumb,
Amid the gladiators halt and numb."

In the early spring of 1861 he rode with his wife in a sleigh from Amherst to Springfield; a heavy snow-storm blocked the highways; in often getting out of the sleigh, as the difficulties of the road required, he took a chill which resulted in a violent attack of sciatica. Such attacks recurred at intervals during the rest of his life.

In July and August he took a carriage journey to the White Mountains with Charles Allen, whose brotherly fidelity and equable temperament yielded to him always a wholesome and grateful companionship. The two friends drove in a buggy up the Connecticut Valley, stopping sometimes for a night or a day at a friend's house. Mr. Bowles was struggling against his old enemy, a weakness of the bowels. He found something of tonic in the long days out of doors, the restful, unexacting companionship, and such scenery of river and meadows and hills as was well suited to soothe a weary brain. By every such outing he made some gain, which soon was lost upon his return to work.

In the autumn he went for a month or two to Dr. Denniston's water-cure in Northampton. A lady who made his acquaintance there says:

"He was the life of the whole company. Bent over with sciatica, suffering day and night, he gave cheer to us all, though probably no one of us was suffering more than he. He helped in all the common amusements, and was quick at all games. He had a happy and delicate way of receiving kindly attentions from women, without any sentimentality. To everybody his manner was gracious, but especially to plain and unattractive people,— he had a knack of drawing them out, so that they became agreeable and entertaining. Dr. ———, a minister, was there at the time, sick and miserably depressed, and Mr. Bowles seemed to put new life into him. With myself and my husband there began a friendship that never was broken or clouded. He had in him a great deal of the boy,— sportiveness and playfulness. There was a genuine reverence and seriousness, but it was his habit to mask it. All his personal ways were delicate and dainty. In his pronunciation there was a touch of Yankee intonation,— a slight flatness of the vowels,— not disagreeable, just enough to give a relish of the native soil."

In November he went with his wife to New York, where they took rooms at the Brevoort House, and were both for a number of weeks under the care of Dr. Fordyce Barker. Upon their household had rested a succession of shadows. Following the three older children, there had been born three others, who all died at birth, and another time of anxiety was approaching. The event was happy,— a son, Charles Allen, was born, lived, and throve. Following these months of rest, there came to Mr. Bowles enough recuperation and steadiness of nerve to enable him to face and fully measure his own condition and necessities. A more radical treatment was necessary. The situation as he and his associates saw it may be illustrated by a letter from Mr. Bryan and the answer to it.

SPRINGFIELD, January 14, 1862.

MY DEAR BOWLES: In the name of the *Republican*, Amen! Once more pardon me for saying to you what my sense of duty compels me to say, without knowing whether it will be acceptable to you or not.

I am satisfied from your note of Sunday, and from other facts as well, that you are in no condition to come back and take up the oar of labor next month, and that it will be a most suicidal act for you to attempt it.

Figuratively speaking, you are a steam engine, and you have been driven beyond your physical capacity. The machine worked well for a long time, and carried its load so easily that the constant additions made to this load by the growth of years were not noticed, until it had been overloaded and strained in some of its most vital and intricate parts; but when it began to falter, it was discovered that the frame was not so strongly built as we had supposed. Is it policy to attempt to keep this machine running while rebuilding and repairs — acknowledged necessary — are going on? Shall we fit a cog here and a bolt there while the wheels are revolving, and thus run the risk of so complete a wreck as to be beyond repair? Or shall we stop the machine and thoroughly rebuild, depending in the interval upon such motive power as can be brought to bear upon the machinery to be driven, albeit that power should run imperfectly and unevenly? I ask you, boldly, shall we thoroughly rebuild, and run as best we may while the rebuilding goes on, or shall we patch up and patch up, exposing ourselves to the risk of a total break-down?

You must not entertain the idea of going to work this spring. I beseech you not to think of it. I pray you take warning by the past. You cannot ward off disease by simply resolving that you *will* ward it off. You have not the physical strength sufficient to meet the severe demands heretofore made upon it, and why renew the tax upon it in its enfeebled estate?

But to come to the point. Without attempting to be dictatorial or presuming, I have to say affectionately and earnestly, you must go abroad. Dr. Holland must come back to the editorial room as soon as his lecture season is over, and give time and attention enough to the *Republican* to keep it in as good shape as possible. We shall have our yearly settlement made up in a few weeks, and then Ben can be spared to go abroad with you, and I do not think you can find in the whole circle of your acquaintance a more judicious, useful, and interesting companion than he would be for you.

I am actuated by a desire to accomplish mutual good, in thus writing you, and have not stopped to ask myself whether my epistle will be well or ill received by you. My appeal comes from a grateful and affectionate heart, and I hope it may be received in the same spirit in which it is made. Will you heed it? Will you look the matter fairly and squarely in the face, and resolve to "rebuild"?

That the God of all goodness may guide and direct you in this matter, and spare you to yourself, to your family, and to the world, in a full measure of health and strength, is the prayer of your friend,

CLARK W. BRYAN.

BREVOORT HOUSE, NEW YORK,
January 17, 1862.

MY DEAR BRYAN: Your kind letter is only another evidence of the constant and generous thoughtfulness of yourself and my other associates in business. I thank you very much for its substance, and more for its spirit. I should be mean and ungrateful to resent it in any way. The subject had been already on my mind most seriously. I had foreseen the possibility that I could not resume my active life, as I had hoped, this spring, and had contemplated the alternative of going abroad quite early, say in March, to come back in early Fall. I believe I have made up my mind to do it, if my fears and not my hopes are realized in the condition in which I find myself a month hence. But I do not wish to consider the matter foregone till after I have returned home, and been there a few weeks at least. As to how and with whom I shall go, if go I do, that may also be left. I am well enough and courageous now to go alone; and I cannot think it wise to take Ben from the office merely as a companion. My absence will fall more heavily, on the whole, on you than on any one else; and so would his — and that is reason enough why we should not both be gone together. Rev. Dr. Storrs and his wife have some idea of going. If they do, I should wish no better company. If they do not — and I must go — somebody will turn up or I can push off alone. Ben would be the most advantageous companion possible, — he would relieve me of all thought and care, and everything of that sort, and be truer to me than anybody else, — I know all that; but he must not go. That I consider settled. You get along splendidly without me. I shall have no fears or anxieties on that score. I should only feel oppressed with the serious care and work thrown upon those I love, and in whose health and happiness I have a personal interest, both selfish and unselfish. But we must follow what seems to be the necessary and wise course, on the whole. And what that is we will let February develop. I hope to be home the whole of that month, and if I must go, to do many things that shall lighten my absence for others.

. . . We send much love to your wife, and though I have not written half I feel of your tender thoughtfulness and kindness to me on this and all occasions, I know you will believe that I do feel it all, — that it even burdens me while it blesses me with its great weight. Good-bye —

Ever yours,
SAM'L BOWLES.

The following weeks confirmed the necessity of the foreign journey, and brought Mr. Bowles to the point of taking his brother as a companion. It is hard for a half-sick man to leave home and wife and children. Europe had not for him the strong fascination which charms and draws so many Americans. The appeal of its associations and its art, the background of a mighty past which colors all its atmosphere, spoke to him less strongly than the stirring American present, with which his life and labor and affections were blent. To go abroad among foreigners while the nation's fate hung in doubtful balance, was to all true Americans more than a common exile. But to put the ocean between him and the *Republican*, to find such restorative as there might be in the green lanes of England and the Alpine snow-peaks, was the best hope for him and for the work and friends he loved. His last weeks were crowded with preparations. Dr. Holland was recalled to the office to take the helm. Everything in the paper which its chief could foresee and plan for, was arranged. The household with all its inmates was provided for with scrupulous care. The good-byes were said, the home was left, and at New York the brothers went on board the steamer, the younger looking with vigilant care to the elder's comfort. The farewell letter to the wife was written in the last minutes; — and, utterly worn and weary, his last act one of provision for a needy friend, his last word one of courage and comfort for his family, he gave himself passive at last to the rough, kind cradling of the ocean.

# CHAPTER XXVII.

## LETTERS: 1861–1862.

*To Charles Allen.*

January 12, 1861.

I THANK you for your note. I only except to its apology. You and I are beyond hesitancy in expressing an interest in one another's welfare. Some months ago I came substantially to the conclusion you express. But I am in doubt as to the form the absence shall take. To go off alone, to Europe or elsewhere, would destroy half the benefits of relief from work — perhaps all of them. I am not self-poised enough to travel alone, without wife or dear friend, and get comfort and good from it. My wife cannot well go just yet anywhere. She could hardly go abroad any way. None of the three or four — two or three — other people I could travel with happily, can leave. The way does not seem to open. So I wait. Meanwhile I mean to spend the winter as easily as possible, spending another week in New York with Mary, and perhaps several in Washington. Also a week in Boston. I mean also to ride regularly, and eat and drink more carefully even than usual, — and *work much less.* Then if, when spring opens, there comes no substantial relief, I shall break away more thoroughly — go abroad, if circumstances invite — make a trip to the Plains — spend some weeks or months in the country or at a water-cure — or make a long trip on horseback, with Mrs. Bowles in the carriage, through New England. I duly appreciate the incapacity that is on me, and hope I shall prove man enough to conquer it, both morally and physically. We will see. Meanwhile I thank you again for your kind interest and its expression. But don't encourage in me the selfishness of sickness. Dr. Johnson says, you know, that every man is a rascal as soon as he is sick.

Mrs. B. and I now hope to run up and spend Saturday or Sunday with you — we will do what we can. I keep better since I am home; yet my head is a constant pain.

*To Miss Maria Whitney.*

January 15, 1861.

I yield more readily to the inward suggestion to let you see what I said about Holland's book, because but for my acquaintance with you it could hardly have been written. What is yours could hardly be told; yet I am sure you are one of three or four women to whom I am indebted for my rebellion at Dr. Holland's Miss Gilbert as a "representative woman." The nub of the article is in the concluding remarks; yet if you have time — and are not to read the book — pray read all, and catch some idea of what the volume is.

I find I bring back very pleasant memories of my New York visit; though most of the days were broken through the heavy weights I carried. Home brings soothing and sleep; but I foresee a long struggle is necessary to conquer my nervous weakness. Yet there is a certain illumination with the disorder that is enchanting at times.

I hope I didn't shock Mrs. P—— with my freedom and almost irreverence. Few women command my respect so thoroughly as does she; and still she stimulates a sure antagonism, and challenges an opposition that I am certain to be ashamed of, the moment I have gone away.

I inclose your thought of the other day, as developed by Emerson. Yet I am sure he has somewhere brought out the other truth — that we are never sure of our knowledge, nor of our ideas, till we have aired them in speech or on paper, and thus looked at them from outside ourselves. But Emerson is catholic to all truth; that is his merit, and his demerit as an efficient reformer. To reform, one needs to hold firmly and present savagely a single truth, or one side of truth, and this

Emerson is too well poised, too broadly cultivated, to do.— I have thought a good deal of your suggestions on the loss of feeling and knowledge through their expression, for they interested me. There are some subtle distinctions to be drawn here, yet I do not know but you were nearer right than I. But all this will keep.

*To H. L. Dawes.*

February 26, 1861.

I thank you for your notes. But I can't go on and help save the Union. There are patriots enough at Washington now to do that business. I have thrown my sciatica, but I am o'er weak, and could not stand the fatigue and excitement of your capital city in this "crisis." Moreover, I am afraid I haven't a vital interest in the present row. We shall come out of it, sooner or later, safe and sound, and not a bit sooner for my fretting. I have a great faith in everything but the Republican party, and that, if it chooses, "may go hang." It seems to care a deal more about getting Mr. Seward out of the cabinet than anything else just now. Lincoln is a "simple Susan," and the men who fought a week at Chicago to nominate him have probably got their labor for their pains. But no matter — Seward is a necessity; Chase or Banks ought to be, and really are, if the machine is to run its four years; but let the New Yorker with his Illinois attachment have a fair trial. I mean to be as loyal as possible, and that isn't very loyal; for you know I do love to find fault and grumble, and thank God I can afford to. There are a few friends so demented as to want office, whom I desire to help; and for that I may go to Washington a few weeks hence, and then I shall retire to nurse my health, and mayhap for that go to Europe, and try the only perfect government on the globe — that of Louis Napoleon.

What was apprehension about Andrew is now conviction. He *wobbles* like an old cart — is conceited, dogmatic, and lacks breadth and tact for government. Yet withal one of the cleverest, good-naturedest, and heartiest fellows alive. We were right at Worcester last August; and the people will yet see it and perhaps acknowledge it.

As to compromises, our people must do *for themselves* and for the border states *all they can afford to do.* They can afford a national convention, and should have proffered it early — not accepted it. So they can afford to grant the Adams propositions. It is not concession to traitors. It is only spitting on our hands to take a firm hold of the government. My instincts rarely fail me in politics, and they are sure here. It is not probable I should see this thing differently at Washington; but I am glad I am not there. I can keep cool here, and calm, and am reading poetry, and pitying my friends who can't. Heaven bless and keep you, and bring you home happy.

This letter reads strangely, twenty-five years after it was written. Lincoln "a simple Susan," Andrew a good-natured incapable, compromise the way of safety, the Republican party the weak element of the situation, and the crisis only a transient panic,— and this the judgment of a man whose "instincts in politics rarely fail him, and are sure here!"

Yet any one inclined to pronounce this confident prophet a fool above all his fellows, will do well to remember that Lincoln himself, on his journey to his inauguration, said: "This crisis is all artificial. It has no foundation in fact. Let it alone, and it will go down itself." The time was full of baseless hopes and baseless fears. But this letter illustrates one characteristic mistake of Mr. Bowles during the years just before the war. He failed to fathom the depth of that contest of principles which underlay the surface currents of politics. He did not habitually see that slavery and freedom, justice and injustice, were mustering for a great decisive struggle. Perhaps none had that insight except the men who were themselves animated by a profound devotion to the cause of the oppressed,— and he was not one of those men. He, like many of his countrymen, needed the schooling which the war was to give—a schooling by which some profited and some did not.

*To Charles Allen.*

June, 1861.

The horseback trip [in company with Edward B. Gillett] was wound up to-day by a ride from Westfield. On the whole there was much pleasure and I trust some good in it. I have found out where the weak and where the sound spots in me are, and that's something. The boils the exercise brought out, and which were the chief drawback to the happiness of the excursion, show a poor state of blood.

We rode about twenty miles a day, had excellent weather, were treated with marked civility by distinguished citizens on the route—spent Sunday at Lebanon Springs, and saw the unkissed Shakeresses, and pitied them, but did not want to kiss them—dined with Esq. Colt at Pittsfield—and came over the mountains from Sheffield on Tuesday and Wednesday.

Now, how are you, and what of the book, and our trip to the White Mountains? I am ready to start any time and go horseback or with a carriage, or if you prefer by the public conveyances. Until we start I shall loaf around home probably, but not going to the office much, if any. Tell me what you can and wish to do, and then I will fit my case to correspond.

It is worth while to give a specimen of the letters (very few) which passed between the editor and his friend the congressman on the subject of appointments. The following is a fair and sufficient illustration of the grounds on which, before the days of "civil-service reform," Mr. Bowles recommended men for office:

*To H. L. Dawes.*

July 6, 1861.

I have made some inquiries in regard to a new man for the Westfield post-office, and the result is that if you decide upon that course, and will not appoint Mr. R——, you cannot do better than recommend Mr. T——. He is a young merchant, very popular in the village, of high character, a strong and hearty worker; and while he has been a moderate supporter of R——, his father-in-law, H——, who is one of the leading men of the town, has been a chief supporter of W——. So far as the rival factions are concerned, no choice could probably be better; while in all other respects there could be no fitter or wiser appointment. He represents the vital elements of society and politics, and is himself an efficient worker.

How is the Huntington post-office? If you seek a new man there, Edwin Bowles will be found a satisfactory selection. He is a young man of twenty-three, has been the real postmaster for some years, and probably will be, whoever receives the appointment. He is a second cousin of mine, but that ought not to hurt him. I do not know that I ever saw him—certainly I have not for years. And I only suggest him for such a contingency, or embarrassment, as you find yourself in with regard to Westfield.

Heaven help you through these hot days at Washington. Gillett and I had a right good time on our horseback trip; and next week I am off to the White Mountains with Charles Allen. Good-bye.

July, 1861.

MY DEAR ——: . . . You must give if you expect to receive—give happiness, friendship, love, joy, and you will find them floating back to you. Sometimes you will give more than you receive. We all do that in some of our relations, but it is as true a pleasure often to give without return as life can afford us. We must not make bargains with the heart, as we would with the butcher for his meat. Our business is to give what we have to give—what we can get to give. The return we have nothing to do with. It will all come in due time—in this world or another. We shall have our dues. One will not give us what we give them—others will more than we can or do give them—and so the accounts will balance themselves. It is so with my loves and friendships—it is so with everybody's. There is no call for any of us to *humble* ourselves before each other. To do right, to be generous, forgiving, kind, charitable, and loving, is not humility—it is only justice

VOL. I.—21

and truth to the God in us. We do not need so much to bargain with others as with ourselves. We should measure our
own powers and our duties — see what we can do — what is
most pressing — and do what we can — taking care always to
keep ourselves in good heart and body for the service of
life. It is as bad to overdo as to underdo. In doing a chief
duty, we must not neglect others, even if they are lighter. It
is not faithfulness to wife or husband or children to neglect
brother or sister or friend. Our faithfulness to the lesser duties
gives us strength and capacity and usefulness for the higher.
If, for instance, one can take full care of a child in four out of
twenty-four hours time each day, we do wrong to give him any
more time, to the neglect of other even if lesser duties. We
had best cultivate ourselves by other occupations for the twenty
hours, so that we can do all the child requires in the allotted
four. The length and intensity of devotion and care are of
less account than its intelligence and usefulness. But I may
not write more; and this is very stiffly written, for I am not
bright. Have patience with me till I am stronger and better.

*To his Wife, on his White Mountain trip.*

PLYMOUTH, N. H., July 20, 1861.

. . . I have been too lazy and unambitious to do anything
all the forenoon, but have lain on the bed most of the time,
reading the paper a little, sleeping a little, and dreaming awake
a good deal — wishing I was stronger and better, and able to
do more for my wife and children and friends. It is a week
last night since I left home, but it seems twice as long, and I
so much want to see you all again. It does not seem as if
I could wait another fortnight, without seeing home and all its
fond joys again.

Charles has been sick for the last day or two, so that he has
not enjoyed his food or his travel very much; but he is recovering now, and I expect to see him eat a hearty dinner. I hope
to have another letter from you before we start away this
afternoon, and to learn from it that you are much better.
I have read Dr. Holland's " Renunciation," on Mrs. Flutter
Budget and repose. It has its lesson for both you and me,

though he has not fairly and properly put the question in issue. Sympathies and passions are greater elements of power than he admits. All they want is to have judgment equal to and directing them. No matter how powerful, how acute they then are — the more so the better. But sympathies and passions that run away with us are oftener a curse than a blessing. You and I both need to strengthen our judgments and chasten our sympathies and passions — not to subdue them, but to wisely direct them. Don't you think so ?

We begin this afternoon to enter into the beauty of the mountain scenery. What we have seen is but the taste and suggestion — the shadow of coming grandeurs and beauties. But regret that you are not here, to see with your own eyes and enjoy it all as you can only — much more than I do — is ever present with me. I should be so much happier in seeing and feeling how greatly you enjoyed the scenery. But we won't sorrow too much over that. You can come another time, when I am better, and better able to enjoy it, and minister to your enjoyment of it too.

Tell everybody I am very well, and having a good time — as I am.

NORTH CONWAY, July 24.

. . . It is three days since I wrote you, partly because I have not been where I could directly reach you, and partly because I could not summon will enough to do anything but eat and drive. I have been tired and dull, and leading rather an animal life. . . . My sleep is still unsatisfactory, disturbed and broken by dreams, but still I feel that I am growing better every way. . . . By your birthday I trust not only to be with you, but to be driving down by the sea-shore in your company. The last two weeks of August at least I want to spend at the salt water quietly with you. The temptation and duty to go abroad decrease; but if I do not I shall probably be absent from home nearly if not quite all the time till November, and then you and I must begin to think of going to New York for a while, you know.

We do not meet any very attractive people, and few that we have ever seen before, and have made no new acquaintances.

I have no disposition to see or talk with strangers, and Charley is a little too shy to commence, though he has done something in that line. These Boston people about here are hideously plain. There are plenty of fine clothes, but a handsome face is a *rara avis*. As Charley says, we shall have to take to liquor for exhilaration.

I send a blue flower from the top of Mount Willard, with my love. Remember me as ever to the children; if I felt well enough I would write them — to Allie, Mother, and "all friends and relations." Don't forget Mrs. Cook in my remembrances; her notice of Mrs. Browning was very good. Good-bye — don't forget to be selfish in taking care of yourself.

GLEN HOUSE, July 25.

This has been the most beautiful day since we have been in the mountains. The sun has shone out steadily all the day, there were few clouds, and the highest mountains were clear and distinct to the very top. The drive from North Conway was pretty hard and long (five hours) over a muddy and hilly road. We stopped to see Glen Ellis Falls, — a charming waterfall, better and brighter than the Falls of Minnehaha in Minnesota, — and got here before two. I was quite tired, and had a bad headache, but since dinner, a nap, and tea, am better. We are right at the foot of the great mountains — Washington, Adams, Jefferson, etc., and their forms roll up against a clear sky to-night most proudly. There is not a cloud, and such mountain scenery I never looked upon before. We have promise of a beautiful day for the ascent of Mount Washington to-morrow — more beautiful than any for some weeks.

 . . . On the whole, I feel that I mend. But you must not be impatient at slow improvement. It will probably be long ere I get real well again. The nervous weakness of years' acquirement is not to be broken in a month, or two, or three. But I feel the old blood tingle once in a while in my veins, and I long sometimes to get into action again. The war news stirs me, and I want to be in the midst of the fray. If I were well, I should certainly go down into the midst of the

camps, and see this great spectacle of the century. But good-
night. Love to all.

GLEN HOUSE, July 27.

I am just up, and have a moment before breakfast and the
closing of the mail to report myself as well and happy, and
" renew the assurances of my distinguished consideration " to
my wife and children. We had a delightful day upon the big
mountain yesterday. We started at eight, and did not return
till five. The stimulus of the horseback-riding and the rare
mountain air was wonderful; it was like champagne, and
everybody was full of glee and joy. Charles got up a flirtation with a pretty Portland girl, and I contented myself with
civilities to a married woman and an engaged one. We dined
at the Tip-top House, and a stereoscopic picture was taken
with us in the foreground.— My sciatica is slowly wearing
away apparently, though I feel it some every day, and also
when tired some rheumatic feeling in my other leg. But it is
less than it was, and I do not worry about that. If I could
only sleep straight through the night, without waking or
dreaming all the while, and feel I had had enough of sleep
for once, I should be happy. But I hope I am getting the
better of that.

LITTLETON, N. H., July 29.

This is the third stop we have made since I wrote you last,
and now we are again in the Connecticut valley, with our faces
set homewards. The river looks beautiful and familiar, and
we shall keep within sight of it for the week's drive that is before us. . . . I have not seen the *Republican* for more than
a week. Only one copy has been sent to me since I left, and
now it is of no consequence, for I shall soon begin to find it
wherever we stop. You need not speak of this, however. I
presume it has been forgotten in the excitement.

We are now out of the mountains, and it has been a delightful experience in all respects — one which I am very sorry you
could not enjoy with me. I will try to tell you about it all
when we get back. I wish you would give my love to Mrs.
Cooke, and thank her for her pleasant note. I will try to

answer it before many days; but in fact I am in no spirit for
letter-writing, and have a dozen letters now unanswered. I
have written only one or two notes besides those to you since I
left home. Charley is bright and happy; Poney keeps up his
vigor and spirits, and you will think I have grown fat and
happy. I will write again to-morrow, and I hope a better
letter. This flower I found near the Crystal Cascade. Is not
this fern beautiful? The woods are full of just such. I am
glad you are getting interested in the soldiers; it will do you
good if not them. I meant to have told you and Mrs. Cooke to
see that ——— [a soldier] had every desirable comfort that he
had not, at my expense; and so far as can be now, I wish it
may be. Tell Mr. Bryan and Mr. Gillett that I shall try and
write them in a day or two. But good-night — Heaven bless
you.

HANOVER, August 1.

I did not write you yesterday because I was ill with a bowel
difficulty. It kept me in pain and fretted from two o'clock in
the morning till night, and I could not have written a cheerful
letter — so I wrote none. We drove from Littleton to Bath in
the morning, and staid five or six hours — I lying on the bed
the most of the time, and Charles writing his law reports; and
in the evening we drove on to Newbury, Vt., and spent the
night. I went to see Sophy J—— at Bath, and found her very
well; she was glad to see me, gave me some late Springfield
papers, and sent her love to you. We stopped at a charming
old-fashioned tavern. I slept quite well for me, and I came
out recovered this morning, though not very bright. We
started at seven o'clock, and drove thirty miles at once, before
dinner, to this place. I was very tired and sleepy, and after
dinner had a little nap. At three o'clock I got your last night's
letter, and was quite cheered by it. . . . I find Mr. H——
and his family here at the hotel; also Lucy M—— (Mrs.
F—— of Brattleboro) and her husband, on his peddling tour. I
called on her to-night; she was prettier than ever, and appears,
on the whole, very well.

. . . I am glad you did what you did about ———, though
I do not think it well for him to have much money. What I

meant was that you should see he had clothes and little comforts for camp life. However, I reckon he can be safely trusted with $15 or $20, and I am glad, I say again, that you got it for him. . . . I want to take you off to the sea-shore with Pone and the top-buggy, all by ourselves. I shall wish to be at home for a few days first, and I also wish to go down to Boston for a day or two and see Col. Lincoln. You need not be afraid of my fretting about office affairs, or the sight of the paper disturbing me; I am vastly indifferent to all that, while I am ill; but I like to see the news, and know what is going on about home, like other folks. . . . Don't do too much, dear Mary, either in housework or labor for the soldiers. Save yourself. You will find you can do more in the long run by doing a little every day, regularly, than by long and hard days of work at intervals of excitement. I don't want to be preaching to you on these subjects, but you do need constant thoughtfulness and care concerning yourself. . . . Do, do think of all this, and act cautiously; avoid all work, all excitement, all writing, at night. Let the evenings be given up to quiet amusement and pleasure, and then you can sleep and be refreshed. There, I won't preach any more. . . . While L—— is with you, you must ride out often, and make her visit pleasant in any quiet and unexciting way. I would not have any set " companies," but invite in one or two to your ordinary tea, perhaps every night. It is best, too, that —— is coming. When she comes you had better inquire if she has left any unpaid bills behind her, and have them settled. See, too, that she is comfortable, without extravagance in clothes, and let her stay in peace with us for the present; something will turn up for her before the end of the season. . . . I send you a *Harper's Weekly* that I bought and have read to-day. The illustrations will interest both you and the children. Dickens's new story is finished in it; I have read only this, the last chapter,— but it is as sweet and touching and charming as his last chapters always are.

I feel as the three months' soldiers do, I suppose, that, though I ought to go away again, I want to go home first, and see the dear home friends and scenes. It will be delightful to look you all in the eyes again, and see our pleasant parlors, and the corner snuggery by the bedroom, with you in the arm-chair. Would you like to come up to Northampton on one of the trains on Monday, and drive home with me?

Don't tell anybody what I say about myself, except that I am pretty well, getting very lazy, and enjoying myself very much.

*To Charles Allen.*

SPRINGFIELD, August 8, 1861.

. . . Our trip is a blissful memory to me. I enjoyed it more than I expected to, and am sure it has done me good. I cannot hope it is equally so to you. I was too much in a sub-jective mood to give as much pleasure as I took; but you can have the satisfaction, if it is one, of having " laid up treasures in Heaven," and having further cemented a friendship which has run many years with unalloyed comfort to me, and I trust has an indefinite number of such yet in store for it.

*To his Wife.*

[From Dr. Denniston's water-cure, in Northampton, October–November, 1861.]

What a dismal day and dreary rain! I hope it don't fill your heart and our home with sad and blue thoughts, but that you reach out to the " Beyond," where reunion and happiness are. The carpet-bag arrived yesterday morning, and opened its treasures of comfort, beauty, and love. The flowers were but little faded, and I gave them, after admiring them in detail, to Mrs. S——.

. . . Mr. H—— had a lot of grapes from Cincinnati yesterday. We all had some for dinner, and A—— has just brought me a private plateful to-day. The elder Mrs. D—— gave me a fine basket full of big apples, which are a great treat for me. Everybody is kind to me, and I only hope I de-serve the thoughtful attentions I get from all, acquaintances as well as friends. It is very pleasant, and does a little something towards making up for absence from home and those who love me most and best.

. . . I am about as well as two days ago, and am getting
somewhat impatient at the slow improvement. Yesterday I
was quite blue and discouraged, but feel better and brighter
to-day; but now the novelty of the life has worn off, I suppose I shall find it a little harder to be reconciled to the slow
improvement of the water-cure, and grow impatient at the
restraint and the inability to do what I yearn to.

. . . I hope there are a good many people whom I shall
know and love in this world. I do not suppose people on the
whole are better or worse than myself; and as I want to be
loved, and believe there is something in me worthy of love, I
believe there is something in others for me to love. I don't
expect to find perfection, and shall of course be subjected to
disappointment in some cases, by people turning out to be
what they do not at first appear to be. But that does not harm
me. We are blessed by what we give more than by what we
receive. We need returns, to be sure, but we can often live
on what we give of affection and faith and trust.

. . . Yesterday I drove Miss C——, one of our patients,—
a friend of Miss L—— from New Bedford, who has come back
since you were here,—to church and back, and meantime
myself went in and saw M—— and M——, who didn't go out.
I was too nervous to sit still in church ; besides, I can't bear to
exhibit my lame back to a miscellaneous crowd.

Let me know what the cows are doing ; and be sure that
Michael feeds them fully up to my directions — two quarts of
provender to each, each night and morning ; a half-bushel of
roots (turnips or mangels) at noon, and as much hay and other
stuff as they will eat clean, all the time.

There is not much new to write of life here. Yesterday I was
engrossed with Mr. Tiffany and Mr. Bryan all day; to-day, Mr.
Osmond Tiffany called, and I found Austin Dickinson and John
B. Stebbins down street, and had a little talk with both, and
made a short call on Miss P——. I also drove out Mr. Delano
for half an hour, and offered to drive out with his wife, but she
was busy with household affairs. Miss L—— and Miss C——

drove out with Pone yesterday afternoon, and have gone again this afternoon.

Do not encourage anybody else to come up and see me. I want more quiet than I have. I will send for the children, if I feel like entertaining them, for Saturday; if not, they must await my return next Wednesday evening or Thursday noon. Do you get ready to go to New York on Friday, the day after Thanksgiving. I will get some one to go with you if I am not able; but I expect now to be able to go.

Mrs. S—— is delighted with your basket, and blesses you for it. Get another for yourself in its place. I play a game of chess every evening after tea with little Mary S——, and she beats me now, after two or three reverses. By the way, do you see the *Harper's Monthly*? Tell Mrs. Cooke, if it comes to the office, I should like it after she is through, for the children. I want them to read the illustrated articles; they are interesting and instructive. In the November number is a sweet little poem, too, "A Game of Chess."

Bear me in sweet remembrance to all friends, in and out of the family. Console the children with kisses — let them have "larks" and be happy, if "pa" and "ma" can't. Finally, dearest sister, be calm and peaceful, and as happy as you can be. "Thou knowest that I love thee"—and so, good-bye.

*To Charles Allen.*

BREVOORT HOUSE, NEW YORK, November, 1861.

Mary stood the ride much better than I feared. Of course it was hard, but she didn't give out. We are cleverly quartered in the fourth story of the Brevoort House — up three flights — in a very quiet and retired part of the house. We have a nice parlor and bedroom, ample in size and elegantly furnished, with three windows looking on to Fifth Avenue. We go to bed at ten, get up from seven to eight, breakfast at nine, and dine at five; taking our meals in our parlor all by ourselves. It is somewhat cosy, but very odd. We are as genteel as may be, but after all it is quite a prison-house. Mary has not been out, or down-stairs, and cannot go. I hobble down-stairs three or four times a day, and outdoors for a little walk once or twice. I have got out as far as Broadway three times, but have to stop and rest there before coming back.

Dr. Barker has been in to see us several times, and has got us both under his care — promising to bring us both out right. Mary is pretty well, and hopeful I think, and I am better this week than last — less headache and more sleep, and walk and stand about as usual.

Mr. Dana came in to breakfast with us yesterday. Mrs. Dana has also called, and several others of our friends. I read the papers, some books, and do a little light editorial work. . . .

Let me hear from you as often as may be. Tell me all about yourself, how you live, and what you do. I long to have you well settled in Boston. I believe it will be the beginning of a long and prosperous business for you. Youth may not come to us, save through our children, but health returning, and prosperity staying, we will have deeper joys, though soberer.

*To C. W. Bryan.*

BREVOORT HOUSE, December, 1861.

Our friends cheered us by their sympathy beforehand, and now swell our thankfulness by their rejoicings — and none more than you and your wife. " We make a note of it." I wonder if ever baby was born, the object of more anxiety beforehand and felicitation afterward. Probably not, sir. It is a " big thing," sir, as the boys say; and the young man evidently appreciates his being here, and don't intend to make any less noise in the world than he has done already. He sounds a regular Chinese gong for five minutes before going to his meals, and as these occur about once in fifteen minutes, as nearly as I can estimate it, there is considerable of a sensation about all the time. However, we all manage to make ourselves pretty comfortable, and Mary improves day by day. She is quite cheery and comfortable, and perhaps the following bill of fare for her dinner to-night will illustrate her condition better than any amount of rhetoric.

A bowl of stewed oysters.
4 slices of buttered toast.
A bowl of tea.

And there wasn't a " smitchel " left.

All which please repeat to the sympathizing family, to cheer them up during the Christmas solemnities. Young master Charles Allen — to be called Al, or Allie, out of regard for our home " nuss "— sends his love to his brother and sisters, to his grandma, to that excellent maiden who will be expected to bring him up " by hand," as Pip was—to his aunts and uncles and cousins—and last but not least to all the members of the " firm."

I get myself up straight now the first thing in the morning by an half-hour's faithful and painful walking and family gymnastics, and then by taking care not to let it get cold I keep the machine upright all the day. But the rubbing and the exercise don't leave me much strength or pluck for anything else, and I sleep well for me.

There's a'—that's all there is to say about personal matters. For the rest, I believe just as Hood does—he's right on all the gooses. Except that I am rampant for war with England, and a savage one at that [this was between the seizure of Mason and Slidell, and their surrender to the British government]— confiscating all English property here, and putting the John Bulls through the hardest sort of sprouts. They see that if we maintain the Union intact, we shall have a high tariff on things we can raise and make; that they must buy cotton and provisions of us, while we shall want none of their truck, and so they must be continually paying us specie — and thus we come up to the head of the commercial world. Hence their ugliness, their sympathy with the South, and their desire to break us down. But good-bye— love to all, and many thanks for unnumbered blessings.

*To his oldest Daughter.*

BREVOORT HOUSE, NEW YORK, December, 1861.

MY DEAR SALLIE : Mother devolves on me the duty of writing home to-night. We are both as well as usual, if not better. Mother, I think, is quite as well as she was a few days ago, and quite as well as she has been any time since we came to New York. I am quite straight now, and have been for some hours, but I shall probably yield to the pressure of fate, and be crooked by to-morrow morning. But I think the straight is getting the better of the crooked a little every day, and I hope will overcome it altogether by and by. There is not much new with us to-day. Grandpa comes in every day to see us, and talks wisely, and goes away. Cousin Kitty calls nearly every afternoon, and almost always brings Mother some pretty flowers. She left a beautiful little basket of them this afternoon. Flowers are very cheap here ; you can buy a little bit of a bouquet for ten cents, and a little basket like this of Mother's for twenty-five cents, and a large basket for $1 or $2. Mother's little basket contains two rosebuds, several carnation pinks, some mignonette, and other little flowers. We got your long and nice letter of family news this morning, and were glad to hear you were all doing so well. It seems to me that Aunt Allie is putting on airs ; tell her she must be humble, like a good Episcopalian, and not snub people who are two hundred miles off, and sick, just because she is in authority. Tell Michael to be sure and feed the cows just as I told him. . . . Do you go to Mr. Townsley, and have him make you a new pair of boots. But when you wear your rubbers, wear your old boots under them, if you can. Be careful and not have the house too hot — 68° to 70° is as warm as it ought to be at any time. That is all the good advice I have got for you to-day.

Mother and I both send love and kisses to all.

NEW YORK, December, 1861.

MY DEAR CHILDREN : Mother and I wish you all a " merrie Christmas." We are sorry we cannot be with you, to help make it merry, and be made merry too, in return. But you must make the day as happy as you can for yourselves, for each other, and for all around you. We shall think of you all as happy and enjoying your Christmas-trees, your Christmas visiting, your Christmas dinner, and your Christmas givings and receivings. You can remember us, too, as very quiet down here at the Brevoort House, but as very happy, too, in pleasant thoughts of you all at home, in the possession of a new and pretty little baby, and in the faith that we shall soon return to our dear home and family and friends, in good health, and find you all well and happy as of yore. Mother is much better to-day, and is feeling very happy indeed. The baby behaves himself better than he did,— mother's appetite is improving,— and in a very few days she will be able to sit up and to come out into the parlor. It has rained here all day, and a little snow has fallen too. But the rain wouldn't let it look white, and so we shall have no real winter for Christmas. You, I suppose, have had snow all day, and will have sliding and sleigh-riding for your holiday.— I grow better every day, and have stood up straight nearly all day. The rubbing man I guess will cure me, and by the New Year's day I hope to say good-bye to the old broken back.— Give Mother's and my love to Grandma and Aunt Allie and all the uncles and aunts and cousins, and all the dear friends in Springfield. We kiss you by telegraph, and with much love we bid you good-night.

### To Charles Allen.

SPRINGFIELD, February, 1862.

. . . Tell Lincoln [Ezra], with my love, what I write. I mean to write him in a day or two, though I have nothing new to say. It is the same old thing, as Emerson says,— men and prophets have tried it, and found nothing new or better — to love and be beloved.

### To Miss Whitney.

January, 1862.

. . . How can you utterly desert the country, these pure and beautiful days of winter, and lose these magnificent stretches of vision — the long, white meadows sentineled with trees — the vacant stretch of the river, with its quick life beneath a calm surface, like the great human soul with its outward peace and inward beating — and away beyond the gray and blue hills, with their curtain of hoar-frost, like the white veil that heightens bridal beauty — and the evening reddened light of the sun, that even Gifford never yet transfigured, set off on the eastern horizon with the cold gold of the rising

moon — that same moon now grown round and full like our
friendship — whose first faint outline we looked at together
from Fifth Avenue two weeks ago yesterday morning — how
can you leave all this and more, the pure bracing air, the
still, calming hush of Nature? *You*, country-bred, country-
loving — you are unloyal — you are "secesh" against your
birthright — you sell yourself for the mess of pottage, the routs
and excitement of the city — the adoration of men and women,
the fascinations of gas and furnaces. I know what you will
say — you will shut me up by telling me that warm and loving
hearts are sweeter than the cold beauty of Nature, shine it ever
so brightly — that — that — well, state your own case. I am
not going to convince myself. I stick to my upbraiding. And
I do wish you could parade my western piazza with me in the
first flush of morning, and again in the rich red of sunset —
where the eye travels its twenty miles at one look — and then
for exercise walk off upon the open plains, bounded by our
familiar friends, Tom and Holyoke, beckoning us to their
embrace with the old loving sunny sides and the gilded tops.
Can you stay away? We will try that you shall miss nothing
if you will come.

The weather and the country are very beautiful, in truth,
since we came home. I never knew that I loved the country
so much in the winter before. Only I get nobody to enjoy it
with me. Mary is shut up with measles and baby, and is not
strong for walking. M—— is not enterprising enough, and so
I have to push off on the road solitary and alone, save my
thoughts. If, now, you and ——— would come and join me,
how we would rollick under the inspiration of cold Nature and
warm humanity!

I am trying to read a little, yet it is only a little. I exhaust
my little nerve power in a few hours of writing and talking,
and when reading time comes, I am too weary even for that.
There is nobody to read to me — nobody that I want, and so I
get on slowly. John Brent is good, though — you must read it.
Winthrop belonged to the men of "fine forces," and he recognized them in others, and portrays character and experience,
nature and art, with most subtle and sweet power. Then the

scenes and experiences described are new and fascinating and refreshing, as much so as pure soul after long travail with dirty humanity; as —————— after boarding and Broadway femininity; or, to come to your apprehension, as hot whisky to a parched throat. I am only a third through with John Brent, and only wait for you to join me. Shall you read it in New York, or wait till you get home? Do you want my copy? Then I have attacked Dr. Walker's sermons, which I have been waiting for for some months. I have much respect for and faith in him — have you? I have read only one, and that was on The Mediatorial Mystery, and left it mystery still. The others will fit me better, I hope; and if they do, I shall ask you to read too. Thank you, too, for Mr. F's [Frothingham?] sermon; it has wonderfully fine passages — beautiful and exhaustive of the philosophy of life; but I read it too late to appreciate it all. Events have thrown its material pictures out of line. I copy [in the *Republican*] some of the exquisite passages. But I am not satisfied yet; let me read more of him before I pass opinion upon him. I do not feel the presence of that greatness I worship yet. I have got out my neglected Macaulay (history) also, and hope to resume that. This is the sort of reading that widens and greatens me; it confirms me in my philosophy of history, my views of life and progress. The God in History, when recognized to the extent of faith, gives us all patience and charity, even with those who differ widely from us, and denounce us and our opinions. The statesmen and politicians of England, in the formation period of her polity, are the same types as those we see about us now — the conservatives, radicals, and middlemen, of every grade and shade. But you know my opinions on these and kindred subjects; though I suspect I am really more of a radical and progressionist than you believe me. I have talked with you of men more radical and hot and impatient, and so probably have not done justice to my own tendencies. Then, too, you must remember I have necessarily schooled myself to coolness and philosophy, and to the look ahead. Otherwise my life would have killed me years ago.

Brent, Walker, and Macaulay are my reading for the present. Think of me in each.

Bless you, my dear friend, for opening to me so freely your religious life and faith. Had I not been gradually recognizing it for the last two or three months, I should have been astonished to find it is so great a thing to you. And I am surprised and impressed that yours was that common experience of revelation and rest by a sudden flash, as it were. There must be, I suppose, preparation and thought; but the finishing stroke seems God-given, and fastens itself in a way that must be wonderfully impressive. As to my own opinions, it would be pretty difficult to describe them. Perhaps you have done it as nearly as it can be done — yet I do not wholly recognize it as my condition. All these things have seemed very much a muddle to me — my mind never could solve them. I can generally average and condense the intelligent views and opinions of others on most subjects; but here the wide divergence of great and good men, the contradictions of revelation and science, the variant testimony of all our sources of information, have been too much for the grasp and condensation of my mind. So I have just put it all aside — and waited. I have striven to keep my heart and my head free and unprejudiced, open to all good influences — ready to receive the gift, but perhaps not reaching out for it — and not reaching out, perhaps, again, because when I made the effort I felt a sickening feeling of hypocrisy, mixed with the apprehension that to go ahead was for me to go back. And that the faith of the fathers and the testimony of good men forbade me to do. So I have seemed forced to be content to grow in goodness in my more practical way, and to leave theories and faith to time. I try to make my life show the result of Christianity and godliness, if I have not the thing in its theoretical form. Patience, charity, faith in men, faith in progress, have been lessons that I have been learning these many years. Purity of life too has been a steadfast aim. Measured by my fellows, I have been successful — more successful than many who have firmer foundations, or affect to have. But this consciousness is injurious to me. It is leading me to be content. It is perhaps reconciling me to a little sin. And indeed I do not expect ever to be perfectly good, or to find any other person so. I do not see how that is possible

with any nature. That is, I mean by goodness, purity of soul —
perfect purity in thought as well as action. Deeds may be commanded, though that is rare, and I do not know that I ever
saw or expect to see a person who can do it, — but the thought,
never, it seems to me, so long as we are human. Indeed, does
God expect or demand it of us? We cannot *crucify* our earthly
desires, — that has been tried, and it was semi-barbarism. They
are the elements of growth, of usefulness, of progress, almost
as much as the yearnings of a higher and holier nature. Strike
out from the world the deeds or that portion of them done
through the promptings of what may be called the human side
of our nature — ambition, selfishness, passion, love, hate, etc.—
and the world would stop, retrograde. There is not *force*
enough in the divinity within us to carry on the machine. Does
not God understand this better than we do? Are we not made
as we are with a view to produce the greatest results? Let any
candid mind, honest but severe, examine the motives which
lead it to the execution of its highest and noblest deeds — I
imagine it will find subtly but not always feebly working there
some elements of selfishness, pride, ambition, desire to appear
well, make an impression, gain the applause of the multitudes
or *the one*. Did you ever think of that? I have, and watched
myself and others — and sometimes I have thought there was
never an *absolutely* pure action — pure I mean of any human element, wholly divine. And why should there be? Can human
beings become divinities — wholly, exclusively? When they do
they will cease to be human, and go hence. So I learn patience
and charity, even for myself. All progress, all good, is but an
approximation. The end is never reached, never can be, perhaps never could be, — but the effort should be continuous
and earnest. It should also be *intelligent*. It should not be
self-upbraiding and morbidly dissatisfied with itself. Praise is
said to be useful to others — is it not to ourselves from ourselves? Justice is the better word — we should be just and
generous to ourselves. There are some people — are you not
one? — charitable and loving and generous to everybody else,
but hard and severe to themselves. This is cruel, wicked. It
limits their happiness and their usefulness. One of our first

duties is to ourselves — to make ourselves happy. Then we can
make others happy, and make them grow, and grow with them.
Of course, indulgence is not always the way to make ourselves
happy — and yet there are some indulgences that we should
permit ourselves. The philosophy of life is understood by but
few. Our humanity makes us oftener blindly practice and
illustrate it, than spread intelligent theories. We practice
better than we preach. Mr. Staples's sermon had some fine
illustrations bearing on this point — the protests and conquer-
ing protests of human nature against dogmas and creeds and
theories, that seemed to be of God at the time, — you remember
them. There is no end of the application of this philosophy;
the difficulty is in the *intelligent* application. Give one man the
doctrine I have enunciated, and he would run away to the
devil under it. And in the application of it, there will occur
thousands of cases full of doubt and trial — questions of Love
and Duty — Duty to ourselves and Love to others. . . . And
indeed in the application of any rule there would spring up a
new crop of questions below the first — and so on and on.
Here is the field for our higher intelligence, our purest justice
to ourselves and to others. Every one must be a law unto
himself. If I should tell you what to do, in the case of
———, it might be impossible for you to do it — it might give
too little to yourself or too little to him. — And all this is life.
We grow in all ways and by all sorts of means — here by indulgence, there by restraint. But I think you, and such as you,
as often do yourselves wrong by restraint as by indulgence, by
being unjust to yourselves in your great desire to do no injustice to others. . . . I have meant to speak generally, and
to utter very generally my views of religion and life and
humanity. Perhaps you think it is low — that it betrays lack of
faith in humanity as well as faith in God. Consider it again and
you will think otherwise. I have great faith in man, and the
faith in God is perfect, only it cannot describe and take hold of
the object. But I have run away from my religious life. I know
what I want and lack — it is a higher inspiration. It would
not change my theories, but it would lift up my life, give it
more play, more richness, more power for daily good.

*To his Wife before sailing for Europe.*

BREVOORT HOUSE, Tuesday night.

DEAREST: We are in the midst of a snow-storm, but the Cunard steamers wait for nothing, and besides it will probably be clear to-morrow. I was very deeply drained by the last few days at home, but surprised that I was able to stand so much. There was a cheery crowd of men at the depot; the Briggses and Merricks were on the train; and I had a pleasant call at New Haven with the Whitneys, and got in here in good season at night, and went to bed by eleven o'clock, and had a fair sleep for me. To-day I have been about a little, but not so much as I had proposed. The weather was bad, and I could not go over to Brooklyn without too great fatigue, and so I cut that and some other calls I had intended to make. I find it very easy to say good-bye to friends after the hard strain of parting with home and its nearer and dearer ones. On the whole I feel better and cheerier about my going away than I have done. I have faith that it will all work out rightly and happily for my and our happiness and health. At any rate, we must both act and live as though we expected and believed that. But as I have kept clear of emotional indulgences since I left home, I will not get back to them now, for if I do I shall break down. You know how I feel and what I should say if I yielded to the impulses of the heart and the occasion. . . .

BREVOORT, 9 o'clock, Wednesday.

DEAREST: Now good-bye for a few months. We shall come together again, healthier and happier — both better I trust for the separation. Don't shut yourself up. Go out, circulate around, see your friends, and know always that I never shall be so happy as when I know you are well and happy and enjoying all that life gives you of home and friends and beauty and love around you. . . .

——— has just come in to say good-bye. He will write you. He accepts our offer. I am very glad of it. Now send him and ——— the money regularly, and tell nobody. . . .

Kisses and love for children, and love for every friend.

# CHAPTER XXVIII.

## THE CIVIL WAR.

UNTIL April, 1861, politics was but an incidental and minor interest of the American citizen. The people of the Northern states plowed and reaped, builded and traded, and were absorbed in the interests of the family and the neighborhood. They read the newspapers, talked over the news of the day, went to town-meeting or to the polling-place once or twice a year, and seemed to leave the affairs of the nation mainly to congressmen, editors, and wire-pullers. Then the aspect of the country changed as suddenly as when the curtain rises on a new scene in the theater. These men of peace left their plows and shops and forges, and by hundreds of thousands enlisted for the discipline of the camp and the perils of the battle-field. The flower of the population resolved itself into an army. Back of that army lay the resources and the hearts of the entire community.

The people of the South fought to vindicate their political independence and in defense of their homes. To the typical Southerner, always attached to his state and his section more than to the Union, the defense of the Confederacy against invasion was as natural an impulse as was his forefathers' maintenance of American independence against Great Britain. A minority had opposed secession as politically inexpedient. But the moment the invasion of Northern armies was seen to impend, the instinct to defend their firesides roused the whole white population into a resistance as united and as resolute as ever a people made. The slaves remained peacefully at their work, save when the approach of the Union armies tempted the more adventurous to flight. Many of them, when emancipated in the course of the war, enlisted in the Union armies, and showed abundant courage as well as capacity for discipline. The masters of the slaves did not venture to enroll them as troops, but families were freely entrusted to their fidelity on many a lonely plantation.

The people of the North had not their independence to fight for, or their homes to defend. Secession, if successful, would have left to the Northern communities the same independence as to the Southern. There was no immediate menace to Northern firesides. But what was menaced was the unity of the American nation. By a marvelous instinct the common people of the Northern states realized that the breaking up of the Union was an ultimate danger to the personal freedom and safety of all its present and future myriads. It was the first step in the dissolution of a great social order into warring atoms. They recognized, by an intuition deeper than logic, that the welfare of each household in the land was bound up with the organic life of the nation. They saw in the stars and stripes the imperiled symbol of the common good and the common right. To defend that they staked their fortunes and their lives.

The North began the war in a temper of passionate ardor and hope, looking for speedy victory. The defeat at Bull Run was a bitter disappointment; but after the first shock came a bracing of the sinews for a longer effort,— very long, they thought, it could not be. Then followed the organization and slow training of McClellan's army; the schooling of the nation in patience; a confident expectation that the Peninsular campaign in

early summer of 1862 was to be the decisive stroke;—
then the seven days' struggle, and the heart-sickening
sense that it had failed. Fresh calls for troops followed;
then the rebels' invasion of Maryland and their repulse
at Antietam; — the successes in the West, the resistless
march down the Mississippi and its tributaries, to meet
the conquerors of New Orleans;—but for the brave
army of the Potomac fresh repulses, and the slaughters
of Chancellorsville and Fredericksburg. So went
the tremendous alternation, hope now drooping at
delay, now flushed by triumph. The story was not single but million-fold, as in the homes of East and West
the eyes of fathers and mothers and wives and sisters
were fastened on their soldier in the field, while they followed with scarce less eagerness the fortunes of the cause
to which they had given so much.

Slowly turned the doubtful tide of war. Lee's army
taking the offensive met at Gettysburg a great disaster;
thrown again on the defensive, again it held at bay
the overwhelming numbers which the North poured
against it. Vicksburg fell and Port Hudson; — "the
father of waters," said Lincoln, "flows again unvexed to
the sea." Grant, the conqueror of the West, was called
to lead the final assault on the rebel capital; then came a
summer of multitudinous slaughter;— meanwhile, Sherman's victorious march through the heart of the exhausted
South,— then the winter before Petersburg, besieger and
besieged locked in the last grim clutch,— until outnum-
bered, starved, overborne, but dangerous to the last,
Lee's army fell. The agony was ended,— the nation was
one, and free.

The North's first impulse of loyalty to the Union
became mixed as the struggle went on with both finer
and coarser forces. It fought at first for an unbroken
nationality. Soon rose in many minds the purpose, not
only to preserve but to purify that nationality,— to make

an end of the legalized wrong against a race. That purpose was opposed for a while by the legalists, the timid, the selfish — but it prevailed; and the North fought through the last half of the war for universal freedom as well as for national unity. At bottom the South was fighting for the power to hold men in slavery, and the North was fighting to break down that power.

Yet other motives had large place. The North had a great material stake in the contest. To the West, the possession of the lower Mississippi by a foreign power meant commercial vassalage. While the South was utterly impoverished by the war,— its one product, cotton, being shut off from market by a blockade which also excluded all imports,— the teeming population and manifold industry of the North were not exhausted by the drafts of the conflict. Its shipping was driven from the seas by the Confederate cruisers, but its commerce went on though under foreign flags. Its farms and factories and shops and colleges were full and flourishing. The equipment and supply of the armies created temporary activities; general business throve; the expansion of the currency gave a feverish activity to trade. Great fortunes were made out of army contracts, honestly and dishonestly; and the poor cloth sometimes furnished for uniforms gave a new name, "shoddy," for sudden and ill-gotten wealth. The volunteers of the early years were largely from the best class of citizens; but as the supply of such recruits slackened, recourse was had to large bounties; forced drafts were made; and the men thus enrolled, and those who enlisted for the high pay, were of an inferior class. Politics became more passionate than rational, and a class of politicians flourished who traded on passions which they did not share.

But in its broad aspect it was an ennobling period. Men learned to live for something larger than self. The

air was charged with a religion which made men willing
to die for men. Life was exalted. Its outlook was wider,
its temper more heroic. Men woke to consciousness of the
higher relationships,—they felt as never before that

> " 'Tis not the whole of life to live,
>   Nor all of death to die."

No state took a heavier share of the common burden,
and none was more forward and resolute to push the
war to the highest issues, than Massachusetts. She contributed none of the great commanders, but the Massachusetts regiments were always recognized as among the
finest material in the Northern armies. The high intelligence of the rank and file made them easily amenable to
discipline. There was a brain and a conscience behind
every musket. The proudest historic names were on the
muster-rolls. In its politics the state was more than
Republican,— it was Radical. Its representative public
men were such as Andrew and Sumner. The tide of
patriotism lifted people above the barriers of sect. In
communities like Springfield, where a social partition
line had run between Orthodox and Liberals, it almost
disappeared when men of the different churches shoul-
dered their muskets in the same ranks, while at home
their wives and sisters were working together to provide
supplies or raise funds for the Sanitary Commission.
The humanitarian spirit in literature assumed a new
form. For many years, poets and reformers had decried
war as much as slavery. Now Humanity was seen as a
warrior goddess. Emerson and Holmes and Whittier sang
battle-songs ; Hosea Biglow's verse no longer satirized
war, but was charged with the passion of those who
fought and the pathos of those who watched.

The higher life of the nation in the war was epitomized
in Abraham Lincoln. With all his heart he loved peace

and abhorred violence. His whole instinct was to govern by appeal to right and reason. But when the higher powers had set the great issue to be tried by the ordeal of battle, his resolution was inexorable, his patience inexhaustible. The joy of combat was foreign to his nature. It was the suffering of the people, as much as his own responsibilities, that furrowed his face with wrinkles. He scarcely felt the conscious thrill of victory before he bent every energy to heal the wounds of war. He had grown and lived among the hardest materialities of the West, and amid the selfishness and pettiness of practical politics. He had an easy-going tolerance for men and practices far below the ideal standard. Yet the bed-rock of the man was moral fidelity. His was a careful and considerate conscience, guided by reason, amenable to logic, scrupulous to look well at all sides of a question. He was thoroughly teachable; he listened to every speaker; he let the preachers preach to him, and gave his ear to statesmen of every shade of opinion; he talked freely with plain men and women; he consulted Sumner, as the barometer of the nation's conscience; he turned to Seward's diplomacy when a foreign complication was to be averted; he utilized the fiery energy of Stanton and the financial genius of Chase. His administration in its details was under a perpetual storm of criticism, but the people never doubted that an honest man was at the head of the government; and his homely common sense, his humanity, his humor, won for him more and more their trust and love. By nature deficient in that faith which is buoyant confidence, he was rooted in that deeper faith which is unswerving fidelity. Accustomed to guide himself by logic and by the outward sight, rather than by spiritual vision, there grew in him under the schooling of events an awed sense of some divinity guiding the affairs of men. His service to his country was perfected by his death. Martyrdom gave to his worn and homely figure the last touch of radiance in the eyes of his countrymen. A nation's highest treasures are the heroes in whom something of ideal greatness is realized, and who become the guides and prophets of its future. The greatest of America's servants to-day is Abraham Lincoln, as he lives in the hearts of the people.

To trace in detail the story of the war is a task which does not belong to these pages, save at the points of special contact with the history of the *Republican*. Americans never read their newspapers so eagerly as in those days. Every household had either members or friends in the ranks of the armies. Women were concerned no less deeply than men in the war, shared vicariously in its worst sufferings, made its greatest sacrifices, and breathlessly watched its daily fortunes. The newspaper was the medium through which all these anxious hearts looked out on the strife. So newspapers as a class prospered and grew. The *Republican* prospered, though its limited means forbade any such splendid enterprises of news-gathering as the great city journals achieved. The New York *Herald* is said to have spent half a million dollars for its war news. The *Republican* could afford no " special war correspondents." It had occasionally a soldier's letter ; and it had one series that ran through the whole war, in which, under the name of " Dunn Brown," Rev. Samuel Fiske, who served in the ranks of a Massachusetts regiment, described his experiences in a pithy, off-hand style, full of spirit and humor and color. But the leading feature of the paper was the daily report of the various campaigns, a story read then with breathless interest, but which is now to be studied as it has been winnowed and condensed into histories of the war.

The effect of the war while it lasted was to magnify the function of news-giving and relatively lessen that of shaping opinion. Fighting once begun, the people needed little leadership except in the field and the cabinet. The press scarcely needed to give education, beyond the story of what was passing. Such other education as was needed was not so much the imparting of new ideas as the articulate expression of those sentiments which already lay more or less clearly in the readers' minds. When the nation was nerving itself for the final effort, the *Republican* (August 27. 1864) said of "The Journalist as a Leader":

"His power does not lie wholly or chiefly in the ability to convince or the gift to persuade. He has marvelous resource in the mere power of expression. There is virtue enough at this hour in the yeomanry of our country to save it, but it is dumb. It is his duty to give it voice. Heroism unuttered is robbed of half its force. . . . The journalist can unite all those who have high and generous thoughts, even though they may have them unconsciously, by giving utterance to those thoughts, by making his readers feel that thrill of sympathy with the virtue of others which shall quicken their own. There is a world of self-sacrifice, of endurance, of resolve in the masses, to which the leader has only to appeal. Their very silence is listening for his voice. Their voiceless thought is a sword which it is his privilege to unsheathe. Their courage and self-devotion are motive forces like steam or water power, waiting for his pen as for the machinist's hand to bid them put their shoulder to the wheel.

"The vast majority in this country are men of moderate means and simple habits, to whom the interests of labor and the rights of mere manhood are vital. It is of the first importance to them that this war should close not by concession or compromise, but by the victory of the right. Inured to hardship and privation, their whole life is a moral tonic that has strengthened them for the hour. They have muscle enough to fight their battle, they have thrift enough out of their modest industry to pay its cost, they have energy enough to use their resources effectively and well. They want merely that the press should be true to its mission, to lead them to the charge. Men of action, they wait for the men of words. Let them not wait in vain."

The *Republican* did its own part manfully and well. It reflected and expressed the unfaltering determination with which the people of Massachusetts, like those of the whole of the North, carried through the costly work of the war. Its instinct toward criticism and extreme independence was subordinated to the great necessities of the time. It not only upheld without faltering the Union and the war; it supported with equal steadiness the government of President Lincoln. In that government there was a great deal to provoke criticism. A peacemaker by every instinct of his nature, and almost wholly without administrative experience, Lincoln found himself the nation's captain in a gigantic war, and the chief administrator in a governmental system the work of which had been suddenly and immensely increased. Military interests sometimes suffered because the supreme commander was a civilian and a politician. There were mistakes and groping and terrible waste of resource. The heaviest burden of the nation was that its toils and sacrifices seemed so often thrown away by bad generalship. The President underwent fierce and frequent criticism. But the mass of the people stood by him through all, because they were certain of his patriotism and his honesty. The *Republican* stood by him always. He had none of that brilliancy and magnetism which were apt, as in the case of Douglas, to win the paper's sympathies; his faults were often those of slowness and hesitation, with which it was not wont to have patience. But, because it recognized his entire moral soundness, and his position as necessary leader in the great work in hand, it supported him through evil and good report.

It is unnecessary to write any detailed history of the opinions expressed by the *Republican* in those years: it will be enough to outline its course on two subjects—slavery and party politics. That stumbling-block of intelligent consciences, the conflict between the legal and moral aspects of slavery, passed out of sight while secession gathered to a head, and in the outbreak and first shock of the war; and then it reappeared. The first object of the war was to put down the rebellion and restore the authority of the government. That was the view which Lincoln maintained. But soon a sentiment found expression that the war should be openly directed against slavery as well as against the rebellion; that it should be made avowedly a war for emancipation. This sentiment was strong in Massachusetts and in many parts of the North. The old Abolitionists and anti-slavery men were reënforced by others who thought that the former legal rights of slavery had been canceled by the slave-holders' rebellion. In opposition to these, the President for a time, and the more conservative of the Republicans, as well as the entire Democracy, maintained that the sole object of the war was to restore the supremacy of the Constitution, and bring back the insurgent communities to their former status; and that the obligations of the Constitution regarding slavery and all other matters were in no whit impaired by the defection of one section from its allegiance. This view was held for a time by the *Republican*. It thus argued the matter, October 2, 1861, under the heading " Shall it be a war of emancipation ?"

" About half the sermons preached on the late day of National Fast—and by the leading city preachers, who are accounted the representative men of the various sects — assume that God requires that the war should be made a war of emancipation, as a condition of success, and that the defeats and failures hitherto encountered are in consequence of the neglect of government to fulfill this condition. Not Dr. Cheever alone, but Dr. Bacon, Dr. Cleveland, Dr. Tyng, Dr. Bellows, and a host of other titled and untitled divines, of all denominations, took the same view. . . . Let us not rashly accept a conclusion involving such tremendous consequences. If we adopt it, the war is no longer a war for the Constitution and the Union. It sets aside the Constitution; it is a counter-revolution at the North against the revolution at the South. It releases the South from its constitutional obligations and makes the contest one of sections and institutions." Those, says the paper, who believe that the Constitution is " a covenant with death and an agreement with hell " may consistently call for a war of emancipation. " But those who adhere to the Constitution and the laws, and seek the restoration of the Union as the fathers made it, can join in no such revolutionary cry. . . . This is neither the time to discuss amendments to the Constitution, nor to violate any of its existing provisions. If it were certain that the rebels could be more easily subjugated, as some confidently assert, by proclaiming general emancipation, we are to remember that it is characteristic of the just man (and the just nation as well) that ' he sweareth to his own hurt and changeth not.' . . . It is taken for granted by the divines who have furnished us a text, that God designs the damage and destruction of slavery by this war. We hope so. But let us follow Providence instead of undertaking to dictate or direct its course. The struggle that is upon us opens daily with wider scope and greater power, and the more extensive and formidable it becomes the greater will be its effect upon the monstrous social crime in which the rebellion has had its origin and from which it derives its malignant spirit. We need not fear that it will not be sufficiently damaged if we adhere with unflinching fidelity to our constitutional obligations; and the supposition that we need to break our oaths, and to violate the very instrument in defense of which we fight, in order to assist the divine plan, shows distrust rather than confidence in the power of Providence to accomplish its own ends. No,—let us walk firmly on the straight line of duty and right, and trust God for results."

It is unnecessary to elaborate here the objections urged against this view:—that it was very tender of the technical rights of the master, and wholly oblivious of the moral rights of the slave; that the familiar plea of the legalist against the humanitarian was out of place when final appeal had been taken to the arbitrament of force; and that it was an odd interpretation of a man's constitutional rights which allowed you to shoot him, but forbade you to set free his slaves.

As the war went on, the question of slavery in various practical aspects was forced upon the government, which for a time decided questions of detail in favor of liberty, while avoiding any sweeping measures. The return to their masters of slaves who came within the lines of the Union armies was forbidden. Slaves actually employed in the service of the rebellion were declared free. Then Congress enacted that all slaves owned by rebels or the aiders and abettors of rebels should be free as soon as they were included within the lines of our armies. But when General Fremont in Missouri, and afterward General Hunter in South Carolina, issued proclamations of freedom to all slaves of rebels within those states, the President disapproved and canceled their action. Eventually, a vehement pressure was brought to bear upon the President to declare all slaves of rebels free, by virtue of his military authority, as a measure necessary to the successful prosecution of the war. During the summer of 1862 the more radical Republicans plied the President with all forms of importunity and sometimes with reproach and invective. The *Republican* opposed this demand as unnecessary and useless. It said, August 30, 1862:

" The gist of the whole case is this : we have emancipation by law; the law will be enforced and the slaves freed as fast as the armies penetrate the Southern section ; a proclamation of military emancipation could be enforced no farther,—therefore there is no real foundation for the issue which some of the Republicans attempt to raise against the President, and the only way in which General Fremont and the rest of us can help enforce the law and free the slaves is to go into the field and defeat the armies of the Rebellion.  Every victory is a victory over slavery.  Every victory is a grand proclamation and act of emancipation.  We have emancipation as a law.  The musket and the cannon must enforce it. . . .  If emancipation is proclaimed as a war measure, it can be realized as a fact only as fast as the adverse section is subdued, and thus much is already secured by the act of Congress.  Neither laws nor proclamations execute themselves."

Lincoln meanwhile was anxiously brooding over the question whether the war should be directed against slavery.  His moral repugnance to slavery, and his oath to maintain the Constitution;—the people's will as interpreted now by enthusiasts like Sumner and Phillips, now by the Conservatives;—the need to satisfy the Northern conscience, the need to hold the loyalists of the border states,—these were the conflicting considerations with which his mind was laboring.  At last he reached a conclusion, which he shared with no counselor, until he read to his cabinet the proclamation of freedom, and told them his purpose was fixed.  The supreme constitutional duty, he reasoned, was to save the nation's life.  The rebellion which imperiled that life was supported by the labors of four million slaves : to declare freedom to the slaves was to strike at the sinews of the rebellion, and was thus justifiable as a military necessity.  That was the logic he used with himself and with the nation ; but an instinct finer than logic told him that the hour was come, and that the people would support him in abolishing the

VOL. I.—23

great wrong. On the 23d of September, 1862, appeared
the proclamation of emancipation. It was moderate and
guarded ; three months were allowed the rebels to return
to their allegiance before the final decree of freedom
should be issued; it was to apply, if issued, only to the
communities in actual rebellion; and it was based on
grounds not of absolute right, but of military necessity.
But it pledged the government, at a near date and upon
a contingency almost sure to be realized, to maintain the
freedom of the great body of the slaves. The President
when he issued it declared in effect that the war was to
be for emancipation as well as for the Union. His action
temporarily weakened his party; it helped to give New
York to the Democrats; it shook the loyalty of many
Unionists in the border states. It did not impair by a
man or a musket the fighting force of the South. The
slaves took no advantage of their new theoretical rights,
until their masters were conquered by the Northern
armies. But the proclamation declared to the world
that the contest was for human freedom. It formally
invoked to the Union cause the mightiest ally,—the
justice of men and of God.

The *Republican* welcomed the proclamation heartily, if
not with entire consistency. It said, September 24 :

" The President's action is timely — neither too soon nor too
late. It is thorough — neither defeating itself by half-way
measures nor by passionate excess. It is just and magnanimous — doing no wrong to any loyal man, and offering
no needless exasperation to the disloyal. It is practical and
effective — attempting neither too little nor too much. And
it will be sustained by the great mass of the loyal people, North
and South; and thus, by the courage and prudence of the
President, the greatest social and political revolution of the
age will be triumphantly carried through in the midst of a
civil war."

When, with the opening of 1863, the final decree of freedom was issued, the *Republican's* comment was:

" Theoretically we are pursuing emancipation as a means; practically we are pursuing it as an end. Practically we must pursue it as an end, until the end come. . . . Let every loyal man feel grateful that he has two good and great ends to look for and to fight for, instead of one."

The course of party politics requires notice. In the first summer of the war, with the autumn elections in view, the *Republican* strongly urged that old party lines be ignored, and no issue recognized save the prosecution of the war and the maintenance of the Union. It pleaded that the issue of "no slavery in the territories," which had furnished the central article of Republican doctrine, had been completely submerged by the greater issue of the war. It called for a union of men of all parties upon that single question. The response to this was very wide and very hearty. The chief of the Democratic leaders were ready to agree. The Boston *Post*, Benjamin F. Hallett, and even Caleb Cushing, were strongly in favor of waiving party lines in support of the government. The call for the Republican convention had been worded in very liberal terms, but it was issued by the party committee, and the purpose was manifest to secure the renomination substantially of the party ticket. In both parties the professional politicians controlled "the machine," and the desire of the people for an unpartisan union lacked practical leadership. The *Republican* made the novel suggestion that in the emergency the editors of the Boston daily papers should issue a call for a Union convention, which would cut the ground from under the feet of the old parties. But Boston journalists, who had never agreed upon any point, could hardly be expected to agree upon this. For one of them to suggest such a convention would have been enough to secure the opposition of all the others. The party organizations were maintained. The Democrats met first, and, in the absence of their ablest leaders,— Butler being in the war, and Hallett and Cushing absent,— a set of small men managed the convention, adopted strong Union resolutions, but denounced the Republican party and took a highly partisan tone. The Republican convention, under the presidency of Mr. Dawes, was both patriotic and catholic in its spirit; Governor Andrew was renominated with enthusiasm, and places on the ticket were given to a Democrat and a Bell-Everett man,— both of whom ultimately declining, the nominations were bestowed upon Republicans. The convention's temper and action were praised by the *Republican*, but with regret that no escape had been found from a party contest. The election that followed was spiritless, but Governor Andrew and his associates were chosen by a majority of 34,000 — two to one.

In New York there was in 1861 a Union ticket, headed by an old Democrat, Daniel S. Dickinson, which defeated by a great majority a partisan Democratic opposition. In other states, then and afterward, during the war, there were some similar fusions. But in general the two parties kept up their organizations.

In the autumn of 1862,— a time of general discouragement,— the Democrats carried New York by a close vote, electing Horatio Seymour governor. Pennsylvania, New Jersey, Ohio, Indiana, and Illinois gave small Democratic majorities. The Republicans had a reduced majority in the national House, and the Senate was still theirs by four to one. The Democracy in general maintained throughout the war an attitude of protest against the Administration for errors and usurpations, and for its growing tendency to an emancipation policy. The tone of Democratic speeches, newspapers, and conventions varied according to time and place from stanch support of the war to denunciation of it. The "War Democrats" sometimes voted for the Republican candidates, sometimes carried their own party for the war and for a merely legitimate criticism of the Administration. Whatever there was at the North of sympathy with the Southern cause allied itself with the Democracy, and sometimes controlled it, as when Fernando Wood was a magnate in New York City, or when Vallandigham led his party to overwhelming defeat in Ohio in 1863. That the Democrats as a body were disloyal is disproved by abundant facts. The great state of New York was governed by that party during the latter half of the war, and in the presidential election of 1864 the party cast forty-five per cent. of the popular vote of the country. But whatever there was of devotion to universal freedom, and of unreserved allegiance to the national cause, found its most congenial place among the Republicans. To most members of that party, its success became identified with that of Union and freedom; the whole passion and fervor of the war-time assured their party fidelity; and it was in those years that the party name became so dear to the hearts of earnest men, that its ascendency was safe, against whatever errors it might commit, until a large part of that generation should have passed away.

In the summer and autumn of 1862, when Mr. Bowles was in Europe, and the paper was under Dr. Holland's control, it came into an attitude of pronounced hostility to the management of the Republican party in the state. The radical element of the party were in the ascendant, and Sumner was their hero. There was among them, before the emancipation proclamation, a very critical disposition toward Lincoln. The state convention in its

resolutions said not a word in commendation of the
national Administration, and lavished all its praises on
Senators Sumner and Wilson. The *Republican* declared
in great disgust that the convention had been managed
exclusively with a view to Sumner's reëlection. That
reëlection it opposed. It declared that Sumner was a.man
of but one idea; that as a practical legislator he was
gravely deficient; that Massachusetts desired no senator
who was not thoroughly anti-slavery, but that she also
wanted a man of broad views and business capacity.
Throughout the state there was a good deal of sentiment
unfavorable to the dominant radicalism. It took form
in a " People's convention,"—a kind of last rally of old-
fashioned, highly respectable Massachusetts conservatism. It nominated General Devens for governor, and
Charles Francis Adams for senator. But the Democrats
damned the movement by indorsing its candidates, while
resolving against "secession and abolition" as equal
evils, denouncing emancipation "in the name of civilized humanity," and opposing pretty much everything
that the best people of the country had at heart. The
name of Mr. Adams—absent as minister to England—
was promptly withdrawn by his son John Quincy, in
accordance with his father's previously expressed wishes.
The *Republican*, which had been sympathetic toward the
People's movement, though never fully committed to it,
gave it up on seeing the sort of alliance which it received
from the Democrats. It expressed a preference for Mr.
Sumner over "any man who is likely to be nominated
against him," and for the Republican ticket as representing a better cause than its rival, while it continued to
protest against the folly of party divisions at such a
time. At the state election the Republicans kept their
old advantage.

Mr. Bowles spoke afterward in private with strong regret of the course of the *Republican* in opposing Sumner's reëlection. The hand of the chief soon appears in the paper after his return in November, 1862; it becomes broader and calmer in its tone, with more of news and variety. From this time on, it was to be counted with the progressive rather than the conservative element of the Republican party. It had felt the teaching of the times. Its chief had brought back from his half-year of exile a fuller health, a broader and calmer vision, a finer sensitiveness to moral elements. The next chapter, giving his European letters, will show how he chafed at being absent in the crisis of the nation's struggle; but that absence, with its rest for body and mind, its long and silent musings, its new perspective of events, served as a preparation for the higher leadership he was to take in the new era of the nation.

The *Republican* was in harmony with the Republican party during the state election of the next year; there being little controversy, and Governor Andrew being chosen again, by a vote of more than two to one. But the paper exhibited its independence by opposing some of the party nominations for the legislature, supporting in one case a Democrat, and in another Daniel L. Harris, a bolting Republican. In local elections its advice always was to vote for the best man, on whatever ticket his name might be found.

The Democratic National Convention of 1864, which met at Chicago in August, contradicted itself. By its nomination for president, it approved the prosecution of the war: by its resolutions, it advocated peace. General McClellan was an excellent representative of the war Democrats. He was an undoubted Unionist; he had shown high merits in the field; and he had suffered from the Administration a damaging interference with his military operations, and finally, in consequence probably of his open hostility to the President's emancipation policy, a removal from command. The resolutions upheld the Union and the Constitution, but mainly complained of the usurpations of the Administration, and disapproved of the continuance of the war. They called for an immediate armistice, to be followed by a convention of the states, or other peaceable measures for the restoration of the Union. McClellan, in accepting the nomination, ignored the platform, and declared strongly for the persistent maintenance of the Union. His associate on the ticket was George H. Pendleton, of Ohio.

The only serious opposition to the renomination of President Lincoln by the Republicans came from a group of captious Radicals, who met in convention and nominated General Fremont. He had after the first years of the war been kept out of active service; by the Administration's jealousy of him as an emancipationist and a popular leader, said his friends; by his own false pride and ambition, said others. His candidacy was soon abandoned. The Republican convention, meeting at Baltimore in June, gave its voice without division for Lincoln; joined with him for the second place Andrew Johnson, of Tennessee, in recognition of the Southern loyalists; fully indorsed the emancipation policy; and declared in favor of the constitutional abolition of slavery, and the prosecution of the war until the rebellion was wholly subdued.

The *Republican* (August 2) summed up the issue between the parties, thus: Peace, it says, is sure to come soon, but what kind of a peace depends on the presidential election. "*Shall this peace be what the nation has fought for, or what the rebels have fought for?* This is the grand vital question of the presidential campaign,

by the side of which all others sink into nothingness."
When McClellan was nominated, it said of him, Sept. 18:

" With respectable talents, a pure character, and patriotic
purposes, he is wanting in that high moral sense that perceives
the truest truth, and that high moral courage that does and
dares in its behalf. He waits, he hesitates in the presence of
great opportunities; he compromises with time and with truth;
and he is no fit man to deal with the sharp exigences and the
sublime occasions of this hour. He wants and would try to
save the country; but he would hinder rather than help the
people, who *will* save it in the long run, despite their own
occasional fickleness and faint-heartedness,—because he fails
to see and use quickly the moral and material agencies by which
it is to be saved, and because he is no match for the men who
are bent on its ruin. . . . The platform is weak in words
and wicked in intention. It lacks vigor, sharpness, and high
principle. The breaking purpose shines through every sentence.
Its words for the Union are hesitating, guarded, shuffling;
while its clamor for experiments that would endanger it, its
want of condemnation for those who have struck at it, and still
hold aloft the bloody flag of disunion and destruction, and its
petty arraignment of those who are wielding the power of the
government to sustain and secure it, all show that the real
sympathy of its authors is with the enemies rather than the
defenders of the Union. . . . We are very sure that neither
the ticket nor the men who will vote for it — all of them — are
so mean as their platform seems to us."

In Massachusetts, Governor Andrew was again renominated. The vigor and success of his administration,
the great-heartedness of the man, and his popularity as a
" war governor," left no room for successful rivalry.
The presidential campaign, somewhat doubtful in the
early autumn, moved at the close to a clearly foreseen
result. Men cast their votes for President Lincoln less
under the feeling of a doubtful contest than with a
solemn sense that the people were accepting and ratify-

ing the prosecution of the war at whatever cost, till union and freedom were won. Only Delaware, Kentucky, and New Jersey gave their electoral votes for McClellan. In a total of four million votes, Lincoln had a majority of 400,000. New York was for him by a narrow margin of 7000; Illinois by 30,000; Ohio by 60,000; and Massachusetts led the column with 127,000 for Lincoln to 40,000 for his opponent. The day after the election, November 9, the *Republican* said:

" The appeal to the avarice and cowardice of the people was a strong one, and it was vigorously plied by the opposition. The burdens of the war are fearful, and they are severely felt. The people would rejoice with joy unspeakable in the restoration of peace. But they have rejected all solicitations to a premature and dishonorable peace. They have declared that they prefer any sacrifice of ease, property, life, to the sacrifice of the Union and the surrender of the nation to the slave-holding oligarchy. The decision is honor and safety to the country and to all who have contributed to it.

" Let the victors be magnanimous. The great body of the Democratic party have meant well for their country in their votes against the Administration. Copperheads and sympathizers with treason are but a fraction of that party, and the party has lost by its concessions to their influence. The masses of the Democratic party will still stand by the country, fight its battles, and rejoice in its victories. Let their patriotism have generous recognition, and let them still further exhibit and attest it by ready acquiescence in the decision of the majority, and by cordial support of the Administration indorsed so strongly by the people."

The completion of emancipation, by extending it over the whole Union and making it irrevocable, had been inaugurated early in 1864, when the Senate passed the Thirteenth Amendment, abolishing slavery. In the House it failed of the necessary two-thirds vote. The Republican National Convention insisted on " the utter and complete extirpation of slavery." The *Republican* declared (November 10) that by the reëlection of Lincoln, and yet more explicitly by the congressional elections, which gave the party more than two-thirds of the House, the destruction of slavery was assured.

" The amendment will be adopted by the next Congress " [it was in fact adopted by the old Congress in its final session], " and the people will ratify it with eagerness and delight the moment they can get a chance. Thus will slavery be legally and constitutionally abolished throughout this Union. This result of Tuesday's effort is even more important in its ultimate consequences than the reëlection of Mr. Lincoln. It is the crowning glory of the peaceful victory of the day. It is a triumph for all time. It settles the vexed question which has brought war, bloodshed, and debt upon the nation, and precludes the possibility of another rebellion in behalf of slavery. The grand triumph is nearly completed. Let us thank God and push on."

The political questions of the time have offered the salient points for quotation and comment in this chapter. But the war itself is the great drama which is seen through the daily pages of the newspaper file from April, 1861, to April, 1865. There it all stands vividly out — the four years' experience which so deeply impressed the lives of all who shared it. There is the first eager and passionate rush against the foe; there are the first defeats, the disappointments, the perplexities, the evergrowing sacrifices; then the deep breath of anticipated triumph when one week saw Gettysburg won at the east and Vicksburg captured at the west; the brightening hope; then the industries of peace recovering and multiplying themselves in the midst of war; the dogged, desperate rally for the last tug of the Wilderness and Petersburg; the equal valor of North and South; the myriads of lives lost and homes desolated; the new manliness wrought by heroic endurance into North and South alike; the birth of a race into freedom, the restoration of a people to unity.

# CHAPTER XXIX.

## In Europe.

*To the " Republican."*

London, April 28, 1862.

ONLY five days have gone since we landed at Liverpool, yet they seem as many weeks. . . . It is curious to notice how many of these Englishmen I seem to know as old acquaintances. *Punch* and Thackeray and Dickens and the *Illustrated News* have made one-half of them as familiar to my eyes as my home neighbors. We had a faint Lord Dundreary on the ship coming out. The custom-house officers that boarded us in the stream were unmistakable as if they had borne printed labels. . . . The village butcher, the magistrate, the member of the town council, the hotel waiter, milord Tom Noddy's valet let loose for an afternoon, Betsey the cook, and Mary the chamber-girl, all pass before you in familiar guise. You almost unconsciously nod your head as they go by. As yet I get my waiters and ministers of the established church sadly mixed up. They dress just alike, and so far I have to give the preference for impressiveness of manner and mental alertness to the waiters. Certainly a big man in white canonicals, who mouthed a lot of incoherent stuff at a popular audience in Westminster Abbey last night, would do the world and his Maker better service in bringing bread and cheese and pouring beer in a country inn than in disgusting and befogging people from a pulpit in the matter of the highest import to their happiness. But a shoemaker I saw at Chester was the very St. Crispin

himself, and it was by great effort of will that I kept myself
from rushing into his arms as if he had been a "long-lost
brother."

So, too, does Nature come to you here in half-friendly and
familiar forms. She is new, yet old. She reproduces to your
mind the descriptions of poets and moralists that you had
read and forgotten long ago. You look and wonder where you
ever saw the same before; confident you have, yet sure you
never could,— as stern and strange events call to mind a
dream thereof not till then remembered. The wide, green
fields,— greener far than even New England meadows,—
bright with yellow cowslip and white daisy; the long hedge-
rows of hawthorn, sprinkled often with sweet-brier; the holly,
the yew, the dark, mournful cypress and juniper, soberly sway-
ing in grand masses as if keeping time to the slow, deep
beatings of a widowed heart; the spreading bushes of the
rhododendrons, filling the ground for rods and rising to ten or
fifteen feet in height, bursting with the buds of the white, or
putting out the green leaves with the wealth of scarlet bloom;
the parks of oak; the little white cottages, covered with blossoming peas or flowering vines; the low, dark, stone parish
church, moss-covered and ivy-crowned; the surrounding
church-yard with the low-lying monuments of half a dozen
generations, grass-grown and time-faded, but still hallowed by
a posterity that lives in the same cottages that they lived in,
and will lie where they lie; the long, narrow pathways through
the fields; the stile where Mary's lover sat and sung for her,—
all "stand dressed in living green" before you, and call up
memories and associations and persons that have lain buried
and forgotten for half a life-time. You rub your eyes, and look
for the people who ought to be among the familiar scenes,—
for Mrs. Poyser and her children coming home from church,
for Maggie Tulliver running away to join the gypsies, for
Adam Bede stalking sternly forth to his work or to search for
his lost Hetty, for the lovers walking arm in arm through the
fields, or sitting fondly under the hedge, regardless of all curious eyes, for the cruel gamekeeper in pursuit of the skulking
poacher, for the humble but devoted country curate going

about doing good, "passing rich on forty pounds a year." They are all here, and I have seen some of them, and shall see the rest before I leave England.

*To his Wife.*

London, April 29, 1862.

. . . I have on the whole enjoyed the stay here. But I am glad to go away — I should be sick of it in two days more. I have taken in a general sense of the city, and am indifferent about details. We shall probably spend four or five more days here in June, to see the great Exhibition, then complete and in order, the British Museum, Windsor Castle, and one or two other specialties; and yet but for the country of England I could hardly be tempted back. I cannot begin to tell you, Mary, how beautiful that is to me already, and how rich its promise is for June. You know how "Plainfield," and that part of West Springfield where the market gardens are, look in their best estate; and this gives you the best suggestion I can think of, of all England. It is literally a garden. The hedges, the evergreens, the ivy, the flowers, are rich with rural beauty; and then it is such a comfort to a *tired* American — tired of our fret and hurry and unfinish — to see something done and completed and polished.

As for my health — the first eight or ten days of the voyage pulled me down considerably, but ever since I have been improving, and now I am surely better than when I left home. I get thoroughly fatigued physically every day, without commonly too much nervous excitement or exhaustion, and this has a favorable effect upon my sleep. I think I get more of it, though still the great trouble is broken and dreaming nights. I am, on the whole, quite satisfied with the improvement I have made in the short time I have been away. At Paris we shall settle down into a more quiet and regular life than we have lived in England, and I expect to enjoy that city much more than London. But I look forward to our proposed week on the Isle of Wight, another week in the Lake country of northern England, and the month or six weeks in Switzerland, with the largest anticipations of pleasure and improvement. The great drawback, however, to it all is that you are not here to see and participate in this new life. I knew it would be so, and yet the feeling is greater and more ever-present than I anticipated. Hardly an hour goes by that I do not see something that I wish you in particular to see and enjoy; and it is a constant fret that I cannot have you by my side, and feel not only my enjoyment of it, but yours in addition. When I was on the steamer, I thought I never would bring you across the ocean, and was glad you were not with me to suffer the torture and discomfort; now it seems to me as if I could not let you stay away another month. I want all my friends with me — one for this and one for that,— but you for all; you who have had so little of the outward life of society and nature, but are so greedy of it. Well, well, we won't chafe any more than we can help about it; the true course is to make the best of things as they are, and seem selfish that we may grow into the power to be generous by and by. But I do wish I had the power of interpreting what I see and enjoy to you more literally than I have. That would give some satisfaction in seeing and enjoying so much that you do not share. But you must take it all in results — in the blossoming, I trust, of a richer life. We cannot share our daily food with those far away, but they may have the effects of it in health and strength. But this is philosophizing, and cheap at that, instead of gossiping.

*To the " Republican."*

LONDON, June 15, 1862.

. . . I have avoided England's politics and politicians, and let alone the questions that now embitter America toward them; and so I have found generally both pleasure and profit in my travels. I do not expect to find any country or any people I like better, and I do not know that I want to. They are nearer to us than any other — more like us — with more of our traits, more of our faults, and more of our excellencies, than any other nation; and all the meanness of her government, all the jealousy of her aristocracy, and the selfishness of her commerce cannot crush out the sympathy her intelligent, independent, progressive middle classes feel for us, now and always. Perhaps I may sum up England with the sarcasm of Macaulay, or Sidney Smith, or somebody else, on her greatest philosopher and states-man (Lord Bacon), and say she is at once the greatest, wisest, and meanest of nation-kind. [Of course "every intelligent school-boy" can correct this quotation, and give the authorship rightly — and he shall be left to do it!]

### To Charles Allen.

BADEN-BADEN, July 7, 1862.

You see I have taken you at your word, and not written — but I can't stand it longer — I must send my message of friendship to you across the water, to give you visible evi-dence of my constant thought of you, and to prove to you that the old fire still burns. One day last winter, as I was walking up Sixth Avenue, New York, two plainly dressed Germans met each other near me, and the cold air instantly grew warm with their cordiality. One said: "I t'inks of you every day." That seemed to me the perfection of compli-mentary friendship. I believe I can say the same of you. This banishment only brightens into stronger relief all my home treasures, all my home friends — and especially during the last month, the anniversary of our expedition to the White Moun-tains, have I had recollections of you and that experience brought keenly to mind. I have lived those days all over, and found new pleasure in the remembrances of them.

Your letters were very grateful to me — I have had two, I be-lieve — and I hunger for more. I want to know all about your-self, your life and prospects, and then about "the folks'" both with you and at Greenfield. Also your views about public affairs, and any gossip of personal or public nature that gets to you. I have no correspondent but you for all that latter class of subjects, and I do not read the papers much, and try not to think greatly about politics and revolutions at home — and yet I do not care to remain in entire ignorance, and your summaries and gossip will just suit me. So, if you can keep up a one-sided correspondence, pray do so.

For myself, there is not much to be said that Mary has not probably told you already. I write to her pretty fully every

week, and little or nothing else.  Now that I have commenced,
I want to write an occasional letter, say once in three or four
weeks, to the paper, especially as Frank [the younger brother
was called sometimes Ben, sometimes Frank] doesn't take to that
thing as he promised to.  But I shall hardly do enough in that
business to harm me.  A fellow like me must have some little
outlet, and I can't talk the lingo so as to amuse myself with
the people; there are no women to chaff with, and to rub your
mind out of its morbidity — what was hunger with us at the
White Mountains last year in this respect is famine here and
now — and I have no disposition to read beyond the guide-
books and old copies of the *Republican*.  It could hardly be
otherwise than an interesting and instructive summer to me;
the journey is full of material, and I only want *society* and a
little more head to be quite content and happy. . . . I
have got through with my sight-seeing experiences, and am
now fairly launched on the summer's plan of out-door life,
which I have great faith will build up the weak points in my
system.  I must expect it to be slow work, for the decay was
slow.  Nobody knows how I have abused my brain but myself,
and I therefore ought to be the most patient with its maladies.
The daily life is simple and virtuous enough to suit an an-
chorite.  I go to bed from ten to eleven, get up from seven to
nine, breakfast on weak coffee and bread and butter (and such
bread and butter you never saw in America for goodness) with
eggs, fruit, or a little meat — one of the three generally — in
addition.  Then for four or five hours out-doors in excursions,
looking at the shops in the cities, and lounging in our room.
If an early breakfast, a light lunch of bread and butter or fruit
at eleven, and a dinner of soup, beef or mutton, and bread and
butter at five, with a little beer, light wine or porter, for drink.
Then more walking and sauntering around till bed-time.  I
am drinking no hot and rebellious spirits at all, and very little
of the light sorts, and these only at dinner.  Could a man be
more virtuous and live?  There are very few Americans to be
met abroad, and those few of little interest.  I had a very
charming Sunday and Monday with Carrie D——, at Sheffield,
and at Edinburgh a strong-minded Miss Bird, who writes books

VOL. I.—24

and reviews, and did write some letters for the *Republican*, made herself very agreeable to us. I met her at Erastus Hopkins's, some years ago, when she was in America. Also at Edinburgh the County Parson fed me and chatted with me. Beyond this I have had no society but my brother, and he isn't a talkative chap, you know. I ought to except Paris, however, for there at dinner we always met two or three clever young Americans, and Mrs. Bigelow and Mrs. Doremus, of New York, gave us two or three pleasant evenings.

But the women of Europe don't fascinate me very much. It is easier to be virtuous among them than I supposed. You see occasionally a pure and pretty English girl that reminds you of our young American beauties, but the Continental dames have few attractions any way. At Paris and these German spas the most beautiful and best got up are the demi-monde, but they savor too much of high art to beguile such a lover of the natural and true as I. But the demi-monde are a class to which we have no counterpart in America; they are respectable disrespectabilities, lead the fashions, and give the tone to the society in the outside, superficial world. You ought to see them on the street, in the gardens, and around the gaming-tables at the watering-places. There are many things I see that would greatly entertain you, but I cannot write of them. Paris is a perfect George T. Davis place,—he would be in heaven there, after getting the hang of it. But I must cut this short. Tell Lincoln about me, and give him and his my love. Let me be remembered also to our pleasant friend Miss B——. Ditto to Judge Chapman. To L—— and your mother much love and many good wishes. Also remember me to the Greenfield home.

*To Miss Whitney.*

INTERLAKEN, SWITZERLAND, July 26.

. . . August 14 is Mary's birthday; you will get this letter—"errors excepted" as the merchants say—before that date, and if you can get away from home, I want you to go down that day and make her a surprise visit—tell her you have come to keep her birthday with her. I will pay you

some time, or try to; and if I don't and can't, only let it go to
the saintship accumulation, and the individuals of coming generations that get your disembodied soul will be the bigger and
the richer for it. Then — at that time or later, after your summer visitors have flown — I want you if you can to go down
and stay a long month at Hotel de Bowles — play with the
children, happify the mother, and ride the horse — and leave
the aroma of your spirit for me to fatten on when I come
back. Don't you think you can do it — and that it will do you
good ?

. . . I have to thank you very, very much, my dear friend,
for your late little visit to Mary. Could I quote to you what she
writes of it, I am sure you would feel repaid for whatever of
sacrifice or trouble it cost you. Yours is the priceless privilege
of making others happy — no life is cheap or barren or lonely
that is so rich in gifts of this sort as yours. . . . I am eager
to talk to you of the several leading topics of which you write,
and in which I either have been already interested, or you
interest me freshly. As to *writing* of them, that is impossible
now. My convictions are not clear and positive enough to be
stated concisely, and I shall not yield to the temptation of writing at length till I am stronger in health and fresher in spirit.
There are some considerations in my mind on the question of
immortality, as well as upon the origin of language, that it
seems to me you do not sufficiently take into account. Nor do
you, I believe, quite fairly state the most intelligent and reasonable view of the future state as felt by its believers. The great
idea of it, the great want of it, is Rest. Nobody is happy in
this life, save idiots, and the feeling that creatures of such
capacities and endowments are entitled to a higher life and a
more peaceful one, it seems to me, lies at the bottom of most
of the popular belief in a future existence. How rest in its
higher sense is compatible with growth and progress, perhaps
no one of the believers can tell; nor can we tell, any of us, of
other mysteries that we believe in. Certain it is that the
laws of life in the other world, if there be one, must be different from those here ; we must put off all that weariness and
striving, all that want that torments us here. God there,

must be to us all that our dreams and ideals are here.  . . .
I am willing to wait.  My views of this life would be the same
under either view of the other,— there I agree with you most
fully.

.  .  .  Mary will tell you as to my health — it is so-so-ish —
not so good as we hoped, but yet improving.  I keep very
much on the surface of life, as you will see from all my letters.
The days go by listlessly,— and the best sign is that I grow
lazy and indifferent to all but the going home.

*To his Wife.*

INTERLAKEN, August 3, Sunday.

The week has introduced me to some of the finest scenery
of the Alps.  Our excursion along the necks of the higher
Bernese range — Jungfrau, Mönch, Eiger, Wetterhorn, etc.—
was a most fortunate one.  The weather has been fine all the
week, warm, summery, clear, with pure, fresh air — a new
moon o' nights, and starry heavens such as we never see at
home, save in those clear winter nights when the stars crowd
and jostle each other, they are so thick.  . . .  The two really
novel and indescribable features of Swiss scenery are the high
snow-peaks and the glaciers of snow and ice extending down
from them through the gorges, and the waterfalls.  The latter are
most exquisite, and shake their coquettish beauties at you at
every turn.  More than anything else they surprised and delighted me.  The mountains themselves, that is, the higher ones,
are simply great masses of rock, bare and bald, save where covered with snow, and majestic and overawing rather than picturesque and beautiful.  The verdure of the lesser mountains and
valleys is wonderfully rich, timid in height, but thick and exquisite in variety and color.  The turf seems more like moss
than grass, and it is as thick with little bright wild flowers as the
heavens are these nights with stars.  The mountains of rock
and snow seem strangers to you, you cannot grow friendly
with them, they frown rather than smile, like an orthodox
divinity; but the little meek-eyed flowers are as sweet and familiar as the "Suffer little children" of Jesus; you are on

loving terms at once; and you only want, at least I only
wanted, the presence of human love and friendly hearts and
faces to feel full delight in their company. But the tantaliza-
tion I have often before expressed robbed all of half its
pleasures. I can't seem to be a complete humanity, and I
think I suffer quite as much as I enjoy in the presence of these
novel sights and rare spectacles of nature. After all, human
nature is the most fascinating of nature to me. I want something that speaks, and that in a familiar tongue, and with a
sympathetic heart. " Come over and help us " — do! . . .
There are lots of English everywhere, but so long as they let
us alone, we do them. I shrink from getting into serious conversation with any one, most of all with an Englishman, for he
would be sure to want to talk about the war, and that is a theme
I cannot talk with any one about, friend or foe. The English,
however, do not make themselves especially obnoxious to us,
I ought to say, and I had an amusing experience with a man
and his wife at lunch, the other day. I called for some English
porter; the woman looked at the man, and he at her, and both
at me, with an expression half of astonishment and half of
delight. Finally he spoke : "I beg your pardon, but did you
say *porter* ? " "Certainly, sir." "But do they have it here ? "
" Yes, sir ; and very good." The woman's eyes fairly danced
with delight, and she immediately offered me a cold boiled
potato that she didn't want. When my porter came I begged
them to taste of it, which they did with increased satisfaction,
and since then they have treated me with great condescension.
They have evidently erected a monument in their hearts to me
for having introduced to them the fact that their pet home bev-
erage could be had in Switzerland. The gentleman invited us to
join in a waltz in the public room, last night, and offered to get us
partners, but we declined as out of practice. I must learn to
waltz after my French and German are acquired. These are
the only acquaintances I have made among the English on
the continent, and our discourse has confined itself so far to
porter and dancing! . . . Frank found "the girl he left
behind him" on the Wengern Alp, seven years ago, when he
was sick and she took care of him. She is now married,

and has a pretty baby. I was introduced, and made my profoundest bow. She gave him a souvenir in the shape of a watch-case, and he has returned the compliment with one of his purchases, sending it by her husband, whom he found down here.

*Monday morning.* . . . In the evening, my conscience, and bad weather which forbade walking, drove me to the English chapel, and I had my usual bad luck — a stupid, unelevating sermon, all about the brazen serpent and the Israelites and the severity of God! I took some money to pay for the preaching, and then was so disappointed and disgusted I resolved I would not give a cent, but I had not courage to pass the plate-holder, especially as he turned out to be Mr. Brown Stout, as I call my English porter acquaintance. So I gave in, and paid!

*To his Wife.*

GENEVA, August 31.

. . . Saturday, rode on horses three hours (from Visp, in the Rhone Valley), walked four hours, to Zermatt — cloudy, bad weather. Sunday, beautiful day — God's invitation to " go up higher " — so we went — Unitarians piously; Orthodox protestingly, hurt their consciences and stopped half-way — saints went on, and had magnificent views of glaciers and snow-peaks, whereof I have written on the spot, in a sheet inclosed.

[*Inclosure in Pencil.*

Gorner Grat, near Zermatt. 10,200 feet high. Dearest Mary: This commands the finest Swiss view — the highest mountains, the most snow, the largest and finest glaciers. On every hand, the mountains covered with snow, — before us the higher hills, twelve, thirteen, or fourteen thousand feet high, covered with thick snow-fields, piled up in immense drifts and of the purest white. The chasms between are filled with compact ice and snow, stretching down into the valleys, and feeding the rivers with vehement torrents. Such a panorama of rocky mountains and hard and unrelenting " virgin nature " I never saw before — never imagined. No trees, no grass, — here and there a flower, — all else barren land, or rock, or snow, or ice. It is vast, impressive, sublime — not soft, not picturesque, not poetical, not soothing, but wonderfully impressive. Of all the scenes in Switzerland, this is the grandest, the greatest, the most sublime. . . . I wish you could be here for an hour or two — you and all our friends. So vast, so imposing, so wonderful a scene cannot be expressed in words or sketch,— it must be felt through eyes in an acheless head to be understood. The egoism of my headache is a great drawback to me — one never gets out of himself with such a malady. But still it is great — it almost lifts me out of myself, and that is the best tribute I can pay to its vastness and magnificence. But a good-morning to you, dearest — I think of you all among all sights and in all experiences.]

This was a great experience. Monday repeated the sight, Orthodox going this time, and finding no sin. Tuesday — big day — up at two A. M.— off at three to cross the St. Theodul pass into Italy — sunrise on the hills — immense thing —"must be seen to be appreciated," as the man said of his monkeys. Stopped at seven for second breakfast " à la fourchette," with five-tined forks,— then on to the snow for three hours — up, up, up,— snow for miles on all sides, thousands of feet deep,— stopped on summit at stone hut to warm,— 11,000 feet high,— highest point we have been,— twice as high as highest White Mountains,— found at hut large party, including two or three women, making the trip from other side. For two hours in crossing the snow, we had to be tied together,— strung on a rope six feet apart, guide ahead, so as to prevent any one being lost off by falling into the crevasses, great cracks in the snow and ice, fathomless, across which we jumped. Danger not very great, just enough to be exhilarating. Snow cold, struck to bowels; sick — ate sugar and brandy — didn't do any good. Down into Italy, through splosh, and under the bluest of skies — very blue — struck down and met the snow striking up, and was blue all over and through. Got to dry land about noon— better — dined and pushed on — tramp, tramp,— rode a mule an hour or two — harder than walking — Ben sick and parted company with his dinner,— but on, in shadows of night, till nine P. M.— eighteen hours on road! — when we reached Chatillon, and supped on fresh figs and grapes. Wednesday, general sense of stiffness and stupidity through company — breakfast of fruit — rode in carriage fifteen miles to Aosta, and agreed to call it a day's work. This, Italy — dirty, nasty, goitre and cretins abundant — worse than Switzerland or Germany — and yet through dirt occasionally a sweet face and an Italian eye, borrowed of heaven's own blue. Thursday, rainy, but off for the great St. Bernard Pass — bought grapes for two cents a pound, same kind that B. K. Bliss sells for seventy-five cents, and ate, and ate — also peaches and pears — turned ourselves into fruit-jars, covered with umbrellas to keep the air and the rain out — long walk, eight hours, all rain — last two hours hard climb — struck snow-storm before we got to the hospital, and made the last half-mile under a blinding squall — had to put our noses to the path and move on. Warm reception at hospice, dry clothes, fire, and supper. Bleak, dreary place — scene of Longfellow's Excelsior. Morning, still rainy — saw the St. Bernard dogs, big yellow and white fellows — saw the building where they stick up the dead bodies of people lost in going through the Pass in bad weather — a ghastly, grinning collection of skeletons in all stages of decay — among the rest a mother and child in her arms — air so rare and pure up here it is not necessary to bury, and so they dry up and fall to pieces as they stand around the walls. Down back into Switzerland — walked an hour and rode five to Martigny, in valley of Rhone. This was Friday, and Saturday we intended to walk (nine hours) over to Chamouny, but the weather was still bad, and we turned off here by rail to pass the Sunday, recruit our strength and our purses, get some clean clothes, and wait for fine weather. And so here we are — place where John Calvin ruled and preached, and a great musical *fête* going on of Sunday, — grand concert in Cathedral, Protestant church — processions, flags, salvos of artillery; and to-night a banquet and a torchlight procession and illumination. We have spent two hours at a concert — marvelous chorus singing — and came out to write. That's all, I believe. As to health, up and down — bad days and good days, but think I can feel steady improvement.

*To his Wife.*

CHAMOUNY, under Mt. Blanc,
14th Wedding-day, September 5.

So I celebrate the blessed anniversary! The morning is wet and foggy, mountain flights are forbidden; I have been dreaming over open fires and reading old *Republicans;* now I vary the action, but keep ever the thought of thanks for the past and hope for the future — for our past and our future. New health courses in my veins, and that, too, gives joy. Push back the tragedies to-day — room for the joys, for pleasure, for happiness, for thankfulness — for life, for wife, for home, for children, for friends! If I were a poet, I would write a love-song; if I had a voice, I would sing it; I am a man, and I feel it! God grant you all feel it with me to-day; that my renewed content and happiness subtly communicate itself to you, and that in the Connecticut valley as in that of Chamouny, there are joyous hearts inspired by the same love and faith and hope! . . .

*To his Wife.*

. . . Such love was hardly ever given to man before, and it has kept me up by its exaltation when all other resources failed. We are all lifted up by the good opinion of others; and though, of course, I can never dream of reaching the high pinnacle to which your idolizing idealism exalts me, I am sure it never has made me for a moment careless of your happiness. It has always been a stimulant, an inspiration, a call to betterment, and the only grief it has produced has been that I was unworthy of such adoration. . . . I do not talk much about these things, because it is of no avail, and because such talk is apt to run into morbidness, and spend itself and satisfy itself in mere talk; but I think and act a good deal. My life, if it has character and eloquence in it, expresses itself best in action. Words are born largely of intellectual stimulations and contact; the life, which is yours in its daily effort and thought and striving, has deeper roots and firmer hold, and may be trusted longer.

*To his oldest Daughter.*

VEVAY, SWITZERLAND, September 15, 1862.

MY DARLING SALLIE: Your many dear little letters deserved special answer long ago, but I felt you would have patience with me and not expect "line for line." But I see even you are giving out, and demand recognition, and count up what I have written others, and remember that I have written you nothing. But here goes now, and you will forgive past neglects, won't you? Your letters have given me great pleasure and much news. I have been glad to notice the care and scholarly perfection of their composition. Now you must seek to acquire elegance and ease in writing, and also in expression. These will come with practice and familiarity with language. There is no better discipline than writing compositions, and I hope you like it well enough to seek every opportunity and excuse for exercise in it.

I do not know what I can tell you about myself or my travels that will be new to you. I confess to Mother so fully of all my daily doings and undoings that there is nothing left. To be sure, there are details of excursion, and daily experiences, but these are long stories, and can hardly be written in letters. Some time I hope to tell you some of them, though you know, too, that I am not so good as Mrs. Cook at story-telling. This is a bright and beautiful morning, and I anticipate great pleasure in going out into it. I am still in my room, and have just eaten my breakfast here, consisting of three pounds of grapes, and of nought else. They were beautiful grapes, eight great bunches, greenish white in color, turning to yellow on the sides exposed to the sun, and very rich and sweet. How I wish I could lay down a great basketful for you and the other children and Mother and Aunt Allie, in our dining-room.

. . . Our hotel is located right on the banks of the lake — Lake Leman or Lake Geneva,—a small garden and yard in front lead directly to the water, and boats are always ready to take people out to ride. We mean to go to-day, and I shall try to learn to row, so that I can beat "Aunt Maria," as I believe you call her, when I come back. You should see the water of the lake,—it is so exquisitely pure and blue. The

Rhone River comes in at one end, dirty and muddy as the
dirtiest " soap-suds " on washing-day; but it soon settles and
clarifies, and when the river goes out at the other end, it is as
pure as crystal, and blue as the bluest sky you ever saw. It is
a charming sight to see this transparent and richly colored
water dancing and foaming as it rushes out of the lake into
the narrow river-way right through the city of Geneva. No
matter how much dirt is thrown into it, nor how many muddy
streams pour into it — it turns all to purity and crystal — just
as, a minister would say probably, a pure and true life changes
everything and everybody that comes into contact with it into
truth and goodness.

Only think,— two months from to-day, November 15 — if no
accidents happen, I shall be at home. I shall clasp you all in
my arms, and once more the old home circle will be full, and
we will be happy together! Won't that be nice? I think of it
every day and every hour, and am growing dreadfully impatient for the day and the hour. There — I have filled up my
sheet, and yet have not said half the things I had to say to you.
But they will keep till I come. You must give great love to
Sammy and Mamie and little Charlie — wonderful baby — but
we always have wonderful babies at our house, you know —
and to Aunt Allie and Grandma and all. Please, too, hand the
accompanying sheet to Mrs. Bowles, with my most affectionate
regards. I kiss my hand to you across the land and over the
ocean! Good-bye. Your fond and proud father.

*To Miss Whitney.*

VEVAY, SWITZERLAND, September 20, 1862.

What will you have — if you can get it? A pound of fresh
grapes, a row on the lake with me, or a stroll out among the
vineyards and the groves, and up the hill-sides? Come, and
you shall have your choice — all three if you are greedy.
There are grapes enough to share with you — I should suffer
no lack; and as to the other things, why, your company
would be better than the room! We would " welcome you
with open arms," and take care not to shock you by closing
them — if we could help it!

We count our remnant of Europe by days, and the heart beats quicker with every lessened day. The passage is engaged by the Boston boat of November 1. . . . It was "awful jolly," as an Englishman would say, the way Mary's birthday went off. I fairly clapped my hands with glee at the news of how it all came out. Thanks to you for hieing so quickly to do your part. The whole thing was as good as a play. . . .

I have been learning to row lately, so as not to be ashamed when you take me out in your boat. We men so hate to have a woman more clever than we are in anything but worsted work, playing the piano, and darning stockings. I have become quite proficient in short practice ; that is, I have splendid blisters on every finger-joint. This lake is charming boating-ground, and I wished my flannel-skirted boat-woman was here to do the work for me while I sat enjoying the *dolce far niente* at the end of the boat. My laziness would have overcome my pride, and the woman's rights should have been indulged for once.

But all this is not replying to your late letters — as fresh and delightful and suggestive as ever. My brother wonders if getting married would spoil such a woman as you. For you see he reads and enjoys, too. But you must excuse me from going over Swedenborgianism, slavery, the war, and all the solemn questions, and sad, too, started since Eve tempted and Adam fell. I shall do so much better justice to my profound and philosophical and altogether original views, when I can see you face to face. You and I would hardly differ as to the negroes, on a full statement of our respective views ; however, I shall always appear to you somewhat conservative on most topics — while almost everybody else finds me radical — because that is what you rather need from me ! My mind of late years has a pestiferous way of seeing pretty much all sides of questions ; and though both from nature and principle I am identified with the progressive and radical side, I still do not forget there is another, and when I come in contact with such as you, I am apt involuntarily — especially if I love them — to give them the benefit of it. The only difference that I notice between us just now on this particular topic is that while you are willing to trust God on all other questions connected with the war, you are not as to slavery — and I am willing to trust him on that and not on the others. In other words, I feel sure that my views of his purposes as to slavery agree with my wishes; while as to others, I am in sad doubt. There can be no doubt that slavery is done for — that the war growing out of it must and will end it. To be sure, I am impatient with the progress of both Abe Lincoln and the Almighty — but what can we do? But we do not free ourselves from responsibility for the evil by running away from it. Would a father relieve himself from a child's sins — partly the result of his education and toleration — by driving him out of his house, or letting him run away and riot to the full in his wickedness; when by holding him in his household he could alternately flog and nurse the sin out of him, as rapidly as digestion and grace could operate? Tell us that, my fair logician. But then, in the present case, slavery goes by the board in our day. All the suffering and bloodshed and cost will atone for the past, and give us an immediate entrance into the heaven of Freedom. *How*, don't ask me. The winds will blow, the rains fall — but I cannot make them, or foretell them, or explain them — but they *do* and they *will*.

. . . Will anything come out of your study of Swedenborgianism? It has certainly much to appeal to such natures as yours, and yet I think the ceaseless, querying, arithmetic part of your brain will reject it. Christ will grow more to you, surely. For, looking at him without any but the mere mortal eye, there is no such other character in history. As Artemus Ward said of Washington, his principal distinction is that there is nobody else like him. . . . I often wonder if when people forget Theodore Parker's iconoclasm, his negations, he will stand out as Martin Luther and John Calvin do — the founder of a new church, a new faith. There is a chance of it. He was much like them — had he lived earlier he would have burned his enemies, as Calvin did, and gloated over it. He came as near it as the times would allow. But of all this by and by.

*To the " Republican."*

VEVAY, SWITZERLAND, September 22, 1862.

Two months and a half since we gossiped together, *Republican* readers! How you have escaped, and how I have the discipline of ministers to "a mind diseased," for insisting on not forgetting you, nor letting this right hand forget its cunning. You must know that even these superficial gossipings of my European summer are forbidden indulgences, and have to be done on the sly. Then — as we would not be lugubrious and tell you of the low and sad side of the summer — how can we talk gaily of pleasures and places, of lazy life in luxurious countries, to men and women whose hearts' blood is pouring itself out for the sake of our common heritage of country and government? It seems but cruel mockery in us to tell you of sweet Alpine valleys, of snow-crowned mountains in midsummer, of lovely lakes and poetic cataracts, of daily journeyings that have no end but rest for eye and mind, and ease for body — no object but comfort and pleasure — while such things be at home. We would rather you would forget we are here and not there — we would rather forget it ourselves. But the days of exile are numbered — we count the few that separate us from our country with impatience. She may not need our presence, but we need hers. The torture of absence to every right-feeling American at this time is indescribable, no matter how feeble might be his presence and his contribution to his nation's struggle for civilization and right. It robs the day of its glory, the night of its rest — it puts a blur upon the face of nature. We see everywhere and in everything struggling, bleeding America — friends fallen and falling, hearts desolated and homes despoiled; and we are not there even to give the sympathy we feel, or gain that which we crave. Here there is none asked and none to be had. Europe is in ignorance or in opposition. England suffers in her only sensitive spot, her pocket, and turns upon the country that she feared in prosperity and hates in adversity; while famished but still blatant Southerners flaunt at the hotels, and poison the sweet surface of this republican Lake of Geneva with the presence of their banner of barbarism.

Two months and a half suffice most American travelers for seeing the whole continent. We have revolved in a narrow space — two weeks in the Black Forest portion of Germany, and two months in Switzerland. But our views have been mostly a-foot; and instead of glances we have had sight — instead of impressions, conviction. Our tramp in the Black Forest country was a fitting prelude to Switzerland. Its scenery is a sweet proem to the Alps. . . . Save the fruit trees, that line the roads here as generally throughout Germany and Switzerland, there is often not a tree or a shrub to be seen that is not an evergreen of deepest, darkest hue. The effect of the long succession of hill-sides, dotted with these firs as thickly as they can grow, sending out their sharp needles into the air at every angle — sometimes proud and erect to heaven, then drooping as if in somber sorrow, and again with hesitating horizontalism — is magnificent and grand in the extreme. You think of Mrs. Browning's

> " Hills running up to heaven for light,
> Through woods that half-way ran;
> As if the wild earth mimicked right
> The wilder heart of man;
> Only the hills are greener far,
> And gladder, than hearts ever are."

Yet one of these hill-sides, when in shadow, symbolizes and sympathizes with, as no other scenery I ever beheld, the deep, unutterable pathos of humanity. It looks out upon you like a great human soul in imperishable and unspeakable sorrow. These woods, too, are the paradise of mosses and ferns. The amateur in these should make a special pilgrimage to the Black Forest. The mosses, thick, soft, and of every hue of green, shaded with yellow and red, are not content to cover the ground with a carpet that no tapestry can rival, but often mount the trees themselves, and clothe the trunks and branches with their fascinating resurrection life.

Our tour of Switzerland has been quite full and satisfying. It is certainly a very delightful country when the sun shines. But for its full appreciation, besides, are needed an anti-dyspeptic stomach, a stout pair of legs, and a head that is not forever egotistically reminding you of its existence. . . . No country has such contrasts, such variety of natural scenery,— the grave and the gay, the beautiful and the sublime,— that which woos with soft poetic grace, and that which oppresses by its majestic severity. Health seems, however, to be in all its veins; the mountain air is tonic, like perpetual champagne; it sets the soul free from the flesh, the body falls away into forgetfulness under its inspiration, while the lower heights and the valleys, and particularly the lake shores, are almost universally soft, dry, and equable. . . . Switzerland, if you come near to her, lasts, while the rest of Europe is lost in your soul or only remembered as a faint dream.

. . . These later weeks in Switzerland, it may interest personal acquaintances to know, have told favorably upon my maladies. The brain forgets itself sometimes, and the nights are not all profaned by wakefulness.

The more fruitful half of Mr. Bowles's working life may be dated from his seven months of European travel. No immediate recovery showed itself. He returned to work when he was yet by no means fit for it. He was unable for years to do his old amount of labor, and, as his letters will show, he continued for some time to be doubtful of the issue of his case. But in the half-year of absence and rest there had been a refilling of the exhausted springs, and from this time he slowly regained some measure of the old vigor. It was by far the completest and longest rest he ever gave himself, and under conditions the most favorable. The very isolation from society which he so constantly lamented, gave the jaded brain that rest from stimulation which it needed, and which it never would have accepted voluntarily. If his enjoyment had been fuller his rest would have been less.

The journey included several weeks in Paris, some days in the Netherlands, a trip up the Rhine, and a walking excursion on the Moselle. His letters show with

what thoroughly American eyes he looked on all he
saw,— how entirely he belonged to his own country
and his own age. In Paris he goes on Sunday to the
American chapel, hears Dr. McClintock preach on general and special providence, and writes to a home correspondent of that favorite old problem of theologians.
In writing of the churches everywhere, he speaks of
hardly anything but the preaching. Almost his only
mention of Westminster Abbey is a complaint of the
dull sermon he hears there. Cologne Cathedral is disposed of in five lines. He was too wholly a child of the
present to respond to that spirit of the past which
speaks through the antique services of cathedrals and
the incomparable architecture of the Middle Ages.
Neither history nor art touched him with any such
power as living humanity and external nature. It is
deeply interesting to trace the growing effect upon him
of high mountain scenery. At first, the snow-peaks
strike cold and alien on his tired and sensitive heart.
Even the Jungfrau and her sisters are to him simply
" great masses of rock, bald and bare, save where covered with snow." When he reaches the Gorner Grat,
before the Matterhorn and Monte Rosa, he fully owns
the sublimity of the scene, though still with a subdued
regret for more soothing and picturesque effects. At
Vevay, when the sights he has witnessed have had time
to settle to right proportion in his mind, he writes:
" Switzerland, if you come near to her, lasts, while the
rest of Europe is lost in your soul or only remembered
as a faint dream." In later years, when he had re-
visited Europe, and had seen and described the western
" Switzerland of America," he wrote to a friend: " I
ascribe my later growth of heart and head in great part
to the inspiration of high mountains. There is nothing that sinks deeper, spreads wider, lasts longer."

VOL. I.—25

## CHAPTER XXX.

### OFFICE AND HOME: LETTERS (1863–1865).

TO the *Republican* as a business enterprise the war brought increased circulation, larger profits, and the power to strengthen its working force. It had little rivalry in its immediate field. One after another, several dailies had been started in Springfield, but none of them could maintain themselves against so strong a competitor. The last of these was the *Argus*, a Democratic paper, which was set up for the Buchanan campaign in 1857, but soon went down. After this, the *Republican* had no rival in Springfield, until, in January, 1864, the *Evening Union* was established and became a permanent institution, though for its first eight years an insignificant one. The *Republican* gave a cordial paragraph to the *Union* at its commencement, saying that there was room and opportunity for such a paper. When the *Argus* died it had chronicled the fact under its regular heading of "Deaths." But it never recognized the existence of its local rivals, save at their birth or death, by so much as a word. All of them found a large part of their material in a warfare against the *Republican*, but they never could get the satisfaction of a syllable in reply. No journal had livelier controversies with other papers than the *Republican*, but it would not wage them in its own town.

The firm of Samuel Bowles and Co. continued down to 1872 to do a general printing and binding business as well as to publish the *Republican*. It was one of the first houses in the country to begin, in 1861, the manufacture of photograph albums, and within three years it was at the head of the business in the United States, employing one hundred hands in this department alone.  Leaving as heretofore the general business mainly to the care of his partners,— among whom had now been included for some years his brother, Benjamin F. Bowles, in special charge of the finances and accounts of the concern,— Mr. Bowles was now able to so enlarge his editorial staff that the daily work of the *Republican* was provided for independently of his personal presence, leaving him free to do as much or as little as he felt able.  His genius for selecting, training, and using men now came into full play. He gradually surrounded himself with a group of young men, some of whom became permanent members of the staff, while the greater part, after two or three years of training, were graduated to other fields of service. The *Republican* office came to be recognized as a school of journalism.  It educated its pupils so well that their services became more valuable than the paper could afford to employ in its subordinate positions.  The staff was brought to complete organization in 1864.  Dr. Holland's connection with the paper closed about this time, though in 1864 he contributed another series of Timothy Titcomb letters under the title, " Letters to the Joneses."  Mr. Hood was, after Mr. Bowles, the leading editorial writer.   William M. Pomeroy was made the managing editor — a man whose fidelity and judgment Mr. Bowles could thoroughly trust, and in whose hands the paper was safe against any reckless steering.  Under Mr. Bowles's training he grew to marked skill in the range of work which his chief once sketched in these terms: "To know what news is, and where to find it, and how to present it; to detect the truth from falsehood among rumors and speculations; to perceive what is probable and what otherwise; to learn how to write a paragraph and turn a news item and make a heading; to insure freshness and correctness in detail; to know what to put in and what to leave out,—to learn, in short, how to *edit* a paper, is something very different and very much more difficult than to know how to write for one. There are many good writers in this country, but there are very few good editors." At this time Joseph H. Shipley was night editor. Charles H. Sweetser, afterward editor of the *Round Table*, gave place after a few months of service to Edward H. Phelps, who took charge of the local department, including the whole New England field. At this time, and for a number of years, the literary editor was Mrs. Frances H. Cook, a lady of fine intellectual accomplishments, and a thorough and careful worker. Some of the ablest reviews were written by Mr. Hood, and outside contributors were occasionally employed in this department. The paper still gave that large consideration to literary topics which it originally derived from Dr. Holland. Of its regular correspondents the most noticeable was "Warrington,"—William S. Robinson, whose Boston letters covered most of the years between the birth of the Republican party and the Greeley revolt. He was strongly anti-slavery and radical, often a long way beyond the paper itself in these directions, well informed in all the personalities of politics, a sharp controversialist and a dangerous foe, and caustic to a degree which gave constant exasperation to a large part of the paper's readers. In the *Republican's* salad he was the cayenne pepper. The Washington correspondent was D. W. Bartlett, under the signature of "Van." Outside of its regular force the paper had contributors not a few,

some of whom first won in its columns a reputation
which grew beyond the provincial field.  Among its
writers at different times were Bret Harte,— who was
first introduced to an Eastern audience in its columns,—
Edward King, Frank B. Sanborn, Washington Gladden,
David Ames Wells, Prof. A. L. Perry, Charles H. Webb,
Alice Cary, Mary Clemmer Ames, Kate Field, Caroline
S. Whitmarsh, and Adeline Trafton.

In 1860, besides Mr. Bowles and Dr. Holland, there
were only three men in the editorial office; in 1864, Mr.
Bowles had a staff of seven assistants; and in 1877, the
last year of his life, the number had grown to fourteen.
Until the changes in the office in 1872, Mr. Pomeroy and
Mr. Phelps remained his chief lieutenants.  For this
period of about eight years, he was more the master of his
own time than ever before or after.  The paper was still
his absorbing interest, but no longer to the same degree
as before his inexorable taskmaster.  He lightened his
labor, too, by learning to dictate his articles to a stenog-
rapher.  Ultimately he used the same method in most
of his private correspondence.  But in the case of his
editorials, he at last, after several years, directed his
amanuensis to write in long-hand, except in the case of
brief paragraphs, saying that the quicker method tempted
him to be too diffuse and careless.  Whatever work he
did on the paper he did at high pressure.  "I have known
him," says one of his assistants, "to keep five good compositors steadily engaged on his copy."  Every man on
the paper felt the chief's eye on his work.  "Sometimes,"
says one of them, "he would take up the file of the paper
for a week when I thought I had been doing pretty well,
and go through my work, and completely riddle it.  It
was fine training for me."  The daily stint was no
light one in those times.  Mr. Shipley, the night editor,
thus describes his daily routine: "I went to the office as

soon as I was up — about noon. The afternoon was
spent in reading the general exchanges, and woe to me
if I overlooked anything! Then I had charge of the
night work, from 7 P. M. to 3 A. M. That was the regular
labor assigned to me, and Mr. Bowles said, ' You'll find
it about enough; but if you see anything else you can
do, try it.' So I did try my hand at condensations, then
at editorials, etc., and his praise and encouragement
helped me on."

In 1864, the residence on Maple street was exchanged
for one on Central street, which had been built and
occupied by Francis Tiffany, the pastor of the Unitarian
Church, and a personal friend of Mr. Bowles. The new
house was larger, better built, and more commodious
than the old one; it stood in close neighborhood to the
beautiful cemetery, and was surrounded by shade-trees
and shrubbery. Mr. Bowles threw himself with hearty
enjoyment into the work of finishing and planting the
grounds. He had a relish for the cultivation of the earth,
and no mean knowledge of the farmer's and gardener's
art. Here was his home for the rest of his life, here his
children grew up, and here was exercised a generous hos-
pitality to a various and brilliant circle of guests.

The best illustrations of the personal and home life of
this period are given by his private letters.

*To F. B. Sanborn.*

Feb. 16, 1863.

If the *Commonwealth* enterprise were mine, and I desired
alike its success and its power for good, I should make it the
representative of the extreme right of the Republican party,
— of Sumner, Andrew, Chase, Stanton, Amasa Walker, etc.,—
and not of the Wendell Phillips school. I would have it very
positive, earnest, and enthusiastic, sometimes perhaps a little
*malignant,* but bearing, on the whole, with as much patience as

possible, with the more laggard and conservative elements of the party,—with Lincoln, Seward, and with Boston, etc.; and remembering always the chief duty of giving the most constant blows to the common enemy,—that there are various ways of fighting battles in this world,—that strategy, flank movements, patient waiting and pleading, and even *digging*, have their uses and their reasons, as well as open front assaults, and that, though the latter was our style and choice, we must not forget that those who used the other means were also our allies. I should be full of the "Come up hither!" and not repulse by too much denunciation and want of candor our friends and allies. Such a paper, properly published and edited, and backed by somebody's pocket for a year or two, will soon become self-supporting and a power in New England and Boston, and very likely make the basis of a daily. Such we need, Boston needs, and New England needs.

You propose to grasp too much in your details. You would want a sheet of twice the size, and that is not possible now. It seems to me you should seize two or three strong points: 1, political position with the foremost Republicans; 2, identification with the use and development of the negro, theoretically and practically; and, 3, literature of choice and original character. Thus, I would—keeping the paper of form and size as now, for the present, but giving it the typographic air of a journal of the 19th instead of the 18th century—give up the first page to political selections, documents, speeches, public opinion, etc.; the second and third pages to editorials —not too many, say two of a column and four of a quarter-column, and half a dozen shorter and biting editorial paragraphs—and correspondence and news; and the fourth page to literature. As to correspondence, a weekly letter from Washington, and one from New York, or once a fortnight perhaps as well, should be your chief reliance. These should be written by people of sense as well as talent—no Gurowski stuff, except as an occasional salad—should be gossipy, speculative, and newsy; that from New York should make art and literature leading themes, and may be by a woman—better, indeed. They should both be paid for, at $5 each. As to army correspondence, when you can get some good, and from leading points, have it. Poor is abominable, and rather than that read and select from the New York papers. For news, there should be a compact review of the week of say two columns, and then a column or so of items, fresh and piquant,—nothing more. Let the farmer, the mechanic, and all other specialties, slide — make your paper for *men and women*, not for specialists. And yet, if you can have once in a while a strong, suggestive, fresh article on special and side themes, right well. But don't have a paper of *departments*. As to literature — variety, freshness, and a higher character than any American paper has, or ever had. Avoid, as a rule, continued stories, though they may be very well as an exception, if very, very good. A good, short, piquant story of three or four columns once a fortnight, and for the rest, reviews of new books, selections, choice discussions, literary reminiscences, etc. You ought to make this the second great feature of your paper, and *keep the negro out of it*. Let it be such that people will, must, take the paper for that alone, if rejecting the other.

There, that will do, I guess. I hope you will be " master of your situation," and be able to say *no*, not only to everybody else but to yourself. A newspaper should have its own individuality and conscience apart from any man, and the "able editor" is the man who can respect that more than his own passion. If you succeed, you will find you must keep somewhere near the people, not abreast, but not so far ahead as not to be seen and appreciated. A great newspaper is not a reformer, not a radicalist, but may be and should be a leader — a go-between for the head men and the masses. But this is not to your purpose now, though it should not be forgotten. In laying the foundation, it is well to be conspicuous and ultra. A minority is always more radical than a majority. But don't put yourself out of the pale of the world. An individual can be Wendell Phillips or M. D. Conway, but a newspaper cannot, and have circulation and tolerance.

As to times and men, of what use to prophesy or pass judgment ? The present duty is clear — to push on the war, conquer all we can, as fast as we can, and stir up the "social institution" of the South as deeply as possible. We may have to stop, or be stopped, any time. The future is not clear. But what we want is to make sure that slavery shall be destroyed, whether there be peace or war. The white man seems to have failed us, and so the black man, as yet; but God is on our side, and it must come right. Butler is playing poker with fortune, and plays as always desperately. He is to be trusted as far as he gives security. But he is a bold, bad man, with quick instincts, sudden resolutions, and desperate resorts. He makes great successes and great failures. It is disgusting, the way some of your people favor him, yet he deserves praise, recognition, and authority — and yet must be watched. I see no reason to question Banks. He ripens more slowly than I expected, and has done nothing yet. But he believes in God and progress and regeneration, and will not cheat us. Give him a fair chance. He may fail — he may not dare enough — sometimes he distrusts himself and the people and hesitates — but when his moments of inspiration come, they are all right.

I wish you would come and see me, and then we would talk over all these matters. I am glad you are married, and are taking strong hold of life. I wish you every success, and am sure you have the opportunity and the power.

This is rapidly, badly written — but I hope you can spell it out. You will find it difficult to get such correspondents as you wish, or such other writing; but keep your purpose high, and they will come after a while. A newspaper is a slow growth, and there is a great lack of ready newspaper talent in America.

*To Miss Whitney.*

May, 1863.

. . . The Atwater farm property is put before me again by Mr. A.'s pressing my purchase. It is quite temptatious, but too big for me. Yet I shall coquet with it a little. I have of late a passion for *real* property, knowing that it survives wars, crises, and even death — and that the rest of my possessions hardly will.* Mary is pretty well this week, and we are both busy with spring cares and work. This afternoon we have our usual Saturday dinner with some old boyhood friends of mine. I love to keep up, after a fashion, all the old acquaintanceships, and revive my young friendships and feelings. They freshen life, and they serve greatly to keep us in sympathy with our children's wants and feelings and fancies. It is not much that I do for my children, but I never want to lose sight of myself at their ages — then the little I do can be done more intelligently.

There is need of new patience and faith in the war. I am glad I do not see Mrs. ——— often. She has always all the badness of things and people. And I had rather not know, since I cannot largely help. The fight goes on till slavery is thoroughly uprooted — that seems to be it. And we must carry it on, so far as possible, with negro soldiers. The government seems to realize this. Organize the negroes, and put them to service, offensive and defensive; make them work out the freedom of their race.

I shall read Faustina, because it stands for something to you. I feel strongly, however, that I shall not like it. The closing sentences seem the key, and such stories I do not like. They lessen what is waning too fast in me for my happiness — trust and faith in man and woman. They sap that reverence for woman — that holy worship — that was early and deep in me, but does not seem so strong as it was. I cling to all and every thing that freshens and inspires it. The characters, the books, the people, that strengthen the waning faiths of hard experience, that bring back youth and ideals, that bring the good and the great and the unselfish into prominence and activity — rather than the opposites — are the characters, the books, the people, I seek and need. I am afraid I don't have so much faith in myself as I used to, as I ought to, as is best for me and my content. Perhaps that is the trouble. So much higher do people rate me than I deserve that it causes me to react against myself. But don't *you* dare to put me lower! To you and

---

* In fact, however, it so happened that a part of Mr. Bowles's real estate investments proved ultimately an embarrassment, while his newspaper was a steady source of revenue during his life-time and afterward.

Mary and the children I must always be great — else the school would be dismissed!

June, 1863.

. . . How warm and sticky the days are getting; it frightens me that the summer comes on so fast and far, and we have had no horseback rides. But the nights are compensating to those who are then alive and fresh. These splendid moonlights will be gone ere you get to Hastings, and won't distract you from man's identity, and geologic strata, and such! I am glad of it, for your sake! It must be trying for such many-sided people to be tempted in all ways at once! Commend me to your narrow, one-stringed fiddles of humanity for content and peace and happiness.

Fix it as I will, my days seem crowded and hurried with care — always more left over than is done. The mere running of a daily paper like the *Republican* produces friction enough to keep one set of nerves on the stretch. There is always some line somewhere that grates on somebody,— a name wrong in a marriage, a birth that didn't happen, that the "editor-in-chief" and nobody else must hear all about, and apologize for and correct. Hood's absence, too, gives me a large share of the detail. Think of your friend collating religious intelligence! But that is one of the things I do well. I have a soul for the petty strifes of parishes, and take delight in disciplining good men— to say naught, as you know, of good women.

Did I tell you Mary's delicious scheme for a piano present to —— failed? It was too bad. It required $50 each from some six or eight to insure it, and only two or three were prompt and hearty. The rest absolutely refused.

Sunday, June, 1863.

Talk of Hastings-on-the-Hudson! You should see Springfield-on-the-Connecticut, this blessed June Sunday morning! It is the "perfect day." The rain is over, the green at its full, the sun not too kind,— the love of friendship, not of passion,— and the bobolink's song comes up from the lower meadow and steals in the open window. The air is the breath of roses and grass and leaves, cool and sweet, and only silence is

golden. To speak above a whisper would seem sacrilege —
would break this sacramental beauty of morning. Come and
see if it be not so. But speak not, upon your peril. You cannot, with all your tongues, including Greek! improve upon the
still small voices of the lower orders,— the pushing vegetable
life, the grasshoppers, the birds, the frogs,— all ripening into
ultimate disagreeable, fretting, anxious, exacting man! No;
I reject the development theory! The growth is backwards.
Reverse Darwin and Huxley, and I will believe. Pity the poor
bird, happy now, that should be a girl, anxious and unhappy
about her spring bonnet. Let us " go to grass " rather than go
on to more unhappy man.

Our company is gone; we are alone with our garden and the
baby and Pone. I have cut "morning service," and am going
to drive with Mary and the small boy — he with a dreadful
mumps-looking face, because of teeth that will come, and yet,
fearing their fate, hesitate—and in the conflict hurt.

There is nothing else fresh in our lives. Mary is really better
and stronger and happier,— and I grow buoyant under the
inspiration.

It is pleasant to feel that you are having such a gay time
with your friends. We try to think it would be even better
here,—but I am afraid don't succeed in the delusion. However, we do what we can; and what more would you ask?
" She has done what she could " was the finest epitaph ever
written. I shouldn't hunger for any other, if I could reach that.
—When you have tried them all, come back to us, and try us
over; and be the morning like this you shall be content — for
the last of such mornings is the finest that ever was, and
sends the soul to its higher level. Beside, there be fresh strawberries and green peas here, and I am sure the carnalities are
not wholly extinct in you. You will come back from Greek and
Pre-Adamite-dom and Braceville, to breakfast — I am certain.

And so, nothing new — we give you the old ; we have nothing
better: it is our best.

June, 1863.

We do not permit our selfish satisfaction that you are not to
leave us for so far and long to cover our grief with you at the

loss of the beloved and blessed sister.  Believe that both Mary and I are touched with the tragic fate that has fallen upon her, away from home and friends, and are in deep appreciation and sympathy with you.  That remorse that death brings to those that are left has been often in my mind, deeply and sadly, of late; and I am sure it is much easier to be the one to go than to stay.  It is inevitable to every tender heart, however self-sacrificing and devoted it may have been.  Do all we may or can, none of us can do everything,— and there will ever be the after-thought that we might have done more, tor- turing our lives, and mocking the bliss of the memory.  And yet could we know the heart away, we should probably find it blessing us for what we had done, and with never a thought that we could or should have done more for it.  Only we, fortunately, know our failures; and, alas, how well we know them!  And yet, out of our very selfishness, out of our very neglect, God buildeth us up; so that what we do perform for kindred and friends takes on larger power and gives deeper bliss than if in a narrow way we had given more hours and thought and service to the beloved.  It is a shadowy, tender line between service to ourselves and service to others.

But think of other things in connection with the sister. There must be many a pleasant, grateful thought of your deep sympathizing natural exchanges, of her life as locked with yours, of her memory, and of her character.  Gather hold of all that enlarges and ennobles her place in your heart, and do not let the black cloud overshadow or dim it.  She will be ever to you an inspiration and a guide.  Only think of what you might have done for her and did not, to prompt to clearer duty hereafter.  I always think of this lately,— I hardly know why, since I am no more likely to go first than those who will most miss me,— that I must not do, or omit to do, that which if one among those to whom my life is locked should die, would leave a sting and a sorrow in my whole life.  Of course it does not always check the hasty word, the unjust thought, the neglected duty; but " it helps weel," as the Scotchman said.

I want to know more about your sister.  We must talk largely and freely of her.  She must indeed have been large-headed and large-hearted to have taken such a hold upon all your family, and upon your nature especially. Pray let me know her fully, and learn to admire and love her character and her soul.

These are hot, oppressive days. In spite of much discomfort, I am pretty well, in some respects better than usual. I cannot get away, as I meant to before this, because I must wait and see where the draft strikes in our establishment, and what havoc it will create. I hope to run away Saturday or Monday for an exploring tour along the coast, to get a snuff myself, and find a spot for Miss Easter and the children for two or three weeks.

*Evening.* Affairs are so threatening all around — riots everywhere, and confusion and doubt — that I shall not think of leaving my post till the air is clearer. A bold, decisive, military suppression of the New York mob would have settled everything; now, the draft must be abandoned, or several cities put under military surveillance.

EAST EDEN, ME. [Bar Harbor], August, 1863.

. . . The point of doubt as to recovery lies in the liver, I think, — the rest may be managed with time and care; *that* may be so dulled as to defy all effort, as it probably does all ordinary medication. It is at least a rather settled, hard case of nervous dyspepsia, — and I, as well as all my friends who propose to stick to me, have need of all patience and indulgence with its caprices, its vagaries, and its incapacities. One thing I have strongly resolved on; to resort to an effort of will as rarely and as lightly as possible for any purpose of reading, writing, or working. My will has carried me for years beyond my mental and physical power; that has been the offending rock, — and now, beyond that desirable in keeping my temper, and forcing me up to proper exercise and cheerfulness through light occupation, I mean to call upon it not at all, if I can help it — and to do only what comes freely and spontaneously from the overflow of power and life. This will make me a light reader, a small worker, and a poor and irregular correspondent. Will you, my friend, to whom I owe so much, and who appeal

to me so strongly in all intellectual and emotional ways, have
patience and indulgence with me in this resolution,— and help
me to carry it out?  I cannot always write to you, even when
there is time and much to say, because it is hard to come to you
with mere nothings; you inevitably appeal to my best, and I
shrink from and put off writing to you often because I cannot
make up my mind to give you poor thought or none at all,
and there is spirit and power for nothing more.  The indis-
position to read, or even to be read to, is quite singular with
me.  This fortnight I have been here I have read nothing; and
M—— has only read to me once for half an hour, and then
with no interest at all on my part.  I do not think well to yield
to it altogether; light, instructive reading is better than loose,
morbid thinking,— and yet even here I am sure the path of
safety is not to force myself beyond the point of full pleasure
and lively interest.

M—— has enjoyed her trip and visit very much; though I
have been able to contribute nothing to it save the bringing
her.  She has fitted in well with the rest of the company, and
entered heartily into all the excursions and amusements.  She
is disposed to be too grateful for the opportunity.  Such gifts
are of the smallest and cheapest of generosities.  The things we
omit to do —what we withhold — often cost the most.  The unseen gifts are the largest; those of charity, love, forgiveness,
patience, and self-restraint, and of these people give me more
than I can possibly give them.

Under favorable stomachic influences, I find my muscular
power quite fresh and responsive.  I have taken several rough
walks of six and eight miles with good effects on the whole;
and yesterday I led M—— up a high mountain,— an hour and
a half up and an hour down.  She faltered a little going up,
but stood it on the whole well, and comes out to-day better than
ever.

I long to be at home again.  Every absence endears more
and more the valley and its possessions to me.  I feel there
some power, some ownership; away, I am " nothing to nobody," and nobody anything to me.  There is my native soil—
my field, my life —all that I have done, all I can hope to

do — and there the six feet by two of Mother Earth that is all I can hope to call my own beyond the fleeting years of this generation.

The following letters were among those written to his wife, when she, with Miss Whitney as a companion, was in New York at the Brevoort House, again under the care of Dr. Barker, at the time of the birth of another son, named Dwight.

October, 1863.

The children are first-rate — never better — fact, and no rose-coloring. I am pretty well — a trifling cold, and the old headache, but better than usual,— happy and hopeful, as befits a man with the elements of joy in his life that I have.

Great crowd here to the convention. Springfield all full, and running over into Chicopee and Holyoke and perhaps Northampton. Great many Unitarians this year, especially sisters, who like to visit the Connecticut Valley at this beautiful season of the year, and get free board. Mr. Putnam came this noon, the Robinsons to-night. Mr. P. has not come home to tea ; gone probably with some of the sisters of his flock who are up here with him.

Everything going on rapidly at greenhouse and barn; both will be pretty much finished this week; then, ho for grading, draining, fencing, planting! Margaret's nephew, or " niece," as he introduced himself to me to-day, has come from " over the say," and I have set him at work. He starts off like a steam-engine.

Let me have a word every day from one of you, to know how you get along — don't write much yourself; it exhausts head and heart, and makes you nervous more than anything you can do.

The weather is beautiful — between nine and five. Mornings and evenings, cold and damp, and grapple with you like a vice. I am *so* glad you are out of this wretched climate.

Live well — count every joy and comfort twice — and forget those you miss — but don't forget your always loving husband.

My most profound bow, my heartiest faith, to the contents of the other blue dress!

During these weeks the *Republican* is unusually brilliant; there is no mistaking the chief's presence and inspiration. The discussion of the war prospects is wise, steady, and hopeful. The Unitarian National Convention is reported intelligently and sympathetically, apparently by Mr. Bowles. The summing up is by him, beyond doubt. It is warmly commendatory. "Not a stupid thing nor an unpleasant thing was said." Some of the talk was too fine-spun for edification. "In the discussions, especially on the last day," when the topics were such as optimism, the question whether all evil is but disguised good, etc., "there was manifest the old effort, ever recurring, to get upon God's side of the universe, and see the Infinite through finite eyes, in which originate all the puzzles and contradictions of the theologies. Perhaps those who attempted it thought they succeeded, but it cannot be done, and all inferences from what men suppose they see on that side are phantasms and fallacies." "The talk against creeds amounts to little. Unitarians are just as strenuous in their negations as others are in their affirmations, and have no more toleration for the ideas they think false than other Christians." As to the mooted right to the name of Christians, says the paper, that name belongs to whoever accepts Christ as an infallible teacher (as, apparently, no speaker in the convention refused to do).

*To his Wife.*

October, 1863.

Everybody is well; children, cow, horse, and all,—just as well as they can be; and the world moves on as well as it can with you out of it. There is a hole here in this circle, and will be till you come back; but considering that, we are all as well as could be expected. I have been very busy to-day. I had to send Pomeroy to Pittsfield, and am only afraid I can't get him back in time to send to Amherst, and going myself is out of the question. This forenoon I rode to Chicopee on business, stopped at Henry's coming back — downcast but comfortable, and sister still there — and then to the cattle-show on the Park for a little while. This afternoon, in the garden for an hour, at the office for an hour or two; a call on Mother, who has a cold; and then home to entertain Mr. Flint, secretary of the Agricultural Board, at tea. He has gone now, and I am writing in haste for the mail at nine o'clock, after which I shall go to the office for a little while. Mrs. King won't give up Kate, the washerwoman, and Sarah is doing the washing and ironing. Doesn't that fructify your economical soul? I don't hear a bit of family news. —— and his wife are here,— saw him for a moment; didn't find humility written on his forehead. ·Bryan is in Boston, or was to-day. Mrs. —— as frigid as an iceberg. We are growing dreadfully apart — and because she can't wait till I outgrow dyspepsia, and will insist that I shall treat her with at least as much consideration as she *thinks* I show some other people! Ah, well! People won't twit me much longer on having so many friends. That crime is passing from my soul!

I am going to introduce hominy to the Hotel de Bowles. I suppose you will begin by turning up your dainty nose at it, and end by eating an extra share! Then I am going to have baked instead of fried fish-cakes! You see I believe — as to eating — that it is worth doing well, since it must be done. Yet what unspiritual business it is! I don't see how a sentimental young lady can stand seeing her lover eat, especially if he eats like Thackeray or —— or some other people I wot of. I have dropped one or two promising friendships myself on this score. Vulgar but absolute necessity! Don't vex your economical spirit now, but have what you want, and be comfortable. What's the use? There's money enough; pray enjoy it. Then, you know my perversity: if I find you're doing some self-denial for the sake of half a dollar, I shall certainly squander two, in order to balance it.

Mary, don't you let my fretful, downcast moods annoy you. They are unworthy of me, and I ought to rise above them, and control them. But sometimes they master and overpower me.

I want to give it all up sometimes.  Nobody can understand the spell that is upon me.  It cannot be described — it doesn't seem as if anybody else can ever feel it.  Consider me if you can as a little child, sick and peevish, wanting love and indulgence and petting and rest and peace.  There, this ought not to have been written.  But it can't be unwritten, and it is too late to write anything else.  It is morbid ; but there's truth, sometimes the clearest, in our morbid reflections.  Health is too often independence, selfish philosophy, and indifference.

My heartiest love to Maria.  Get and give as much comfort and pleasure as you can,— between you.  You mustn't urge her too much to stay with you when I am also with you.  It will be a disappointment to me to miss her altogether, but she has other friends — and she is giving us our full share — more than we can repay — and after her Sunday vacations she will come back fresh and hearty for your entertainment.

Keep up good courage ; believe all is well at home — that I will take as good care of every detail as possible ; and above all feel ever that my thought, my love, and my prayer are with and for and about you.

November, 1863.<br/>8 P. M., Tuesday [Election day].

Busy with election returns, and you must take a word.  Everybody well at house.  Children never better, high and low.  All but baby over at Amelia's to tea — that is, all the children.  The boy has got his new cap, and is as proud of it as his mother is of him.

My going to New York this week depends upon what I hear from you.  I stand ready for marching orders.  Let me hear from you constantly and at once.

Are you interested in our election news ?  Have you read to-day's *Republican ?*  The Republican bolt against the reign of Judge Shurtleff, Trask & Co. is triumphant.  Harris chosen [D. L. Harris, to the legislature], and Sturtevant defeated by a tie vote with Bond.  I am afraid there is a great deal of hard swearing against "Sam Bowles" around in secret places to-night.  The whole is the choicest bit of fun I have had this long while.

If you and Maria can take the responsibility, buy the three dresses,— seven yards for Mamie, nine for Sallie, and nine of Empress cloth (double or extra width) for Allie. The latter dark-green or brown. Then you may stop the millinery and dry goods department till you get home and well.

The baby grows fat and rosy — talks better and acts more like a man. All owing to the excellent example of his fond father and your loving husband.

Wednesday.

I am *real* tired to-night, but very well for me. It was like old times, staying up at the office last night till after midnight, coming home and sitting over the fire, eating grapes and drinking mild brandy and water, all alone, for an hour, and then to bed. I slept well notwithstanding, and called the girls and the children at quarter past six. George Reynolds and his teams and men have commenced grading to-day. The green-house begins to assume form and character. My rural fence has got to go over. Nell took a French breakfast this morning, or rather an American breakfast in French style, and got up in time to avail herself of an invitation to Amelia's to dinner. I was bidden, but could not go. She reports a pleas-ant time ; she staid all the afternoon. Lizzie Rice came up here to tea, and has gone with Allie to Church — capital C — expecting to hear the Rev. Dr. Huntington, who is reported in town.

The children are well and happy ; Sallie cyphering ; Mamie and Sammie playing cards and checkers with Nellie ; and the grand boy asleep with Mistress Keen brooding over him.

I was busy all the morning with the Weekly and election returns. This afternoon I had a long horseback ride,— out nearly to Chicopee and back,— a fine sunset, and clear and cold air, which I am sure has fitted me for a good night.

That was a brave feat of yours yesterday, and I am glad of it. But be very careful. Don't let your impatience lead you into any rash actions. Wait a little longer, and you will be paid for all your suffering and trial.

Everybody inquires lovingly for you. Everybody is waiting anxiously and hopefully.

Miss Whitmarsh I do not see yet.  She and Lizzie are growing together.  They were off in the woods, this morning,
painting.

So you have our life in brief: just as good as being here,
isn't it?

Courage, care, patience, Molly!

Sunday, November, 1863.

We have fine weather and fine spirits to-day.  It is odd
for me to be here and not there, for over Sunday, and I am
not reconciled to it quite. . . . Mr. Shipley came up to
dinner, and I have had a long walk with him.  Mother has
seen the greenhouse and garden and barn, and approves.  The
small boy is rollicking with the Easter down-stairs.  He is really
getting to be a very fine boy, well-behaved and reasonable.
He was on a spree last night, however, and I tried my hand at
getting him to sleep, walking back and forth upstairs.  He was
eminently good-natured so long as I pictured to him the
delights of horseback riding and whipping Pone; but when I
subsided into drivel, or nursery songs, he was impatient and
wanted to go back to Allie.  He promised to behave himself
and go to sleep if I would take him back, and the bargain was
kept on both sides.  Allie said he grew restless once in a while,
but on her reminding him of his promise to me he would sub-
side and go to sleep again.

November, 1863.

It is good for sore hearts to see your hand of writ again, to
read your overflowing words of tenderest love, and to know
strength and life are coming back so cheerily and rapidly
to you.

We have heavy, dreary rain to-day, spoiling all my plans for
work.  With fine weather, I should have seen the end of things
by to-morrow night, and dismissed most of the men.  Now I
am afraid I shall have to go " right in the suds," as the washer-
women say.  But go I shall and must.  I must have the rest and
recreation and sight of you.

I must tell you both of an interview I had with Miss ———
to-day.  I had to decline one of her letters, which " pitched into "

the editors of the *Republican* personally. She didn't like it
much ; but I took high ground, and she couldn't quarrel very
well. But I guess she won't like me quite so well, after this.
Women don't like to be crossed better than men.

The children are all well, and full of " charades," or rather
small acting plays for Friday night. Charley Allen was here
two hours last evening on his way from Greenfield to Boston.
I shall go down in the evening train. But it is day before
Thanksgiving, and the trains will be full and late. I ought to
be in 65 by twelve o'clock, but don't worry if I am not for
an hour or two later. I would come in the day train, but I
am *so full* — it is impossible. I expect you both will be glad
enough to see me to intermit the usual discipline. I shall be
tired and cross, I presume, and shall require great indulgence
and the proper amount of feminine petting.

December, 1863.

BELOVED WIFE, AND PROUD MOTHER ! All well at this end
of the rope, and nothing new. I am up to my ears in work
under the hill; had nine men and six horses all in harness to-
day — grading, making embankments and grape-borders, setting fences, drawing sand and turf, transplanting, etc., etc. I
have been out nearly all day superintending and clearing
strawberry beds,— and I am the better for it. But I see so
many things I want to do that I almost despair. I shan't stop
till the snow shuts down on me.

Sleep — sleep — let Mrs. R. and Maria experiment on the
baby. Don't fret over him — they can't harm him — only you
can, and that by nervousness and anxiety and overdoing.
This is solemn truth — heed it, an' thou lov'st him and me. For
the rest, be of good cheer, and wait. Think over all the joys
in your life, and how few have *so* many, and how many so few
sorrows. Get all the comfort you can from Maria, and give
her all you can in return — and you can give her a great deal.

December, 1863.

I wish you could breathe this clear, cold air. There is tonic
in it beyond bark, iron, and quinine ; soothing beyond opium ;

strengthening beyond beef tea. We will save some up for you. I will try to bring you some.

Babies all well and hearty, individually and aggregately. School is in progress, and the three are in it with zest. Skating too has opened.

I enclose Mr. Pomeroy's grateful letter — perhaps you can pick it out, when you sit up. If not, it is of no consequence, though it helps to know him.

I dine with Curtis at Walker's to-morrow — nobody else. To-night Briggs gives a supper to his friends because of his election as alderman. Sallie wants to know why I am not elected to anything. The children will begin to look upon me with contempt, unless I hold some office. So the American mind is early debauched by respect for office as such. What could I say to her, save that the people didn't seem to want me, or perhaps it was because I wouldn't give suppers? Henry treated at the hotel, which was well for Amelia's carpets.

I pray you prosper in strength, freedom from pain, and hope and courage. The children send abundant love and kisses. "Even more I," as Paul says.

Dec., 1863.

DEAR GIRLS IN 65 : It is good news you send to-day. Keep on getting better. There is nothing so good to put babies to sleep as a strong arm around them and a strong will behind it. The connection between weak and nervous mothers and nurses and sleepless and nervous children, is just as quick and sure as the play of the magnet—the joy or sorrow of two loving hearts.

I am so weary with a long day outdoors, digging and weeding! I have only just now — dark — put on whole clothes and "washed up." You must excuse the few words in which I write, and be assured of the sympathy and the love behind them.

It has been a sweet, soft day here, and everybody is well. The boy never looked heartier or handsomer. He is practicing on *Yes* and *Mamma*,—but all his efforts at the latter melt sweetly into *Papa*—so ravishingly! The children are all in high glee, and the town calm.

It is so provoking my Tuesday letter did not reach you yesterday. I wrote you each, as I did also last night. Be sure I give you something every night — of the written word — while the thought is full and constant, and always as you would wish.

And so, love and grace be with you.

December, 1863.

The good news you send us, my dearest wife, to-day, is quite cheering. It gladdens my heart very much ; and everybody rejoices that there is such a promise of your early return. Home is waiting and yearning for its lost head. But pray be cautious; a little overdoing now, a little fussing and anxiety, and too much care of baby, will pull you all down again. So put clogs on your outstretching wings. Be content to keep them folded a little longer, so when you do fly, it shall be clear to Springfield.

I have had a long, full day at office and house, but have been well sustained, and am very well for me. The family are in fine condition. The school term closed to-day, and a vacation of two weeks opened. You will hear now oftener from the children. They are very busy, you know, during the last weeks of school term. And it is not so easy for them to write ; it is a larger undertaking than for you or me. They don't think of you any the less often, love you any more feebly, re-joice less keenly in your new joy, or sigh less warmly for your return, because they don't put it all in writing daily. You know there are higher and holier expressions of love than poor words can give.

The work in the garden goes on apace. I have borrowed more money. If I go on long at this rate, you will have to go on short allowance of gowns and gaieties next year. But the time for dividends at the office is coming, and the album busi-ness is good. So have a plate of fresh toast, if you please.

I shan't come down to-morrow night, unless you get into sorrow or trouble. It was hard for me to give it up, and I only did to-day ; but I must husband every hour here at home while the frost and snow hold off. So wait patiently and lov-ingly, as I will try to, till Wednesday night.

*To Miss Whitney.*

December, 1863.

I return you Rénan. Keep it if you will. Hood's review will be rather orthodox-y — suiting our readers better than I, I reckon; but you wouldn't do it and I couldn't. Tending baby and sick friends, and trying to satisfy clamoring outsiders, isn't favorable for high theology, is it? It seems to me Rénan is very puerile and ridiculous in parts, and very magnificent in others. Some of his suggestions are harder to swallow than the miracles, but his general conception of Christ is large, comprehensive, perhaps as high as any yet written, though not above some felt. But it is comforting to people with free and vagrant heads to feel that there is even a Christianity back of and without Christ, and to which he seems rather interpreter and disciple than founder. Do you see the story that Strauss has recanted — come over to Orthodoxy — converted by his critics? Odd, is it not? What is certain in this life but Death and Love?

[Probably 1864.]

. . . We shall have to be counted converts to your Mr. Frothingham: we went again on Sunday,— he was a trifle too radical for Mary, but he on the whole voices my philosophy more fully than any other preacher I ever heard. I don't see why he isn't Theodore Parker improved; he has all his philosophy and spirituality, and little of his hot temper, gross conceit, and bigotry. Yet because of these lacks he will have smaller power. The congregation seems large and growing, and he has a more hopeful, successful air. . . . Frothingham was on the whole the greatest enjoyment in New York. There were drawbacks on all else, and even on that — but that possessed me more, made me forgetful, for the time, of my own wants, my egoism — which was well.

I have changed my habits somewhat now, under Dr. Barker's suggestions. I come to the office about ten, and stay till four,— intending a walk and light lunch from twelve to one,— and dine at five. I mean to do all my work, and read all my papers, at the office in those hours — and for the rest, exercise, home cares, and amusement. Pray for patience and persistence in well-doing for me. These seem to be the necessities of the case.

January, 1864.

. . . I have glimmers of health enough to read. It is like a peep into heaven. There are so many things I want to read, and so much enjoyment and consolation in the reading. And yet, reading is not my life, and never can be, unless it is remade. Still, when there is power enough in the brain, I think I shall read more and to better purpose than ever before.

February, 1864.

Parker's book is out [Weiss's "Life of Theodore Parker"], but not here, and I have sent for copies for you and me. We shall both want to read it and own it. I have read the *Examiner's* review of it with interest. That side of his character which you felt, and a few others, the affirmative, constructive, as well as the sentimental and soft and pious, is now coming out only to the world. And so now we shall begin to see, as never before, his effect upon religious thought. But I do not yet realize that he made a new religion; and yet it is much more than likely that he will take his place along with Luther and Calvin as remedying and improving the defects of the old — seeing more clearly than his contemporaries the religion that Christ established, out of the Heart of the Great Father. It impressed me that Parker only began his real work at thirty-five. All before was getting ready. He began at the age where I left off. I didn't get ready — he did. Only so, he won his great glory, — only so, I won my small one. If I had waited to get ready, I should have done nothing. There was not fire enough in my stomach to have done it save as it was forced on me in the puerile passion of youth. So oddly are lives contrasted, and work done — only one should not think of one's little self when reading of the great Parker.

But how very sad it is to see that such great-headedness and great-heartedness — so much nobility — carries along with it, as by a necessity of its very power and greatness, so much meanness and hatefulness! Or must we carry the burden and blame over on to our poor humanity, which can only be waked

up through such debasing and marring of true greatness? So
it would seem. Ah, but Christ escaped this law, this necessity,
that belongs to all other great men and reformers in history;
yet how he has projected himself into and over the world's
life! Calvin imprisoned and burned; Parker came as near
it as our civilization would permit — but Christ "forgave them,
for they knew not what they did." Yet he did drive the
money-changers from the church, and he did denounce Phari-
sees as generations of vipers; and there is where he was
human!

. . . I do not know what there is that I can do for you in
the preparations for California. I would do much, everything,
— I suppose the best service is to keep out of the way, and not
interrupt the flow of preparations, or depress by vain sorrow.
You will wish to carry a little library, a few choice books, such
as you will fall back on and read and re-read. Now these I
wish to furnish, and you must let me, and tell me what they
are. I think of Mrs. Browning — in full; Emerson, ditto; Whittier, the poet of liberty and humanity; Dana's "Household
Book of Poetry," which has so many of the gems of all ages and
countries,— and now, what else? I am ashamed to say I don't
know you well enough to enlarge the list with confidence. Any
novels, and what? There must be more, and as you have not
been generous enough to me to let me freely enough into your
book tastes and dependencies to enable me to tell, you must
now, by catalogue. The more, the happier I.

*To Charles Allen.*
May 9, 1864.

I shall delight to have you notice Frothingham's book for us,
and he would, doubtless, be pleased, too; and if he would
think of it to tell his publishers to send his books to us, they
would always have a friendly notice.

I really don't see why you should fash yourself about my
blackguard way of editing the *Republican*. You tell me only
public facts, such as you would tell anybody, such as are at the
getting of us all. I use them as I see fit, and am responsible.
The only difference between you and me is that you abuse and

blackguard in court, where the law, which you fellows have made, protects you; while we blackguard in the papers, where the law, which you make, doesn't protect us! I think you are savage and harsh in court; but that is none of my business. Let us each be responsible for our own individualisms, and for no more. You will have a heavy load if you undertake to carry mine.

Bushwhacking is very annoying to guerillas, but it is sometimes the only way to fight them. Defended on strictly legal principles in court, we should be beaten in the suit. But if we break down their character, expose their misdeeds, and make them notorious — we have driven them out of court; at least, out of the jury-box. Our plan is to stimulate and foment this investigation at Washington; and for this nothing is so useful as newspaper talk. The members don't care a copper for your private letters, but what you print sets them agoing always.

Come down this way, and drink some rum, and confess that there is more than one way to do a thing, sometimes.

*To Miss Whitney.*

Sunday, September 4, 1864.

It is 10 1-2. I have had my bath, my hour on horseback, my breakfast, a half-hour (for digestion!) with the papers, have picked vegetables and fruit for dinner — won't you come and dine at one? — have put on my blue suit, and after worshiping you for a few moments, especially, shall go to church. Mary has been bustling about all the morning, doing the work of her three girls, and getting them and the children off to church and Sunday-school. The baby, your baby, has made his advent this morning in short clothes and leather shoes — the second stage of babyhood. He is well, too fat almost to be beautiful, and M—— says has "killing eyes." When you come back, he will fascinate you as a young gentleman, and you can try your theology dodge on him, if you dare!

This week we have here a great cattle and horse show, by the New England Society; and think of it,— in the stress of war time,— it is likely to be the grandest agricultural exhibition ever known in New England. Hampden Park is almost covered with sheds and tents for its accommodation. The town will be running over full, and where and how the crowds will sleep and eat, I have no idea. We expect nobody in particular, unless George Morgan comes, but can hardly avoid filling all our spare room. Had I felt up to it I should have invited Governor Andrew and his staff, but the burden would be too great on me in my weakness.

Sherman has finished his splendid campaign with Atlanta, and the tone of the North stiffens and grows brave. But for politics and politicians, we should substantially get out of the woods this fall. Lincoln's triumphant election, if it can be accomplished, will be the final *coup de grace;* it will raise up at once a reactionary party in the South — a peace party that would be controlling, with the aid of our arms. But now, all is uncertain in the political field, though growing better apparently. Do you notice that the *Anti-slavery Standard* and the *Liberator,* the representatives of the old Abolitionists, are both earnest for Lincoln ? Yet a new crop of radicals have sprung up, who are resisting the president and making mischief. Chase is going around, peddling his griefs in private ears, and sowing dissatisfaction about Lincoln. Oh, how little great men can be — the larger the smaller. Or is it only the contrast, the conspicuousness ? Or, again, does nature compensate for great gifts in one direction by withholding in others ? You are a moral metaphysician — study it up !

But the bell rings — and I kiss my hand to you !

Dr. Osgood, of New York, preached for us last Sunday and to-day. I didn't get reconciled to his manner, and his matter is not so overpoweringly good as to make one. Our people are utterly at sea as to a minister; the man they want they can't have, and there is no one in sight that is satisfactory. The Northampton society does not settle any one yet, as I see. It is a shiftless, lamentable state of affairs; the evil I do not quite comprehend, nor can I see the remedy. But I have been long thinking that the minister should be more the center, the leader, the teacher, of his people; that they should gather around him as disciples, somewhat as of old in Asia, in Greece and Rome,— going to hear him and joining in his work because they believe in him, what he teaches, and his ways of doing good,— rather than centering in a church organization around a few lifeless dogmas, and having for associates people whom you have no sort of sympathy with, whose principles of life are in most cases wholly at variance with your own, and for a minister mayhap one equally discordant with your spirit; or if not with yours, then with that of half the rest of the parish. Most of the earnest and best work of our lives is not done with the people who go to the same meeting with us; with them we are often wholly at variance; while in other parishes we find those of like spirit and faith, and along with whom we yoke in the best labor of our life. The church organization seems to me a failure — at least that we have outgrown it, or are fast outgrowing it. Did you ever think of all this — and what?

This is a quiet day, cloudy and now rainy — full of the Fall feeling, and with a savor of sadness all in and over it.

Sunday, October 23, 1864.

. . . To-morrow I hope to go to Boston for a day or two. It will be my first night out of this house since we moved into it, more than three months ago. Is not that unusual steadiness for me? But the truth is, I have no pluck to break away; I yield cowardly to the little daily duties and cares, and don't seem to have the ambition or the power to clear them off and get away. But I mean to, and I will,— for I am growing dull and narrow, and getting below — farther below — my soaring friend in California. And I must keep within *reaching* distance, at least.

Election prospects continue to look well. So, on the whole, does the military situation. The inner circles have great faith in Grant's going into Richmond very shortly. But he is more anxious to catch the rebel army than to take the town. The two things would be the signal for the downfall of the rebellion. "Phil Sheridan" is our latest hero; he has this last week shown the highest quality of a military commander,— the power to wrench brilliant victory from a terrible defeat. He is a little fellow, of Irish parentage, with brains enough to steady his conceit, but not to conceal it.

Do you begin to hear about " Emily Chester," the new novel ? You will have seen Mrs. Cook's notice of it. I inclose Gail Hamilton's, and mark Frank Sanborn's in the *Commonwealth.* And the book itself I will try to send you by another steamer. It seems to have power and merit. The author is said to be a Baltimore girl, and this her first writing. How genius compensates for experience. How this dower of great insight divines all hearts, all trials, all experiences. It is this power which is genius, and distinguishes it from talent.

*To Charles Allen.*

November, 1864.

This winter caught my cabbages, grapes, roses, and a' that, and in rescuing them I am losing Boston this week. Sorry ; but agriculture and horticulture first. Colfax is to be here Friday ; how long to stay, I do not know.

I took my old post election night, and sat through from six P. M. to six A. M., and survived it capitally, suffering much less than I feared.

There is nothing else new with me. I am organizing anew, somewhat, at the office, with a view to still more relief for myself. I want things to go whether I am around or not, so that I can stay away days, evenings, or weeks, even, if so be I am in the mood. But I think we have some good papers. To-day's, for instance, was about as good as any of the "metropolitans." " The Case of the Florida " was Ashmun's.

*To Miss Whitney.*

WASHINGTON, Feb. 1, 1865.

Yesterday was a great day in our history. Congress then perfected the abolition of slavery through the amendment of the Constitution. The scene in the House was of deepest interest. The floor swarmed with distinguished individuals besides the members,— the leading senators, members of the cabinet, Chief-justice Chase, prominent generals, leading anti-slavery men from all quarters. All hung with impatience on the result. Hope fluttered. Doubt floated on and off like a cloud. But the Opposition wavered, broke, and the sky cleared away in a complete triumph. Then such an outburst of feeling — such enthusiasm and applause! The galleries rose to their feet — so the members. The ladies floated their gauze handkerchiefs and clapped their gloved hands. The soldiers shouted and cheered. The members on our side threw up their arms wildly and embraced each other. Joy rioted in crazy expression for some moments. The occasion was historic; the thought sublime. The day opened a new dispensation. To-day a negro has been admitted to practice in the Supreme Court. And the work goes on, or rather has just begun.

. . . It is delightful to see how Massachusetts looms up in these times. Never was her influence greater, or so much confessed. Never was her position, as the first of Christian democracies so conspicuous. I feel more and more content to live and die in her embrace — more and more proud to be a small element in her progress, a small influence in her power. And really there is no state where so much of all the real comforts of life — material and spiritual — can be secured as within her borders. We who live there hardly realize all this. It is only when we get away, and see what life is elsewhere, and hear the testimony of men and women who know her from afar, by observation and study and comparison, that we can appreciate and acknowledge our fortune. You must never give up Massachusetts, nor that best and sweetest part of it, the Connecticut Valley. Its comforts and advantages and its power are to be more and more realized and confessed as the new day of the nation ripens into fullness.

*To his Wife.*

WASHINGTON, Sunday.

I wrote you of the melancholy morning yesterday. The evening turned out quite dissipated, altogether quite a contrast, and unexpectedly. I went out to walk and to do an errand for Mr. Walker, and met Mr. Colfax on his way to Mrs. Lincoln's reception. He insisted on my going along, and there I met the Bankses and a few other people I knew. General Banks next insisted we should go together to the reception of Mrs. Sprague

(Miss Chase); there we met much the same people, though rather more select. I came to the hotel, then, to find Walker over his sickness, and getting up. Then I went to Mr. Dana's to dine, and again met Mr. Elliot, M. C., from New Bedford, and we had a pleasant evening till 8:30, when I went to meet Mr. Colfax and his mother at Dr. Peter Parker's (who is a returned and retired missionary and doctor in China) where I had a pleasant half-hour. From there at 9:30 we went to Mr. Seward's reception, which was more select and brilliant than either of the others. I met here Mary Morgan, daughter of Mr. George Morgan, and Mrs. Stoekel (Eliza Howard) with whom I had agreeable talk. At 10:30 we left, Mr. Walker, General Banks, and I, and we three went off and got some *steamed oysters*, and home to our hotel at midnight rather used up by the various dissipations. To-day we have been to the Capitol to hear Rev. Mr. Channing preach, and a beautiful old Quakeress from New Bedford exhort, and afterward to call on Senator Sumner. Now I am resting (!) before going out to drive with Mr. Ashmun. So you see I am rather alive and "going it." I am pretty well to-day, and Mr. Walker is quite recovered, and our visit bears more cheerful promise than it did. Your first note of Friday reached me last night. I am glad to note your enterprise in going out daily. I hope you will keep it up. Take one hour or two every day for outside life, and you will be better and stronger and do more inside in the other twenty-two for it — depend upon it.

*To Miss Whitney.*

HOME, Sunday, March 12, 1865.

. . . Our society is still pastorless, and finds nobody that suits it, that can be got. Our weekly ministrations are feeble and uncertain. We want John Ware, who went to Baltimore last year and who is not quite satisfied there; and it looks now as if we should wait another six months or a year, in hopes of getting him. At any rate, there is no disposition to settle an ordinary man. Our people were never stronger or more generous than now; they offered Mr. Ware $3000 to $4000 salary, and $500 outfit, if he would come.  Mr. Wasson fails at Cincinnati by reason of ill health, and is coming back.  Very likely we shall have him to preach for us more or less during the summer.  But this vagabond condition is very unsatisfactory even to me, so little dependent as I am on "the minister."  I find I am longing for regular, dependable preaching, and a leader reliable and faithful, in our pulpit.  We hardly know, indeed, how much we appreciate a good pastor, and in how many ways we count on him, and make him useful to our lives till we are without him.  Tiffany I find I like more and more as he is farther removed — he was so true and genial and cultured and really pious.

Your letters of the 3d and 13th February have come since I wrote last.  They show better health than any you have written in a long while.  It is delightful to find you entering upon your second year with so much courage and hope and freshness, and with a strong conviction too of your usefulness — able to see you have done something — as I have no doubt you have done much, everything, — and to comprehend how much still you can do in the year that remains.  It is a great thing, in any life, to have this feeling that our work is useful, to feel that we can command and comprehend it, and to have, from whatever combination of motives, a *heart* for it. The first requisite, I insist, for all life, for all work, is health — at least good digestion.  After that, of course, motive, object — but that *first*.  I have not got beyond that yet in my study of the science of the ebb and flow of the soul-life.  All things are easy, possible, — I am brave for all life, I am almost equal to it, when good digestion waits on appetite, and sleep on both. When they fail, all fails, all is impossible — motives are blurred, objects fall away, and I am only and absolutely disagreeable — to myself most, to all much.  Nothing has so taught me charity as invalidism.  I am ready to pardon anything to man or woman who can prove a clear case of dyspepsia, sluggish liver, or impotent sleep.  Even murder would be excusable in my eyes under such provocation, for there are moments in my life when everything that is insane and wicked seems possible. Let me add now, however, that the thaw and rain cleared off

Friday night, and carried off my extra neuralgic headache, and since then I have been as well as I can hope to be at present; certainly not tempted to murder, and even intolerant of the year that keeps you from me!

. . . I have read with interest the book notices in the *Atlantic* for March. Bushnell's new book ["The Vicarious Sacrifice"], I have heard otherwise well spoken of. I wish I could read it. The little I have read of his previous books always pleased and elevated and instructed me. But I have not got to book-reading yet. Last night, however, I was hungry for something and turned to my old friend "Shirley" for relief. I believe I like to read the last few chapters at least twice a year. Her love-talks — conflicts rather — with Moore are perfectly delicious to me.

Sumner's behavior in preventing a vote on the Louisiana question was perfectly unjustifiable. I shall henceforth be intolerant of him, always. It was undignified, disgraceful.*

* The occasion of this passage was as follows: the Senate had under consideration a bill for whose success President Lincoln was very anxious, establishing a state government in Louisiana. Mr. Sumner was dissatisfied with it, as not conceding enough to the freedmen, and, unable to defeat it if a vote were taken, he united with some of the Democratic leaders to stave off action by parliamentary maneuvers, so that it failed by default. Mr. Schurz has related the sequel. The Washington world believed Sumner's course had made an irreconcilable breach between him and the President. But Sumner received a friendly little note from the President, saying he would call in his carriage to take him to the Inauguration Ball. The carriage came, Mr. Sumner joined Mr. and Mrs. Lincoln, and the company in the ball-room were astonished to see the three come in together, Mrs. Lincoln on Mr. Sumner's arm. That was Lincoln's way of assuring Sumner and the public that he was not going to quarrel.

END OF VOLUME ONE.

LI